GENDER, MIGRATION AND DOMESTIC SERVICE

For my mother, Joan, and my father, Bill

Gender, Migration and Domestic Service

The politics of black women in Italy

JACQUELINE ANDALL
University of Bath

Ashgate

Aldershot • Burlington USA • Singapore • Sydney

Published by
Ashgate Publishing Limited
Gower House
Croft Road
Aldershot
Hampshire GU11 3HR
England

Ashgate Publishing Company
131 Main Street
Burlington, VT 05401-5600
USA

Ashgate website: http://www.ashgate.com

British Library Cataloguing in Publication Data
Andall, Jacqueline
        Gender, migration and domestic service : the politics of
        black women in Italy. - (Interdisciplinary research series
        in ethnic, gender and class relations)
        1. Women, Black - Employment - Italy 2. Women domestics -
        Italy - Social conditions 3. Women, Black - Italy - Social
        conditions 4. Women - Italy - Social conditions 5. Sex role -
        Italy 6. Discrimination in employment - Italy
        I. Title
        331.4'0896'045

Library of Congress Control Number: 00-134478

ISBN 0 7546 1088 8

Printed In Great Britain by
Antony Rowe Ltd, Chippenham, Wiltshire

Contents

List of Tables

Series Editor's Preface

Dr Jacqueline Andall introduced me to this work during a two-week summer school that we both attended on the Greek island of Hydra. She discussed aspects of the research with me and I was fascinated. I am glad that she decided to publish her book with Ashgate because this is a most welcome addition to the Interdisciplinary Research Series in Ethnic, Gender and Class Relations.

The author notes how the gender debate in Italy had been ideologically de-racialised in both official discourse and academic discourse. She argues that the colour blindness of the gender debate in Italy, coupled with her own biography as a black British citizen of Caribbean origin, left her with little choice but to adopt the black feminist perspective that privileges an articulated understanding of race, class, gender relations in preference to the gender atomisation of the reality of migrant black women who work as domestic servants.

Whereas the post-fascist Italian constitution states that female workers are entitled to the same pay as male workers for the same work, the book exposes the contradictions inherent in the sameness of work principle especially in such jobs as domestic service where immigrant black women were more likely to find employment. This contradiction also affects Italian women because the constitution states that they should fulfil their maternal duties along with their public functions. However, the contradiction of work sameness is resolved for middle-class Italian women by the presence of poorly paid immigrant domestic servants who make it possible for the native women to seek sameness of pay outside the domestic setting with men who do the same types of work.

The author argues that the presence of immigrant female workers represents significant changes in Italian history – a history of predominantly white male emigration now replaced with a more recent history of predominantly racialised female immigration. At the same time, restrictive employment practices, reinforced by restrictive immigration policies make it clear that the constitutional protection of gender roles does not apply

viii

to immigrant women at all even though there is great demand for their cheap labour by privileged Italian families.

This lack of protection for immigrant women is made worse because many domestic workers are required by their middle-class employers to 'live in' and such working conditions frustrate their own wishes to fulfil maternal roles of their own. Moreover, the job of a domestic worker remains very insecure given that she could be sacked even after six years of service with no benefits and she could be forced to seek a new job even while heavily pregnant.

This book offers a sober alternative to the sensational pornographic coverage of the presence of black women in Italy. Tabloid newspapers give the misleading impression that most black female immigrants in Italy work in the sex industries but the author de-sensationalises the debate by analysing the hidden struggles for survival being waged by under-paid, over-worked, and de-sexualised black women in Italy's domestic industries.

Dr Biko Agozino
Associate Professor
Indiana University of Pennsylvania

Acknowledgements

This book has benefited from the contribution of a number of people. I would like to thank my mentor, Prof. Gino Bedani, for fostering my interest in Italy, commenting on my research and being a source of constant support. I am also grateful to Prof. Anna Bull for reading the bulk of this research and providing constructive suggestions for improvement. I would like to acknowledge the financial support of the British Academy and thank the research committee in the Department of European Studies, University of Bath, for granting me study leave to complete this work. This book has additionally benefited from the comments of participants at a number of conferences and seminars. I would like to particularly thank the organisers and participants of the ERCOMER conference on migration, Utrecht 1996; the Municipality of Rotterdam's conference on Cape Verdeans and cities in Europe, Rotterdam, 1996; the University of Melbourne's conference on the state of contemporary Italy, Melbourne 1997; the University of Bath's Women's Centre seminar on gender and ethnicity in Europe, Bath 1997 and the University of Miami's conference on Africa/Italy, Ohio, 1998.

This book would not, however, have been possible without the participation of the female migrants of my case-study and I am especially grateful to all of the women who gave up their limited time to share their experiences with me in Rome.

During my fieldwork in Rome, I received assistance from a wide range of people. I would like to especially thank Antonia Bento, Tewodros Bekele, Francesca De Fazi, Teresa Savini and Alfredo Zolla. Residents and staff at Rome's *Città dei Ragazzi* made me particularly welcome. Librarians at the ACLI's national archives and at the CIES research centre provided me with much assistance. For fieldwork assistance in Rotterdam, I would like to say a special thank-you to Pedro Landim and Dr Joke Van der Zwaard. Alfredo Silva was also a great help in Paris.

My frequent visits to Rome have been made all the more enjoyable as a result of time spent with my adopted Italian family. Ancilla Ferrara and Luigi Troina have never ceased to show me the true meaning of friendship and in recent years, their daughter Elettra has added a new dimension.

I would like to thank my sister, Glenys Andall, for being a source of support throughout this project. For computing assistance, I wish to acknowledge Mark Robertson. For introducing me to 'pan', I would like to thank Toussaint Clarke, Hallam Ifill and Michael Toussaint. My Thursday evening sessions with Rainbow Steel Orchestra, Bath, were more than a welcome diversion. Thanks also to my extended family, the Cardiff posse and Eleanor Grant for friendship and support.

Support from my husband, Hari Nada, has been provided in an inimitable way. His challenging questions forced me to clarify my arguments and our debates were lively and heated! I would like to thank him for making a valuable intellectual contribution to the final product.

Finally, I would like to express my gratitude to my parents. They have been unfailing in their support. This book is affectionately dedicated to them, with love and respect.

Introduction

Italy's history has been marked by the widespread transatlantic and European migration of its citizens. By contrast, it is only in the last 30 years that Italy has been defined as a country of immigration. Italy's immigration picture has remained far from static. Indeed, a snapshot perspective of the situation in the mid-1970s would be profoundly different to the snapshot picture taken today. The current immigration situation is characterised by its diversity. Contemporary migrants vary considerably, in terms of nationality, regional settlement and employment location. Despite the fact that both the political elite and the media continue to focus on the latest waves of migrants, there are in fact some settled ethnic minority communities who have moved on to a 'second generation'.

This book, however, seeks to document the early history of Italy's transition into an immigration country and focuses specifically on the experiences of African female migrants from the early 1970s to the early 1990s.[1] At its core, the book tells two stories. One story concerns the African women of my case-study. This first narrative addresses the circumstances of these pioneering women who migrated to Italy, not as secondary migrants or dependants, but as autonomous primary migrants. They were mainly single and some had left children behind in the country of origin. They would be employed almost exclusively as live-in domestic workers. The second story concerns Italian women and Italian society. This second narrative focuses on the experiences of migrant women both as a reflection of Italian women's transformed social roles and as a reflection of Italian society's attachment to a particular conception of Italian family life.

As a 1993 European report on Black and migrant women[2] clearly showed, not only is there fragmentary information available regarding Black and migrant women in Europe, but they have frequently been excluded from general research about women at the European level. This book not only seeks to provide new information about the specific experiences of Black women in Italy,[3] but it additionally seeks to integrate their experiences into Italy's wider gender debate.

The post-war Italian gender debate has been primarily centred within two competing ideological spheres. These can loosely be defined as progressive and conservative, although the groups encompassed within these dual spheres did not pursue analogous ideological or strategical goals. Broadly speaking, the principal actors situated within the progressive sphere were the left-wing national women's organisation, the *Unione Donne Italiane* (UDI), the principal opposition party of the post-war period, the Italian Communist Party (Pci)[4] and the autonomous feminist movement. Within the conservative sphere, the principal actors were the Catholic national women's organisation, the *Centro Italiano Femminile* (CIF), the dominant party of the post-war period, the Christian Democrat Party (Dc) and the Church. Post 1968, the advent of an autonomous feminist movement marked an important new phase in Italy's gender politics. The 1970s were distinguished by the visibility of this women's movement and its ability to challenge not only the then dominant subcultures of Communism and Catholicism, but also wider sociocultural norms regarding women's position within society. In the 1980s, the concept of diffuse feminism was utilised to describe the spread of feminist ideas in a variety of cultural, institutional and political spheres.

Throughout these changes however, one unresolved issue permeated the analyses and strategies of both conservative and progressive spheres. This concerned the ideological and practical tension regarding Italian women's productive and reproductive roles. In the immediate post-war period, there had been some consensus at the political level, within both spheres, regarding the centrality of women's reproductive roles to their social identities. By the 1970s, Italian women had begun to reject this limiting definition, articulating instead the desire to inhabit a multiplicity of social and political spheres. Nonetheless, the process of combining family and work roles has not been straightforward and Italian women have largely experienced their new social identities in a conflictual fashion.[5]

The movement of migrant women to Italy in the 1970s occurred in tandem with Italian women's new aspirations to participate fully in the labour market. Their presence contributed significantly to Italy's new status as a destination immigration country. The characteristics of this female migration were noteworthy for several reasons. Firstly, female migrants to Italy in the 1970s were autonomous primary migrants. Furthermore, their migration was essentially a single-sex migration. This was not simply a new phenomenon for Italy, but additionally marked a new phase in the nature of post-war female migration to Europe. Finally, the new presence of migrant women naturally enlarged the constituency of gender. What the implications of this would be for the wider gender debate in Italy forms a key question of this book. My discussion of this wider gender debate will be related principally to the progressive sphere of women's activism. By the 1980s, this sphere was broadly divided into three areas – political and institutional feminism, cultural feminism and trade-union feminism (Becalli 1994). In this book, I shall focus on political feminism and specifically the activities of the women's section of the Pci/Pds party.[6]

Progressive women activists in Italy have historically been influenced by external political and cultural movements. In the 1970s, some strands of the feminist movement were influenced by the direction of the American women's movement. In the 1980s, the Italian feminist movement's increasing focus on intellectualism was in part precipitated by its proximity to the directions being taken by French feminism. At a similar time in Britain and America, the question of 'racial' difference between women had begun to emerge as an important feminist issue. This led to the development of a Black feminist critique which sought to construct a more inclusive feminism which could integrate the experiential diversity of ethnic minority women. It aimed to fully engage with the manner in which gender interacted with ethnicity and class processes. At the time, the apparent absence of ethnic minority communities in Italy meant that these discourses did not penetrate the Italian context. However, as I shall demonstrate in the course of this book, the new presence of migrant women in the 1970s indicated that these discourses were in fact becoming increasingly relevant to the Italian situation.

This book is thus an exploratory attempt to 'racialise' the category of gender within Italy. The manner in which ethnic minority women's presence will impact on the Italian gender debate has yet to be put under scrutiny[7] and this book aims to make migrant women visible within an Italian gender framework. While the importance of migrant women's agency cannot be entirely eclipsed from the structure/agency dichotomy, sustained attention is paid to structural conditions within Italy as important determinants of their experiences in the country. I shall differentiate Italy's experience from those national contexts where most of the literature on diversity has been pioneered (UK and USA). Distinguishing features will include the significance of Catholicism, the distinctive evolution of political feminism, the importance of the family in relation to comparable countries in Western Europe and a different experience of ethnicity and 'race'[8] when compared to countries such as Britain and America.

How then can we incorporate the situation and experiences of migrant women into the Italian gender debate? What possibilities are there for a more inclusive gender debate in Italy and how might the Italian experience contribute to the wider debate on inclusive feminism? What does migrant women's situation tell us about Italian women's attempts to reconcile their productive and reproductive roles? What conclusions can be drawn regarding the relationship between different women structured both by class and ethnicity? I shall be arguing that a fundamental disparity between Italian women and migrant women[9] concerns the privileging of the labour identity of ethnic minority women over and above other social identities. This is antithetical to the historical experience of Italian women in the post-war period where the importance of the maternal role not only permeated national legislation but was explicitly enshrined in the Italian Constitution. This book thus seeks to investigate the marginality of migrant women's gendered identities, which I would argue is irrevocably connected to their restriction to the paid domestic work sector.

Any understanding of the restrictions the domestic work sector has placed upon African women must be predicated on an understanding of the sector's particular development in Italy. The polarised politics of post-war Italy contributed to the emergence of a national organisation, operative within the Catholic sphere of subcultural influence, which was specifically dedicated to the organisation of domestic workers (the ACLI-COLF).[10] Given the historical problems associated with organising domestic workers into a collective force,[11] this organisation stands as a particularly interesting and perhaps even unique body within the post-war European context.[12] An evaluation of its conceptual and strategical development provides the background framework for an understanding of the paid domestic work sector. While this sector has traditionally been excluded or marginalised from accounts of women's working experience,[13] its survival and indeed expansion in the post-war period needs to be highlighted. The obsolescence of this sector had in fact been predicted by modernist theorists such as Coser (1973) who argued that it was not consonant with modernity. In other European countries, strategies adopted to reconcile reproductive care with the transformed gender roles of contemporary European societies have also generally been based on the use of external paid labour or internal unpaid labour.[14] However, Italy's retention of the archaic live-in form of domestic work warrants particular explanation and not simply because its retention and expansion has created specific forms of social marginality for migrant women. In France, Condon's (1995) analysis of 1968 census data showed that while 38 per cent of Guadeloupean female migrants to France were categorised as 'service-staff', only 6.2 per cent of these were live-in domestic employees.[15] A critical question therefore is why, at an analogous time, were migrant women being recruited to Italy exclusively for live-in domestic work?

To reiterate, the research issues at the core of this book concern the experiences of Black women as workers and mothers, the implications of a racialised gender category in Italy and the organisation and development of Italy's paid domestic work sector. A combination of research methods was utilised to gather data, including semi-structured interviews,[16] questionnaires and field observations (see Appendix 1). The bulk of the interviewing took place in Rome in 1992 and 1993, with some additional interviews conducted in Rotterdam in 1996. The principal groups investigated were Cape Verdean, Ethiopian, Eritrean and Somali (see Appendix 2).[17] The outcome of qualitative interviewing is of course contingent on the analysis and presentation of the results. The notion of 'situated knowledge' (Haraway 1991) typifies the increasing practice of reflexivity in a number of academic disciplines. Haraway (1991, p. 581) has promoted the practice of 'embodied objectivity' in research:

> I would like to suggest how our insisting metaphorically on the particularity and embodiment of all vision ... allows us to construct a usable, but not an innocent, doctrine of objectivity ... The moral is simple: only partial perspective promises objective vision ... Feminist objectivity is about limited location and situated knowledge (ibid., pp. 582–3).

My own location as a British woman of Caribbean origin, with a personal family history of labour migration, has undoubtedly led me to focus my reflections on the manner in which national contexts facilitate or repress migrants' aspirations and agency. Nevertheless, I have attempted to present my findings within the framework of Haraways's concept of embodied objectivity.

In the following section, I present the theoretical framework for this study. I have drawn principally on the literature on diversity and the literature on female migration to situate the experiences of Black women in Italy.

Black Feminist Thought

The concept of gender as a central analytical tool with which to understand women's lives and subordination has constituted a fundamental component of feminist theory since the 1970s. In an influential feminist article published in 1974, Sherry Ortner (1974, p. 67) concluded that 'the secondary status of women in society is one of the true universals, a pan-cultural fact'. It was such writing which encouraged feminist writers and activists to focus on the commonality of women's oppression. By the 1980s, this focus on women's common oppression increasingly began to be viewed as unhelpful because it denied the experiential diversity of those women who did not fit a specific prototype model. One challenge to the concept of women's commonality was articulated via the literature on the condition of ethnic minority women. This literature documented the effects of the intersection of gender, race and class factors in ethnic minority women's lives. It was pioneered in countries with established ethnic minority communities, first in the United States and subsequently in Britain. African-American writers such as bell hooks (1981) and Angela Davis (1982) published seminal works around this theme in the early 1980s. Their work sought to demonstrate how Black women's experiences had historically been marginalised from mainstream discourses on gender. Davis (1982) highlighted Black women's exclusion from the early women's rights campaigns around the issue of the vote in nineteenth century America, while hooks (1981) emphasised Black women's marginalisation from feminist theory and activism in the 1970s. Interactive oppressions were seen to 'provide a distinctive context for Black womanhood' (King 1988, p. 42) and in 1990, Patricia Hill Collins sought to synthesise some of the main tenets of this Black feminist thought.

The literature challenged earlier feminist notions about the globality of sisterhood by exposing the feminist movement's focus on the experiences and concerns of White middle class women (see Amos and Parmar 1984). It maintained that ethnic minority women experienced their subordination through a combination of multiple variables rather than through an identifiable and single system of oppression. The assumption that some women's lives were prototypical, and as such representative of the female gender, was indicative of what the social psychologist Kum-Kum Bhavnani (1993, p. 30) has described as a 'racially unselfconscious feminism'. In point of fact, by being 'racially unselfconscious', the movement was implicitly 'racially' biased. Indeed, according to the African-American Gordan (1985) White feminists were often deliberately racially unselfconscious to avoid acknowledgment of their racial privilege.[18]

The feminist theorist hooks (1989, p. 20) has argued that a focus on patriarchal domination, with its inherent perception of class and race exploitation as subordinate, disguised the fact that 'women can and do participate in politics of domination'. She proposed a deconstruction of the notion of man as enemy and the accentuation of paradigms of domination which could highlight women's capacity to dominate.[19] The work of a number of authors had shown that in a variety of contexts, racism had empowered

White women to act as exploiters and oppressors (Rollins 1985; Hewitt 1990; Romero 1992). Gordon (1985) in fact concluded that this precluded a gender based interaction between Black and White women. Increasingly however, new global perspectives indicate that possibilities for domination exist within and are practised by men and women of all classes and races and a number of writers have emphasised the necessity for all women to recognise this potential (hooks 1989; Brah 1991; Bhavnani 1993). Avtar Brah (1991, p. 172) narrates her personal circumstances to elucidate this:

> ... as an Asian woman living in Britain I am subjected to racism, but as a member of a dominant caste within the specific community from which I originate I also occupy a position of power in relation to lower-caste women. From my standpoint, a feminist politics would demand of me a commitment to opposing racism as much as casteism although I am positioned differently within these social hierarchies, and the strategies required of me in dealing with them may be different.

While many writers have been critical of what they see to be an exclusive feminism (hooks 1981; Bourne 1983; Parmar 1989; Brah 1993; Bhavnani 1993), their arguments are motivated by the desire to transform this into a more inclusive practice. Critical exposure of this issue has thus been used to modify the agenda and practice of progressive female activists. These views have had some impact on feminism, but as Brah (1991) has indicated, there is growing acknowledgement that convergence and divergence in the lives of women leads to different priorities and that this was likely to present 1990s feminism with a series of contradictions.

The desire to achieve a more inclusive feminism has entailed movement away from a hierarchical ranking of oppressions. Current emphasis revolves around the importance of assessing the interconnectedness of different systems of subordination. The sociologist Paul Gilroy (1993, p. 68) has argued for 'a new line of thought that goes beyond 'either/or-ism' into a different conceptual logic of supplementarity. In its simplest form, this might turn on the alternative couplet both/and'. This logic of supplementarity is intrinsic to the logic of Black feminist thought. An early formulation of this can be found in the 'Black Feminist Statement' published by the Combahee River Collective in 1977:

> ... we are actively committed to struggling against racial, sexual, heterosexual, and class oppression and see as our particular task the development of integrated analysis and practice based upon the fact that the major systems of oppression are interlocking. The synthesis of these oppressions create the conditions of our lives (Combahee River Collective 1977, p. 13).

Black women have tended to be located either within the category of 'race' along with Black men or within the category of gender with White women. Proponents of Black feminist thought have argued that these positionings have led to Black women's needs as both Black people and as Black women remaining on the margins of both these sectors (hooks 1981; Davis 1982; Bhavnani 1993). The consequences of either/or conceptual premises for Black women are exemplified in the following citation from Bhavnani (1993, p. 35):

> Gendered inequalities are set up so as to act in competition with racialised inequalities – *either* someone is Black *or* they are a woman. The consequence of this is that Black women are defined into or out of one of these categories, and those of us who refuse such a splitting, who argue uncompromisingly that 'race' and gender are inextricably enmeshed, often end up with our arguments not being heard. In this way, the denials elide into Invisibility – the Invisibility of Black women as racialised and gendered subjects simultaneously.

The desire to establish a framework which ascribes a broadly equal status to a variety of systems of domination nevertheless requires a flexible approach. When attempting to interpret the experiences of those subjects who simultaneously inhabit these multiple spatial arenas, the simple affirmation of the existence of intertwined relationships does not automatically offset the tendency to afford one or other of these categories a more prominent position. While systems of domination may be interconnected, this does not prevent one or other of these systems predominating in specific social and historical instances. Thus, at a given time, gender may assume the status of the dominant oppressive system, while on another occasion, class or ethnicity may rise to the fore. Although there has been a linguistic normalisation of the concept of interconnected systems within the literature on diversity, it may be appropriate to accept that in a given sociopolitical national context, different systems may prevail, albeit temporarily, as the most relevant interpretative mechanism of women's subordination. This does not preclude the inclusion of other systems of subordination. Rather the integrative analysis is retained with the recognition that a range of factors may constantly reorder the influence of the various constructs.

Black feminist thought is grounded in the American and British experience and its applicability to the Italian context will be explored during the course of this book. Although in the 1970s the influence of new wave American feminism on European feminist movements was significant, a linear transferral with reference to 'race' is perhaps less viable. While the manifestation or practical consequences of racism may not be dissimilar in different contexts,[20] the historical dimension of 'race' within the American setting may distort this process. There is a fundamental racial antagonism in the United States, which, in terms of the African-American community has its roots in slavery, enforced racial segregation, and the politics of the civil rights movement in the 1960s. King (1988, p. 53) has argued that these issues have been formative experiences in most African-American's 'socialization and political outlook'. It is probable therefore that the politics of 'race' in North America has influenced Black feminist thought and this is likely to have consequences for the direction of Black feminist writing emanating from the United States. For example, the contemporary theoretical interest in Afrocentricity on the part of some African-American thinkers may not be entirely compatible with Black feminist thought.[21]

Nonetheless the general premises of Black feminist thought undoubtedly have relevance for other national contexts:

> Black feminist thought fosters a fundamental paradigmatic shift in how we think about oppression. By embracing a paradigm of race, class and gender as interlocking systems of oppression, Black feminist thought reconceptualises the social relations of domination and resistance (Collins 1990, p. 222).

Black feminist thought then, does not separate various systems of power but attempts to determine the manner in which these systems function in articulation with each other. There is no shared uniform appellation for this system, rather it tends to be described as a process whereby the systems of capitalism, racism, classism and patriarchy can be seen to interact with each other.[22]

This paradigmatic shift has been reflected in the practical strategies of women's activism in the United States and Britain. While, in the 1970s, a uniform feminist strategy did not exist, certain issues were common to North European and North American feminists. These included a focus on women's sexuality, abortion rights and a rejection of an exclusive mothering role for women.[23] In effect, this constituted an unacknowledged identity politics of White middle class feminist activists. The response of White feminist activists and theorists to this Black feminist critique has been diverse. Some feminist writers have acknowledged the initial tendency amongst Western European feminists to universalise their experience as representative of women (see Barrett and McIntosh 1985). Others have sought to present more inclusive feminist accounts (see Segal 1987; Ryan 1992).[24] The Black feminist critique also contributed to an additional body of literature which documents the differential construction of women's social identities in relation to ethnicity (see Cole 1986; Du Bois and Ruiz 1990; Amott and Matthaei 1991). Enlow (1989) has documented this from a global perspective.

This critique, coupled with trends within anti-racist literature, has furthermore contributed to the development of a new body of literature on 'whiteness'.[25] This has begun to systematically explore how and to what extent a White ethnicity can lead to unacknowledged privilege. In response to Black feminists' critique, Ruth Frankenberg (1993) explored the concept of whiteness through the life histories of White women in America. She found that even their anti-racist 'colour blindness'[26] often led them 'back into complicity with structural, and institutional dimensions of inequality' (p. 143). Power evasion was identified as a corollary of this colour evasion:

> If the sharp edge of color evasion resides in its repression or denial of the differences that race makes in people's lives, power evasion is a permutation of that repression: rather than complete nonacknowledgment of any kind of difference, power evasion involves a selective attention to difference, allowing into conscious scrutiny ... those differences that make the speaker feel good but continuing to evade by means of partial description, euphemism, and self-contradiction those that make the speaker feel bad (ibid., pp. 156–7).

The literature on whiteness has yet to be integrated into the Italian context. Nevertheless, as will be argued in subsequent chapters (see chapters 8 and 9), some evidence of power evasion can be identified in the analyses and activities of those Italian women's associations which have begun to interact with migrant women.

But to what extent are the above discourses relevant to the specific case of Black women in Italy? The perspectives of Avtar Brah are a useful framework for the Italian experience in relation to questions of difference between women. In Brah's (1991) essay on difference and International feminism she raises a number of considerations which appear particularly pertinent to the Italian situation. The first concerns her argument that questions of difference must be framed with reference to the international context, given that we live in a global economic system. Secondly, she contends that while feminism should be concerned with developing strategies which provide women with possibilities for increased autonomy, these strategies should not 'reinforce or reproduce existing inequalities' (1991, p. 169). Her third argument concerns the necessity for securing:

... accounts of why certain sectors of the world economy become feminized, why certain categories of women perform particular kinds of paid work, and how these different groups of women are differently represented within different political, religious, academic and commonsense discourse (ibid., p. 171).

It seems to me that Brah's first concern is directly relevant to the Italian situation since it is the current global economic context which forms part of the equation in explaining the presence of Black women in Italy. Her second question, transposed to the Italian context, raises the question of whether Italian women's increased opportunities for autonomy can be partially attributed to the presence of Black women in Italy and whether this does in fact reinforce inequality between women. Finally, I aim to expand on Brah's concern regarding the manner in which women are differentially represented in a variety of discourses within a given national context. In later chapters, for example, I argue that different constructions of female social identity in Italy point to a rather malleable category of gender.[27] My contention is that it is precisely this explicit structural differentiation between some Italian women and the majority of primary female migrants which will diminish the potential for an acceptable accommodation of difference within the Italian context.

Black feminist thought has framed its arguments in relation to the multiple class, gender and race dimensions of Black women's lives.[28] While these factors undoubtedly affect Black women's experiences in Italy, their migrant identity is of equally important consideration. The literature on diversity principally addresses racism as experienced by ethnic minority citizens of particular national contexts. In the Italian case, we are essentially dealing with women who are citizens of Third World countries. As such, these women frequently endure a more precarious presence in Italy, determined by their migration status and structured by residence and work permits. For this reason, the question of migration remains an important frame of reference for the Italian context and accounts for my decision to draw also on the literature on women and migration. The following section thus provides a brief review of the general literature on female migration and then proceeds to a discussion of Italian models of female migration based on the experiences of Italian female emigrants. This provides a useful and quintessentially Italian framework within which to situate the contemporary position of migrant women in Italy.

Women and Migration

In a pioneering 1983 article entitled 'Women in migration: beyond the reductionist outlook', the sociologist Mirjana Morokvasic provided a critical evaluation of the development of the literature on women and migration. Her subsequent articles (1983b; 1984; 1991; 1995) elaborate and expand on these theories. Morokvasic (1983a) registered that as late as the early 1970s migrant women were not only sociologically invisible subjects but where they were mentioned it was within the framework of the family and in relation to children:

> In important works on migration, the symbolic references to women as migrants' wives and their stereotypical presentation as wives and mothers has led to a conceptualisation of migrant women as followers, dependants, unproductive persons, isolated, illiterate and ignorant (1983a, p. 16).[29]

In reality, there were numerous examples of migrant women engaged in migratory projects to West European countries where they were not dependent on men.[30]

In addition to considering migrant women within the framework of the family, researchers have also focused on the extent to which migration has affected gender relations within the cultures of the migrating communities. Morokvasic (1983a, p. 20) formulated a critique of the ethnocentric approach of those writers who tended to evaluate migrant women in terms of their potential to embrace modernity:

> ... researchers in various parts of the world attribute to migrant women of extremely different origins one and the same simplified cultural background and label it 'tradition', meaning immobility and oppression of women, and oppose it to their own average western model of modernity ... migrant women are placed on the tradition to modernity continuum: the women's path on the continuum is sometimes a zigzagging, sometimes a straight one, but they are all unmistakably striving for the Western, modern and, of course, emancipatory values.

Migrant women's involvement in the paid labour market and a restrictive control over fertility were considered to be important indicators of their modernity. Even when studies began to afford women the status of a social actor, the writers' pervasive ethnocentricity meant that regardless of the conditions of migrant women's employment, it was seen as 'a blessing of modern societies and as a means out of their oppressive traditions' (Morokvasic 1991, p. 77).[31]

In fact, migrant women have tended to exhibit high levels of labour force participation when compared to general trends for women's participation in paid employment in certain European countries. In those European countries which adopted a focused migrant labour policy from the outset (Germany, Switzerland and Austria), the labour force participation of migrant women was almost double that of native women (Morokvasic 1984).[32] French Census figures for 1968 also indicated that Caribbean women in France had higher economic activity rates than both metropolitan French women and most other foreign immigrant women (Condon 1995). Female migrant labour in fact offers specific advantages to employers and Phizlackea (1983, p. 5) has emphasised the attractiveness of migrant women's labour to the needs of Western European capital:

> Migrant and female labour share many characteristics, both have been 'produced' by the demand for labour in certain low-wage sectors of the economy and they are confined to those sectors, often by specific policies and practices which are partially justified by the ascription of inferior characteristics, the consequence then being viewed as vindication of the ideology.

Migrant women have additionally been affected by assumptions regarding their involvement in primary and secondary migration processes. Primary migration has traditionally been viewed as characteristic of male migration, with migrant women seen to be involved in secondary migration processes in the name of family reunification. This view partially explains why when women migrants began to be integrated into migration literature, the family framework was automatically considered to be the most natural context in which to investigate their position. A second area which migration theorists have identified as important thus concerns the family experience of migrant women. General migration theory has shown that the existence of dislocated migrant families in the receiving countries is a typical feature of the migration process (Morokvasic 1991), although historically there have been instances of the migration of family units.[33] But more importantly, Morokvasic found that the conditions of family life for migrants is a consequence of the differentiated manner in which the receiving industrialised countries perceive non-indigenous families: 'The nation state which protects the family and considers it as a basic institution of society applies other principles in the case of immigrants' (ibid., p. 74). This fact goes some way to explain why ethnic minority women's groups have attempted to defend the value of the family for migrant communities, sometimes clashing with views prevalent within feminist discourse which have generally cited the family as an oppressive institution.

Black women's migration to Italy as primary migrants, sometimes, but not always followed by the family reunification of their husband and children provides new evidence of a shift in women's migratory patterns. Indeed, the findings presented in this book entirely confirm Castles and Miller's (1993) hypothesis which posits the feminisation of migration as one of four general tendencies of contemporary migration movements. The extensive primary migration of single and married women from developing countries to Italy points to new developments within the field of immigration. In the 1970s, the refashioning of European migration strategy, where the principal receiving countries justified new restrictive entry policies by pointing to the oil crisis and the ensuing slump in European economies, initiated new trends. Instead of moving labour to capital, capital was moved to labour (Phizlackea 1983). Multinational capital exported production processes to offshore locations where they had access to cheap and non trade unionised labour. Nonetheless, there are certain economic sectors which are not easily exportable and which are in fact what Gibson and Graham (1986, p. 135) have termed 'site-specific'. The domestic work sector is an obvious example of a site-specific occupation, alongside occupations such as construction work.

Phizlackea's (1996) elaboration of a feminist migration and globalisation perspective has demonstrated that despite the introduction of strict immigration controls by affluent countries in the 1970s, a demand for low wage female labour in manual service jobs has remained. She points to three contemporary economic sectors which indicate a peculiar model of current female migratory processes: the sex and marriage industries, the maid's industry and the homeworking of migrant and ethnic minority women.[34] The Italian example fits this model well with the overwhelming majority of migrant women being employed as domestic workers.[35]

Given Italy's emigration history however, any attempt to understand Black women's experience in Italy should also reflect on Italian women's history of internal and external migration. In some ways, this provides a uniquely Italian model of female migration which may condition the manner in which Black women migrants are viewed. Italian women's experience of emigration is likely to have set some precedents in terms of the interpretation of women's involvement in migratory processes. Paola Corti's (1990) research into Italian emigration in the late 1800s and early 1900s argues that the development of a rigid model of Italian emigration not only distorted regional and local realities but that it additionally obscured the central role that women played in these processes. The prevailing model created two principal categories of migratory streams. One was European, temporary and undertaken essentially by men; the second concerned transatlantic emigration which tended to be a family migration. Corti maintains that there was in fact some mobility of women in these temporary migrations and that this mobility formed an integral component of rural family strategies. However, data from those southern communities where emigration was high did show that men migrating alone constituted some 70 per cent of emigrants and that women were more likely to emigrate within the context of family emigration rather than alone. There was, however, large scale seasonal emigration of female wet nurses, domestic servants and textile workers. The seasonal emigration of Italian women was also a feature of later migratory processes in the post-war period. Nevertheless, the dominant precedent of female migration amongst Italian women has frequently been linked to a family migration context. Single-sex female migration had been apparent predominantly in the form of 'team-transfers' such as rice weeders, who would be seasonally transferred to rice-weeding areas.

Italian women's involvement in migration was also marked by regional differences. Alberoni (1970) found that in the 15–24 age category, women from Northern regions outnumbered men in their migration into Milan between 1932 and 1955. Conversely, Southern men outnumbered Southern women in this age group. Women involved in this type of migration moved from rural areas to find employment in industry or domestic service and although some would continue working after marriage, as a rule, this migration of single women was envisaged as a provisional arrangement prior to marriage (Alberoni 1970; Arena 1983). Generally, writers such as Arena (1983) have argued that Italian women's role during migration was to remain in the country of origin and Monticelli (1983) has pointed to the existence of southern villages almost entirely populated by women, the elderly and young children as a result of male migration. The women left behind in the villages were referred to as 'white widows' (Boswell 1996, p. 140).[36] Where women did migrate with their families, they did not always participate in the labour market. In fact, relatively high numbers of Italian women were categorised as housewives in the destination immigration countries. Data collated by the Foreign Ministry in 1981 showed that 74.2 per cent of Italian female emigrants in Brazil were housewives. In Argentina 59.4 per cent were housewives, 66.3 per cent in Chile, 44.1 per cent in France and 36.8 per cent in Belgium.[37]

A dominant migratory model thus linked Italian women very closely to a family driven migration. This meant that there was a limited precedent in relation to the long term migration of single women. This would have some impact on migrant women's experiences in Italy as the characteristics of their migration were so novel. So how did commentators of incoming migration to Italy interpret the presence of migrant women? In one of the earliest published academic articles on migrant women, Gabriella Arena (1978) attributed both the rural to urban migration of Italian women and the labour migration of overseas migrants to Italy to modifications in Italian women's lives. Arena's argument centred on emphasising the manner in which Italian women's involvement in the paid economy had created female work and she was thus one of the first commentators to articulate the important connection between Italian women and migrant women.[38]

It would be at a much later stage that sustained attention would be paid to migrant women's involvement in the new migration to Italy. The early 1990s in fact witnessed the organisation of a range of activities related to migrant women. For example, a number of conferences on migrant women, at the national and local level, were organised and the proceedings published. The 1990 publication by the *Comune* of Milan was the outcome of a conference organised by the *Centro Azione Milano Donne* and the *Comune*. In January 1990, the Emilia-Romagna region also held a conference on female migration to the region. In 1993, Lazio published a report on migrant women's experiences in the region (ISCOS-CISL 1993). In 1993, an academic conference on migrant women's situation nationally was held at the University of Ancona, the proceedings of which were published in book form in 1994. Increased journalistic attention was also apparent in the 1990s.[39]

The Italian academic literature which has addressed the issue of female migrants has tended to focus on the migratory aspects of migrant women's experience (Arena 1983; Raffaele 1992) or female migrant adaptation within Italy (Favaro and Bordogna 1991). Researchers have presented a variety of perspectives related to migrant women's presence in Italy. Campani (1990) has argued that the situation of female migrants is indicative of the future stability and social integration of migrant communities, while Raffaele (1992) viewed migrant women as inhabiting an important mediatory role between tradition and modernity. Favaro and Bordogna (1991) similarly adopted a tradition/modernity continuum to interpret female migrant adaptation with reference to different ethnic groups.[40] Picciolini's (1992) use of what she termed a woman's studies approach to the issue led her to prioritise gender as an explanatory framework for migrant women's situation. She posited a fundamental conflict of interest, not between Italian women and migrant women, but rather between men and women. Migrant women were thus incorporated into the constituency of gender. On closer observation however, it can be observed that this approach lends itself to Frankenberg's (1993) concept of the power evasiveness of a privileged gendered ethnicity (see above). An example of this is apparent in Picciolini's explanation of why migrant women utilise safer contraceptive methods in comparison to their Italian counterparts: 'What lies between their desire for maternity, moulded by their culture of origin, and the concrete reality which prevents them from realising it is a mature awareness which utilises the instruments offered by western medicine' (Picciolini 1992, p. 85). As I will argue in chapter 6, it is often the importance of Italian women's family organisation which requires migrant women to negate their own maternity. Picciolini underplayed this, choosing instead to highlight the benefits of western medicine for migrant women. Her interpretative framework thus prevented her from recognising a rather fundamental arena of conflict between migrant women and Italian women.

Academic focus on issues such as 'push' factors or female migrant adaptation within Italy has not, in my view, given sufficient emphasis to the significance of existing structural conditions within Italy as factors which shape Black women's experience. Part of these structural conditions relate to Italian women's new social identities and the impact this has had on the Italian family. Favaro and Bordogna's (1991) interest in establishing whether the migration of women had led to a redefinition of gender relations focused only on the relationship of migrant women with their respective communities. It is my view that the discussion of gender relations in the context of female migration needs to be broadened to investigate the manner in which migrant women may be redefining gender relations in terms of the national community. The focus on the former displays an ethnocentric concern with the tradition of other cultures. A focus on the latter is more likely to present these authors with the contradiction of migrant women's work functioning to liberate some Italian women from aspects of reproductive labour and simultaneously protecting Italian men from having to engage in this work.

In the conference proceedings of the 1993 Ancona conference, a more informed theoretical and less ethnocentric overview of migrant women's situation was provided in the introductory preface by the editor Giovanna Vicarelli. Here, she argues that the work of migrant women is central and functional to the new economic and cultural conditions of post-industrialised societies. Indeed, migrant women's labour is seen as having the potential to soothe if not resolve the social contradictions typical of contemporary western societies. In addition to such a forceful acknowledgement of the importance of migrant women's labour, Vicarelli recognised that migrant women could not be 'developed' according to the demands of Italian women: '... we need to appreciate that they [female migrants] demonstrate, in their daily lives, that they are capable of being autonomous and having an identity which is not from their past, but is also not that pursued and desired by western women' (Vicarelli 1994, p. 9).[41] This constituted an important progression from the tradition/modernity polarity typical of works relating to the European context and implicit in the work of some Italian authors such as Favaro and Bordogna (1991).

Several papers from the 1993 Ancona conference suggested a coexistence of new and old theoretical approaches. Campani (1994a) for example made explicit reference to the Anglo-Saxon literature on gender, race and class, conceding that Italy was far behind the Black feminist thought of Britain. Piazza's (1994) research, on the other hand, prioritised the importance of gender for migrant women, marginalising, to some extent, their migrant status:

> Because [their] main problem is ... dealing with the present, not simply in terms of the problem of racist attitudes ... but also and above all in terms of dealing with relationships, their relationships with their children, possible changes in their employment. In other words problems which are in some way exacerbated and made more dramatic because they are foreign women, but which, all things considered, concern all women. I think it is important not to place them into an immigration framework, but instead to place them into the general framework of contradictions and difficulties that all women experience (Piazza 1994, p. 220).

An emerging awareness of the potential significance of the relationship between migrant women and Italian women could also be identified in this literature. Adriana Luciano (1994, p. 225) referred to the presence of migrant women in Italy as 'a disturbing presence'. One of the few Italian writers to emphasise Italian women's own recent emergence from traditionally prescribed roles when discussing migrant women, Luciano verbalised the existence of a fundamental gender antagonism between migrant and Italian women which many other studies have chosen to obscure:

> But their presence questions us ... Their availability (compulsory?) for subordinate work that we have rejected questions us. The ease with which we have accepted that they should bear the burden for the contradictions of our civil life questions us: women who are less equal than other women confirming the stigma which has always relegated domestic work to the bottom of the social scale. Their presence represents a challenge ... The fact that these women –

whether they are educated or not, whether they are alone or accompanied ... can only live in our country as wives, domestic workers or prostitutes ... is an issue which concerns us directly. If one of them replaces one of us who has managed to escape such a destiny, with no hope of redemption, our history is taking a step backwards (Luciano 1994, p. 226).

This antagonism will be explored in more depth during the course of this book utilising the two bodies of literature discussed above. I am focusing on a specific model of female migrant identity in Italy. This does not imply that a single female migrant model exists in Italy. Regional economic disparities combined with the range of ethnicities present in the country have led to a variety of coexisting models. The models referred to in Italian migration literature refer to female headed households, family migration units and women who migrate through family reunification policies as wives (Favaro and Bordogna 1991; De Filippo 1994). Whether migrant women are present in Italy as part of a family unit or on their own has significant implications for the model of female social identity to which they will be able to aspire. This book is concerned with only one of the female migratory models referred to above. This relates to the long-term primary migration of single, separated or married women who have been employed exclusively as domestic workers. This category is utilised for several important reasons. Firstly, it constitutes the original female migrant model in Italy and as such represents an early example of modifications in global migratory trends. Secondly, the refusal of migrant women who fit this model to renege on their desire for motherhood has underlined certain problems intrinsic to this model. It is in fact a model which lends itself to a hierarchical construction of women's multiple identities, where a labour identity becomes dominant. Finally, this model stands in antithesis to dominant models of social identity for Italian women.

In relating this model to the discursive elements of Black feminist thought, we need to investigate how the different processes of gender, class and a migrant status interact within the Italian context. I argue that the central link revolves around migrant women's insertion into the domestic work sector. It is largely uncontested that where female migrants are employed, their principal employment occupation is that of domestic worker.[42] I address the conceptual premises of domestic work in chapter 4, but at this stage, it is important to highlight the structural organisation of the domestic work sphere as a major contributory factor to the negation of migrant women's multiple social identities and thus as an important causal factor in the establishment of gender difference within Italy. Domestic work constitutes a low-status occupation, it is principally a feminised employment sector and in its most oppressive form – the live-in sphere – it is increasingly carried out by migrant women. In conformity with a Black feminist perspective, I do not seek to ascertain which of the three processes of class, gender or migrant status stand at the root of migrant women's subordination in Italy. Rather, it is my contention that these processes are inextricably connected and together contribute to migrant women's specific marginality. I would suggest however, that the specificity of the Italian case lies in the importance of the domestic work sector as a central link between these processes.

Notes

1   Excerpts from some chapters have been published previously. See Andall (1992; 1995; 1998; 1999; 2000). Translations of Italian sources reproduced in this book are my own.
2   See European Forum of Left Feminists and Others (1993).
3   A variety of terms are used to refer to the principal subjects of this book. 'Black women' is used as a political and descriptive category to discuss the specific ethnic groups of my case study. Similarly, 'African women' is utilised to describe their provenance. 'Migrant women' is used as a description of their migrant status, and in some cases refers to other ethnic groups not explicitly included in this study. 'Ethnic minority women' is used here to acknowledge a social identity which lies beyond a purely migrant identity.
4   The Italian Communist Party became the Democratic Party of the Left (Pds) in 1991.
5   This has been highlighted by writers such as Kichelmacher (1990) and Bimbi (1993b). Both writers stress the influence of generational differences in determining Italian women's ability to manage these roles.
6   There is some agreement that Pci/Pds women in the 1980s and 1990s became important political representatives of progressive gender activism. Pitch (1990), Bimbi (1992) and Guadagnini (1993) all suggest this.
7   Published research in Italy has mainly focused on 'gendering' immigration (see below).
8   Prior to incoming immigration, the prevalent discourse on ethnicity in Italy was in relation to regional ethnicity and culture.
9   I am not asserting a universal Italian or migrant experience by using these terms. Internal differentiation within both categories is acknowledged.
10 Christian Association of Italian Workers. COLF (*collaboratrice familiare*) is an abbreviated form of 'family collaborator', a modern Italian term for domestic worker (see chapter 4).
11 See Burnett (1977) regarding the problems of organising domestic workers in Britain in the nineteenth century.
12 Escrivà's (1996) research on domestic workers in Spain indicates that Catholic church missions were also heavily involved in the domestic service sector. However she did not find evidence of any national organising Catholic body.
13 De Grazia (1992) does discuss domestic workers in her chapter on women and work under fascism, but points to the absence of a focused study of the 'servant problem' in fascist Italy.
14 See Gregson and Lowe (1993) for an appraisal of the contemporary British context.

15 Condon's (1995) research shows that a more diversified range of jobs was available to female Caribbean migrants to France. Although these were principally in feminised sectors of the economy, one third worked in the health and social service sector and a further quarter in office employment.

16 Gender, ethnicity, class and age are all factors which impact on the relationship established between the researcher and the researched. Moreover, one cannot assume an insider identity simply by virtue of a shared gender, race or class identity (Warren 1988). As a Black woman, I occupied an ambiguous insider/outsider position in relation to the African women I interviewed (see Song and Parker 1995). Interviewees perceived my commonality as a Black woman but also my difference as a researcher, as someone who lived in another country and who was of a different ethnicity. Nonetheless, commonality was exploited as a strategy to secure access to women and was particularly useful when making direct approaches to women in public spaces.

17 Cape Verdeans were one of the first migratory groups of the recent period. Their migration dates back to the 1960s and has been almost entirely female. The East African countries are historically linked to Italy as a result of colonialism. Ethiopian and Eritrean women were both labour migrants and political refugees. Only a limited amount of data was acquired, via questionnaires, in relation to Somali women, thus the bulk of the data reported in this book refers to Cape Verdean, Ethiopian and Eritrean women.

18 Bhavnani (1993) has referred to the EDITing of Women's Studies, whereby the four processes of Erasure, Denial, Invisibility and Tokenism militate against a more inclusive feminist movement.

19 The theory which presents patriarchy as the basic system which creates women's subordinate position is of course representative of only one particular strand of feminist theory.

20 See for examples, the special issue of *Race and Class* on racism in Europe (1991) and Jan Rath's (1993) article on the ideological representation of migrant workers in Europe.

21 Afrocentricity combines elements of philosophy, science, history and mythology to give a perspective on African-American people, placing Africa at the centre of its philosophy (see Asante 1988). One example of this incompatibility may be found in Collins' (1990) synthesis of Black feminist thought where she names Afrocentricity as one of the theoretical traditions which has shaped her analysis. Collins' analysis of Black women and mothering demonstrates a tension between her desire to portray the African-American family in a manner which places value on those aspects of African-American family organisation which have traditionally been negatively represented (see Jewell 1993) and the necessity from a feminist standpoint to develop a critique of the family's impact on African-American women.

22 hooks (1989) refers to this as paradigms of domination while King (1988) refers to an interactive model of multiple jeopardy.

23 See for examples Barbara Ryan's (1992) work on American feminism; Claire Duchen's (1986) work on French feminism and Lucia Birnbaum's (1986) study of Italian feminism. See also Bourne (1983) and Stacey (1985) regarding a respective critique and defence of the British women's movement's focus on sexuality as a mobilising issue within the context of the inclusivity/exclusivity of feminism.

24 There have been others who have resented the nature and extent of this critique. Ryan's (1992) work on the women's movement in America, indicates how some White feminists had grown tired of being criticised by both the White male establishment and ethnic minority women.

25 See Bonnett's (1996) review of the literature relating to 'whiteness'.

26 She defines this as 'a mode of thinking about race organized around an effort to not "see", or at any rate not to acknowledge, race difference' (Frankenberg 1993, p. 142).

27 Contradictory discourses do not of course exist only across ethnic boundaries but also within such boundaries. Annalisa Pasero (1991) for example has documented how Mussolini's advocation of a family-based role for women in Italy warranted substantial modification in order to prevent the miscegenation of the Italian race in Italy's East African colonies. The creation of all-white brothels, in contrast to the family-based role of women being promoted in Italy, was perceived to be a preferable alternative to interaction between European and African cultures.

28 These are seen to be three principal but not exclusive analytical frameworks. It is acknowledged that other factors such as age, sexuality and disability may shift the nature of the principal interlocking identities for many women.

29 Although Dumon (1981) in his study of migrant women workers found that immigrant women were increasingly defined and defining themselves as workers.

30 See Bryan, Dadzie and Scafe (1985) with regard to the post-war migration of Caribbean women to Britain, and Condon (1995) with reference to the post-war migration of Caribbean women to France.

31 See Kosack (1976) for an example of this trend.

32 For example the 1970 Swiss Census showed that while economic activity rates for Swiss women was 32.44 per cent, for foreign women it was 46.6 per cent. When this latter figure was broken down by nationality, Southern European female migrants exhibited particularly high levels of employment participation – 77 per cent of Yugoslav women and 64 per cent of Spanish women. These statistics are cited in Kosack (1976) and Morokvasic (1984).

33 Some Italian transatlantic migration at the turn of the century fits this model. See Corti (1990).

34 For a study of the racialised and gendered characteristics of homeworking in Britain, see Phizacklea and Wolkowitz (1995).

35 Some migrant women are also involved in the sex industry. For some discussion of this, see Raffaele (1992), Campani (2000) and journalistic articles by Melandri (1991) and Pajetta (1990c). Pajetta (1990c) also refers to those migrant women who have become involved in drugs trafficking. Interestingly, she cites one of them as saying '... life here [in Europe] is easier and after all if you can't find a job you can always be a domestic worker'.

36 See also Boswell for more on women and their experiences of migration.

37 Cited in Monticelli (1983).

38 This connection was not explored in any detail as her paper proceeded to a discussion of Italian women and employment. A later article did, however, focus more specifically on migrant women in Rome (see Arena 1983).

39 See as one example, a series of articles published in *Il Manifesto* in November 1990 by Giovanna Pajetta. See Pajetta (1990a; 1990b; 1990c).

40 Their research is related to Milan and their scheme categorises Egyptian and Iranian women as traditional, Filipina women as being prepared to adapt and Eritrean women as assuming modern values and attitudes. Implicit within this framework is of course an unchallenged assumption regarding the superiority of the West's modern values and attitudes.

41 Campani (1994a) referred to this as a Third Way for migrant women.

42 Even in the industrial heartland of Lombardy, Campus's (1994) analysis of employment placements for female migrants via the local job centres in Milan in 1990 showed that 76.7 per cent of women found employment as domestic workers, 16 per cent in industry and 4.9 per cent in the tertiary sector.

1   Italian Gender Models

As in other national contexts, there has been a persistent and as yet unresolved tension between Italian women's reproductive and productive roles. In the post-war period,[1] the maternal role of Italian women has historically been privileged above other roles, although more recently there have been moves towards a more equitable accommodation of women's multiple social identities. These trends have led to parallel but differentiated gender models for Italian women and migrant women and in subsequent chapters I will be arguing that, in contrast to Italian women, migrant women's labour identity has been privileged above other social identities. This chapter will establish the nature and direction of Italian debates on women, providing a specifically gendered framework within which to situate the experiences of migrant women. Given that the post-war debate on gender is so vast, I shall concentrate my discussion on providing an account of the tension between family work and paid work with reference to a few limited areas – the Italian Constitution, legislation regarding work and maternity and the empirical realities of women's family and work experiences. The activities of political feminists in the post-war period will also be addressed.

The Constitution

After the defeat of fascism, a Constituent Assembly was elected in June 1946 to establish a new Italian Constitution. The Assembly included members from the dominant political parties – the Christian Democrat Party, the Communist Party and the Socialist Party – and it would be these Catholic and Marxist traditions which would influence the Italian Constitution in different spheres. The most influential Catholic group within the Constituent Assembly was the *dossettiani*.[2] They were keen to include Catholic values into the Constitution and as Bedani (1996, p. 14) has shown their ideal was for the state to 'co-ordinate social relations as understood in Catholic social teaching'. Although the Catholics' strategy was ostensibly amenable to an accommodation of secularisation, their true goal was to 'keep alive the prospects of a Christian

23

civilisation' (Bedani 1996, p. 15). Moreover, organized Catholicism established a range of committees to guide the *dossettiani* in issues such as the role of women in society and this influence can be seen in the nature of articles pertaining to women. There are several articles in the Constitution which refer specifically to women.[3] I shall focus principally on Article 37 as it most evidently embodies the tension referred to above regarding productive and reproductive roles.[4] Article 37 is contained within the section of the Constitution which deals with employment and working conditions and reads:

> Female workers have the same rights and pay for the same work as male workers. Working conditions must allow them to fulfill their essential family function and ensure a special and adequate protection for mothers and children.

The affirmation that women's working conditions should not stand in conflict with their essential family role appears as indisputable evidence of the perceived importance of the maternal role for women – a role to which all other roles were to be subordinated. The discussion which preceded the eventual acceptance of this article confirmed this. On 8 October 1946, the president of the Drafting Subcommittee opened the discussion on the following draft:

> Female workers are assured of the same rights and the same treatment afforded to male workers. Furthermore, they are guaranteed special conditions to allow them to fulfill, along with their work, their family mission.[5]

The Christian Democrat La Pira wanted to add '*prevalent* family mission' (p. 503), while his colleague Moro suggested alteration to '*essential* family mission' (my emphases) (p. 503).[6]

By 1947, the article was being discussed in the Main Assembly as Article 33 in the following formula: Female workers have the same rights and pay for the same work as male workers. Working conditions must allow them to fulfill their essential family function.[7]

The discussion which took place on 10 May 1947 suggested a fairly consensual vision of women's role. The Christian Democrat member of the drafting Committee of 75, Maria Federici, proposed an amendment which aimed to give even greater emphasis to the maternal role. Federici sought to underline the essential and natural aspect of the maternal role: '... we should be surprised that we need to introduce a norm which is so human and natural' (La Costituzione della Repubblica, Vol. II, p. 1571). Indeed maternal care as opposed to parental care was presented as irreplaceable: 'Mothers are irreplaceable for children in relation to their interior development, their spiritual growth, the formation of their moral world' (p. 1572). Numerous Christian Democrats expressed a similar view regarding the mother's duty to care for her child. Moro, for example, referred to the maternal and family role as functions innate to women.

Speaking on behalf of some of the Left-wing members, the Socialist Angelina Merlin did propose to exclude the adjective 'essential', arguing that its inclusion was both superfluous and indicative of a reductive and outdated model of women's role. She insisted that women's role could no longer be seen as one confined to the family:

> We feel that maternity, that is our natural function, is not a condemnation, but a benediction which needs to be protected by the laws of the State without circumscribing and limiting our right to give as much as we know how to and want to in all areas of national and social life … (ibid., p. 1574).[8]

The Socialist Ghidini referred to: 'the fulfillment of her highest office' (ibid., pp. 1575-6) proposing the substitution of 'essential' with 'special'. The Socialists tended to argue that 'essential' diminished the male role while 'special' simply differentiated on the basis of function. Within Christian Democrat quarters, a family wage to be paid to the husband was promoted as an appropriate strategy to allow women to fulfill their natural maternal roles:

> This is where our specific demand resurfaces; … that is that salaries are such that the male worker can, with the income from his work, not only live in a dignified manner, but also form, raise, educate and maintain a family in a dignified way (Maria Federici, ibid., p. 1572).

Thus an explicit asymmetry of roles between men and women was included in the Constitution. While there was some consensus over protecting mothers in the workplace, implicit within this was an inevitable tension as to whether the nature of this protection would or indeed should limit women to a dominant role within the family.

Article 29 of the Constitution did establish the legal and moral equality of spouses but then subordinated this equality to the concept of family unity:

> The State recognises the family as a natural society based on marriage. Marriage is based on the moral and legal equality of spouses, within the limits laid down by the law to guarantee family unity.[9]

Despite Article 29 appearing in the above form, it is worth accentuating that Catholics had tried to give priority to the husband. In the drafting committee, the Christian Democrat La Pira was reported as follows:[10]

> ... despite being perfectly in agreement regarding the moral and legal equality of spouses, he would like the pre-eminent position of the father of the family, as the head of the family, to be more prominent.[11]

There were also some Catholics more extreme than the Dc. Rodi, for instance, belonged to the *Uomo Qualunque* Party.[12] In the debate he objected to the expression 'moral and equal equality of spouses' because: '... it is clear that we are before a harmonious law of the universe and that this harmonious law has sanctioned, based on natural criterion, the supremacy of the husband over the wife'.[13]

While the Dc was often cautious and anxious to accommodate the Left as far as it could, the Catholic right often represented a more widespread view. The ideas of the Catholic right were in fact consonant with the ideology of the Church which had adopted an unambiguous line with regard to women's employment. As Pope Pius XII stated in 1945, 'Women who do go out to work become dazed by the chaotic world in which they live, blinded by the tinsel of false glamour and greedy for sinister pleasures'.[14]

The finalised articles of the Constitution reflected a tension between granting women legal and moral equality while simultaneously privileging women's maternal role above other potential roles and social identities. It has in fact been argued that this intrinsic ambiguity explains the enduring conflict regarding the social construction of women in post-war Italy (Bimbi 1993a).

Maternity and Employment Legislation

An account of post-war maternity and employment legislation is utilised here to ascertain the nature of the state's regulation of these issues in the post-war period. This background information does not simply illuminate the situation for Italian women but is again an indication of the gender context which would also define migrant women's opportunities and circumstances. Like Article 37 of the Constitution, it could be argued that maternity and employment legislation pertaining to women displayed a desire to protect Italian women's maternal role, with an ensuing subordination of their paid employment function. More recently, the evolution of feminist debate within Italy has influenced state legislation, leading to an acceptance of the need to legislate for greater equilibrium between Italian women's work and family roles.

Protective maternity legislation offers a useful indication of the state's perception of the value of the maternal role. When compared to other European countries, Italy's protective maternity legislation is, in theory, quite generous.[15] Law 1204, which regulates the protection of working mothers, was introduced in 1971, replacing an earlier law dating back to 1950 (law n. 860). Italian maternity law provides for five months of benefit at an income replacement of 80 per cent (Art. 15). The mother is entitled to a further six months of benefit at an income replacement of 30 per cent (Art. 15). At this stage, the father is permitted to substitute for the mother, but only if the mother expressly waives her right to the benefit.[16] During the child's first year of life, the mother is entitled to two hours less work each day (Art. 10). Provision for protection during pregnancy and up to seven months after birth stipulates that women should not do heavy or dangerous jobs (Art. 3). Early maternity leave must also be granted if the woman has health problems related to the pregnancy, if the working environment is considered harmful to mother or baby and if the working mother cannot be moved to a more suitable task within the firm (Art. 5).

These provisions demonstrate a clear desire to facilitate the maternal process. However, there is a tension between the formal regulation of this issue and its informal practice. One of the problems of the maternity legislation is that access to its generous benefits are limited. The provisions do not cover self-employed women, women on short term contracts, women in the informal economy; and categories of workers such as domestic workers and home-workers are only partially covered by the legislation (see Art. 1). In one of the few studies which address the legislation's functioning in practice, Romito (1993)[17] found that most female employees remained at work until the beginning of their maternity leave. Conversely, those women not eligible for maternity benefit tended to continue to work until a few days before birth. In a number of cases, those women employed on short term contracts did not have their contracts renewed. Some women employed in the informal economy were dismissed, while others simply resigned. These findings evidently demonstrate that those women who remain outside the scope of the law suffer severe disadvantages in terms of job protection during and after pregnancy. Those women protected by the law, on the other hand, not only find good legislative provision but are further protected by a generalised consensus which prioritises the maternal role. According to Romito's (1993, p. 588) study, early maternity leave to women protected by the law was often offered and accepted in a fairly liberal way:

Consider the perfectly healthy teacher who stayed at home, fully paid, on the grounds of an alleged threatened miscarriage. None of her family, friends, or colleagues seemed to object to the fact that she and her doctor lied in order to give her the possibility of staying home. The very eagerness with which the leave was requested and accorded suggest that the home is still considered the more appropriate place for a woman, even if she is employed; therefore, a little cheating is acceptable as long as it results in her being led back there.

Some writers have pointed to the ambiguous implications of generous maternity provision in Italy, arguing that it contributes to employers' reluctance to employ women. Padoa Schioppa Kostoris (1993, p. 132) for example sees the 1971 maternity legislation as symptomatic of a policy which 'pays no heed to market reactions or to the perverse effects on the weak party it was supposed to protect'.

The concept of protection in relation to maternity is additionally evident in legislation regulating women's employment. For example, the fascist regime not only legislated to restrict women's employment (e.g. law n. 1514, 1938), but also legislated to protect women from dangerous and unsuitable jobs (law n. 653, 1934). It was only in 1963, that a law was promulgated (law n. 7) to prohibit employers from dismissing married women. This marked an important legislative watershed for Italian women as this law indicated a move away from the belief that being a wife and mother was fundamentally incompatible with paid employment.

Nonetheless, the protective concept inscribed into legislation regulating women's employment was perpetuated by the 1977 Equal Treatment Law (law n. 903). Historically, legislative acts had been based on a recognition of women's difference, understood in terms of women's *weakness* and legislative norms thus tended to be inspired by a culture of protection rather than one of validation (Farinelli 1993). The 1977 law was seen as an important landmark, outlawing direct and indirect discrimination against women in employment (Art. 1). It is to be noted however that various categories of women were not protected by the provisions of this law. Thus, women and girls hired as domestic workers for the normal functioning of family life were not considered to be in need of protection. While recognising and promoting equality for women in the workplace, the law indicated that the legislators were unable to fully relinquish the view that women workers required a paternalistic form of protection.[18]

Debate in the 1980s concerning women in employment culminated in the 1991 law n. 125.[19] It signified a new historical phase in the theoretical approach to women and employment through a consideration of women's difference as a value as opposed to a limitation. The law sanctioned the use of affirmative action to eliminate disparities regarding educational and professional training and to provide access to employment. The legislation also sought to challenge the organisation of work where this was seen to have an adverse effect on women. As Farinelli (1993) has shown, the law recognised the plural composition of the workforce, implicitly rejecting the traditional social prototype of the employed worker. The law additionally paid attention to gender roles within the family. This had the explicit aim of promoting: '... through a different organisation of work, conditions and work times, the balance between family and professional responsibilities and an improved division of such labour between the two sexes' (Art. 1/e). This was a particularly critical ruling. It constituted a clear legislative attempt to propose an organisational remedy to the practical difficulties of women's double presence.[20] Not only did it recognise that the reconciliation of a family role and a paid work role could be facilitated by a reorganisation of working structures, but perhaps more significantly, the legislation theoretically sanctioned the idea of assisting women to combine these roles. Furthermore, the legislation called for reproductive labour to be shared more equally between men and women. In so doing, the 1991 law recognised that women's disadvantaged position on the labour market was not exclusively a consequence of the manner in which paid employment was organised, but that it was also a direct consequence of women's responsibility within the home. While the former area could be modified by a commitment to the reorganisation of working structures, the latter area could only be modified by reducing women's responsibility in the family arena. This implied much greater participation from men in reproductive labour and the innovation of this piece of legislation was its formal recognition of this fact.

Conceptual Premises and Empirical Realities

The above has addressed the ideological premises of state legislation and as Caldwell (1991a) has observed, legislative change in post-war Italy provided women with new and different opportunities. Nonetheless, legislation does not necessarily reflect actual experience, and the following section will consider Italian women's experience of family and work roles. This is used to ascertain the impact that the values and ideologies discussed above have had on Italian families in the post-war period.

The Italian family has generally been noted for its cohesiveness (Paci 1983; Ginsborg 1990).[21] This cohesiveness has not only proved to be important within the sociocultural sphere but it has also led to the establishment of a valuable socioeconomic model of development in the form of family run small businesses (Ginsborg 1995). Nonetheless, rural depopulation, urbanisation and industrialisation have all contributed to structural changes in the Italian family (King 1987). Despite this, links and obligations to the family have not disappeared (Turnaturi 1987) and even though the traditional extended family is no longer common, the geographical proximity of families, together with emotional and economic ties have remained (Paci 1983). In fact Ginsborg talks of a familism specific to Italy.[22] In comparison to many other West European countries, the Italian family does appear remarkably resilient. It has a comparatively low divorce rate and a low number of single parent families. In 1990 figures for children born out of wedlock were 6.3 per cent in Italy, compared to 27.9 per cent in the UK, 30.1 per cent in France and 46.4 per cent in Denmark.[23] Italy has also become noted for the phenomenon of the 'long adolescence', where 80 per cent of Italians aged between 15 and 29 still live at home and where almost half of 29 year old males still do so.[24]

There has been a wealth of sociological literature dealing with the Italian family. Saraceno (1988) has pointed to a body of research which focuses on the asymmetrical interests of individuals within the family unit. These asymmetrical interests suggest a potential reduction in the cohesiveness of the Italian family or at least the need to develop strategies based on external assistance to sustain family cohesiveness. At a conference on the Italian family held in 1985, Golini (1986) suggested five areas which could be viewed as the cornerstone of transformations within the family – the sexual revolution, the change in women's status, the existence of divorce, the availability of contraception and the growing central importance of the couple. The prominence of gender implicit within his explanatory framework suggests that modifications in women's lives and aspirations have had an important impact on the Italian family.[25]

Italian women's experience of labour market participation in the post-war period has been determined by both cultural and economic factors.[26] In the immediate post-war period, women's social identity was closely intertwined with their biological role as mothers.[27] Family equilibrium and cohesion was based on women's unreserved devotion to the family unit (Belotti 1986). In recent years, there have been attempts to define a contemporary social identity of Italian women. The results have focused on generational differences between women which explain the coexistence of a variety of models of female identity

(Bianchi 1990; Kichelmacher 1990; Bimbi 1993b). According to Bimbi (1993b) the oldest generation of women (born in the 1930s and 1940s) represented a traditional model of female identity, which was intrinsically connected to their biological roles as mothers. The generation born after the war, on the other hand, would eventually legitimise a new model of female identity which was detached from an exclusive family identity. However, in the 1950s and 1960s, female employment was still viewed as a secondary identity for women, and its economic advantages were considered a supplement to the main (male) breadwinner's wage (Battistoni 1986). Thus, until the end of the 1960s, the dominant role for women was that of a housewife and mother (Bimbi 1993b). Cultural factors supported this type of family organisation. In her study of poor working-class women in Naples in the 1970s, the anthropologist Victoria Goddard encountered discouragement and even active opposition to women's waged employment 'even where economic circumstances made their monetary contribution necessary' (Goddard 1987, pp. 173–4).[28] While in other European contexts working-class married women would engage in paid work through economic necessity, in Italy it was not uncommon for men to take on a second paid job while their wives remained as housewives (Saraceno 1987).[29]

The nature of women's participation in the labour market has thus been partially determined by cultural considerations. This tended to mean that female identity was more clearly centred in the family than in labour market participation (Cammarota 1984). But the specific characteristics of the Italian labour market also contributed to this situation. Both Del Boca (1988) and Bettio (1988b) argue that models of female employment participation for other countries are not entirely applicable to the Italian situation and that Italy is in many ways a special case.[30] It has been suggested that institutional factors and labour market segmentation may be the most appropriate explanatory factors for understanding the nature of women's labour force participation in Italy (Bettio 1988b).

While the Italian labour market is formally governed by inflexible and universalistic legislation, at the informal level one finds various forms of 'micro-social regulation' (Reyneri 1989). In line with this national framework, the organisation of women's labour in the official labour market tends to be on a full-time basis, with more flexible working arrangements within the informal economy. Where other European countries have frequently utilised the part-time supply of women's labour to provide cheap and flexible labour, small firms and the unofficial sector have assumed this role in the Italian context.[31] Eurostat data for 1989 indicated that only 10.9 per cent of Italian women were employed on a part-time basis, compared to 43.6 per cent of British women and 60 per cent of Dutch women.[32]

The rigidity of the official labour market, coupled with an absence of comprehensive external services for working mothers with children have undoubtedly affected women's employment decisions. Historical and cultural explanations have been used to account for the state's deficiencies in terms of welfare provision for the family. According to Bimbi (1993a, p. 151): 'The mystique of the family led to the idea of a private world that was self-sufficient in meeting the needs of everyday life'. It has also been argued that it is not simply an absence of appropriate service provision which has a negative impact on women, but also the organisation of work and work times (Saraceno 1994). Although writers such as Battistoni (1986) have suggested that women's weak situation on the labour market can no longer be fully explained by the centrality of their family role, other studies have indicated that family factors still condition women's employment choices (see Del Boca 1988; Bianchi 1990). Results from commissioned research by the Equal Opportunities Office (*Commissione nazionale per la parità e le pari opportunità tra uomo e donna*)[33] showed that working mothers tended to reduce their productive working time to attend to the needs of the family, while working fathers tended to *increase* time dedicated to productive labour to provide for the additional needs of the family. These results therefore suggested a perpetuation of the sexual division of labour.

To conclude this section, I would argue that there would seem to be an enduring conflict between women's productive and reproductive roles in Italy and this, along with the value attributed to the institution of the family, can be used to account for the demand for migrant women's labour as domestic workers. This argument must be considered in the light of changing welfare structures, not simply in Italy, but more generally in Western Europe.

In a paper which attempts to define the features of a European welfare state, Cochrane (1993) has demonstrated how global economic competition means that welfare policies in European countries have to rely increasingly on market solutions. He argues that welfare budget expenditure has moved away from universalistic forms of service to individual and private provision and he identifies a tendency towards state *regulation* rather than state *provision*. While this may be true at the general European level, a more specific interpretation of the Italian welfare system model can inform our understanding of the demand for migrant women's labour as domestic workers. Paci (1989) maintains that while there has been significant public regulation of welfare in Italy, there are large gaps in its private regulation. I want to focus on this latter point in relation to the family in Italy, as it is of some relevance to the question of migrant women.

The emphasis of the Italian welfare system with regard to the family has focused on the family as institution rather than on the question of female emancipation. This has meant that a comprehensive network of services which could benefit the individual and the family by minimising domestic obligations and thus facilitating women's paid employment does not really exist (Zanatta and Mirabile (1993).[34] According to Dell'Orto and Taccani's (1993, p. 109) evaluation of Italy's welfare system: 'The family has been recognised as an irreplaceable resource and family care has been officially approved as part of the welfare umbrella'. Indeed, the sociologist Bimbi (1993a) has developed the concept of a 'gift relationship' to describe Italian women's relationship to welfare provision. Paci (1989, p. 227), on the other hand, has argued that the dual public and private welfare system was initially acceptable to Italian families:

> True, the state did not offer extended and efficient social services to families, but this in a sense was 'reciprocated' by the job possibilities offered to the head of the family through the clientelistic route within the 'guaranteed-corporative' area.

Paci (1989) acknowledges that this acceptability was based on a vision of the Italian family which assumed that a reliable network of parental assistance and a clearly delineated gender based division of roles would provide for the social protection of the family. A changing Italian family called for a different style of welfare provision:

> Recent surveys ... show a rapid spread in the 1980s of a more modern family model, characterized by the loss of the 'extended family' ... and, above all, a much larger and steadier supply of female labor than before, in spite of a competitive and difficult job market and the high rates of female unemployment. Under these new conditions ... what is needed is a policy of available and efficient welfare services across the nation, which the Italian state has neither wanted nor known how to offer (ibid., p. 229).

The new trends of the Italian family and their impact on welfare provision for the family are clearly relevant to the labour migration of women. The concurrent challenge to Italian women's 'gift relationship' to welfare provision and European governments' concern to reduce welfare expenditure have encouraged the development of alternative strategies within Italy. Recourse to domestic service can therefore be viewed as a redistribution of certain aspects of domestic labour to migrant women, with the state regulating rather than assuming responsibility for the provision of this service. This form of redistribution is symbolic of what Dell'Orto and Taccani (1993) have described as a prevalent 'do-it-yourself' approach to care issues in Italy, which is premised on the low levels of confidence in the social services.

But we need to understand why this particular form of private regulation gained currency in Italy and not in some other European countries. Using Britain for comparative purposes, one significant disparity between the two countries concerns the structural organisation of women's employment. In Britain, part-time labour and social services provision have generally been used as adjustment mechanisms to structural changes in the family.[35] Italian women, on the other hand, are normally employed on a full-time basis and have historically relied on informal family care networks and available social services provision to combine family and work roles. But the choice of *live-in* domestic workers for Italian women still needs to be explained. It is my view that socioeconomic and historical factors can be used to account for the *possibility* of this choice. In Britain the domestic servant class had virtually disappeared by the end of the Second World War (McBride 1976; Burnett 1977). In Italy, however, the enduring poverty which existed in parts of Italy in the post-war period meant that there was a regular supply of cheap indigenous labour to meet the demand of the middle and upper classes. As Italy developed economically and women were able to find employment in other sectors, the indigenous supply of domestic labour for the live-in sector began to dry up. It began to be replaced in the 1970s, by a cheap female migrant labour force. When the structural changes that had been taking place within the family led to a demand from different class sectors of the society, the model of the live-in female migrant was already in place.

The existence of the demand for live-in workers in Italy shows the extent to which the society was dependent on the unpaid labour of women as full-time housewives or as part-time welfare providers. It is furthermore symptomatic of an inability to conceptualise an alternative model to the pre-existing one. In effect, live-in domestic work replicates in structure the traditional role of the wife and mother. Nonetheless, the implications of this transformation indicate an enduring need for a figure which embodies the wife/maternal function. Thus the conceptualisation of care remains linked to a feminine figure whose availability to provide care for extended periods of time is paramount. The unpaid labour of the housewife is being transformed into the paid labour of the domestic worker. However, just as the unpaid labour of the housewife was subordinate to the paid work of men, so too can we witness the subordination of domestic workers to the paid labour function of both Italian men and women. In attempting to embrace new multiple identities, Italian women are increasingly unwilling to permit the demands of the family to totally define their aspirations and roles. This has led to a progressive rejection of their role as unpaid informal carers. Migrant women's labour in Italy can thus be seen as a functional response to the structural changes which have taken place in Italy in the recent period.

Italian Women's Political Activism

The political ideology underpinning legislation affects the contents of national legislation. In these matters the state is far from ideologically neutral. In Italy debates about women were profoundly influenced by the presence of the influential and active machinery of the Catholic church. It attained sustained input into questions related to women's roles and identities, demanding 'a public centrality for the family' (Caldwell 1991a, p. 27).[36]

The two dominant political forces of the post-war period, the Christian Democrat Party and the Italian Communist Party had important roles in defining the parameters of women's changing identities. As political parties, they were of course operating within wider strategic constraints. However, throughout most of the post-war period, the Christian Democrat Party's position with regard to women was intrinsically linked to the institution of the family for which the Dc proclaimed outright support.[37] The Italian Communist Party, on the other hand, assumed a less static position with regard to women.[38] This section of the chapter is not however concerned with political parties' approach to women but rather with the nature of women's political activism within Italy. The following brief overview of progressive women's post-war activism is intended to establish a historical framework into which political initiatives developed by, for and with migrant women at a later stage can be situated (see chapter 9).

Women's political activism in the post-war period has been widespread and varied. The two principal organisations of the immediate post-war period reflected the emerging political polarisation of post-war Italy. Two parallel national women's associations, influenced by the competing ideologies of Communism and Catholicism, dominated the arena of women's political mobilisation in the immediate post-war period. These were the Communist and Socialist affiliated *Unione Donne Italiane* (UDI) and the Catholic affiliated

Centro Italiano Femminile (CIF).[39] There were also women's sections operating within a number of political and cultural formations.[40] The year 1968 marked a watershed in the nature of women's activism with the emergence of an autonomous feminist movement. This was firmly centred in the progressive arena of women's activism. While initially treated by the political forces 'as a substantially marginal, elitist, and fairly insignificant phenomenon' (Ergas 1982, p. 263), it was soon to become a visible political actor.[41] It has routinely been described as reaching its peak in the years between 1976-1978 at the height of its mobilisation over the issue of abortion (Calabrò and Grasso 1985; Ergas 1986; Birnbaum 1986; Pisciotta 1986). During this period, the feminist movement was able to challenge the hegemony of both the UDI and the women's section of the Pci as protagonists of the progressive sphere of women's activism. I want to briefly highlight some feminist perspectives on the question of maternity and domestic work given the relevance of these two themes to this book.

Although some feminists paid substantial attention to the question of domestic work in the 1970s, this was limited to the unpaid domestic work of Italian women. The paid domestic work of both Italian and migrant women remained largely absent from their analyses. Their analysis of housework as productive work led to calls for a salary for housewives.[42] While feminists formulated an analysis of unpaid domestic work at the expense of paid domestic work, they did pay some attention to the question of maternity. Not surprisingly, feminists reacted against the dominant construction of women's social identity as a fusion of maternal and family roles. As one feminist collective asserted: 'Women must be able to refuse marriage in order to achieve full independence'.[43] The discussions around maternity which emerged from a conference on women held in Assisi in 1975 fully demonstrated the conflict that feminists were beginning to feel in relation to motherhood. Motherhood was seen as denying women their true personality. As one woman stated: 'I have the feeling that my rejection [of a child] is certainly not a free choice ... Perhaps I am not rejecting the child itself, but the role in which the child would today constrict me to'.[44] Influenced by the collectivist values of the 1970s, some women even saw the rejection of maternity as a gesture of solidarity for woman, in that it could transform the collective destiny of women.[45]

As a result of feminist mobilisation for the legalisation of abortion, which was achieved in 1978, feminists became noted for their attachment to the importance of choosing *not* to be mothers. In some ways then, the needs of migrant women and the theoretical evolution of Italian feminism stood at different stages with regard to maternity in the 1970s. Migrant women were struggling to find the space for a maternal identity in the 1970s (see chapter 7), while Italian feminists were still locked into an ambiguous, if not overtly negative appraisal of the mothering role. By the 1990s, this position had fundamentally changed,[46] although as I will illustrate in later chapters, with limited benefits for Black women.

In the 1980s the feminist movement was unable to sustain its position as a mass women's movement.[47] However, feminism certainly did not disappear. Rather, its activity and visibility became more diffuse.[48] By the 1980s, the relationship between autonomous feminist groups and the institutional sphere of progressive women in the form of the UDI and the Pci's women's sections was also undergoing an important transformation (see below).[49] While the feminists of the 1970s had preferred to assume an autonomous position in relation to political party structures, the younger generation of feminists sought to 'bring feminist values and perspectives into party politics' (Guadagnini 1993, p. 176). The Pci was seen to be the most accessible party, partly because of a new political direction in the 1980s where it had committed itself to paying more attention to new social movements.[50] Furthermore women activists operating within the progressive institutional sphere were becoming more detached from their parenting ideological structures.

While the events of the 1970s have been widely documented, rather less attention has been paid to the evolution of progressive women's activism in the 1980s and early 1990s. During this time, two broad forms of feminism developed. Cultural feminism was centred in the Women's Bookstore in Milan and promoted the concept of women's difference, whilst political feminism developed within political parties and trade-unions (Beccalli 1994). However, these were not separate feminisms. Women within political parties, and especially Communist women, drew on the work emerging from within cultural feminism for their own political feminist practice. In her paper on women and the Italian party system, Guadagnini (1993) has argued that the nature of Italy's partyocracy meant that power and influence could only be achieved by working within the parties. This section of the chapter traces Communist women's attempts to do just this, first within the Italian Communist Party and subsequently within the Democratic Party of the Left. This discussion provides the framework for an assessment of Pds women's eventual political work with migrant women (see chapter 9). It seeks to establish whether the specific evolution of progressive women's activism in the political sphere boded well for the inclusion of a racialised gender category in Italy.

The Pci/Pds's Women's Section

An important concept for cultural feminism and which was seen to typify the new intellectual direction of Italian feminism[51] is the theorisation of the philosophical concept of sexual difference, derived from the writings of the French psychoanalyst Luce Irigaray. This concept presents a critique of our acceptance of the universality of things that are, in point of fact, masculine and patriarchal. Adriana Cavarero has written widely on this concept and its implications for women in the Italian context:

> The consequence for woman is that she cannot recognize herself in the thought system and the language of a neutral subject which does not contain her – and indeed excludes her – without accounting for that exclusion. The universal, presuming to hold true for the excluded sex as well, erases the logical space of originary differing ... (Cavarero 1993, p. 192).[52]

This theory thus posits an essential female difference which has been negated in the language and structures of contemporary society. This analysis in itself was not unduly problematic, but 'the underlying strategy [was] somewhat obscure' (Beccalli 1994, p. 105), and when subsequently practised by Communist women, the language which they adopted was frequently criticised for being 'impenetrable to outsiders' (McCarthy 1997, p. 351). Nonetheless, as De Lauretis (1988:28) has argued, the ideology of cultural feminists had 'unprecedented influence' on the progressive political thought of the Pci. The ensuing discussion will demonstrate Pds women's proximity to feminist theory, by documenting its attempts to transfer these concepts to the political arena. I shall focus on two areas. Firstly, a brief account is given of the nature of Pci/Pds women's organisation within the party. This is undertaken to place in context the organisational decisions adopted by the Pds women's section in relation to migrant women in the early 1990s (see chapter 9). Secondly, I discuss the Women's Charter (*Carta delle donne*)[53] written by Communist women in 1986. This is used to highlight their absorption of feminist theory, their position on work and the family and their general strategical direction.

The internal women's committees (*commissioni femminili*) of the Pci/Pds have assumed a variety of roles in the post-war period. Initially intended as a forum which could attract the female masses to the party, it subsequently provided a forum which would address issues specific to women. These separate spheres allowed women the space to debate issues which were marginalised at the mainstream level. An enduring problem however, was the difficulty encountered in influencing the dominant party structure. The VII congress of Communist women held in 1984 marked the beginning of important transformations in Communist women's relationship to the autonomous women's movement and to their parenting structure, the Communist party. This transformation was encapsulated in the sanctioning of the concept of autonomy.[54] Autonomy marked the desire for a new relationship with women outside the party. As the prominent Communist Boccia (1986, p. 47) wrote in the Communist women's journal *Donna e Politica*:

> As long as Communist women saw that women's activism was principally in the movement, to talk of autonomy (including the relationship between Communist women and the party) meant guaranteeing autonomy for the movement; and allowing Communist women to choose the movement as a main reference point for their own politics.

Autonomy would also mean the elaboration of a 'woman's view' not only on issues considered to be pertinent above all to women, but also on wider issues. It was anticipated that this would give women greater political credibility and would also constitute a response to the ghettoisation of women's issues and women's analyses.[55]

The 1984 congress also proposed the formation of a new committee – the committee for the emancipation and liberation of women. This was to be equal in status to the other committees of the Central Committee. It aimed to be a forum from which the autonomous viewpoint of all Communist women, those working on specific women's issues and those working more generally within the party could be expressed and developed. It reinforced Communist women's desire to have their specific analyses debated by the party at large and was also an attempt to integrate the activities of Communist women within the party. As my key informant stated: 'We want to have our own elaboration, but we want our decisions to be taken up by the party' (interview, Pds). The problems that Communist women encountered in exploiting the powers of this Committee were instructive. The principal difficulty concerned the lack of interest manifested by those women elected to the managing bodies of the party who were automatically members of this new committee. The organisation of this committee had presupposed that as women, they would necessarily be interested in women's politics. Low attendance at the meetings of this committee indicated that this was not the case. Communist women moved on a stage:

We said that we have to take into account that there are some women active within the party who want to construct a discourse as women. There are others, on the other hand, who think that work with women should be done outside the party and they therefore are active in feminist centres. Then there are women who think that politics is in some way neutral and thus whether you are a man or a woman is irrelevant and therefore they preferred mixed politics (interview, Pds).[56]

My subsequent references to the activity of Pci/Pds women in the 1980s and 1990s pertain to those women who had chosen to work within the 'women's area' around the issue of a gender-determined presence in politics.

The true innovations of the 1980s were closely related to Communist women's engagement with feminism. Livia Turco, the national women's representative emphasised the significance of this in an interview published in the Communist paper *Rinascita* in 1990. She referred to the 'providential encounter with specific areas of feminism' (p. 63) – including the Women's Bookstore in Milan and the Virginia Woolf Centre in Rome – from which she had grasped the importance of the practice of the relationship between women and the use of your own sex as a primary reference point and as a means of affirming one's strength.

As the Communist activist Boccia observed, it was the acceptance of the theory of difference and the presentation of the Women's Charter which signalled a choice 'to propose feminist practice as the basis for the political presence of women within the party' (Boccia 1989, p. 3).

In organisational terms then, initial problems had centred around the difficulties encountered in influencing the directions of the wider political party in terms of women's issues. Furthermore, a tension could be identified between competing spheres of influence, the party on the one hand and the autonomous spheres of women's progressive activism on the other. Once this tension had been resolved through the concept of autonomy, Communist women would adopt a different approach to their organisation within the party.

The Women's Charter

The Women's Charter exemplified the duality of Communist women's presence within the party. It signalled at one and the same time women's desire to be a part of the party and their extraneous position from it.[57] It was the beginning of Communist women's political application of the concept of difference, marking an important transition in the reconciliation of feminist theory and political practice for Communist women. In an interview published in *Rinascita*, Livia Turco outlined its aim:

> To put down the foundations of a party inhabited by women and men, to construct a society for both sexes, where political and social citizenship is redefined starting from the principle of sexual difference and not on making women the same as men. Being in politics, advancing proposals of a general value but which at the same time express a gendered practice and culture.[58]

To achieve this, women would have to locate themselves differently within the party, although there was certainly no prescribed manner in which to do this:

> ... for all of us it was no longer a question of the importance and significance that the 'woman question' had within the party, but of the sense one gave to one's own identity, history and political passion. From the moment that being a Communist woman was no longer equivalent to a Communist man ... for every woman the central issue was that of *how to be in the Communist party as women* (Boccia 1989, p. 4).

The Communist Women's Charter outlined the principal objectives for women working within the party. It was not conceptualised as a definitive document, rather it appeared as 'work in progress', to be amended and improved in the light of the communication that would be generated by women who responded to its contents. It covered a range of issues (e.g. peace issues, the environment, intellectual work and women's work). I shall focus here on the relevant issues for this book – women and employment, maternity and female solidarity.

The Charter clearly demonstrated Communist women's approach to employment:

> *Work is an essential component of our identity* ... A new attitude towards work has developed in women, whether they are young or old, educated or not, in the North or in the South. It is no longer considered only as an unpleasant economic necessity. *Work is desired, wanted, and stubbornly sought after* (Sezione femminile della Direzione del Pci 1986, p. 29).

Italian women's new relationship to paid work indicated that the progressive forces considered this an important arena on which to base their political work. This was not to be at the expense of maternity. A new consciousness with regard to maternity envisaged it as an integral rather than exclusive component of women's social identities:

> Maternity is assuming a new place in many women's lives. It demonstrates the awareness and the desire which has developed in us to live a full life, without having to choose, from time to time, between affection, maternity, work ... (ibid., p. 36).

A recognition of the social value of maternity was called for, but there was also an awareness that women occupied a transitional stage with regard to issues such as sexuality and the desire for maternity. Communist women thus appeared to have a clearer focus with regard to work, while maternity constituted a more complex issue on which to determine a clear theory and strategy.[59] Substantial debate was however afforded to the need to reconcile productive and reproductive labour. This was formulated as an attempt to reduce the 'tyranny' of productive working times. It was argued that the rigid model of productive work organisation had devalued other equally important times such as reproductive time and leisure time.[60]

The Women's Charter was specifically addressed to a constituency of women. But how did it intend to deal with differentiation within the category of gender? In the introductory premise to the Charter, Livia Turco clearly identified the women with whom Communist women desired dialogue:

> We intend to meet women in parties, women in feminist movements, women in associations, in trade unions, intellectual women and individual women. *But above all we intend to consult and involve 'ordinary women'*, those whom we meet in our everyday lives, ... those who are weaker, more alone, more exposed (my emphasis) (ibid., p. 4).

Communist women thus aimed to establish dialogue in a variety of spheres, but they highlighted the importance of dialogue with ordinary women. This was unlikely to be an easy objective given their proximity to an intellectualised Italian feminist thought. In point of fact, Communist women had already decided to relate to a more educated category of women. In an interview for *Rinascita*, Turco stated:

> During the last stage of membership, there has been an admission of more educated women, with higher qualifications, between the ages of thirty and forty; these are the women active in politics ... At the time of the Charter there was a discussion amongst us: should we focus on the majority of our female members or ... focus on women in society? The latter option prevailed, even

though we have never stopped talking to all our members, at least in our intentions (Turco 1990, p. 64).

This decision indicates the difficulty of appealing to 'ordinary women' within their own ranks. In fact, there was already some awareness that Communist women had neglected their relationship with women in civil society:

> In order to construct a party of women and of men, I think that a lot will depend on us and whether we will be able to construct a widespread network ... with women in society. Because I think this is fundamental if we want to be active in politics ... often we spoke amongst ourselves and we did not establish a true and widespread relationship with society (interview, Pds).

Communist women would no doubt have positioned migrant women within the category of ordinary women. However, at this stage of their theory and practice migrant women were still an invisible social category. But the contents of the Charter indicated that Communist women did seek female alliances beyond a national constituency of women. However, this related to a European female constituency and to women in the developing world. The lack of reference to migrant women in Italy indicated that they were invisible despite a growing presence (see subsequent chapters). This was acutely apparent in the article by Rossana Rossanda, a then prominent Communist figure, who in discussing the value of the Communist Women's Charter in the first issue of the women's journal *Reti*,[61] pointed to the marginalisation of [Italian] women by highlighting the category of 'race': 'Immigrants, blacks, everyone seems to be obviously entitled to rights, whilst the *apartheid* against women is taken for granted like the changing of the seasons (Rossanda 1987, p. 40). In the editorial of this first issue, Boccia (1987, p. 3) had also written:

> The images that we habitually receive from society are all populated by male figures: Italians, workers, young people, drug addicts, Catholics, Communists, Southerners, etc. When a society represents itself, the illustrations and images which are used, unequivocally assume a male shape and profile.

In the light of Boccia's statement, Rossanda's assertion that 'Immigrants' and 'blacks' (just male, or male and female?) are seen to have rights but women (inclusive of migrant women?) are not, graphically demonstrates the manner in which migrant women can remain invisible – not explicitly included in either category but implicitly included in both. In fact, it is possible to argue that the direction of Italian feminist thought and Pci/Pds women's acceptance of the concept of difference lent itself to the exclusion of ethnic minority women. As De Lauretis (1988, p. 31) has argued, the direction of Italian feminist thought 'makes little space for differences and divisions between – and within – women ...'. The view amongst Pds women activists that 'female liberty can only be constructed with women' (interview, Pds) had implications as to whether progressive women's activism would be able to accommodate ideologically the racialised gender of migrant women. The articulation of an essential female subjectivity did not seem open to an accommodation of migrant women's difference. If one were to be more optimistic however, it could be suggested that Pds women's organisational position within the party, where they has struggled to articulate their *dual* interests as women and as left activists, would facilitate the acceptance of migrant women's dual interests as migrants and as women.

Conclusion

This chapter has provided some insight into the Italian gendered framework of the post-war period – a framework into which migrant women would ultimately be situated. The first half of this chapter suggested that Italian women's maternal role has historically been protected in the post-war period and this has impacted on Italian women's opportunities to participate in the productive labour market. I also argued that cultural factors supported the ideology of maternity, leading to women's social identity being closely constructed around the ideal of the mother. The new aspirations articulated by Italian women in the late 1960s and 1970s led to a tension between their expression of reproductive and productive roles which has yet to be fully resolved. This must be seen as a contributory factor to the demand for migrant women's labour in the 1970s.

The second half of this chapter has documented aspects of Italian women's political activism, focusing on the 1970s and 1980s and the endeavours of Pci/Pds women. I have argued that Pds women's activity constitutes one strand of progressive women's political activism and that their activism is grounded in feminist theory being produced in more autonomous women's spaces. The nature of this theory is rooted in the concept of an essential female difference which allows for an incorporation of a racialised gender category, but principally from the perspective of gender. It is my view that this will tend towards a negation, rather than an accommodation, of migrant women's somewhat more complex multiple identities.

Notes

1 For an account of Italian women's situation before this time see De Grazia (1992).
2 They were so named after the Catholic intellectual Giuseppe Dossetti and included Aldo Moro, Giorgio La Pira and Amintore Fanfani. See Bedani (1996).
3 See for example Arts. 3, 20, 29, 31 and 37.
4 See Caldwell (1991a) for a discussion of the debates surrounding Article 29.
5 *La Costituzione della Repubblica nei lavoro preparatori della Assemblea Costituente,* Camera dei deputati, Segretariato Generale, 1971, Vol. VI, p. 503.
6 Togliatti, leader of the Communist Party, accepted this amendment.
7 See Discussion of Article 33 held on 10 May 1947, ibid., Vol. II, pp. 1571–80.
8 Merlin also made reference to the necessity for greater attention to those working women excluded from protective maternity legislation. Merlin highlighted the case of homeworkers, but paid domestic work was also a category which could have been mentioned.
9 Saraceno (1988) attributes this contradiction to the difficult compromise that the political forces of the immediate post-war period had to undertake and to the coexistence of different family models.
10 The debates in the 75 Committee stage were reported, not recorded verbatim.
11 *La Costituzione della repubblica nei lavori preparatori della Assemblea Costituente,* Camera dei Deputati, Segretariato Generale 1971, Vol. VI, p. 655.
12 Many ex-fascists found a home in the Common Man's Front in the immediate post-war period.
13 *La Costituzione della repubblica nei lavori preparatori della Assemblea Costituente,* Camera dei Deputati, Segretariato Generale 1970, Vol. II, p. 943. The aula debates are verbatim.
14 Cited in Caldwell (1991a, p. 22).
15 In practice however, women's experience of the labour market, as outlined below, frequently excludes many women from these generous provisions.
16 This provision was not part of the original 1971 law but was included in the 1977 Equal Treatment Act (Art. 7).
17 Her findings are based on two studies. The first concerned interviews based on a questionnaire with a sample group of 200 pregnant women, the second concerned in-depth interviews with 25 pregnant women. Both studies were carried out in Trieste.
18 One example of this was the prohibition on women in manufacturing industry from working at night, although it was possible to overrule this through collective bargaining channels. See Ballestrero (1984).
19 The law was entitled 'Positive action to achieve equality at work for men and women'.
20 See Bimbi (1989) for a discussion of the double presence hypothesis.
21 Clearly we cannot speak of a universal Italian model as family experiences are mediated through differential class and regional positionings.
22 He defines familism as follows: '... the typically Italian version of familism consists of extremely cohesive family units, a relatively weak civil society, ... and a deeply rooted mistrust of the central state. (1994a, p. 288).
23 Cited in Ginsborg (1994b, p. 285).
24 Cited in Rosci (1994, p. 301).
25 Bettio (1988a) has suggested that a change in the value of children to the family economy has also led women to opt for greater labour market participation rather than larger families.

26 Regional economic differences and employment models have had some impact on women's employment models. See Bolasco et al. (1985).

27 Parca's (1964) analysis of the letters women sent to problem pages in the 1950s and early 1960s indicated that women's lives tended to be defined in terms of the men whom they strove to please in order to achieve the goal of marriage.

28 Women considered their partners' reluctance to support them in paid work to be motivated by loss of reputation (Goddard 1987), jealousy and the desire to have them at their beck and call (Cutrufelli 1977).

29 Surveys conducted in the Turin metropolitan area demonstrated that some 90 per cent of multiple job holders were men (Contini 1989, p. 241). De Grazia (1984) found that the number of married multiple jobholders with children was much higher than the number that were single, widowed or divorced.

30 Balbo and May's (1975) paper had indicated major discrepancies in employment patterns between Italy and other European countries. The most important difference concerned the definitive departure of married Italian women from the official labour force. Padoa Schioppa (1977) also refers to this as an anomalous trend.

31 In the mid-1960s, in a bid to maintain Italy's competitiveness and to reduce the power of the trade unions, an economic strategy of industrial decentralisation was adopted. This effectively forced women out of the official labour market and into the informal sector of the economy. As a means of evading trade union control, large firms began contracting out to smaller firms. New small plants were constructed which principally employed women and employers also subcontracted out to homeworkers. In the late 1970s, 60 per cent of those involved in underground manufacturing were thought to be women (Del Boca 1988). For two studies on women's involvement in homeworking see Cutrufelli (1977) and Goddard (1996).

32 Cited in Altieri (1993).

33 This was carried out by researchers from ISTAT and the IRP (Istituto di Ricerche sulla Popolazione) and was published in 1994.

34 Regional distribution of services is very varied. Regions such as Emilia-Romagna generally have good service provision, but even here migrant women are employed exclusively as domestic workers. Although recognising the inefficiencies of the welfare system, it is perhaps oversimplification to argue, as Hoskyns and Orsini Jones (1995, p. 63) have, that 'Italian women are very house proud and like to have a helper in the house ...'.

35 More recently a resurgence of the use of paid domestic labour by the middle classes in the form of nannying and cleaning has been noted (see Gregson and Lowe 1994).

36 See Caldwell (1978) and Caldwell (1991a) for a more detailed discussion of the church's input regarding women.

37 For an internal account of the relationship of the Dc to the family, see Russo Jervolino (1990).

38 For a discussion of this see Caldwell (1978); Hellman (1984); Beckwith (1985) and Birnbaum (1986). For internal accounts of the party's relationship to gender and the women's movement see Tiso (1976); Tiso (1983); Seroni (1984). For Togliatti's post-war writings on women see Togliatti (1965).

39 For useful primary documentation of the UDI organisation up to the early 1980s see Michetti et al. (1984). For an overview of the CIF in the post-war period, see the internal account by Ravasio (1989).

40 For example, the Pci, the Dc and the ACLI all had women's sections.

41 There have been many accounts of the Italian feminist movement. For two useful accounts which also include primary documentation see Calabrò and Grassi (1985) and Bono and Kemp (1991). For some accounts written in English see also Pasquinelli (1984); Birnbaum (1986); Hellman (1987) and Caldwell (1991b).

42 See the 1973 Lotta Femminista document published in Bono and Kemp (1991) pp. 261–2. See the argument against a salary for housewives articulated by another feminist group Movimento Femminista Romano also in Bono and Kemp (1991), pp. 262–4. Some have considered this demand to be part of a wider strategy of feminist mobilisation rather than a realistic goal (see, for example, Birnbaum 1986). What Bono and Kemp (1991) refer to as the dangerous ambiguity of the salaries for housewives debate was heightened by Catholic women's subsequent mobilisation around this issue.

43 Movimento Femminista Romano, 1973. Documentation in Bono and Kemp (1991, p. 262).

44 Cited in Fossati (1976, pp. 70–71).

45 See the testimony of B. cited in Fossati (1976, pp. 74–5).

46 For a good overview of the trajectory of Italian feminist ideology in relation to the maternal and the mother-daughter relationship see Giorgio (1997).

47 This was the result of both internal difficulties within the movement and external factors such as the retreat into private life and the concomitant decline in collective participation.

48 See Calabrò and Grassi (1985, p. 79).

49 See the documentation regarding the UDI's XI Congress held in 1982 in Michetti et al. (1984). This was an important turning point for the UDI as it loosened its ties with the Pci in order to enjoy a more profitable relationship with the autonomous women's movement.

50 During the 1970s, the Pci had begun to relinquish the view of workers' struggles as paramount. At its XV congress in 1979, it accepted the autonomy of women's movements (Thesis 77) although Thesis 81 called for 'a firm alliance between the workers' movement and women's and feminist movements'. See 'La politica e l'organizzazione dei comunisti italiani. Le tesi e lo statuto approvati dal XV Congresso Nazionale del Pci. (1979). By the time of its XVII congress in 1986, there was greater recognition of women's autonomy. See for example, Thesis 30, XVII Congresso del Partito Comunista Italiano (1987). For a view of Communist women's position regarding these theses see Mancina's (1986) article in *Donna e Politica*, where she argued that the Pci accepted ideas at the theoretical level but had difficulty incorporating them into the culture and action of the party.

51 Both Del Re (1989) and Caldwell (1991b) have highlighted this trend.

52 This reference is to the English version published in Kemp and Bono (1993). The Italian version is published in Cavarero (1987).

53 Its full title was 'Women's Strength from Women' (*Dalle Donne la forza delle donne*).

54 See *Alternativa Donna – Atti della VII Conferenza delle Comuniste* (1986).

55 For an example see Grazia Labate's 'La crisi dello stato sociale: Il punto di vista delle donne' (1985).

56 See also the article published in *Noi Donne* by a group of Communist women critical of this Committee. An example of the tone of the article can be seen in the following citation: 'The women's committees speak for all Communist women. Yet not all women members of the party are involved in them. Are the women who are not involved in the women's committees perhaps men? ... What is the point of Communist women mobilising as women against F16's given that the whole party is against F16's? Peace, environment, the fight against organised crime are not women's objectives' (Cavaliere et al. 1988, pp. 9–10).

57   It is to be noted that Communist women saw their new strategic and intellectual perspectives as valid for the party as a whole. They would subsequently feel vindicated by the events which took place in 1991, when the party changed its name to the Pds. According to a key informant: 'In some ways we anticipated the turning point. For example, the idea of having relationships beyond Communist women, thus to have a relationship with feminist women, with women in associations. The diffuse Left, as it was subsequently called after Occhetto's change of direction, had not only been raised by us but had been practised by us. And we were the only ones within the Pci which had constructed that piece of experience, because the Charter was the outcome of a very intense relationship with various experiences, not just Communist women' (interview, Pds). This position was explicitly stated in the Communist women's document prepared for the important XX Congress of the Pci. See *Carta di Donne per il Partito Democratico della Sinistra.*

58   See 'La differenza è già una politica. Intervista a Livia Turco', *Rinascita*, 19 November 1988, pp. 12–13.

59   See chapter 9 for a discussion of Pds women's conference on maternity held in 1992.

60   Communist women's reference to this issue in the Charter would culminate in their important legislative proposal of 1990. The proposal was entitled 'Women Changing Times (*Le donne cambiano i tempi)* and aimed at a radical and utopian transformation of current use of time (see Sezione Femminile Nazionale del Pci 1990).

61   *Reti* replaced *Donne e Politica* as the journal of Communist women in 1987. This reflected the change amongst Communist women. Although acknowledged as a journal promoted by Communist women, it positively welcomed contributions from women outside the party.

2   Italy and Immigration

This chapter provides a general overview of the immigration situation in Italy and highlights a number of variables which have contributed to the development of a migratory model specific to Italy. Castles (1995) has proposed a tripartite conceptual model to categorise the response of highly developed countries to immigration. Firstly, the differential exclusion model, whereby migrants are integrated into specific areas of society, but are denied access to other areas. This would normally mean integration into the labour market but exclusion from citizenship, political participation and welfare. Secondly, the assimilationist model, which aims to impose a one-sided process of adaptation onto migrants, making them indistinguishable from the majority population. Finally, the pluralist model which accepts migrants' cultural and social diversity and gives them equal rights. Italy cannot be definitively positioned within any of these models, in part because many aspects of the Italian immigration debate have yet to be properly defined and some have yet to emerge. The difficulty in establishing an Italian model can be partly attributed to the late institutional response to the issue. Prior to state intervention in the 1980s, the voluntary sector was the principal regulator of immigration. Its intervention however, was largely informal and uncoordinated. In the late 1980s, Favaro and Bordogna (1989) argued that Italy's vision of immigration was governed by three stages. Stage one attempted to control entry, stage two attempted to control the duration of the migrant workers' stay and stage three provided incentives for the migrant worker to return home. Bonini (1987) argued that Italian migration policy was marked by a dual and contradictory approach, characterised by hospitality and understanding, but also a desire to control the phenomenon. These definitions were both valid, but in the early 1990s, the Italian model was also being shaped by wider factors. Italy's legacy as a country of emigration, the prominence of the voluntary sector and women's involvement in the migratory process were important factors which differentiated Italy from Northern European models of migration.

Labour Migration Theory: Interpreting the Italian case

Labour migration in the context of Western Europe's advanced industrialised economies has been categorised by some theorists as a structural necessity for post-war European expansion (Nikolinakos 1975; Miles 1982). The economic advantages of introducing a migrant labour system were seen to lie in the avoidance of reproduction costs, the acquisition of a labour force with limited rights and the erosion of the strength of the indigenous working class through the fracturing of class solidarity (Miles 1982; Phizlackea 1983; Cohen 1987). Explanations of migrants' decisions to migrate have broadly been treated within two schools of literature. The functional or equilibrium perspective emphasises microeconomic processes and specifically the decisions of individuals who migrate for self-betterment. The structural perspective stresses macroeconomic processes where exploitative global relationships produce the conditions for labour migration (Gibson and Graham 1986; Goss and Lindquist 1995). Italian interpretations can be categorised principally in relation to the latter perspective where discussion of the Italian experience has been formulated using the supply-push and demand-pull framework of analysis. In most cases, supply-push factors were seen to be dominant (Sergi 1987; Venturini 1988; Melotti 1990; Bonifazi 1992; King 1993). Some writers, however, sought to highlight peculiarly Italian factors within this push-pull framework of analysis. Pugliese (1990b) for example, argued that this framework was reductive in relation to Italy as it was the structure and segmentation of the market which warranted investigation. Calvanese (1993) emphasised the regional diversity within Italy arguing that, dependent on regional location, migrants could be seen to assume a variety of substitutional, competitive and complementary functions within Italy. Nevertheless, the overwhelming consensus regarding the significance of push over pull factors to explain the presence of migrants in Italy has shaped the nature of national and regional policy. In the early 1990s, this encouraged policy makers to promote development in the sending countries, with an implicit agenda to stop further immigration to Italy. This in itself was unlikely to stem migratory flows, as structural development in the sending countries would produce interim imbalances which, in the short-term, were more likely to contribute to rather than reduce emigration flows (Martin 1995).

Early responses to immigration to Italy indicate that the notion of invasion was prominent. In the introduction to the 1986 Censis[1] study on immigration, the sociologist Collicelli referred to the 'massive invasion' and the 'massive entry of foreigners' (p. 4). This notion was also identifiable in the work of

Giorgio Bocca (1988, p. 7): '... here we are struggling with a new invasion, poor and peaceful, permanent and uncontrollable'. By 1990, there were some attempts to reverse this perception. Nadio Delai (1991, p. 96), then director of Censis, argued that impressionistic estimations of migrant numbers tended to multiply the reality tenfold.[2]

Nonetheless, the notion of an invasion and the weight attributed to push factors were also utilised to explain the presence of undocumented workers. This, despite the fact that the existence of undocumented migrants needs to be clearly related both to the structure of the Italian economy and to Italian political culture. Schioppa Kostoris (1996, p. 291), for example, has highlighted the importance for the Italian economy of the society's imaginative ability 'to operate outside the rules of the game'. She has argued that Italian prosperity has been partially achieved as a result of 'a collective propensity to ignore general principles and dominant ideas and to circumvent laws, affirmative actions, and economic policy rules' (p. 291). This puts a rather different construction on undocumented immigration. As Petracou (1996) has argued in relation to Greece, another recent southern European destination country, an undocumented status allows migrants to adjust to a society where the hidden economy and personal affiliations are important employment models for the indigenous community.[3]

Demand-pull factors within Italy were initially given limited prominence in academic accounts of immigration. In an interpretative model designed to accommodate the specificity of Mediterranean immigration, the economist Venturini (1988) argued that there was only implicit demand for migrants within the sector of low-skilled, menial, marginal and illegal jobs. She argued that Italy's post-war productive growth had not generated 'additional labour requirements' (p. 134), distinguishing the internal market into which national workers sought entry and where domestic unemployment existed from the external market, where labour was in short supply and to which migrants could gain access. Venturini's theoretical interpretation appears inadequate for a number of reasons. Firstly, by advocating a clear distinction between the two markets, she minimalised the demand for migrant labour in sectors such as construction, domestic service and agriculture by referring to them simply as implicit demands. Furthermore her focus on the human capital of the migrant as a determining factor in terms of employment destination failed to take account of the extent to which structural institutional barriers can affect employment destinations. Her argument that migrants should increase their human capital by 'learning the language, the informal rules of the labour market and generally integrating into society' (p. 143), tended to underplay the importance of the reception context in determining migrants' eventual employment location.[4]

One sector where there has been an uncontested acceptance of demand is the domestic work sphere and in the early-to-mid-1990s, writers such as Pinto (1992) and Ambrosini (1995) began to demonstrate that demand also existed in other economic sectors.

The Gradual Response to Immigration

Many of the women included in the case-study below were present in Italy at an early stage of its immigration history. It is therefore useful to have some understanding of the general social and political climate regarding immigration prior to the social and political attention it received from the mid 1980s onwards. The onset of immigration flows to Italy began in the late 1960s and early 1970s, although there is some evidence of even earlier flows within particular migratory groups such as the Chinese.[5]

In a report to the European Parliament on the rise of racism and xenophobia in Italy, Laura Balbo noted that while immigration in Italy had actually been ongoing for a number of years, it only seemed to really affect public consciousness in the late 1980s (Balbo 1990). Two special issues of the Censis publication *Note e Commenti*,[6] published in 1986 and 1988 respectively, also suggest that reaction to immigration occurred essentially in the late 1980s. In the introduction to the 1986 publication, the sociologist Collicelli argued that immigration to Italy was still a fundamentally hidden phenomenon. She viewed the situation at this time as an almost unintentional balancing act, beneficial to all concerned:

> The characteristics of this immigration ... mean that for now there is neither a total rejection nor, on the other hand, any great tendency towards recognising the foreign presence and its legalisation. An attitude of rejection would damage our economy and above all certain industrial sectors. ... On the other hand regularisation and recognition, as well as also damaging our hidden economy, would probably provoke significant cultural problems (Collicelli 1986, pp. 6–7).

What is of some significance is that only two years later, a quite different perspective is put forward. In the 1988 Censis publication, the same researcher stressed that immigration had now developed into a central issue: 'Today, the issue of foreign immigration has acquired a new centrality because of the extent of its "visibility"' (1988, p. 3). Thus within only two years, what had been perceived as a marginal and peripheral issue had assumed a new central position in sociocultural and political terms.[7]

In the 1970s, there were only sporadic articles relating to incoming immigration. For example, it was reported in the Communist newspaper *L'Unità* (14 September 1978) that the number of Italian emigrants were declining and that Italy had now begun to import labour. Even then, there was an awareness that Italy was unprepared and the government and the trade unions were said to be developing ways of dealing with the situation. Valentina Strada also raised the question of Italy's new status as a country of immigration in an article in the weekly magazine *Panorama* (21 November 1978). She attributed this partly to the needs of the Italian economy but also to the restrictive immigration policies operating in some other European countries. Prodi, then neo-Minister for Industry, linked the issue of immigration to the problems of Northern Italy's industry, arguing that employment in certain industries was no longer attractive to either Northerners or Southerners. He maintained that Italy now had to make a crucial decision based on whether it aspired to be a closed society with limited growth, or a society with increased growth potential but which would need the labour power of immigrants to achieve it (*La Repubblica*, 2 December 1978). Prodi's comments indicated not only the acceptance of pull factors within Italy but saw this as compatible with domestic unemployment given Italians' reluctance to work within specific economic areas. These examples of intermittent reporting on immigration can be compared to an inverse trend in the late 1980s when unremitting reporting occurred.[8] Up until 1990 there was little coordinated knowledge about migrant communities living in Italy. The organisation of a major national conference on immigration held in Rome in 1990[9] was clearly envisaged to rectify this lacuna.[10]

The slow response to immigration may be partly attributable to the fact that women constituted a substantial component of Italy's migratory body in the early stages. As I will demonstrate in subsequent chapters, they were not a very visible force, enclosed as they were within the confines of their employers' homes. The lack of response to their presence suggests that female migrants were not considered to be culturally or economically threatening to Italians. But this low key response also had implications for these women. The novelty of this female model of migration, where the majority were autonomous primary migrants, combined with the general lack of attention paid to incoming migration in the 1970s, led to migrant women being absorbed into a typically male migration framework. This allowed for the pre-eminence of their labour function and it would be at a much later stage that some attention would be paid to the gendered implications of their migration to Italy.

Italy's Legacy as a Country of Emigration

Italy's legacy as a country of emigration undoubtedly contributed to the manner in which the response to immigration developed. It is as a result of this legacy that we can define aspects of Italy's response to immigration as theoretically pluralist (if not in reality), as Italy's own experience led many to articulate a moral obligation not only to treat migrants well but to respect their cultural difference. Italy has had extensive experience of a diverse range of migratory processes (external migration, internal migration and return migration). This historical legacy is important. Early studies of the Italian situation optimistically anticipated some sensitivity on the part of the Italian public regarding immigration:

> ... Now that the newspapers are filling up with news regarding foreign immigrants and their problems of settlement, those who have experienced analogous periods in other contexts feel they are witnessing something that is repeating itself, like a 'déja vu'.
> And it seems natural to ask oneself: but isn't Italy a country which is traditionally 'flexible, tolerant, adaptable and accepting of others, pragmatic and not dogmatic' for which so many anthropologists and sociologists have praised it? (Collicelli 1988, p. 5).

Bocca's (1988) work posed essentially the same question in its title: *Are Italians Racist?* In the introduction to a legislative proposal produced in 1988 by a group of Communist Party senators, it was argued that it was time to move on from asking whether Italians were racist or not and to begin the move towards a multicultural society. The document subsequently reinforced the idea that Italy's own migratory history should be intrinsic to such a development: 'To know the history of our emigration abroad in fact means a better understanding of the feelings and needs of the foreign workers in our country' (*Atti parlamentari* n. 1272, 1988, p. 2).

It was as late as 1972 that migration statistics in Italy showed a positive balance, with more Italians returning than leaving the country (King 1993). This meant that the issue of emigration was still of relevance to Italy in the 1970s, and this was confirmed in a Censis report: 'the emigration phenomenon continues to be a national problem of significant importance and the issues linked to it appear to be difficult to resolve' (Censis 1986, p. 8). Moreover, the growing importance of return migration to Italy in the 1970s also had an impact on incoming migration. Regional consultative bodies *(consulte)* on emigration were established nationally after a national conference on emigration in 1975 (Pugliese 1990b) and conferences on emigration continued into the 1980s. The significance of this for migrant women relates to the fact that during the 1970s, the emphasis within the general sphere of immigration was not focused on the incoming migration of foreign nationals, but rather continued to address a national constituency of emigrants and returnees. This had longer-term implications since when attention was eventually paid to incoming immigration, the initial tendency was to treat Italian returnees and African and Asian migrants in much the same manner (see chapter 3).

Finally, the very history of the post-war phenomenon of internal migration in Italy – its patterns, even the fact of its necessity – was indicative of an entrenched inferiorisation of Southern Italians. In the many Italian writings which cite Italy's experience of emigration as one which should facilitate a more positive reception for African and Asian migrants, the pre-existing racism towards Southern Italians is either forgotten or left out of account.[11] It was in fact as late as the late 1980s that Italy was still being defined by some as a pre-racist country:

> We certainly cannot take for granted that we will not become a racist society (in our institutions, in our practice, in our everyday relationships, in our values), but nor is it true that we are racist today, in the same terms as other European countries. Attention and cognitive investment and debate are crucial in this phase which for the moment is one of pre-evaluation, pre-formulation, perhaps *pre-racism* (Italia-Razzismo 1990, p. 3).[12]

Immigration to Italy

In this section I offer a brief statistical overview of the national picture of immigration. Data presented must be read with an understanding that they present only a partial view of the phenomenon, as figures refer only to those migrants legally resident in Italy. Furthermore, the collation of official data normally includes all foreign residents. In some cases, figures for 'non-EC' migrants are then presented separately as a subgroup of the total figure of migrants.[13] My principal intention here is to highlight the gender variable in relation to the national picture.

In 1992, Home Office data indicated that there were 925,172 migrants registered in Italy, 778,254 from outside the European Community. Men represented 57.31 per cent of all migrants and women 42.69 per cent. However there were regional differences regarding the gender distribution of migrants:

Area	Women	Men
North	39.65%	60.35%
Centre	47.37%	52.65%
South	45.87%	54.13%
Islands	35.31%	64.69%
Total	42.69%	57.31%

In Tuscany, Umbria and Campania, women migrants in fact outnumbered men. Moreover, the gender composition of specific ethnic communities categorically demonstrated the existence of single-sex migration for both men and women. My own data, referring to 1990, showed evidence of dominant female migration in the following communities: Cape Verde, Ethiopia (including Eritrea), Somalia and the Philippines. Women represented 80 per cent, 60 per cent, 63 per cent and 63 per cent respectively of these communities. Conversely 97 per cent of the Senegalese community and 93 per cent of the Tunisian community were male.

There is limited reliable data referring to the earlier stages of migration to Italy. In the 1970s, foreigners were distinguished by continent as opposed to ethnic grouping. In the period between 1975–84, there was a clear rise in the number of foreign nationals resident in Italy, with 186,413 resident in 1975 and 403,923 in 1984. In 1975, African residents comprised only 4.6 per cent of this total figure and Asian residents 8 per cent. The largest foreign contingent – 60 per cent – consisted of other Europeans. By 1984, these percentages had changed to 10 per cent, 14.7 per cent and 52.7 per cent respectively (Censis 1986). The 1971 and 1981 Census created a single category of 'foreigners' and differentiated them in terms of regional residence. The figures indicated a total of 121,116 foreign nationals resident in 1971, 54 per cent of whom were female and 210,937 foreign nationals resident in 1981, 53 per cent of whom were female (Censis 1986). These figures suggest a consistent rise in the number of foreign nationals present in Italy during the 1970s and 1980s. They also suggest that at this early stage of migration, female migrants were quite prominent.

Two of the oldest communities of migrants to Italy are the North Africans in Sicily and women migrants working nationally in the big cities. While the North African fishing community in Sicily was a well established community, this was clearly a specifically regional migration.[14] The migration of women to Italy had more of a national dimension, with women migrating to cities such as Palermo, Naples, Rome and Milan. Home office data[15] showed the gradual increase (with the exception of 1970) in the numbers of migrants working as domestics in Italy:

1969: 6,333;
1970: 5,750;
1971: 6,987;
1972: 8,608;
1973: 9,255;
1974: 10,387;
1975: 10,937.

Evidence of the significance of women's migration during the early stages of incoming migration to Italy can be found in the 1978 Censis study of foreign workers in Italy. Numerical accuracy was seen to be an impossible feat, consequently figures pertaining to the presence of foreign workers were given in estimates. The Censis study estimated that there were between 40,000 to 60,000 North Africans in Italy (Moroccans, Tunisians and Algerians). While all the male groups are referred to by nationality, migrant women from a variety of ethnic backgrounds were subsumed under the category COLF (domestic worker). The category of COLF was estimated to stand somewhere between 70,000 and 100,000 and incorporated women from 'Cape Verde, Mauritius, Seychelles, Eritrea, The Philippines and Somalia etc.'. The use of 'etc.' to describe other nameless ethnic groups is patently indicative of the seeming irrelevance of the nationality of migrant women, and the implicit unproblematic nature of women's migration. Subsuming these different nationalities under the category of COLF clearly demonstrates that from a very early stage, the social identity of migrant women was inextricably connected to their exclusive labour function as domestic workers.

By the end of the 1980s, the immigration situation in Italy had undergone substantial change. New and different migratory groups had begun to enter Italy supporting Castles and Miller's (1993) hypotheses regarding the acceleration and differentiation of contemporary migration movements.[16] Table 2.1 shows the principal migrant communities present in Italy as at 31 December 1993.[17] One area of continuity, however, was identifiable in the

Table 2.1   Foreign nationals residing in Italy

Morocco	97,604
Yugoslavia	72,377
USA	63,960
Philippines	46,332
Tunisia	44,505
Germany	39,923
Albania	30,847
UK	29,091
France	26,993
Senegal	26,368
Egypt	24,555
China	22,875
Brazil	21,075
Poland	21,075
Sri Lanka	19,722
Somalia	19,553
Romania	19,385
Switzerland	18,187
Spain	16,956
Greece	16,545
Ethiopia/Eritrea	14,050
Ghana	14,021
Argentina	13,978
Ex-USSR	11,947
Iran	10,743
Peru	8,879
Colombia	8,287
Pakistan	8,159
Dominican Republican	8,122
Austria	7,809
Japan	7,623
Netherlands	7,390
Nigeria	6,719
Mauritius	6,665
Bulgaria	6,228
Bangladesh	6,136
Portugal	5,683
Cape Verde	5,676
Lebanon	5,673
Czechoslovakia	5,592
Turkey	5,411

Source: Caritas di Roma (1994).

persistent demand for migrant women's labour as domestic workers. Melotti (1990) estimated that domestic service constituted 50 per cent of the paid work undertaken by migrants in the major cities.[18]

Although, as will be argued below, a restrictive approach towards immigration began to emerge in the late 1980s, a 1991 government decree regulating incoming flows for 1992 made provision only for domestic work or other types of work where no labour was forthcoming from within the national territory. In 1992, a total of 31,629 authorisations for employment were made. Of these 53.8 per cent went to women. In some regions the percentage for women was substantially higher (Emilia Romagna – 66 per cent; Lazio – 61 per cent; Abruzzo – 64 per cent) (Caritas di Roma 1993). This confirmed the continuing possibility of entering Italy as domestic workers in the early 1990s.

The Voluntary Sector

The voluntary sector indisputably played a major role in relation to the new migration to Italy. The most important Catholic voluntary sector organisation is the Caritas whose self-defined role is that of 'a pastoral body of the Church, singularly concerned to spread a sense of solidarity among the Christian community and amongst citizens' (Di Liegro and Pittau 1992, p. 21). There are many other voluntary sector associations who work with migrants, some of whom fall within the Protestant voluntary sector. Nonetheless Caritas has assumed a particularly prominent national role. It has an extensive network of organisations which offer primary assistance to migrants. This proximity to migrant workers has given it privileged access to migrants and in this way it has acquired the status of an authoritative voice on the question of immigration. In 1983 it opened a reception centre for migrants in Rome but had been involved with migrants since the 1970s. Its first major publication in 1990 was entitled 'Planet Immigration: From conflict to solidarity', co-written by Monsignor Luigi Di Liegro, head and prominent figure of the Roman Caritas, and Franco Pittau a Catholic Trade Unionist.[19]

The involvement of the Caritas in immigration has been particularly significant. The Catholic ethos underpinning its commitment to migrant workers conflicts sharply with the development of restrictive trends towards migrants prevalent in both Italy and Europe. The work of the Caritas is based on the Catholic virtue of solidarity, which emphasises the necessity for assisting the needy by providing immediate humane action. As the head of the Roman Caritas Di Liegro stated:

Migration is inevitable in a world where the demographic, economic and social differences have become so acute ... we must stop thinking that we have already done too much. Various politicians and administrators think this and so do many ordinary people, but it is not true (Di Liegro, Caritas di Roma 1993, pp. 18–20).

The practical contribution of the Caritas has been impressive. The Rome Caritas' expenditure on social services has been steadily increasing.[20] Services which are of specific relevance to migrants concern medical assistance, accommodation provision in hostels and refectories where free meals can be obtained. The cost of running the canteens incurred the greatest expenditure. In 1989, 8,084 people used this service in Rome, 79.8 per cent of whom were foreign nationals.[21]

The implications of this assistance-based approach has some implications for the management of immigration. Caritas' early involvement with migrants set certain precedents which, in some instances, have been emulated by the state.[22] Caritas has thus been able to influence the debate on immigration. More significantly, in the eyes of many migrants it assumed an important status. An interview with a voluntary sector worker indicated that some migrants clearly equated the possession of a Caritas document with that of a residence permit: 'Before the Martelli law[23] there were very few residence permits. All the women who came to us had a Caritas Card and they thought it was an official document' (interview, YWCA). This is clearly symptomatic of the different roles that the state and the Catholic voluntary sector played during the early stages of immigration.

Popular and Political Responses to Immigration

It has been argued above that a popular response to immigration became prominent in the mid-to-late-1980s. In 1977, a DOXA[24] survey indicated that a majority of Italian respondents attributed the coexistence of domestic unemployment and the presence of migrant workers in Italy to the lower labour costs of the latter group (65 per cent) and to the fact that Italians had begun to avoid manual work, aspiring instead to tertiary sector employment (61 per cent). Not surprisingly perhaps, 85 per cent of Communist Party respondents attributed recourse to migrant labour to their lower employment costs while 72 per cent of Christian Democrat respondents attributed it to Italians' reluctance to engage in manual work.[25] The results of later Italian surveys carried out in the 1980s and early 1990s marked the beginning of new trends.

Bonifazi's (1992) study of surveys carried out by the Institute for Population Research (IRP) and the DOXA suggested that early receptive attitudes towards immigration were being replaced by the fear of invasion.[26] The fact that Italians generally overestimated the number of migrants present in the country no doubt contributed to this (see Delai 1991). Data produced by the IRP confirmed that between the years 1987 and 1991, there was a considerable negative shift in public opinion towards migrants. Already in 1987, 49.7 per cent of the population felt there was an excess of migrants living in the country. By 1991, this figure had jumped to 74.5 per cent with 61 per cent of respondents feeling that immigration brought 'only or mainly' disadvantages. The IRP surveys also indicated a desire for the eventual repatriation of migrants. Sixty-two point nine per cent of the population felt that foreigners should eventually return to their own countries.[27] The late 1980s were in fact accompanied by a growth in racist incidents. In a publication of the British Institute of Race Relations, entitled *Inside Racist Europe*, the head of the Institute talks of a 'Euro-culture of popular racism' (Fekete and Webber 1994, p. vi). Italy seemed to be no exception to this. The racist assaults perpetrated in Italy have been brutal and indiscriminate and have led to serious injuries and deaths within ethnic minority communities. Two days after the murder of an African agricultural worker, Jerry Maslo, the then Minister for Social Affairs, Rosa Russo Jervolino, announced that the government was debating the introduction of a fixed limit to new entries and added 'We must nip racism in the bud' (*La Repubblica* 27/28 August 1989, p. 1). This revealed a somewhat facile cause-effect analysis of the motivation for racism and demonstrated an implicit tendency to understand, although not condone, the perpetrators of racist violence.[28] My argument here, is that by the late 1980s, the early 'laissez-faire' (see Ambrosini 1995) attitude to immigration was being replaced by a more stringent and restrictive approach. While in the 1970s there may have been an acceptance of migrants' economic utility because of the impact of Italy's modernisation on the employment aspirations of Italians themselves, by the late 1980s migrants were beginning to be seen as both economically and culturally threatening.

A different picture, however, emerges in relation to migrant women, who generally encountered a more positive reception context. From a cultural perspective, this may have been attributable to their religious proximity to Italians. For example, Cape Verdians and Filipinas, both early migrant settlers and predominantly female, were Catholics and therefore were not considered to embody the Islamic threat of North African men.[29] But it may also be accredited to their employment location within the domestic work sphere.

Migrant women were principally employed in the live-in sector which had been *vacated* by Italian women. Although some penetration of the hourly paid sector by migrant women had become possible by the 1980s (see chapter 6), Italian women appeared to have more advantages in this sector. In this way, migrant women were not perceived as being culturally or economically threatening to Italians. Nonetheless, all migrants – both men and women–were subject to an increasingly hostile environment from the late 1980s.[30]

The political response to immigration came officially via the introduction of legislation in 1986 and then in 1990.[31] In December 1986, law n. 943 was the first national legislative response to the phenomenon of immigration.[32] The law was intended to regularise the situation of migrants thereby resolving the problems of undocumented immigration. In fact, the law was popularly referred to as *la sanatoria* – an amnesty. Article 16 made provision for migrants to regularise their situation if they were irregularly employed or present in the country. This article thus dealt with one of the fundamental requisites of the legislation – the importance of regularisation to subsequently manage the phenomenon more evenly. The 1986 legislation additionally sought to guarantee certain cultural and social rights for migrants (Art. 3), again demonstrating adherence to a pluralist model. Two important provisions concerned firstly the recognition that enforced unemployment would not automatically translate into the revoking of a residence permit (Art. 11), and secondly Article 4 gave explicit support for family reunification, albeit subject to rather ambiguous conditions (see chapter 7).[33] Article 5 made provision for the establishment of special unemployment lists for migrants registered at job centres. However, for any new vacancies, migrants would have to wait for at least a month until the unavailability of Italian workers had been confirmed. The law was plainly being used to protect the interests of Italian workers who, as emerged clearly in the DOXA report referred to above, were concerned about competition from migrants in the sphere of employment. Law 943 clearly also subscribed to the idea of linking socioeconomic development in the country of origin with immigration in Italy. Thus Article 9 provided for the establishment of projects which would integrate 'the re-entry of non-EC migrants to their countries of origin'. The 1986 legislation thus appeared to conflate a number of conflicting aspirations: a pragmatic response to immigration via the institution of an amnesty, a humanitarian and receptive approach to the issue by indicating support for migrants' cultures, the protection of the status of Italian citizens via job protection and finally, the provision to facilitate migrants' return to their countries of origins.

The 1990 Martelli law was developed with the contribution of a variety of agencies. These included the relevant government ministries, trade unions, voluntary associations and migrant associations. The approach to be adopted was again intended to be both humanitarian and pragmatic[34] and the ratification of the law in 1990 received 90 per cent approval in parliament (Martelli 1991). Law n. 39 of 1990 again made provision for an amnesty (Art. 9). The Martelli law put migrants on a more equal footing with Italian workers in relation to employment via the local employment offices. Although provision was made to implement structures to deal positively with the phenomenon,[35] the 1990 legislation was also an attempt to tighten controls on entry and to severely penalise any contraventions of the law. For example, in line with trends in other European countries, shipping agencies and airline carriers would be penalised if they failed to inform the police authorities of the presence of foreign nationals who did not comply with Italian regulations for entry (Art. 3.ix).[36] The legislation was additionally more stringent regarding the expulsion of migrants who violated prescribed norms (Art. 7).

The 1990 legislation established a close link between the issue of entry visas to Italy and the requirements of the national economy. Entry would be programmed bearing in mind four criteria: the requirements of the national economy; the financial resources available and the existence of administrative structures to ensure the adequate reception of migrants; the number of requests for employment permits by non-EC nationals already present in Italy; the state of international relations and obligations (Art. 2.iv).

The fact that the amnesties of 1986 and 1990 failed to achieve the desired response confirms the argument suggested above, whereby migrants' integration into the undocumented sphere was symptomatic of the segmentation of the labour market.[37] More generally, national legislation appeared to be determined in relation to male migrants, referring, as it did, to 'the (male) worker'. Not surprisingly, as Bonini (1991) has argued, this meant that subsequent institutional interventions were aimed principally at African male migrants. I will expand on this in more detail in relation to the Lazio region in chapter 3.[38]

From a political perspective, the issue of immigration was also becoming intensely politicised as a result of the activities and intransigent position of the Northern Leagues under Umberto Bossi. This party adopted an explicitly anti-immigration stance, not simply to gain votes, but also to gain national prominence for its status as a new party. In an electoral manifesto outlining the party's views on immigration, the League's position was unequivocal:

We are convinced that it [immigration] does not constitute an economic advantage for rich countries or for poor countries: the former, because they have to sustain extremely high costs to integrate immigrants ... the latter only find themselves stripped of their work force without obtaining in exchange technology and suitable financial means on which to base their economic development ... Our position of harsh criticism towards migratory policies also derives from a particular conception that we federalists have of man. The human being is not simply an economic agent, but in fact, he or she is also made up of affection, cultural values and identity, which can find their best expression in their respective historical and environmental collectivities (Lega Nord 1992, p. 2).

Bossi (1992) argued that Italians should show solidarity to themselves first, maintaining that Italy's dysfunctional political system prohibited the extension of assistance to others. The prospect of a multi-cultural society was abhorrent to Bossi and legal migrants at best would be offered 'not so much mythical "rights to citizenship and participation" but a minimum level of dignified treatment' (Lega Nord 1992, p. 5).[39]

In the late 1980s, the then principal opposition party, the Italian Communist Party, adopted a quite different position. In a 1988 law proposal to the Senate, it sought to guarantee migrants a series of rights. One pioneering proposal concerned an article punishing racial discrimination (Art. 6).[40] The party's draft law also proposed a provision whereby migrants would be allowed to renew their permits on a five yearly basis to ensure greater stability. Article 9 aimed to give migrants the vote at local elections after three years of residence in Italy.[41] This proposal stands out as fairly visionary at a time when there was a growing negative attitude towards the presence of migrants. In the ensuing years, the now Pds identified the Italian public's experience of migration as an 'invasion' as a crucial area on which to base their political work, attributing the responsibility for the legal/illegal polarity to government policy: '... the distinction between "legality" and "illegality" does not reflect the identity or behavioural characteristics of migrants, but political decisions and positions of the governments of the receiving countries' (Pds 1991, p. 5).

Although an anti-racist constituency was also mobilised in the late 1980s, the general popular and political mood towards migrants was unquestionably moving in a negative direction. As Bonini (1991) has suggested, the changing circumstances of incoming migration generated a sense of panic in Italy, contributing to this negativity.

Conclusion

This chapter has presented an overview of the Italian immigration situation up to the early 1990s. It suggests that an evolving Italian model of immigration was shaped by a range of factors. This included Italy's own history of emigration, but also the prominence of the voluntary sector and the specific characteristics of Italian immigration. It would be premature to posit a definitive model, but in relation to Castles' (1995) conceptual model, it might be suggested that paradoxically, the Italian model up to that point, partially fitted both the differential exclusion model and the pluralist model. The pluralist position has, in my view, been conditioned by Italy's own experience of migration whereby a vocabulary of the rights to cultural difference, equal opportunities and mother tongue language teaching has been prominent. The differential exclusion aspect relates to the nature of migrant workers' integration into the Italian economy. Integration into the undocumented sphere offers only inclusion into the labour market but exclusion from other social benefits. In the case of migrant women, inclusion into both the documented and undocumented sphere of domestic work can be described as a form of differential exclusion. The nature of this work fully integrated them into a labour environment while implicitly and explicitly excluding them from other social spheres.

An historical overview of Italian immigration suggests that women have played an important part in incoming flows. As the gradual response to immigration indicates, women have on the whole been perceived to be a much less problematic grouping than migrant men.[42] The growing hostility towards migrants, perceptible from the mid to late 1980s, was generated by a series of factors. Firstly, the growing presence of migrants, and particularly visible male migrants. Secondly, the focus on push factors tended to portray migrants' presence in Italy as superfluous and finally the discourse of the Northern Leagues exacerbated this negative climate. By the end of the 1980s, migrants thus faced a generally more unfavourable social environment when compared to the 1970s.

Notes

1   Censis (*Centro studi investimenti sociali*) is a high profile research centre which conducts research into social and cultural issues in Italy.

2 These discussions were a result of the difficulties academics encountered in attempting to define the characteristics of immigration to Italy. In the 1980s, scholars frequently worked with fragmentary or contradictory data. Some of the methodological issues related to immigration research in Italy have been highlighted by Amaturo and Morlicchio (1990).

3 The political scientist Zincone (1993) has also emphasised the widespread administrative discretion existing in Italy which creates and contributes to the persistence of undocumented migrants.

4 Portes and Borocz (1989) have proposed a tripartite model of reception – handicapped, neutral or advantaged.

5 See Melotti (1990) for a more detailed discussion of this.

6 *Il Quindicinale di note e commenti*, to which reference is made here, is a publication outlet through which Censis publicises its work to a larger audience.

7 Stefano Petilli (1993, p. 627) describes this increased awareness towards the end of the 1980s as a departure from an 'agnostic' phase to one of 'attention'. See also Bonini's (1991) article on Italian immigration policy where he argues that the phenomenon was ignored by the institutions until 1987.

8 In fact some of this coverage was published as press surveys by the government. To give one example, the second volume produced covered the three month period between March and May in 1990. It was 690 pages long and contained a wide range of articles on immigration taken from a variety of newspapers (see *Presidenza del Consiglio dei Ministri* 1990).

9 A Censis study was commissioned specifically for the conference. This was published subsequently in book form in 1991. See Censis (1991).

10 Academic interest in the phenomenon had also grown significantly. A bibliography produced by Istat in 1991 showed that from the 1970s to 1984, there were 95 articles covering aspects of immigration to Italy. By the late 1980s, the increase in academic attention was particularly pronounced. Ninety-five articles were published in 1988 alone and 136 in 1989 (see Istat 1991).

11 The French sociologist Wieviorka (1993) has argued that weaker forms of racism are to be found in some of the southern European countries because of their own experiences of migration. He suggests anti-southern sentiment as the dominant racist sentiment in Italy.

12 Italia-Razzismo was an organisation established in the late 1980s to provide information about the immigration phenomenon. Its members included a number of politicians and academics, including Norberto Bobbio, Laura Balbo and Giovanni Berlinguer.

13 The data used here is taken from the statistical dossiers that have been published annually by the Caritas di Roma since 1991. Their tables are based on data provided by the Home Office. I also collated my own data from the Observatory on Employment (Lazio) in 1992. This data refers principally to 1990 and 1991, and allowed me to disaggregate figures for the ethnic groups with which this study is concerned.

14 Taamallah's (1981) unpublished research in the early 1980s estimated that there were 13,200 Tunisian residents in Italy in 1980. Men totalled 96 per cent of the Tunisian community, 84 per cent of whom were based in Sicily.

15 Cited in ECAP-CGIL (1979).

16 By acceleration, they refer to the growing volume of migration and by differentiation they refer to the range of immigration types that governments have to deal with – e.g. labour migration, permanent settlement or refugees.

17 In order to contextualise the case study below, I am presenting data which refers to the early 1990s. For more recent data on the contemporary immigration situation see King and Andall (1999).

18 Employment for men was more diversified, although it consisted principally of low level tertiary work. The employment of men was also determined by the nature of regional economies. Hotel and restaurant work, seasonal agricultural work, construction work, industrial work, street hawking and fishing were all areas in which migrant men could find work.

19 References to this work are to the second edition published in 1992. Further information regarding the organisation's role can be found in the introductions to its annual statistical dossiers.

20 While some of these services are specifically aimed at migrants, other are provided to the needy in general, although migrants increasingly constitute a significant portion of this group. In 1986, 3.4 billion lire was spent on the provision of services, 4.8 billion in 1987, 6.3 billion in 1988 and 14 billion in 1989 (Roma Caritas 1990).

21 The influence of Caritas in the sphere of immigration has come under some scrutiny. Some Catholic voluntary sector organisations felt that it was developing excessive contacts with political parties and other authorities (see Macioti 1990). Other forces viewed the nature of Catholic voluntary sector participation as an attempt to substitute the state (interview, CELSI-CGIL). Di Liegro and Pittau (1992) have categorically refuted these allegations.

22 The Catholic strategy contrasts with the ethos prevalent in some of the Protestant voluntary sector organisations. The Federation of Protestant Churches, for example, aims to support individual migrants in achieving a position of autonomy. This philosophy was illustrated during the 1990 national conference on immigration. Rather than speak for migrants, the federation's representative Anne Marie Duprès forfeited her slot to allow a migrant woman to speak. See Duprès in Presidenza del Consiglio dei ministri (1991, p. 432).

23 This law is discussed below.

24 Institute for Statistical Research and Analysis of Public Opinion.

25 DOXA, Bollettino, 30 November 1977.

26 His results are based on the results of three surveys carried out by DOXA in 1987, 1989 and 1991 and two further studies carried out by the IRP in 1987 and 1988.

27 Interestingly 51.3 per cent were in favour of allowing migrants to vote in local elections. This is perhaps not surprising given that the rights of Italian emigrants to vote in Italy has remained topical. See for example Guido Bolaffi's article 'Emigrati e voto' in *La Repubblica*, 3 July 1993, p. 8.

28 See Ter Wal's (1996) excellent account of *La Repubblica*'s news reporting of the occupation of a disused pasta factory in Rome by male migrants. She clearly demonstrates the manner in which its discourse 'played a crucial role in the reproduction of ethnic prejudice' (p. 62). Her results conform to Van Dijks's (1993) thesis regarding the denial of racism to be found within elite discourse not only as a strategy of 'positive self-representation' (p. 179) but also as a strategy of defence.

29 In his 11 hypotheses regarding migrations and minorities in the 1990s, Castles (1993) has argued that Muslim immigrants have become the main targets of racist discourse.

30 Anti-racist organisations did attempt to counter racist tendencies through anti-racist mobilisation. In October 1989, for example, a national demonstration against racism was held in Rome, promoted by the trade unions and other associations.

31 The 1990 law, popularly known as the Martelli law, was first issued as a decree law (n. 419) in 1989 and was converted in law (n. 39) in 1990.

32 See Favaro and Bordogna (1989) for a critical reading of this law.

33 These were important rulings as both of these issues have been used to limit immigration in other European contexts. France for example, temporarily used the withholding of family reunification entry visas as a means of preventing further immigration (Castles with Booth and Wallace 1984).

34 As Martelli himself stated, the legislators would not adopt a rigid fortress type position but '[we cannot] carry on the back of our country all the pain of the South of the world' (Martelli 1991, p. 56).

35 This would include for example the establishment of reception centres (Art. 11.iii) and the appointment of 200 social workers, 80 sociologists and 20 psychologists to work in the employment offices (Art. 12.i).

36 For example, in Britain, the Carriers Liability Act was introduced for the same reason in 1987.

37 See Pugliese (1990a) for more detailed discussion of this point.

38 The most recent immigration law (n. 40) was introduced in 1998 (Disciplina dell'immigrazione e norme sulla condizione dello straniero). See Bonini (1998) and King and Andall (1999) for a discussion of its contents.

39 Bossi (1992) argued that the League's policies were consonant with that of the European Community. Gallagher (1994:463) reinforced this claim by arguing that the League's position no longer appeared 'out on a limb' given the European Community's restrictive attitude towards migrants. However, some distinction should be made. The European Union has undoubtedly moved in a restrictive direction, but, theoretically at least, it purports to ameliorate the situation of ethnic minorities already living within the Union and seeks to guarantee a series of fundamental rights. While the League's position was similarly restrictive to outside entry, it argued only for *minimum* protection for migrants within Italy and promoted a clear sub-text for repatriation. For more on the League's immigration position see Bull (1997).

40 A government decree law was eventually introduced in 1993 which established penalties for racial, ethnic and religious discrimination.

41 It is to be noted however, that the party failed to include this provision in the 1998 immigration legislation when it was in government.

42 This would begin to change in the 1990s with the increase in African and East European female prostitution. See Campani (2000).

3   Setting the Scene: the Regional Context

The previous chapters have addressed the issues of gender and immigration from a national perspective. However, Italy's regions present quite different social, economic and political characteristics (Levy 1996). Regional case studies cannot therefore normally claim to be representative of the national picture. Nonetheless, the uniformity of migrant women's employment at the national level means that much of the evidence presented in the case study below is in fact generalisable to the national picture. Research undertaken on the experiences of migrant women domestic workers in Milan (Favaro and Bordogna 1991), Bologna (Palazzi 1990) Naples (De Filippo 1994) and Palermo (Cole 1997) all confirm this. Nevertheless, despite evidence of regional uniformity regarding migrant women's employment location, the different regional economies and service infrastructures are likely to influence not only the type of Italian families employing domestic workers but may also condition future employment opportunities for migrant women. In this chapter, I shall focus on the regional dimension of gender and immigration. The first section will address trends in Italian women's employment in the region. The second section will establish the general characteristics of incoming migration to the Lazio region, emphasising employment disparities between male and female migrants. I will then proceed to an assessment of the regional policy response to immigration. It is my view that this response has generally marginalised the experiences of migrant women. Moreover, the establishment of regional consultative bodies which have chosen to adopt a gender-blind approach is likely to signify that issues pertinent to migrant women may well remain on the periphery of social policy proposals.

The Lazio Region: Women and Employment

In terms of women's labour market participation, the Lazio region occupies an intermediary status when considered against the national norm. It is positioned ahead of some of the Southern regions and behind some of the Northern regions (Arena 1978; D'Alessandro 1988) with occupational and organisational models from both the North and the South coexisting within Lazio (Regione Lazio 1988). Nanetti (1988) has argued that the region's low ranking in terms of industrialisation should not be seen as indicative of its economic standing, but rather, the prevalence of its service sector should be utilised as an indicator with which to measure the region's economic well-being. The Lazio region is home to a significant bureaucratic apparatus and the specific features of the region's economy have contributed to a particular typology of women's employment. In the mid 1980s women represented 30.6 per cent of the employed population in Lazio.[1] Paradoxically, the increased presence of women in the workplace since the 1970s has been accompanied by an increase in the number of unemployed women (Regione Lazio 1988) suggesting that only a proportion of Italian women's supply for the labour market has been absorbed.

The overwhelming majority of Italian women in the Lazio region work in the tertiary sector (public administration and services), with a minority working in industry or agriculture. In 1985, 81.7 per cent of women worked in the tertiary sector and by 1987 this figure had risen to 83.8 per cent. The figures for agriculture were 10.1 per cent and 7.2 per cent respectively and for industry 8.2 per cent and 9 per cent. In 1987, the national picture showed that 46.5 per cent of Italian women were employed in the tertiary sector, 26.3 per cent in industry and 27.2 per cent in agriculture (Regione Lazio 1988).[2] Thus, women's employment in the tertiary sector in Lazio was significantly higher than the national average. The region's 1988 report on the socioeconomic situation of Lazio confirmed that the presence in Rome of the state's central administration had led to the high concentration of public administration employees (Regione Lazio 1988) and the dominance of this employment sector for women appears to have had both positive and negative implications. The ISFOL (Institute for the development of professional training) (1988) study showed that the highest levels of employment amongst women are to be found amongst female graduates. Again, this is confirmed by the Lazio region report (Regione Lazio 1988) which highlighted the high level of average educational achievement amongst women in the region as a characteristic which sets it apart from the national average. Only 12.6 per cent of graduates described themselves as primarily housewives while 50 per cent of women with a primary or middle school qualification did so. Only 19.6 per cent of women with a primary or middle school qualification, compared to 75.1 per cent of graduates were employed. This low participation rate amongst the least educated women could be attributed to the nature of available tertiary sector work. Arena (1978) has argued that the prevalence of tertiary work in Rome meant that women usually needed more than a middle school diploma to find work. Nevertheless the low participation rate amongst less qualified women warrants investigation. It implies that there is demand for women's labour predominantly in sectors which require high scholastic achievement. However, the demand for migrant women's labour appears to contradict this inference, since migrant women are employed overwhelmingly in categories of employment which do not necessitate formal qualifications. It would therefore seem more appropriate to explain the low participation rates of poorly qualified Italian women as being partly influenced by the status and conditions ascribed to available employment sectors. For example, while domestic service is perceived as a negative category of employment (see chapter 4), the maternal or familial role is theoretically positively supported in Italy. The argument that the female migrant labour force could be replaced by Italian nationals can therefore only be sustained if important sociocultural factors are marginalised. Within the industrially advanced capitalist economies there are specific employment sectors which indigenous nationals avoid, in part because of the status of particular jobs but also because the employment conditions appear so unattractive. For Italian women, opting for a primarily familial role can present an acceptable alternative to certain types of paid employment, particularly where the sociocultural and financial benefits of such employment appear limited. Reduced employment opportunities within the industrial sector for women in the higher age brackets and with low educational qualifications, is a consequence of restructuring in this sector[3] and is likely to have contributed to a return to female 'inactivity' (Regione Lazio 1988).

Tertiary sector employment in the Lazio region has also influenced the working model for Italian women in Lazio. Most women were employed on a permanent (93 per cent) full-time (91 per cent) basis. Only 9 per cent were in part-time work and temporary work was largely seen as an expedient. D'Alessandro (1988) has attributed this to the fact that the greater part of female work in Lazio is in the services sector where the hours worked are on average shorter than those in other sectors.

Family obligations appear to have a significant influence on Italian women's participation in paid employment. The peak of women's family obligations is likely to occur in the 25–34 age category, in other words when women are likely to have young children. In the 30–49 age group 78.6 per cent of employed women had no family dependants. In the 25–29 age group, 64.3 per cent of employed women had no family dependants. Thus, employment was clearly facilitated by an absence of dependant family members. Marriage also contributed to women's economic inactivity outside the home. A majority of married women who were not employed and were not searching for employment cited personal and family reasons as a significant contributory factor to their primary presence within the domestic sphere. In the 30–59 age group 84.6 per cent of non-working women attributed their situation to family and personal obligations. However, 70 per cent of divorced or separated women worked, with only 19.17 per cent describing themselves as housewives. This can be compared to the situation of married women, where 26.5 per cent of married women were employed and 64 per cent were housewives.

Women's employment in the Lazio region is thus predominant in the tertiary sector.[4] The relatively shorter working hours for permanent full-time positions offered women in this sector some advantages in terms of the organisation of work, whilst creating disadvantages for those women with limited qualifications. Women's employment in Lazio remains fairly limited however. Activity rates for women in Lazio were 30.2 per cent in 1989 and showed a slight increase in 1991 to 31.9 per cent. For men these figures were 55.2 per cent and 55.6 per cent respectively (Regione Lazio 1992b). The family situation of women appeared to be an influential factor in determining women's involvement in paid employment. Certainly, the prevailing model in the region did not appear to perceive women as key breadwinners and only divorced and separated women presented high activity rates. This meant that migrant women's role as main or exclusive breadwinners would constitute a substantial anomaly to normalised practice in the region.

The Lazio Region: Incoming Migration

A significant proportion of Italy's new migrants reside in the Lazio region. According to Home Office data elaborated on by the Lazio region's Observatory on Employment (*Osservatorio del mercato del lavoro*) (OML), on 30 December 1990, there were 781,138 foreigners resident in Italy, and of this total 197,465 were resident in the Lazio region. Women represented 41 per cent of this resident community in the region. Table 3.1 presents data regarding the principal ethnic communities resident in the province of Rome. Table 3.2 shows that Rome attracted the highest percentage of foreign nationals of all the Italian cities. In terms of the Lazio region, some 91 per cent of foreign nationals were resident in the province of Rome (see Table 3.3). Rome

Table 3.1   Foreign nationals* residing in the province of Rome, as at 31 December 1990

Philippines	16,930
Egypt	7,438
Poland	7,185
Ethiopia	6,200
India	5,938
Morocco	5,787
Somalia	4,892
Yugoslavia	4,799
China	4,759
Tunisia	4,498
Pakistan	4,324
Brazil	4,271
Sri Lanka	3,979
Iran	3,109
Argentina	2,610
Cape Verde	2,539
Senegal	1,681
Lebanon	1,591
Nigeria	1,288
Chile	1,162
Ghana	936
Turkey	571
Mauritius	81

*   This table does not include data for foreign nationals from advanced industrial economies.

Source: Regione Lazio, *Osservatorio del mercato del lavoro*.

thus assumed particular significance when discussing the situation of migrants in the Lazio region. As discussed in the previous chapter, while by 1990 immigration data compilation was more sophisticated, it still only provided evidence about legally resident migrants.

A growing literature on the presence of migrants in Rome and the Lazio region has evolved.[5] Since the late 1960s to the 1990s, there has been a succession of different ethnic groups entering the region, differing in gender composition and with divergent experiences of the Italian labour market. This divergency can be attributed to gender, nationality and the period of their arrival. Altieri and Carchedi (1992) found that the first group of arrivals, which they date to the late 1960s, were women migrants from the Cape Verde islands,

Table 3.2   Italian cities with more than 10,000 non-EU migrants as at 31 December 1992

Rome	171,288
Milan	101,884
Naples	35,252
Turin	21,303
Palermo	20,154
Bologna	18,971
Vicenza	17,141
Genoa	15,467
Catania	13,095
Latina	12,592
Perugia	12,352
Modena	11,389
Verona	10,845

Source: Caritas di Roma (1993).

Table 3.3   Foreign nationals in Lazio as at 31 December 1990

Rome	180,093
Latina	9,420
Frosinone	3,103
Rieti	2,274
Viterbo	2,575

Source: Regione Lazio, *Osservatorio del mercato del lavoro*.

Eritrea, Ethiopia and Somalia. There was also a trickle from the Philippines, North Africa and East Africa.[6] In the period from 1975–80, numbers in the aforementioned groups increased through chain migration, coupled with the appearance of new groups from Egypt, Argentina, Peru, Chile and El Salvador. A subsequent wave occurred between 1980–85/6. During this period, there was an increase of North Africans and a further contingent from South East Asia. There were also further arrivals from Eritrea, due to the war with Ethiopia, and Somalia.

Analysis of Home Office data offers a revealing picture of the employment status of Lazio's migrant communities. Data for the province of Rome showed the variety of reasons for which permits were issued. 1990 data indicated that 35.11 per cent of migrants were registered at employment offices while 21.19

per cent were issued with permits for salaried work. The application of a gendered focus, however, is instructive. Twenty-five point four seven per cent of women were issued with a permit for salaried work while 24.86 per cent were registered at employment offices. This compared favourably with the situation of migrant men where 18 per cent were issued with a permit for salaried work and 42.75 per cent were registered at employment offices. A higher percentage of women's permits were issued for family motives (8.79 per cent) when compared to men (2.81 per cent).

These figures pointed to an incongruity in migrant women's employment. Firstly they established that a higher proportion of women than men were employed, and that unemployment was almost twice as high for migrant men. One should not necessarily infer from this that men could not find work in the city. Rather, it suggested that employment opportunities were more easily available within the unofficial labour market. Strozza's (1991) research on migrant workers in Rome for example demonstrated that restaurant related work constituted an important sector of economic activity for these workers. He also found that this sector was overwhelmingly occupied by male migrants.[7] Furthermore, contrary to the situation of Italian women in the Lazio region, where women's presence on the registers of employment offices was substantially higher than men's,[8] migrant women were less likely to be on the registers by comparison with their male counterparts. This is clearly apparent if we take the situation of the specific ethnic groups with which this book is concerned.[9] Fifty-three point zero one per cent of Cape Verdean women had been issued with permits for salaried work, 14.78 per cent were registered at employment centres and 17.72 per cent were arranging employment. This compares with 40.42 per cent and 23.36 per cent respectively for Cape Verdean men, with 15.42 per cent arranging employment. Cape Verdean men were however very much a minority in this community, representing only 17 per cent of the Cape Verdeans resident in Lazio (women 2,111; men 428). A similar disparity was apparent in the Ethiopian community, albeit less marked. While 32.26 per cent of Ethiopian women had permits for salaried work, 18.83 per cent were registered at employment centres. Fifteen point nine five per cent of Ethiopian women were waiting to emigrate. When this is compared to the situation of Ethiopian men, we find only 13.02 per cent had permits for salaried work, 17.37 per cent were registered at employment centres, while a large percentage were waiting to emigrate (35.6 per cent). Ethiopian women represented 53 per cent of its community in Lazio (women 3,304; men 2,896). This slightly different picture when compared to the Cape Verdean figures was to be expected given the different profiles of Ethiopian residents in Italy,

Table 3.4   Reasons for issuing permits to migrant women for the province of Rome as at 31 December 1990 (%)

	Cape Verde	Ethiopia	Somalia
Political asylum	0.00	3.24	3.08
Awaiting adoption	0.00	0.09	0.00
Awaiting fostering	0.00	0.03	0.00
Waiting to emigrate	0.05	15.95	8.26
Arranging employment	17.72	7.20	6.66
Registered at Job Centre	14.78	18.83	50.19
Self-employed work	0.05	0.15	0.96
Employed work	53.01	32.26	14.25
Sailors to embark	0.00	0.00	0.00
Family reasons	8.72	7.60	3.86
Health reasons	0.14	0.42	0.07
Study purposes	1.23	1.00	2.30
Legal reasons	0.00	0.03	0.00
Religious reasons	0.71	1.76	0.00
Tourist reasons	1.14	3.72	6.95
None	1.75	6.69	3.19
Chosen place of residence	0.71	1.03	0.21

Source: Regione Lazio, *Osservatorio del mercato del lavoro.*

where a greater number were political refugees. Among the Somali community, one could observe notable discrepancies by comparison with the situation of other African female migrants. While 14.25 per cent of Somali women had a permit for salaried work, a staggering 50.19 per cent were registered at employment centres. Seven point seventy-seven per cent of Somali men had a permit for salaried work and 42.06 per cent were registered at employment centres. Thus this was the only ethnic group, with which we are concerned, where a higher proportion of women were registered at employment centres. Fifty-seven per cent of the Somali community living in Lazio were women (women 2821; men 2071).[10]

The civil status of migrants is equally significant since it provides information about whether women have migrated autonomously or for the purposes of family reunification. The following Home Office figures refer to the Lazio region and include all foreign nationals. The unavailability of data which differentiated between the civil status of specific groups of migrants

Table 3.5 **Reasons for issuing permits to migrant men for the province of Rome as at 31 December 1990 (%)**

	Cape Verde	Ethiopia	Somalia
Political asylum	0.00	3.76	7.53
Awaiting adoption	0.00	0.00	0.00
Awaiting fostering	0.00	0.03	0.00
Waiting to emigrate	0.00	35.60	17.62
Arranging employment	15.42	1.48	1.74
Registered at Job Centre	23.36	17.37	42.06
Self-employed work	0.70	0.52	2.75
Employed work	40.42	13.02	7.77
Sailors to embark	0.23	0.00	0.00
Family reasons	8.41	2.21	1.35
Health reasons	0.23	0.35	0.19
Study purposes	0.93	2.18	7.10
Legal reasons	0.23	0.00	0.05
Religious reasons	1.64	2.24	0.00
Tourist reasons	3.50	4.87	8.64
None	4.91	15.78	1.88
Chosen place of residence	0.00	0.52	1.30

Source: Regione Lazio, *Osservatorio del mercato del lavoro.*

means that the figures conceal differences between specific ethnic groups. They do however give an indication of general trends. While 62.3 per cent of female foreign nationals in the Lazio region were single, 27.77 per cent were married. A minority were divorced, separated or living with their partners. Even within those age categories where one might anticipate a higher number of married women, a significant proportion of Lazio's female foreign nationals were single – 66.6 per cent in the 25–29 age bracket, 52.97 per cent in the 30–39 age bracket and 54.05 per cent in the 40–49 age bracket. These figures suggested that a substantial proportion of female foreign nationals in the Lazio region were autonomous agents. Employment was clearly critical to their survival as their autonomous migration meant that they could not rely on others for financial support. Indeed, their autonomous migration was likely to mean that relatives in the country of origin relied on their income for financial assistance.

The above data indicates that women were at an advantage with respect to the availability of employment in the official labour market when compared to male migrants. This is further validated by data referring to employment processes at the employment centres. It should be noted that employment via these recruitment centres represented only one method of securing employment.[11] Thus the data offers a partial rather than an overall picture of the situation. It also provides information regarding available sectors of work for migrants. The three productive sectors under which migrants were registered were agriculture, industry and services, plus a non classified section. Data for the Lazio region[12] showed that 4.66 per cent of non-EC migrants were registered as seeking employment within the agricultural category, 84.42 per cent in industry and 6.49 per cent in the services sector. This compared with national figures of 5.54 per cent, 44.92 per cent and 16.38 per cent respectively. However, if we break these figures down by gender, a clear occupational segregation can be observed. Eighty-eight point two per cent of men were registered under agriculture compared to 11.8 per cent of women. For industry the figures were 84.03 per cent and 15.97 per cent and for services 54.84 per cent and 45.16 per cent respectively. The latter figures indicate a degree of parity between male and female migrants in the services sector. A significant disparity could be observed however in relation to industrial and agricultural sectors. Gender polarisation was additionally evident in relation to the period of registration at employment centres. Eighty two point zero two per cent of male migrants compared to 17.98 per cent of female migrants had been registered for a period of between three months and a year. Seventy point seven eight per cent of male migrants and 29.22 per cent of female migrants had been registered for over a year. Men, therefore, experienced longer periods of official unemployment, which points to a certain buoyancy of demand for female migrant labour within the region.

An evaluation of the data which refers to the placement of migrant workers points to levels of demand within specific areas of Lazio's economy.[13] Eight point one one per cent of migrants were placed in the agricultural sector, 22.27 per cent in the industrial sector and 69.63 per cent in the services sector. Men were placed primarily in the industrial sector (42.33 per cent), while an overwhelming proportion of women were placed in the services sector (92.88 per cent). Within the services sector, a further division is made to provide data for the category of domestic work. Within the category of general services, 45.29 per cent were placed in domestic work. This greatly exceeds the national figure of 14.33 per cent. Of those placed in domestic work in Lazio, 62.33 per cent were women.

The above statistics identify substantial disparities between the employment experiences of female and male migrants. Migrant men were, in the main, seeking employment in the industrial sphere. However, as I have indicated above, there was a relatively low incidence of industry in the region. This meant that it was difficult to place migrant workers in this sector, or at any rate that the supply would outstrip the demand. Services, on the other hand, was a buoyant sector in the region's economy and this constituted an advantage for migrant women. The different trends in terms of gender are confirmed by regional figures for the year 1991 where men were placed in employment via the recruitment centres in 45.6 per cent of cases. This compared to a national figure of 77.3 per cent, implying that in Lazio it is more difficult for migrant men to gain employment in the official market than in other Italian regions. The 1991 figures also showed that 82 per cent of unemployed migrants were men. In 1992, 61 per cent of permit authorisations for salaried work in the Lazio region were made to women, against a national average of 53.8 per cent.[14] This points to a particularly marked level of demand in the services sector for migrant labour which offered females a degree of stability within the employment market. However, domestic work does also present some employment opportunities for male migrants, albeit to a lesser degree. This employment sector should not, therefore, be considered an exclusively female preserve. The 1990 national Census study (1991) demonstrated that domestic work featured as a sector of employment even within those migrant groups which were not characterised by a predominant female presence (e.g. Iran, Iraq and Sri Lanka). Male migrants residing in the Lazio region found that their desire for industrial sector work could not be accommodated within the official Lazio labour market.

Although the above data demonstrates that female migrants enjoyed some advantages in securing work via state employment offices, it should be noted that less women than men seek work through this channel. Domestic work can frequently be obtained via alternative recruitment channels suggesting even greater employment stability for migrant women. This indicates not only that the labour supply of migrant women is important for the region, but it also testifies to the possibility of employment in the official labour market. Migrant workers had clearly identified the Lazio region and Rome in particular as a region which could provide employment.[15] This challenged those interpretations, discussed in the previous chapter, which, at the time, tended to minimise the importance of demand in specific areas of the Italian domestic economy.

The Regional Policy Response

The introduction of national immigration legislation in 1986 assigned an important role to local councils regarding the integration of migrants. Until then, the regions had been expected to deal with the new migration in the absence of a national framework of intervention. The Lazio region had already begun to engage with the issue of immigration and it passed regional legislation in the same year. The region's initial policy on immigration had emerged more as a response to the return migration of Italians to the Lazio region (interview, RL1). But in addition to the phenomenon of return migration, evidence of new forms of immigration were already being noted:

> At that time … there was already a small presence of immigrants … In those years, it was not such a worrying problem as it is now but it evolved in such a way that, in 1986, it was felt that there was a need to create a law for emigration and immigration … We created an emigration consultative body which dealt with emigrants' problems as well as immigrants' problems (interview, RL1).

The legislation (law n. 48 1986) was entitled 'Regional intervention for emigration and immigration', clearly indicating the region's propensity to view the issue of immigration as a single issue with limited internal differentiation.[16] This approach was not limited to the Lazio region. Both the Marche and Piedmont regions instituted regional legislation which encompassed both emigration and immigration. Others, such as Lombardy, Umbria and Liguria produced regional legislation specifically on the issue of immigration.[17] Lazio thus fell into the category of regions which assumed that returnee Italian migrants would encounter similar problems to African and Asian migrants.[18] With reference to the British context, Solomos (1989) has shown how a liberal attitude towards the arrival of European workers contrasted sharply with a negative response to Black workers. This led to an increasingly racialised debate which aimed to restrict the entry of Black British subjects to Britain. This suggests that recognition of the diversity within the constituency of immigration is crucial for the development of appropriately tailored social policy. There was, for example, a fundamental disparity between returnee migrants and African migration to Italy around the issue of their legal status. Migrants' citizenship rights within a given country can affect their ability to acquire accommodation, work legally and participate in public life. By 1990, in line with national trends, the treatment of incoming migration to Italy as an issue in its own right had clearly prevailed and new regional legislation was introduced in Lazio in February 1990 (Legge Regionale n. 17 16/2/1990).

The new law separated the two issues of emigration and immigration. In its introduction a programme of initiatives to improve conditions for African, Asian and East European migrants was outlined and specific areas were prioritised. This was followed by a regional plan and the legislation itself. The 1990 legislation did not simply delineate a remedy for the situation of migrants within Lazio, but was also clearly concerned with elaborating policies to encourage migrants to either stay away from Italy or return home. A facile correlation between increased aid to developing countries and a reduction in incoming migration pervaded the regional legislation. The legislation contained implicit acknowledgment of the prominence of push rather than pull factors in explaining the presence of migrants in the region. As a consequence the document contained repeated reference to strategies to encourage the migrant to return home. For instance, although one subsection of the regional plan listed a variety of initiatives aimed at facilitating migrants' social integration, also included was a proposal to develop initiatives to support migrants' return to their country of origin. Such a proposal appeared somewhat out of place in a subsection dedicated to the theme of social integration (Regione Lazio 1992a, p. 12).

Intervention concerning development co-operation targeted specific sending countries:

> Development cooperation in the sending countries of non-Ec immigrants constitutes an important element to stem immigration and promote the choices of those immigrants who intend to return to their countries of origin (Regione Lazio 1992a, p. 16).

This initiative could therefore be interpreted as having little to do with a general commitment to reducing the North/South economic divide and everything to do with strategies for stemming and reversing immigration to the Lazio region.[19]

Nonetheless, a key informant from the Lazio Immigration Office described provisions to assist the effective repatriation of migrants and to prevent their departure from their countries of origin as being migrant oriented:

> There are many foreigners here. However, there is also huge youth unemployment here. So, why do people migrate? Often, some developing countries have problems, in fact, they all have big problems. So, we believe that we can help you in terms of training so that you can train here to be a

plumber, electrician, and then you can go back to your country. The ideal would really be to intervene to stop them coming, because in the end you will find that even here there is no more work. This is the point (interview, RL1).[20]

This view, as well as indicating a paternalistic and limited perspective, also indicated an acceptance of a direct correlation between domestic unemployment and the presence of migrants. This should be regarded as a false correlation given that, as I have already argued, Italian nationals do not accept certain types of employment within the domestic market. Notwithstanding, the region's legislation appeared to be governed by concern about the possible implications of competition in the work place. While it could be argued that a degree of competition did exist between the local unskilled labour force and migrants in the Lazio region, it should also be recognised that up until the emanation of the Martelli law in 1990, the position of nationals, at least in the official labour market, was protected by the 1986 legislation.

In the previous chapter I argued that development strategies will not stem contemporary migratory flows because of the interim imbalances that arise from structural redevelopment. Thus return migration to the sending countries was unlikely to be a realistic option for the foreseeable future. The region's attention therefore needed to be more clearly focused on strategies for the social and political integration of minority communities into the wider Italian community rather than on developing strategies to assist their repatriation.

The regional document singled out five general areas for action: orientation centres, the recognition of civil and political rights, intervention in the social arena, interventions for working migrant women and their children, and interventions regarding migrants' associations. The establishment of orientation centres was intended to prevent social tension and action was intended to encourage:

> the settlement of immigrants in regions where the housing situation is not so tense (the positive experience of the Albanians is to be noted) or where demographic levels are lower or where there is greater economic and productive potential (Regione Lazio 1992a, p. 6).

This statement indicated the Region's adherence to the notion of 'threshold', according to which an almost automatic process of hostile rejection by the indigenous population follows within a given locality or institution when the percentage of foreign or immigrant people reaches a certain level. In 1992, migrants represented approximately 3.9 per cent of the resident population in the Lazio region and 4.8 per cent of the resident population in Rome (Caritas di Roma 1992, p. 168).[21]

The second stated priority of the region displayed a growing awareness of the importance of recognising migrants' civil and political rights:

> It is a case of moving from a position of tolerance to one governed by guaranteeing rights to everyone without any form of discrimination. No one can simply be governed. Everyone has the right to be protagonists of their democratic life (Regione Lazio 1992a, p. 6).

In line with such a position the region placed substantial emphasis on the necessity to promote the various cultures of migrants. It viewed sociocultural intervention as important and promoted various projects intended to protect the cultural identity of migrants.

The third stated priority – intervention in the social arena – promoted training to facilitate migrants' insertion into the labour market. Some contradiction is apparent however, in the promotion of strategies to ensure migrants' insertion into the social fabric of the community with a concurrent emphasis on the long-term goal of encouraging migrants to return to their country of origin:

> In terms of professional training what must be stressed ... is that it must be aimed at encouraging immigrants' insertion into their countries of origin as a means of stemming the migratory pressure (Regione Lazio 1992a, p. 6).

The document proceeded to propose training based on the specific needs of the migrant worker's country of origin.

The fourth stated priority – intervention for working women migrants and children – recognised the pressures on working women from minority communities in carrying out the socialising functions of the family and accepted that society should assume greater responsibility:

> The immigrant woman is called on to carry out a socialisation role for her family and children. This socialisation is necessary, but it not the duty of the woman to ensure it takes place. It is the whole society with all its structures which has to be responsible: with reception facilities, education, and professional training (Regione Lazio 1992a, p. 7).

Thus the Lazio document considered migrant women to have a particularly important input into the socialisation of the family. This did not diverge from some national perspectives addressed in chapter 1. The region seemed to be acknowledging the specific situation of women migrant workers, however the remedial intervention to migrant women's dislocated families (subsidised summer holidays) was a weak long-term strategy which tended to endorse an unsatisfactory situation without proposing remedies to transform it. It is to be noted that only in this subsection, entitled 'Intervention for working female migrants and children', was there specific reference to 'the female immigrant'.

The fifth stated priority of the region, regarding migrants' associations, illustrated support for organisations which permit migrants to develop their own forms of representation. The establishment of migrants' associations was promoted as an instrument to ensure the maintenance of migrants' cultural identity but also as a means of promoting integration into the receiving country.

Article 1 of the regional law (law n. 17 1990) ensured migrants' rights within the workplace, guaranteed social and health protection, endorsed their right to maintain their cultural identity and committed the region to the professional training of migrants. To ensure representation, Article 3 of the legislation made provision for a regional consultative body on immigration and this was established in 1991. In September 1992, this consultative body consisted of 29 members. This included representatives from workers' trade unions (3), employers' organisations (3), organisations working with migrants (3), representatives of migrant workers (6), representatives of associations (4). There were also representatives from the Ministry of Labour and other representatives from regional committees.

The issue of a gendered representation had evidently not influenced the formation of the consultative body. Of its 29 members only six were women. However, more significantly, of the six migrant representatives only one was a woman. This must be viewed as a substantial under-representation of the specific concerns of women. The high proportion of women migrants in the region has already been established. While there were several migrant women's organisations within the Lazio region, suggesting migrant women's propensity to be active in forms of political participation, the dominance of male migrants in terms of institutional regional representation had the potential to misrepresent or sideline their needs. This was not however seen to be an important issue within the Lazio immigration office. As one of the key informants stated: '... The women present within [the consultative body] do not represent women. We made no distinction between the immigrants. They represent immigrants' (interview, RL2).

The legislation promulgated by the Lazio region replicated trends in national legislation. The 1990 regional legislation reinforced Castle's (1993) hypothesis that state policies towards migrants are increasingly complex and contradictory, essentially because governments are attempting to reconcile irreconcilable goals. The strong emphasis in the regional document on strategies to encourage the migrant to return home coupled with the assertion of migrants' rights is clear evidence of this. This implied that the region's contribution to the issue from both a theoretical and practical level would be conditioned by these contradictions. Migrants should be given rights, but how much better if they could be encouraged to leave! Implicit within such a contradictory stance was a view of migrants' labour as surplus to requirements. As I shall be arguing in the following chapters, the high labour force participation of female migrants stood at odds with such an assumption.

Conclusion

The first section of this chapter has highlighted the dominant work model for Italian women in the Lazio region. I have suggested that family obligations significantly affect the nature of Italian women's labour force participation and I have maintained that migrant women's position as head of household constituted an anomaly in the regional configuration of women's employment and family experiences. Statistics provided in the second section of this chapter showed a major discrepancy in the employment patterns of Italian and migrant women. The high labour force participation of the latter group suggested that labour force participation constituted a more dominant social identity for migrant women.

The second section of this chapter also presented empirical data regarding the characteristics of labour migration to Lazio. This demonstrated that the majority of the region's migrants settled in Rome. It also demonstrated that clear gender-based disparities existed within migrants' experience of the labour market. The data presented showed that female migrants enjoyed greater employment stability when compared to their male counterparts. However their employment was decidedly more uniform in comparison to male migrants, confined as it was to the domestic service sector.

In relation to the regional response to immigration, I have argued that the region displayed a propensity to conceptualise migrants as male. This occurred despite both a substantial presence of migrant women workers in the region and the different socioeconomic positioning of male and female migrants.

This conceptualisation was likely to marginalise the specific needs of migrant women. Had a regional policy been drawn up at an earlier stage of the immigration process, it may have been more difficult for the region to sideline women's presence in such a fashion. The dominance of the female presence in the early 1970s might have led to the development of policies which were more clearly focused on the specific needs of female migrants. In the context of the contemporary phenomenon, it is probable that migrant men make greater use of the voluntary services and therefore constitute the group that is targeted for assistance, particularly emergency assistance. For example, accommodation for male migrants in the region is particularly problematic and factors such as these may have contributed to the invisibility of migrant women who appear to have fewer problems because of greater feminised employment demand and the provision of housing with their employment. Nonetheless, as I will argue in subsequent chapters, women migrants encountered a different set of problems which were frequently subordinated to the more high profile problems of male migrants.

Notes

1   In 1988, a publication promoted by the region's consultative body on women (*consulta femminile*) was undertaken by ISFOL (*Istituto per lo sviluppo della formazione professionale*) in collaboration with Rome University. The statistics cited refer to this publication unless otherwise indicated, and refer to 1985. The data is based on the elaboration of data taken from Istat's trimonthly publications on the work force.
2   These figures are based on data from ISTAT.
3   The technological and organisational restructuring which occurred provoked expulsion from the labour market and a greater degree of selection by the employer from the pool of available labour. See Regione Lazio (1988).
4   The presence of a parallel labour market in the Italian context should not be overlooked. In fact the underemployment of women is a further feature of their condition in the region. See Regione Lazio (1988).
5   See Comune di Roma (1988), Caritas Diocensa di Roma (1989) Caritas di Roma (1991) (1992) (1993), Altieri and Carchedi (1992). See also the bibliography on studies published about the region in Istat (1991).
6   Altieri and Carchedi (1992) also confirm my own findings regarding the limited information concerning this period, apart from newspaper reports.
7   Restaurant work is, of course, a sector which can easily absorb labour via the unofficial labour market. See Strozza (1991) and Luisa Natale (1991) for more information on the attitudes of employers in the region towards employing migrant labour.
8   D'Alessandro (1988, p. 278) noted a marked disparity in strategy between unemployed male and female Italians. Women revealed a greater propensity to register at employment centres and to participate in public examinations.

9   These figures are graphically reproduced in Tables 3.4 and 3.5.
10   It is useful to refer to the figures for an ethnic group outside the scope of this study as it confirms the trend regarding demand for migrant women's labour. Forty three point nine two per cent of Filipina women had a permit for salaried work, 18.79 per cent were registered at employment centres and 23.31 per cent were arranging employment.
11   As Reyneri (1989) has shown, although the hiring of staff was legally supposed to occur via these state employment offices, a significant amount of labour market recruitment occurred via electoral clienteles, church parishes, the family and community ties.
12   This data refers to December 1991.
13   This data refers to January/December 1991.
14   There were five other regions where permit authorisations for salaried work exceeded the 60 per cent mark for women (Liguria 64.2 per cent; Emilia Romagna 66 per cent; Tuscany 61.6 per cent; Abruzzo 64 per cent; Molise 63 per cent).
15   Rome is also a popular destination because it is the capital and many embassies and consulates are situated there.
16   The first provincial conference held on the theme of emigration and immigration in Rome in 1986 reinforces this argument. See Regione Lazio and Provincia di Roma (1986) for conference proceedings. Attention to returnee migrants continued into the 1990s. In 1992 for example, a regional conference was held on this issue entitled 'Emigrazione partecipazione. Da emigrati a cittadini'. See ANFE's journal *Notizie fatti problemi dell'emigrazione*, January–March 1992 pp. 12–16.
17   See for examples, the regional legislation of Lombardy (law n.38 1988), 'Interventi a tutela degli immigrati extracomunitari in Lombardia e delle loro famiglie' and the regional legislation of Umbria (law n. 3448, 1987), 'Composizione, organizzazione e funzionamento della Consulta regionale per i problemi dei lavoratori extracomunitari e delle loro famiglie'.
18   There was however also concern that the increased attention towards immigrants would detract from the problems of Italian emigrants. At the 1991 national conference of ANFE – *Associazione nazionale Famiglie degli Emigrati* (an association founded by the Christian Democrats in 1947) – one speaker clearly articulated this (see Bordonaro 1991, p. 9).
19   Other European countries such as France, Germany and the Netherlands have all, at different times, created incentives to encourage the repatriation of migrants. These measures have been largely unsuccessful or, at any rate, did not reach the intended target groups (see Castles et al. 1984).
20   This particular interviewee had difficulty accepting my status as a Black British researcher and constantly shifted between talking about 'you' and 'them'.
21   This compares to a national average of 1.5 per cent. Regional planners in Lazio appear to have uncritically absorbed this notion. This was how the Albanian refugee situation was addressed in 1991, when 1,800 Albanians were dispersed in the region. The positive interpretation of the Albanian operation (see Pucci (1992), failed to consider the special temporary provisions that were afforded to Albanians to the exclusion of other migrants (see Pittau and Reggio 1992).

4 The ACLI-COLF and the Domestic Work Sector in Italy

While the organisation of domestic work as live-in work had largely disappeared from countries such as Britain and France by the end of the Second World War, several southern European countries retained this archaic organisational form into the post-war and contemporary period. Nevertheless, if we are to fully understand the significance of national political and social contexts, it is important not to conceal the internal differentiation within this southern European grouping. This chapter will examine the specificity of the Italian case prior to the migration of Black domestic workers. I suggest that the peculiar political circumstances of the immediate post-war period had important ramifications for the Italian domestic work sector.

Census data indicates that from the beginning of the century until the 1970s, employment in the domestic work sector constituted the principal employment category for Italian women within the tertiary sector.[1] In France and Britain, the First World War had a major impact on the decline of the domestic service sector. A decrease in middle-class wealth and the existence of alternative labour market opportunities for women contributed to the decline. During the inter-war years in Italy, however, 'practically no middle-class families wanted for help' (De Grazia 1992, p. 191). Slower industrial growth as well as fascist perspectives on women's employment[2] meant that Italian women would work as domestics for longer than in several other European countries. Indeed, domestic work was to remain an important employment sector for Italian women into the post-war period, and from the late 1960s onwards, it would perform an important pull factor function for African and Asian female migrants.

One of the aims of this book is to explain why this traditional form of domestic service survived into 1990s Italy. I suggest that this was the result of the conjuncture of a number of separate processes. In the immediate post-war period, when the sector was still the preserve of indigenous nationals, its existence can be related to the continuing poverty of specific regions within Italy as well as to the absence of alternative employment opportunities for women. From the 1970s onwards, the increased labour market participation of Italian women fuelled the demand for domestic labour, expanding what had in essence been a status driven demand, to include the growing needs of middle class women. In the 1980s and 1990s, the buoyancy of the domestic work sector could still be attributed to Italian women's labour market participation but also to the changing demographic profile of Italy in terms of a growing elderly population and the caring implications associated with this. The gradual and ongoing substitution of a national labour force by a foreign labour force can be explained by the low status and intrinsic structural problems of the domestic work sector. Alternative employment opportunities for Italian women and the global forces influencing migration are also clearly relevant explanatory factors.

In chapter 2, I argued that there was a limited response to the early presence of female migrant domestic workers in the 1970s. Their invisibility was undoubtedly symptomatic of their location within an invisible sector of the economy. Nevertheless, the specific historical development of the domestic work sector in Italy also conditioned migrant women's experiences. This chapter therefore focuses on the political organisation of the domestic work sector in the post-war period. This historical perspective is based on the activities of the ACLI-COLF, a national association which represented and moulded the domestic work sector in Italy. Possibly unique in post-war Western Europe, its existence was inextricably connected to the existence of two polarised political subcultures of Catholicism and Communism in post-war Italy.

The ACLI and the *GRUPPI ACLI DOMESTICHE*

The ACLI emerged in 1944 as an organisation for workers which aimed to promote Christian values. It sought to protect the practice of the faith and Catholic morality within the workplace and to assist workers in formulating solutions to their problems based on Christian criteria (Pasini 1974). This reflected Catholic social teaching which was based on the conciliation of capital and labour (Bedani 1995). The ACLI's relationship with the ecclesiastical hierarchy constituted a fundamental and important component of its identity. During the crucial years after the fall of fascism, some elements within the political establishment had hoped to retain the spirit of anti-fascist unity which had been harnessed to defeat fascism. At the political level, this was apparent via the existence of governments of national unity. A strategy of co-operation likewise emerged within the trade union movement, culminating in the signing of the Pact of Rome in 1944. Nevertheless, within this movement, the ideological disparities between the emerging Catholic and Communist subcultures were unable to be subordinated to those issues on which there was common ground – index linked pay scales, agrarian reform and combating the informal economy. As Sergio Turone (1981) has argued, the ACLI developed precisely because of the anti-unitary elements within Catholic opinion and it was in fact the overwhelming victory of the Christian Democrat Party at the national elections in 1948 which strengthened the conservative secessionist wing within the unitary trade union body, the CGIL (Bedani 1995). The ACLI successfully developed an important controlling force within the Catholic trade union sector and initially acted as a representative of the Catholic workforce.[3]

The ACLI's proximity to Catholic ideology could be seen in the philosophy of its internal women's committee, which proposed the setting up of the ACLI-COLF[4] in 1945 during a conference on women and work. The motivation behind the establishment of such a body centred on protecting women who worked outside the home and safeguarding the institution of the family.[5] This conforms to the normalised vision of women's role in this period as discussed in chapter 1. The first ACLI groups of Domestic Workers (GAD) were formed in 1946 and the first national meeting attended by regional leaders took place in June 1947. The minutes offer interesting insights into the preoccupations of these activists and gives some indication of the historical problems associated with domestic work.[6] These preoccupations were of both an organisational and political nature. The meeting recognised that the emphasis of the association had thus far centred on religion and morality but noted that the absence of a tightly coordinated network had not produced the desired results. The national president of the ACLI, Storchi, concerned about the GAD's involvement with other trade union bodies, raised the issue of what future relationship, if any, the organisation should have with both the unitary trade union body and the sectoral Federation of Commercial Workers.

These concerns indicated the significance of political allegiances and alliances at a time of national and international sensitivity to the future political direction of Italy.[7] The period of anti-fascist consensus which had spanned the two dominant political ideologies of Catholicism and Communism was effectively over. Indeed this first meeting of the GAD took place just a month after the Communist and Socialist parties had been excluded from the national government by the Christian Democrats.[8] The minutes of this meeting clearly reflect these national political tensions. Collaboration with other Catholic groups was advocated as a counter-strategy to Communist influence. The representative from Turin, for example, proposed closer collaboration with other Catholic associations involved with domestic workers and suggested setting up a newsletter for domestic workers to counter the existence of Communist propaganda. In some towns, a degree of Catholic collaboration was already in place. The representative from Genoa, Jole Pampolini, reported that a committee had been established with both Catholic Action and other religious bodies. A similar situation was reported by the representative from Bologna, Alma Fontana, regarding links with Catholic Action. The representative from Bergamo, Maria Mazzoleni, confirmed that the 'sector is completely in the hands of the Christian trade union current' (p. 2). Nonetheless collaboration with some Catholic groups was not always a straightforward process and the GAD encountered some internal difficulties within the Catholic sphere. This was largely attributable to the jockeying for control of particular social groups. For example, the representative from Treviso, Alfredo Toppan, reported that there were difficulties between the ACLI and the national Catholic women's organisation CIF. In Brescia, Maria Boselli reported that the ACLI was experiencing hostility from both Catholic Action and the Christian Democrats.

Of course, the principal adversaries were the Socialists and the Communists and there was a clear competitive element to the GAD's work. The representative from Bologna for example, referred to the higher profile of the ACLI when compared to the activities of the unified trade union body: 'The organisation is progressing well, so much so that while the meetings for domestic workers held at the Chamber of Labour never have more than 10 people present, those organised by the ACLI, at religious institutions, on average attract more than 300 domestic workers' (p. 2). When the question was raised about the type of relationship the GAD should have with the Union of Italian Women (UDI), an unequivocal reply was provided by Storchi: 'No relationship must, naturally be held with the UDI …' (pp. 4–5).

The trade union aspect of the organisation's work was clearly seen to be important. Indeed, at this particular meeting, one participant suggested that domestic workers should affiliate to the Federation of Commercial Workers as this would allow them access to an organisation which was already established at both central and local levels. It was argued that this would give domestic workers the support of an important network for the pursuit of their grievances. However, the proposal was unanimously rejected given the limited political control of the Catholics within this Federation. As one participant put it: '… we are not the absolute bosses in the commercial sector' (p. 5).[9]

It is indisputable then, that the GAD saw collaboration with other Catholic organisations as an important means of challenging Socialist and Communist pretensions to organise domestic workers. Although the Communists and Socialists did not have an organisation equivalent to the GAD, they clearly also aspired to have some influence with this sector of workers. In Turin for example, the Communist activist Mariani had managed, with the support of the local UDI, to establish a committee with the employers of domestic workers and had been able to stipulate a provincial contract. This appeared to be the personal work of a committed individual and it therefore lacked the organisational base that the GAD were beginning to develop. Nevertheless, these political machinations had important implications for the domestic work sector in that they sanctioned a view of domestic workers as workers, giving political visibility to a sector which has traditionally been marginalised.

Aside from these organisational matters, the meeting of regional heads of the GAD did address problems pertinent to domestic workers themselves. The association concluded that it should focus on recreational activities and provide general assistance to domestic workers, emphasising issues such as insurance contributions and provisions for illness. Training was also to form part of the GAD's work and courses were introduced in sewing, etc. There was some concern to establish ACLI meeting centres for domestic workers, which emerged in recognition of the fact that domestic workers did not necessarily enjoy meeting under the auspices of nuns. In addition, a propagandist element to the GAD's work was to be developed through the use of the press. In the event, a newspaper for the sector was established in 1947, which from 1949 was entitled *La Casa e la Vita*.

The ACLI-COLF – 1950s and 1960s

The ACLI-COLF established itself in the post-war period as the only national body to occupy itself specifically with domestic workers. Consequently, the domestic work sector came to be ideologically dominated by Catholic doctrine and this was to have particular implications for the type of mobilisation which would take place. Indeed, ACLI-COLF mobilisation was highly influenced both by Catholic ideology pertaining to the family and to Catholic ideology regarding the resolution of labour conflict. These combined to ensure a subordinate position for the domestic worker in relation to the employer. In this chapter, I shall focus on the organisation's development up to its landmark conference in 1973. The 1970s are in fact a useful demarcation point. It was in 1971 that a critical organisational split occurred which permitted the ACLI-COLF to develop in a fundamentally different direction. Furthermore, the early 1970s broadly coincides with the inception of migrant women's migration to Italy as domestic workers. As I shall demonstrate, they would be absorbed into a sector which was organisationally weak and in which the workers' needs had traditionally been subordinated to those of the employer.

The ACLI-COLF's first national congress was held in Rome in June 1952. Focusing on the national situation, the congress motion called for the revision of the legal norms governing the sector in the civil code (see below), longer holidays, clearer limits to the working day and the right to a thirteenth month addition to the annual wage. The second national congress held in Rome in December 1955 accentuated domestic work as a social service, highlighting the important function of domestic work in relation to the family.[10] Three areas were identified for mobilisation. Firstly, there was a desire to properly regulate the recruitment of domestic workers and concern was expressed about the moral consequences for those workers recruited through private employment agencies. Secondly, it was felt that domestic workers required systematic training if a more transparent relationship between workers and employers was to be achieved. Finally, the association aimed to rectify the negative attitude of public opinion in relation to domestic workers. Concerns over training, morality and greater legal protection for domestic workers remained a feature of subsequent national congresses. A further constant was the presentation of domestic work as being intrinsically different from other types of employment because of the role it performed for the family. At the third national congress in 1958, the former national secretary Clara Storchi, rejected the propositions of those who perceived the domestic work sector as a moribund sector or indeed as a sector that should be phased out because it violated human dignity. Citing statistics from the 1951 national census, Storchi argued that there was still considerable demand for domestic workers. Significantly, although she acknowledged that hourly paid work reduced some of the problems of live-in work, she maintained that certain groups still required the services of live-in workers. Families with elderly relatives or children, and professional working women were all singled out as categories requiring the services of live-in workers. Of note however, is that Storchi also singled out those families whose demand for a live-in worker was essentially a status driven necessity: 'There are families whose life-style creates the necessity for live-in domestic staff'.[11] The association's support for the organisation of domestic work as a live-in occupation was also motivated by Catholic moral codes. Live-out work was associated with independent accommodation, which in turn was considered to present morally dubious circumstances. Thus, while the association recognised the difficulties of live-in work, the above factors concurrently encouraged it to view live-in work as indispensable. Consequently, the association's mobilisation revolved around an *improvement* of the live-in relationship. The basis of this improvement would lie in reciprocal respect and duties for both the employee and the employer.

There was a clear propagandist element to how the ACLI-COLF sought to present domestic work to its members. The promotion of domestic work as intrinsically different from other categories of work was inextricably bound up with perceptions regarding women's relationship to the home and family. As Storchi stated: 'we have said that the family is the ideal work environment for a woman and we maintain this'.[12] Storchi herself recognised that certain characteristics of factory work – proper contracts, secure wages and a fixed working-time schedule explained Italian women's preference for factory work above domestic work. Her description of the duties of a domestic worker reinforced such a choice but it was in the very difficulty of these relations and their human, personalised aspect that Storchi viewed the true value of domestic work. Indeed, dedication, subordination and invisibility[13] were values that domestic workers were expected to embrace. Despite calling for reciprocal duties for both employer and employee, Storchi's address to the third national congress indicated that employers would retain the upper hand. This suggested that the needs of both employed middle class women and the status requirements of middle to upper class women were prioritised over and above the needs of working-class women. Papal pronouncements authenticated the ideological position of the ACLI-COLF. In January 1958, Pope Pius XII addressed Roman domestic workers, arguing that the human characteristics of domestic work distinguished it from other sectors.[14] This was in keeping with earlier papal pronouncements. Pius XII had been particularly critical of a formulistic approach to the work relationship[15] and encouraged domestic workers to view their employers 'more as fathers than as bosses'.[16] Catholic virtues of sacrifice were similarly encouraged and like Storchi, the spiritual difference between this type of work and other sectors was emphasised.[17]

In February 1958, the ACLI central administration opened its first national boarding school in Cevo (Brescia). This training school was intended to symbolise a new professional profile for the domestic worker. Training was intended to mould the domestic worker in a particular fashion, with attention paid to moral and professional issues. Courses ran for ten months[18] and were free.[19] Pupils would pay a contribution of L3,000 towards their maintenance but this was effectively reimbursed on termination of the course. As well as receiving a certificate, pupils would receive a prize of L3,000 and be sent on three months practical work experience. There was a clear desire to exert proper moral control over the girls, who were aged between 15 and 20. Parents were allowed to visit their daughters on the second Sunday of every month and only within the confines of the school. Pupils were not allowed any communication with visitors on other days.

While the structural problems of the domestic work sector were afforded some importance, it was clear that part of the problem for the domestic work sector was perceived to be located within the worker herself. In pursuance of the ACLI-COLF's objective of developing the professional and moral preparation of domestic workers, Father Erminio Crippa was appointed in 1956 to provide for the moral and spiritual welfare of the sector. He was to have an influential role within the ACLI-COLF movement and later within the breakaway API-COLF association. Crippa's first publication for the sector was in 1959, entitled *Your Professional Morality*.[20] The representation of the relationship between domestic work and the family contained within this document is of some significance. The document reiterates the dual family role of domestic workers – towards their own families and towards the families for whom they worked. The female worker was urged not to neglect her duties of obedience, affection and respect to her parents. The emphasis on domestic workers' responsibility to their parents, and not for example to their husbands and children, implied that the majority of women working within this sphere were single women.[21] Crippa's document prioritised women's role towards their original family, as daughters. Under a list of obligations, it was clearly stated that should their parents be in extreme need of their presence and assistance, domestic service should be abandoned and the worker should return home. Thus while these women may have been engaged in paid employment, they were left in no doubt as to which role to prioritise. Their family role was ultimately *not* to be subordinated to their paid work role. As I shall be arguing in subsequent chapters, the inverse occurred for migrant women, with a clear subordination of their family function to their paid work role.

In the late 1950s and 1960s, Crippa effectively advocated acceptance of a subservient role. Often his exhortations were justified by biblical references or papal pronouncements, thus appealing to the Catholic sentiments of these workers.[22] An ideal of a gracious acceptance of subordination pervades Crippa's documents. For example, in the event of a disagreement between employer and employee, he advised that regardless of who was to blame, the onus was on the worker 'to break the ice with a smile, a greeting or some form of service' (Crippa 1961). In her discussion of unpaid domestic work,

Picchio (1991) has argued that the role that women perform within the family cannot be easily divided into material and psychological aspects. While one might anticipate that paid domestic work would facilitate such a distinction, it was in fact the fusion of both these aspects which was promoted by the Catholic oriented ACLI-COLF. In so doing, the employment aspect of domestic work was subordinated and instead there was a concern to emphasise the loving familial aspect of the domestic work role to which all women were naturally meant to aspire.

By the time of the fourth national congress held in Pompeii in 1961, the focus on domestic workers' contribution to family life was intensified.[23] A number of structural changes were initially noted, and these were of some significance for future developments within the sector. In particular the growth of hourly paid work was noted as causing new moral and social problems.[24] A new rise in demand for domestic workers among the middle classes was seen as symptomatic of the need to substitute those Italian women who were increasingly employed in the paid labour market. This in itself was seen as positive for the sector. It was assumed that this would entail new demands on the domestic worker herself, and that her transformed duties would lead to a new professionalism. In fact, the changes occurring within the sector had led to better wages for domestic workers, particularly in the big cities. Employers, on the other hand expressed some resentment at the privileges they now had to concede to workers as a result of legislation introduced in 1958 (see below).

The ACLI-COLF continued to promote improved collaboration between the employer and employee. The nature of this collaboration was unambiguously delineated. For domestic workers it centred on perceiving the employing family as a family rather than as an employer. The worker was expected to treat the family's problems as if they were her own. As the following recommendations suggest, the subordinate position of the worker was clear. As well as adjusting her tastes and needs to fit in with the other household members, she was expected:

– to maintain a sense of community, sacrifice and interest in the family;
– not to consider the relationship in terms of salary and toil;
– to consider her duty not as forced assistance, but as a generous gift.[25]

The employment aspect of the job was therefore subtly negated. The employers' duties consisted of treating the domestic worker as a member of the family community, contributing to the general order of the house, avoiding criticism of the worker and respecting the new legislation.

The ACLI-COLF's positioning of the domestic worker in relation to her employer did not reflect a view of the domestic worker as an inferior being but rather as being differentially situated within the employer/employee relationship. In this instance, this subordination was justified because of the primacy of the domestic workers' role in assisting the family unit. In order to sell this particular concept of domestic work to the domestic employee, the ACLI-COLF linked the notion of subordination to specific Catholic values. In a second publication by Erminio Crippa, entitled *The Female Saints of our Work*, this is evident in the emphasis he placed on the sanctification of domestic workers' role. As Turri (1988, p. 90) has accurately commented 'for domestic workers it was a question of joyously experiencing an employment condition which was humiliating or servile as a 'Christian vocation'. Indeed Crippa's (1961, p. 10) document promotes a vision of the employer's home as 'a little church' where domestic workers should conceive of their profession 'as collaboration with the family and a means to love God with all one's soul'. The acknowledgement of the difficulties of practising these virtues indicated that Catholic virtues of privation and sacrifice were being encouraged. Domestic workers were clearly not encouraged to resent, challenge or submit their subordinate role to any form of critique. Indeed, this particular construction of their situation was emblematic of the interclassism promoted by the Catholic subculture.

In marked contrast to any class based analysis of work, Crippa explicitly argued that the female domestic worker was not selling her labour, rather, she was collaborating with a family and thus facilitating the implementation of God's plan. Blatant appeals to women's 'natural' maternal instincts were made to encourage the domestic worker to view her role in a particular vein:

> Don't you feel similar *to a mother*? Don't you sometimes give her a hand and don't you act as a substitute when she is not there? Isn't your life a little like hers, full of sacrifices and lack of sleep, and don't you multiply yourself according to necessity and don't you split yourself a hundred ways to help everyone, making everyone feel that you are there totally for them? (Crippa 1961, p. 16).

Indeed, domestic work was presented as intrinsically *better* than other employment sectors:

> Don't dream of being a secretary in an office; she only carries out one aspect of your profession! At home, you know the vocabulary of everyone … you know the secrets of everyone; at the market, you remember everyone's tastes (Crippa 1961, p. 16).[26]

Because of the dominance of Catholic organisations within the sector, there were limited opportunities to incorporate an opposing ideological framework to discuss the position of domestic workers. Certainly the ACLI-COLF constituted the dominant representative organ for this sector of workers and was therefore able to wield substantial influence. Its proximity to the ecclesiastic hierarchy and its promotion of Catholic ideology during the 1950s was influenced by the national climate regarding trade union activity. What possibilities for change did the organisation envisage? By the time of the fifth national congress in 1964, a commissioned report indicated that there were clear limits to employers' amenability to change.[27] The survey, completed by 400 employers, found that employers were generally amenable to a more modern conception of domestic work. Sixty per cent felt that a contract which stipulated working hours was possible. However, 55 per cent fixed this figure above ten hours per day. Sixty per cent felt that the introduction of such a contract would have negative consequences for the organisation of their family units. Seventy per cent of respondents did however feel that some simplification of domestic arrangements could work to the advantage of the employee. The overwhelming majority of employers (90 per cent) felt that the employee should have better training. However if this entailed any sacrifice on the part of the employers, much less consensus was provoked. Thus, 20 per cent of respondents declared that they would not be happy if their domestic worker attended a course in home economics in the afternoon and 30 per cent of respondents were not prepared to contribute economically to any such course.

The 1964 congress introduced a new appellation for the domestic worker, who would hitherto be referred to as a family collaborator (COLF in its abbreviated form). Such an appellation was considered to reflect more accurately the new professionalism of the sector and emphasised the contribution of domestic workers to family life. At the sixth national congress in 1967, this focus on professionalism was explicitly represented by the theme of the congress which called for the establishment of a professional register for the sector.[28] The philosophy underpinning this decision maintained that given that professional registers were normally established to guarantee standards within those professions whose relationship with their clients could potentially be harmful if not properly regulated (e.g. doctors), domestic workers should also be given the same consideration (ACLI 1967). The establishment of a professional register was promoted as a method of redeeming and conferring some dignity on the profession.[29] Antonio Fontana, a member of the ACLI's research section, highlighted the absence of collective bargaining for the sector as both an obstacle for general mobilisation as well as preventing protection for domestic workers.[30] Despite this position, militant mobilisation was discouraged. Fontana, for example, argued that domestic workers should proceed extremely cautiously. His notion of a Christian revolution was replicated by Erminio Crippa who called for a peaceful revolution.[31] It is worth highlighting that Crippa called for a peaceful revolution despite his unequivocal condemnation of the general conditions of domestic workers which had emerged in a national survey promoted by the ACLI:

> The absence of professional training schools, of public recognition, of a written employment contract and above all the current burdensome work schedule, make of the entire sector a genuine social scandal.[32]

The results of this survey provide a useful insight into domestic workers working conditions in the late 1960s.[33] Of the workers interviewed, 50.25 per cent worked for a family with only one child. Crippa suggested that this figure indicated that domestic workers were probably substituting mothers employed outside the home, but that in those families with a higher number of children, the mother was more likely to be a housewife. This interpretation did not, however, tally with domestic workers' responses to a question concerning the employment status of their employers. In fact, 64 per cent of them stated that their employers were not engaged in paid employment. This figure rose to 70 per cent in those towns with more than 800,000 inhabitants.[34] An alternative interpretation therefore would be to suggest that at this stage of the historical development of the domestic work sector, a majority of the employing families did so not out of necessity, but for reasons largely related to status. It was therefore this type of family that the ACLI-COLF was not only implicitly supporting but to which the needs of domestic workers were also being subordinated. Clearly, in the context of the Catholic/Communist subcultural divide, it would have been politically unwise for the Catholic oriented association to accentuate what can only be described as blatant exploitation of these workers by privileged families. Political expediency may well have encouraged the association to emphasise domestic workers' substitutive function as a response to Italian women's increasing entry into the paid labour market. In reality, its own 1967 survey had indicated that only in 36 per cent of cases were domestic workers employed by such families.

The survey additionally revealed the type of working conditions domestic workers were obliged to endure. Fifty-seven point three nine per cent worked for more than 12 hours a day. When this total is combined with those who worked between 10 and 12 hours a day, this figure jumped to 73 per cent.

Forty-four point four per cent were not permitted a daily rest period. The majority (81.61 per cent) were permitted a weekly rest period, but only for a minority of workers (22.42 per cent) did this take the form of a 24-hour rest period. Eighty-four point seven eight per cent described their work as that of a 'maid of all work', and this figure was as high as 92.1 per cent for those living in towns of less that 500,000 inhabitants. One positive revelation was that the majority of respondents indicated that they were legally registered as workers (83.85 per cent) and this figure was even higher in towns of more than 800,000 inhabitants (90.66 per cent). [35] The distribution of responses to the question asking whether domestic workers themselves thought it was in fact possible to institute limits to the working day is revealing. 28.23 per cent considered it possible against 24.21 per cent who considered it impossible. However, practically a half of the survey group (47.51 per cent) were unable to respond to the question. It seemed that domestic workers themselves considered the privacy of the domestic work relationship beyond the reach of legislation.

I have suggested that the ACLI-COLF's ideology was inherently conservative and that this led to a Catholic interclassist form of mobilisation which underplayed the conflicting interests of social groups. Nevertheless, this should not detract from the efforts made by the association to raise the national profile of the domestic work sector. The number of press releases in the ACLI-COLF archives indicate that this was seen as an important function of the association.[36] The decision to institute a National Day, taken at the 1967 congress, was also intended to raise the profile of the sector and to cultivate public opinion.[37]

Legislation

One of the specific structural problems of domestic work in Italy concerned the legal status of the sector.[38] It had been categorised in the Italian civil code as atypical work. It was thus the duty of the employing family to protect the worker. The atypical status of domestic work thus presupposed a harmonious relationship between employer and employee, where the benign paternalism of the family would suffice as protection for the domestic worker. Significantly the first piece of legislation to address domestic work in the fascist period was concerned with the harm the domestic worker could cause to her employing family. Law n. 1239, introduced in June 1939 required domestic workers to acquire a health card. This was to prevent them infecting their employing families with contagious diseases. A subsequent piece of legislation introduced in December 1953 laid the emphasis, for the first time, on the working conditions of domestic workers. Law n. 940, consisting of a single article, extended the right of a thirteenth month addition to the annual wage to this group of workers.

It was however in 1958 (law n. 339, 2 April 1958) that the first major piece of legislation was introduced with the explicit aim of protecting the domestic service sector. The paternalistic approach had not entirely disappeared. For example, the employer was required to be particularly attentive to the physical, moral and professional needs of minors (Art. 4). Reciprocal duties were outlined for both the worker and the employer. The domestic worker would be legally entitled to a weekly day off, normally on a Sunday, or two half days, one of which was to be taken on Sunday. Article 8 stipulated work hours and rest periods. The worker would be entitled to a suitable rest period during the day and to no less that eight consecutive hours of rest at night. Remarkably, a critical aspect of domestic work was not addressed. Article 8 did not impose any limits to the length of the working day. This was a significant omission, indicative of an enduring structural problem for this sector of workers. This article thus left the domestic worker exposed to the possibility of a 16 hour day, with only an unspecified rest period during the day as protection from exploitation.

There had been earlier examples of stated limits to the working day with regard to women and work. For example, one of the protective employment norms introduced under fascism had imposed limits of 11 and 10 hours respectively to women and children (law n. 653, April 1934, Art. 17). However these norms had not been applicable to domestic workers (Art. 1). The atypical nature of domestic work amounted to domestic workers' exclusion or differential treatment in terms of legislation regulating women's employment.[39] Indeed, as Turrini (1977, p. 38) rightly argues, the Italian domestic work sector has consistently been marginalised from prevailing ideologies concerning women and work:

> While women were integrated en masse into factory work or were expelled as soon as employment problems arose, and while, at the same time, their role as mothers of families was ignored or exalted depending on the type of consensus that one was trying to create, domestic workers continued to carry out their work which did not pose a problem to anyone.

A subsequent legislative landmark, around which the ACLI-COLF had mobilised, occurred in 1969. Article 2068 of the civil code which defined domestic work as atypical work was abolished as a result of its contravention of Article 3 of the Constitution which stated that all citizens were equal before the law. This was a significant ruling since it paved the way for national collective bargaining for the sector. In fact Zannini (1970) has argued that it is only from this point can one really talk of a sector of workers in the legal sense.

Political Change

Before discussing the two critical ACLI-COLF congresses of 1970 and 1973, some mention must be made of the immense sociocultural and political changes which had occurred in the country by 1970 and which would have serious implications for the association. It has been shown above that the ACLI-COLF emerged at a time of heightened political tension. By the 1960s however, the religious and political antagonism of the Cold War had begun to diminish. In the 1960s, the formation of a centre-Left government was one manifestation of this. The second Vatican Council (1962–65) also led to theological change and Pope John XXIII was considered to have some sympathy for the Left. As Barkan (1984) has argued, this influenced the perspectives of certain Catholics who began to see radical change as intrinsic to their religious beliefs.[40] The election of the Left-wing Livio Labor as president of ACLI at its 1961 national congress was indicative of the nature of these changes within the Catholic sector of labour organisation. There were additionally important developments within the workers' movement more generally in Italy. 1969 had proved to be an influential landmark in the post-war history of the movement. Mobilisation in the period that came to be known as the Hot Autumn was to culminate in the 1970 Workers' Statute in which workers made considerable gains.[41] A significant number of Catholic labour leaders were radicalised by the events of 1968–69 and it was in fact at ACLI's 1969 Congress that the membership voted to end its collaterist associations with the Christian Democrats (Bedani 1995). The Catholic labour perspective which centred on the avoidance of conflict and a harmonious employer/employee relationship was increasingly viewed as anachronistic by activists within Catholic spheres.

What were the ramifications of such events for the ACLI-COLF? Bedani (1995, p. 125) has described the tension which existed within its parenting organisation ACLI as a contest between ' … the proponents of autonomy and those who wished to tie the movement more closely to the DC and to the Church'. While the election of the Left-wing Labor in 1961 had marked the beginning of the ascendency of the first group over the other, within the ACLI-COLF the ascendency had been maintained by those who did not want to relinquish their ecclesiastical connections. Thus, in the year of Livio's election, Clementina Barili was re-elected as national secretary of the ACLI-COLF. She, along with Carla Faccincani held the national secretariatship up to and including the national congress of 1970. Both of these two national secretaries would defect to form the alternative API-COLF in 1971.

The Beginnings of Change Within the ACLI-COLF

Until 1970 then, a Catholic-oriented perspective with regard to labour relations prevailed within the ACLI-COLF. This perspective was compounded by Catholic preoccupations with the institution of the family and it effectively prohibited the domestic work sector from evolving in a fashion which was more reflective of the sociocultural and political change which had taken place within Italy. The 1970 national congress was critical for the association. The dominant opposing currents are reflected in the following statements. Firstly, in his opening prayer, Father Erminio Crippa reflected the conservative position: Never has our congress had to take such an important decision ... We ask you to give us all some extra soul so as never to reduce a family to a factory'.[42] Rina Mele, secretary to the Turinese ACLI-COLF, reflected the opposing current: 'We find ourselves at an important turning point ... We find ourselves facing something revolutionary which, however, we want to manage with a great sense of responsibility'.[43] Some contributors clearly still hoped that the divergent views could be contained within the association. But, to a certain extent, the 1969 legal ruling which had granted collective bargaining and a national contract to the sector had also highlighted internal differences.

Employers were also concerned about the future direction of the sector. In 1969, they established their own association called 'New Collaboration' and expressed very clear views on the ACLI-COLF's relationship with the workers' movement:

> ... solidarity with the workers' movement ... should not, in our view, be interpreted too restrictively, [or involve] a rigid and deaf opposition towards other sectors who are equally part of society, and who equally have the right and even the duty to protect and defend their honest needs, and this is said, let us be clear, also for Employers. Otherwise, ... the Employers will also become

defensive on other rigid positions: it is only human that this will happen, but it does not facilitate comprehension and collaboration!

Furthermore the family is not a factory, and there is a danger of creating ... an 'idol' of this 'class solidarity' at the expense of a wider human and Christian solidarity.[44]

Perhaps inevitably, there was some concern about the type of demands domestic workers might put forward as a consequence of their new association with the workers' movement. This 'new collaboration' was indisputably intended to protect the employers' vastly stronger position within the employer/ employee relationship. It was therefore not surprising that New Collaboration sought to privilege the ACLI-COLF as a principal interlocutor with whom a strategy on the contents of the national contract could be developed. Indeed, their choice verified the accommodating posture of the ACLI-COLF in relation to the employers' of domestic workers.

The ACLI-COLF's organisational strategy assumed centre stage at the 1970 congress. In the final analysis, the post-war strategy of the organisation was unequivocally affirmed, and while the concluding document of the congress declared itself open to trade union unity, the ACLI-COLF demanded that the said unions should fully recognise 'the professional and moral values developed through ACLI mobilisation'.[45] The ACLI-COLF leadership was in fact reluctant to engage in a closer relationship with the workers' movement and emphatically rejected the possibility of establishing 'collaterist' links with mixed trade union confederation structures. Although the conservative sector of the association was still dominant at the 1970 congress, its position within the ACLI had virtually become untenable given the opposing direction of its parenting organisation and by 1971, an organisational split had occurred.

In June 1971, the API-COLF (*Associazione professionale italiana collaboratrici familiari*) was formed by the former conservatives within the ACLI-COLF. In July of the same year, the Federcolf was established as an autonomous trade union body for domestic workers, but it was clearly linked to the API-COLF. In November of the same year, the Conference of Italian Bishops recognised the API-COLF and appointed the ubiquitous Erminio Crippa as its national ecclesiastical consultant. Its first national congress was held in 1973 in Milan.[46] In the same month the ACLI-COLF held its eighth national congress. Not surprisingly, the theme of the conference addressed the sector's relationship with the workers' movement.[47] This was a landmark conference in the history of the ACLI-COLF. It reflected the changed ideological mood of the association and offered a radically alternative vision to the particular Christian model that had been adopted in the past.

The 1973 ACLI-COLF Congress

The ACLI-COLF's decision to pursue a new ideological and organisational direction should be considered in relation to the more general changes which were occurring within the sphere of labour relations. The idea of unity for the three trade union confederations was a dominant theme in this period.[48] This was facilitated by the abandonment by some sections within the CISL (Confederazione Italiana Sindacati Lavortori) of the aconflictual model of the employer/employee relationship, and by the CISL's increasing lack of confidence in its collateratist relationship with the Dc (Bedani 1995). In 1972, a federation was instituted – the unitary federation CGIL-CISL-UIL.

As we have seen, ACLI-COLF's parenting organisation, the ACLI, had shifted to the Left in the early 1960s. Speaking at the 1973 ACLI-COLF congress, the then national secretary of the ACLI, Marino Carboni applauded the change of direction.[49] The tendency to greater collaboration amongst the trade union confederations at the national level accentuated the secession of the API-COLF as an anomalous strategy. Indeed, it was perceived as a betrayal by a former national president of the ACLI, Emilio Gabaglio:

> Leaving the ACLI was not only a real betrayal at a difficult time ... but it contained the illusion that one could better face up to one's needs outside a class based organisation and therefore without genuine contact with the working class and its ideas.[50]

There were numerous declarations affirming the new direction of the ACLI-COLF. One Roman domestic worker forcefully emphasised the validity of these new choices:

> ... this congress shows us once again that that terrible experience is over. The decision to remain within the ACLI was the right choice. We have been separated for too long from other workers and, closed up in our ghetto, we have looked out on the future with blinkers, like beasts of burden. Within the ACLI and within the workers' movement we are instead learning how important it is for our own personal growth to be amongst other workers, to listen to other workers, to be ... part of the workers' movement.[51]

The ACLI-COLF had irrevocably centred itself within the new political framework of the ACLI.[52] What would the implications be for the future strategy of the association? The most obvious difference could be found in the association's adoption of a new class vocabulary and its desire to be considered as an integral part of the workers' movement. As we have seen, the ACLI-COLF's pre-1971 strategy had constantly stressed the quintessential difference between domestic work and factory work. Now, equating domestic workers with other types of workers was seen as particularly important: We must have the conviction of being and acting as an integral part of the workers' movement'.[53] This said, there was still some recognition of their difference in relation to other workers. The specificity of the sector (absence of any limits on working hours,[54] live-in work, contact with different individual families and therefore different mentalities) meant that the ACLI-COLF would have to tailor its strategy to the characteristics of the sector:

> [We do] not have the weight that other female sectors might have, but we are no less significant because of this. Everyone has to do their part ... to put us in a position to offer a proper contribution to all those forces of the working class who are fighting to overthrow this society based on profit for the few.[55]

The new direction of the ACLI-COLF did not signify a departure from its Christian values, rather the association was guided by a new interpretation of Catholic social teaching.[56] A new class lexicon was introduced to the congress proceedings in the opening address by Rina Mele. 'Capitalism', 'bosses' and 'the working-class' were all terms which were generously utilised. In contrast to the previous strategy which had presented domestic work as a vocation, this new class emphasis focused on the socioeconomic reasons which coerced women into the domestic work sector:

> We can say, without a doubt, that for the overwhelming majority of family collaborators, the profession is not a choice, but mainly imposed by conditions of necessity dictated by the social and economic mechanisms of capitalism.[57]

Mele was particularly critical of the class position of those who benefited from domestic workers' services and new initiatives were outlined. These included a redistribution of the benefits of domestic workers' labour from the privileged classes to the working class. The strategy to achieve this lay in the wider strategy being proposed by the trade union bodies. In the 1970s, the trade unions had adopted a reform strategy which entailed trade union mobilisation in areas which fell beyond a strict definition of the working conditions of their members. It included, for example, mobilisation around public transport, schooling, pensions and housing (Barkan 1984; Bedani 1995). The ACLI-COLF saw particular advantages to such a strategy as it was entirely complementary to its future vision for the domestic work sector:

The creation of a network of social services, in fact, could be the source of new employment for all female workers in our sector. The type of employment which can guarantee workers a qualified and secure post, employed by local bodies ... in other words serving, the real needs of marginalised people, workers and their families.[58]

The philosophy guiding the new training practices of the ACLI-COLF was diametrically opposed to previous practice. Domestic workers would no longer be trained to graciously accept their subservient position in relation to the employer. There was a patent desire to develop a class-based consciousness amongst domestic workers and to distance the association from its earlier strategy:

> Everyone will understand how our approach to training and professionalism is quite different to the past where we prepared workers for bourgeois families, while today we are called to respond to the needs of working-class families.[59]

A National Contract for the Sector

The 1969 legal ruling which had removed the atypical status of the domestic work sector meant that a national contract could now be collectively bargained for. The early 1970s were thus dominated by discussions regarding both the contents of the contract and who would be involved in the bargaining process. The bargaining platform on which the unitary trade union body based its strategy contained many of the objectives that the ACLI-COLF had consistently advocated in the post-war period, such as a limit to the working day and adequate remuneration.[60] The first collectively bargained contract was eventually signed on the 22 May 1974.[61] The editorial of *La Casa e La Vita* published in the same month underlined its significance:

> It is the first contract for the sector: By itself it has great value and not just because – finally – it equips the domestic worker with an instrument to defend her rights but because it marks another stage in the journey undertaken to remove the sector from the state of marginality and abandon into which it had always been forced (p. 1).

The national secretary of the ACLI-COLF, Pina Brustolin, cited as examples of domestic workers' improved employment conditions a limit to the working day, the recognition of overtime and holiday periods.[62] A positive response to the contract prevailed, despite the fact that, for example, the limit to the working schedule had been set at 66 hours per week or 11 hours per day (Art. 11). Domestic workers nevertheless continued to encounter discriminatory practice when compared to other sectors. In February 1974, the Constitutional Court had confirmed the constitutionality of legislative norms which did not protect domestic workers from being sacked in the event of pregnancy.[63] There were thus clearly a number of spheres where legislative improvement could be made. Nonetheless, this first collectively bargained national contract was considered an important symbolic and practical starting point for the sector.

Conclusion

This chapter has demonstrated that the domestic work sector has historically constituted a marginalised sector of employment, both in terms of employment conditions and legislation. The development of the sector must however be understood in the context of post-war political polarisation in Italy and the desire amongst the Catholic sphere to develop a counter perspective to Communist and Socialist goals in terms of labour relations. The promotion of the sector was monopolised by the ACLI-COLF and its strategy emphasised a peculiarly Catholic conception of labour relations which focused on harmony rather than conflict within the employer/employee relationship. This perspective tended however to subordinate domestic workers to the power of the employers and this inequality was reinforced by equating domestic work with the maternal role; this also contributed to the weak legislative status of the sector. By the early 1970s, radical change in the wider labour movement and the ACLI-COLF, as well as the important 1969 ruling in relation to the sector, signified a new direction. This said, there was still substantial disparity between this sector and other employment spheres. The peaceful Christian revolution advocated by influential figures such as Erminio Crippa had failed to fundamentally transform the structural relationship between employer and employee. Thus, when foreign nationals began their migration to Italy to take up employment as live-in domestic workers, they encountered a sector which was structurally disadvantaged and where there would be ample scope for further exploitation given their status as external migrants.

Notes

1 See Barile and Zanuso (1984) for further information.
2 See De Grazia (1992) and Willson (1993) for more information on Italian women under fascism.
3 The seven founding members of the ACLI represented all the important bodies of the Catholic sector – Catholic Action, Christian trade-unionists and the Christian Democrat Party (see Pasini 1974). This mobilisation was clearly a strategy to respond to the strength of the Communist Party within the unitary trade union body.
4 In 1945, they were referred to as *Gruppi Acli Domestiche*. The change in name to ACLI-COLF occurred in the mid-1960s.
5 See *Il Giornale dei Lavoratori*, 12 August 1945.
6 I convegno nazionale dirigenti del gruppo di categoria personale domestico ACLI, 22 June 1947.
7 This has been documented by several writers. For some examples see Ginsborg (1989) and Bedani (1995).
8 The crucial vote took place on 31 May 1947.
9 Some of these problems were resolved when the CISL (*Confederazione italiana sindacati lavoratori*) trade union body was formed in 1950. It was intended to ideologically and strategically supplant Communist domination of the trade union movement.
10 See II Congresso dei GAD, Rome 17–18 December 1955, documentation in ACLI (1960, p. 163).
11 See Dott.ssa Clara Storchi, 'Il lavoro domestico, vera professione', III congresso nazionale domestiche ACLI, Roma 25–27 April 1958, p. 7.
12 Ibid., p. 6
13 Other studies have highlighted how employers frequently expect their domestic employees to assume an invisible status. See Rollins (1985) and Romero (1992).
14 Dal Discorso, Pio XII, 19 January 1959, documentation in ACLI (1960, p. 148).
15 See for example, Dal discorso 'gli ausiliari del focolare', Pius XII, 6 August 1942.
16 Dal Discorso, Pio XII, 4-5 June 1956, documentation in ACLI (1960, p. 145).
17 See Dal Discorso, Pio XII, 19 January 1959, documentation in ACLI (1960, p. 147).
18 Regolamento della scuola nazionale lavoratrici domestiche, 1958.
19 The school was established with the support of the Ministry for Employment demonstrating that the ACLI-COLF was able to exploit its privileged relationship with the Catholic political sector. The school existed until 1963.
20 For a comparable work from a different cultural perspective see Romero's (1992) appraisal of the publication 'Your maid from Mexico', also published in 1959 in the USA.
21 This is borne out by a survey conducted by the ACLI-COLF. Between 1974 and 1975, 833 interviews were carried out with their own members or those associated with the organisation. Fifty-eight point six per cent of the women were single.
22 For example, he cites Pius XI's recommendations in the 1931 encyclical *Quadragesimo Anno* to 'put aside any sense of envy or resentment' and not to 'scorn one's own social position' (Crippa 1959, p. 87).
23 The theme of the conference was: 'Domestic work, collaboration with the family'.
24 See Schema di relazione: il lavoro domestico, collaborazione con la famiglia, IV congresso nazionale, Gruppi ACLI Domestiche, 1961.
25 Ibid., p. 5.

26   Similar statements advocating the supremacy of domestic work in relation to other employment sectors (teaching, engineering, architecture, nursing and dressmaking) were also made.

27   Inchiesta sui problemi del lavoro domestico condotta tra le datrici di lavoro'. In occasione dei V Congresso Nazionale dei GAD.

28   The conference was entitled: A professional register for the participation of the collaborator to family life and to society, 23–25 April 1967.

29   See 'Sintesti del VI Congresso nazionale delle collaboratrici familiari delle ACLI, *Acli-Oggi*, Anno V, n. 19, 3 May 1967.

30   Ibid., p. 2.

31   See ACLI-COLF, Lo Scandalo sociale del lavoro domestico, Comunicato Stampo, 1967.

32   Ibid., p. 2.

33   The survey was based on the completed questionnaires of 233 domestic workers, taken from the 10,000 subscribers to the sector's newspaper *La Casa e La Vita*. See ACLI-COLF, Indagine statistica sul lavoro domestico, Florence, April 1967.

34   The survey showed that where the female employer was employed, she was most likely to be a teacher (11.65 per cent).

35   These latter figures may indicate the beginning of recruitment difficulties in this sector, forcing employers to pay insurance contributions.

36   In 1967, a round table discussion to determine whether the sector was in crisis was held in Rome and received substantial press coverage. See ACLI-COLF, 'Una Tavola Rotonda delle Collaboratrici Familiari delle ACLI: E' in crisi il lavoro domestico', Rome, 6 April 1967. The 1967 congress was also widely reported in the press. For some examples see *Il Corriere della Sera*, 25 April 1967; *L'avvenire d'Italia*, 25 April 1967, *Epoca*, 7 May 1967. There was even some coverage, albeit mocking, by the Spanish press. The journalist writing for *La Verdad* (27 April 1967) saw it as an example of Italy's love for congresses, and surprise was expressed at just who the protagonists of such a congress were: 'its protagonists are not doctors … or metallurgists … they are creatures of domestic service'.

37   The first National Day was held in Turin in 1968 with the Christian Democrat Carlo Donat Cattin as the keynote speaker.

38   Historical examples from other contexts indicate that this has been a problematic feature of domestic work. The civil status of servants had been largely determined by their dependent relationship on their employers. They were one of the last groups to be enfranchised in both France and Britain (McBride 1976).

39   For example, the 1950 legislation (law n. 860) which regulated the physical and economic protection of working mothers stated that separate legislation would be enacted for home workers and domestic workers, although interim provision was included in a separate section of law n. 860.

40   The leader of the Italian Communist Party, Enrico Berlinguer, had referred to this shift to the Left within Catholic forces in relation to his historic compromise strategy with the Christian Democrats. See Berlinguer (1978).

41   For the text of this statute see Pestalozza (1975, pp. 335–-49).

42   Il contratto collettivo e l'albo per nuovi spazi umani sociali e professionali delle Colf', VII Congresso Nazionale, 1970, p. 2.

43   Ibid., p. 4.

44   Relazione dei Datori di Lavoro 'Nuova Collaborazione' al Congresso Nazionale ACLI-COLF, Rome 23/25 April 1970, p. 4.

45 'I risultati e il documento conclusivo del VII congresso nazionale', *La Casa e La Vita*, May 1970.
46 The API-COLF clearly intended to appropriate the previous work of the ACLI-COLF and this congress was known as the eighth national congress of the API-COLF.
47 'Le collaboratrici familiari nella società e nel movimento operaio, Siena 12–13 May 1973.
48 The three confederations, the CGIL, CISL and UIL were closely linked to political parties. (See Bedani 1995).
49 See 'Il testo dell'intervento del presidente nazionale delle ACLI Marino Carboni all'VIII Assemblea congressuale nazionale delle ACLI-COLF, Siena, 12–13 May 1973, p. 2. This view was reiterated by the Left-wing newspaper, *Il Manifesto*, which simultaneously condemned both the post-war strategy of the ACLI-COLF and the defection of the API-COLF, describing the perspective of Erminio Crippa as a 'suffocating reactionary ideology'. See Al congresso Acli-Colf le domestiche affermano la loro appartenenza al movimento operaio, *Il Manifesto*, 13 May 1973. For further newspaper reports of this landmark congress see *Avvenire*, 10 May 1973; *Il Popolo*, 13 May 1973; *Il Giorno*, 13 May 1973.
50 See *La Casa e La Vita*, May/June/July, 1973.
51 Luigi Guerrini, intervention to VIII congresso nazionale delle ACLI-COLF, 1973, pp. 2–3.
52 It was stated that the ACLI-COLF would no longer maintain a preferential relationship with any of the trade union confederations, although there was some recognition that many individual domestic workers affiliated to the ACLI would probably remain within the CISL. See 'Relazione introduttiva all'VIII Assemblea congressuale Nazionale ACLI-COLF sul tema "Le COLF nella società e nel movimento operaio"', Rina Mele, Siena, 1973.
53 Speech given by national executive member Pina Brustolin: 'Relazione Organizzativa dell'incaricata nazionale: Pina Brustolin', Assemblea Nazionale congressuale, Siena 1973, p. 2.
54 This, at a time when some national agreements had managed to reduce the working week of other sectors by up to eight hours with no loss of pay. See Bedani (1995, p. 172).
55 Ibid.
56 See 'L'impegno delle ACLI-COLF per promuovere e rafforzare la propria animazione cristiana' VIII Assemblea Congressuale Nazionale, Siena 1973, p. 1.
57 'Relazione introduttiva all'VIII Assemblea congressuale Nazionale ACLI-COLF sul tema Le COLF nella società e nel movimento operaio', Rina Mele, Siena, 1973, p. 4. This view was reiterated elsewhere: 'We come from poor families where the work of everyone has always been necessary and essential', 'Le Colf nella società e nel Movimento Operaio, VII Assemblea Congressuale Nazionale, Siena, 1973, p. 2.
58 'Le Colf nella società e nel Movimento Operaio', VIII Assemblea congressuale nazionale, Siena 1973, p. 6.
59 Relazione Organizzativa dell'incaricata nazionale: Pina Brustolin, Assemblea Nazionale Congressuale, Siena 1973, p. 7. The training course for the leaders of the sector also reflected a wider approach, with substantial time dedicated to the workers' movement and socioeconomic development in Italy. See Corso Nazionale di Formazione per Dirigenti COLF, Programma del Corso, Campitello di Fassa 19–25 August 1973.
60 See 'Le Colf verso il contratto', in *La Casa e La vita*, dicembre 1971.
61 The signatories representing the workers were the three confederations – FILCAMS-CGIL, FISASCAT-CISL and UIDATCA-UIL. FILCAMS (*Federazione Italiana Lavoratori Commercio alberghi mense e Servizi*) was affiliated to the CGIL; FISASCAT (Federazione Italiana sindacati addetti ai Servizi) was affiliated to the CISL; UIL-TUCS (Unione Italiana

Lavoratori Turismo Commercio e Servizi) was affiliated to UIL (*Unione italiana dei lavoratori*). The signatory for the employers was 'New Collaboration'. Federcolf, the API-COLF and the ACLI-COLF had all been present at the negotiating table.

62 See 'Una dichiarazione della Segretaria Nazionale ACLI-COLF, Pina Brustolin, sull'avvenuta firma del primo contratto nazionale dei lavoratori domestici', in *La Casa e La Vita*, May/June/July 1973.

63 See *La Casa e La Vita*, May/June/July 1973.

5 Black Women and Domestic Work: the Early Years

Chapters 5, 6 and 7 form the case-study of the book and address the experiences of African women employed as domestic workers in Rome. In this chapter, I am concerned with the early stages of African women's migratory history to Italy. I suggest that, in the 1970s, female migrants were subject to a double invisibility as women and as workers. National gender discourses did not address their specific situation as *female* migrants. Rather, migrant women were located within the category of migration. This positioning contributed to their invisibility as workers because their principal employment location was centred within a marginalised and feminised sector of the economy – domestic work. This chapter examines the 1970s and early 1980s. It is my view that this period stands as a crucial stage in the establishment of a differentiated gender status for migrant women, as it was at this time that one aspect of their multiple interlocking social identities – migrant worker – was constructed as a dominant identity.

Demand Pull Factors

As I argued in chapter 2, there was limited institutional or popular knowledge about migrant workers in the 1970s. As a consequence, there is limited official information covering African women's presence in Rome during this period.[1] In their article on immigration in the Lazio region, Altieri and Carchedi (1992) confirm that information about Lazio's ethnic minority communities in the 1970s is available largely in the form of newspaper reports and a few articles. Newspaper sources must of course be recognised as tending to emphasise what are considered to be the newsworthy aspects of a particular story. Nevertheless, the newspaper articles discussed below provide some information regarding the incidence of and reasons behind migrant women's presence in Rome.

113

In the 1970s, the journalist Isabella de Paz published several articles on migrant women in the Roman daily newspaper *Il Messaggero*.[2] In an article published on 20 September 1976, she offered an overview of their contemporary situation. She described a clear internal demand for overseas domestic labour. Indeed, De Paz referred to the existence of a 'servant crisis', where employers would place themselves on waiting lists to secure the services of an overseas domestic worker. In her explanation of employers' propensity to employ foreign labour, De Paz observed that, initially, Italian women had begun to employ migrant women because of the economic advantages this provided. However, it was noted that, increasingly, Italian women were effectively obliged to resort to migrant women's labour because of the diminishing pool of indigenous women prepared to engage in live-in domestic work. On this point, De Paz (1976a) cited the opinion of an Italian national working for a recruitment agency:

> Today it is a different matter ... Italian girls just cannot be found. No-one wants to go into service any more. Moroccan girls, Eritrean girls, Filipina girls and foreign girls in general are now the only ones going into service (De Paz 1976a).

De Paz's article depicts aspects of migrant workers' conditions which have subsequently become intrinsic features of their experience of the domestic work sector. For example, although it was generally accepted that migrant women were legally entitled to employment conditions comparable with those of Italian nationals, it was also clear that the unauthorised domicile status of some of these workers conferred extensive powers onto employers. In such a situation, the latter could pay migrant workers lower wages and institute a work schedule which violated the national contracts which governed the category from 1974 onwards.

De Paz's (1976a) representation of women migrants focused on their exoticism and visible cultural difference:

> ... Ethiopian women, are reluctant to wear European clothes and they remain attached to their national dress; serious, visibly disoriented ... wrapped in their white drapes, they create a happy absurdity of the stylistic landscape of rich areas ... Their reserved attitude is in contrast to the unbiased happiness of their colleagues from overseas (Filipinas, Thai, etc.) whose character and culture make them always ready to laugh, and who, what's more, are already integrated into the environment.

This cultural representation of migrant women is indicative of an early racial-ising perspective according to which African women's assumed propensity to tradition is contrasted with the 'natural' openness of Oriental women. These apparently innocuous comments attribute certain racialised features to the different ethnic groups of women. This differentiation also permeated the collective imaginations of employers who would subsequently begin to discriminate according to the racialised characteristics attributed to different ethnic groups. Some correlation can therefore be established between cultural perceptions and employment opportunities and conditions (see chapter 6).[3]

Interestingly, the illegality of some migrant women's status was not considered to be particularly problematic. By the late 1980s, the issue of undocumented immigration would become a major topic of concern within Italy. De Paz maintained that even where migrant women were working illegally, their familiarity with Italian conditions as well as the fact that they were 'welcomed', encouraged them to remain in Italy. This statement presents a very positive context of reception for migrant women and certainly De Paz's article does not suggest any evidence of popular hostility to their presence. This may have been due in part to the exoticisation of migrant women,[4] but may also have been conditioned by popular acceptance of the need for their labour. At any rate, as female workers, they appeared not to have been perceived as either a cultural or economic threat.

A subsequent article by the same author published on the 4 October 1976 highlighted the paradox between the migration of Italian nationals to work as au pairs abroad and the shortage of domestic workers that this had created in Italy. However, there was also evidence of Italian employers' actual preference for foreign domestic workers, largely due to the greater potential for exploitation when compared to indigenous workers. As the head of the USILD,[5] a trade union grouping for domestic workers stated:

> [Employers] are not inclined to employ Southern domestic workers, because they consider them to be inexperienced and untrained. They prefer the solution of the coloured [sic] domestic worker if only for the fact that the foreign woman adapts to living in out of the way areas … and she does not 'complain' if the entire domestic load is off-loaded onto her: cleaning the house, shopping, preparing meals, looking after the children.[6]

The preference for foreign domestic workers was additionally contingent on the construction and perception of their primary function as labour-related. The owner of a recruitment agency for domestic workers is cited as saying: 'Those Italian women who are available have difficult family and personal situations, problems which impact on the running of the household' (De Paz 1976b). The implication was that the personal or family needs of migrant women would not be expected to impinge on the smooth running of the Italian employers' household. This could only be achieved if other aspects of migrant women's identity were negated. While the USILD highlighted the mismatch of skills between southern women and the requirements of potential employers, it seems likely that some of the legal gains made by the sector and the extent of labour politicisation during this period meant that Italian employees were seen as potentially more problematic.

De Paz's articles also suggest that there was a generalised assumption that migrant women's presence in the domestic work sector would replicate the experiences of Italian women. In discussing the problems Italian women faced within this sector, the owner of the placing agency stated:

> Many [Italian] girls would be happy to work as domestic workers so that they could move to Rome and find, subsequently, different jobs, more consistent with their training. Just like foreign girls, this occupation would constitute a provisional solution, but they are not accepted.[7]

This assertion virtually implied the perpetration of discrimination against potential Italian domestic workers. In fact, the explanation for employers' preference for foreign nationals is implicit within this statement. For Italian nationals, domestic work would frequently constitute a temporary employment arrangement until alternative employment became available.[8] As I will demonstrate below, for migrant women domestic employment represented much more than a temporary solution. For the majority of African women working in the region, domestic work has constituted a restrictive sector of employment with limited opportunities for penetrating other employment spheres. Thus, rather than representing a temporary work solution, it has assumed more the form of a transmutating anchor, simultaneously offering partial stability and security (for legal workers) and a restrictive employment niche with adverse long-term implications.

In an article published two years later in 1978, there appeared to be some awareness of the problems implicit in accentuating a strictly labour-related role for migrant women. In this article, De Paz focused on some of the difficulties of domestic work for migrant women, emphasising particularly the extent of their clandestinity and the difficulties they encountered in attempting to reconcile a maternal role with that of live-in domestic worker (see chapter 7).

These accounts suggested that demand for migrant women's labour was substantial, and that this was partly attributable to their weaker position within the labour market when compared to their Italian peers. Recruitment via agencies and ecclesiastical organisations[9] can be seen to be indicative of the nature of this demand. However, it was not simply a mismatch of skills or Italian women's greater legal protection which contributed to the demand for migrant women's labour. A further important factor lay in the continuing low status of domestic work, despite the ACLI-COLF'S efforts throughout the post-war period to rectify negative public opinion towards this sector of workers.

An assessment of the general perception of domestic work and domestic workers in the post-war period suggests that the low status attributed to such work meant that Italian women would seek alternative employment where possible. Transformations occurring in the domain of women's employment in Italy facilitated this. As Del Boca (1988) has shown, in the period between 1963 and 1970 female employment decreased as businesses restructured. There was a reversal of this trend in the 1970s when a turnabout in the decline in women's labour force participation occurred (Beccalli 1985). A number of factors accounted for this, including modifications in women's education and aspirations. Although some of the industries in which women had traditionally been employed contracted, there was a parallel expansion in sectors such as electric machinery and shoes. Italian women were additionally absorbed into the parallel unofficial labour market and the small firm sector.[10]

Employment as a domestic worker compared unfavourably with employment in these alternative sectors. The presumed benevolence of the employing families, visible in legislation and in the ideology and activities of the ACLI-COLF up to the 1970s, did not seem to reflect the actual experiences of Italian women engaged in domestic work. The following discussion of Italian women's experiences in the sector is useful for identifying recurring problems attributable to the sector itself, and also helps to explain why the internal market was unable to fulfil the demand for domestic workers.

Throughout the post-war period, internal migration had featured as an integral aspect of the domestic work sector. Domestic workers frequently migrated to the cities from agricultural or underdeveloped areas of the country (the Veneto, Friuli Venezia-Giulia, Abruzzi, Molise, Lazio and Sardegna). As was stated at the 1973 ACLI-COLF congress:

> Emigration has almost always been imposed on us ... We have had to migrate because we needed to work and we could not find work at home. Quite the

opposite of choosing, it must be recognised that we have almost always been forced to leave our homes, we have been sent away by underdevelopment.[11]

The fact that internal migrant workers, typical of most migratory processes, were absorbed into unpopular employment sectors, gives some indication of the status of the profession. Indeed, at the 1973 ACLI-COLF congress, the extent of internal migration amongst domestic workers was cited as an explanatory factor for the weakness of the sector: 'because it is from here [immigration] that we can begin to understand the reasons for our marginality and weakness'.[12]

A national study of the domestic work sphere was promoted by the ACLI-COLF in 1974.[13] This study was based on the experiences of Italian domestic workers who were members of the ACLI. It demonstrated that the vocational and missionary role promoted by the Church and the pre-1971 ACLI-COLF bore little relationship to domestic workers' own perception of their involvement in this sector. Seventy per cent of those interviewed stated that they worked as domestic workers because they could not do anything else.[14] Seventy-three point three per cent of domestic workers perceived their employment as domestic workers to be temporary, or had at least perceived it to be so in the past. While 58.6 per cent were single, 33.1 per cent were married and the remaining workers were divorced. A majority had either attended some primary school classes (30.8 per cent) or attained a primary school diploma (37.7 per cent). Thus 68.5 per cent of those surveyed had received only an elementary level of education. Fifty-six per cent had been unable to continue their studies for economic reasons. A relative majority of those interviewed came from the South (Campania, Sicily and Sardegna – 37.4 per cent). Forty-five per cent of the survey group had worked as domestics for more than 10 years, 7.2 per cent for under a year, 10.4 per cent between one and two years, 12.4 per cent between three and four years and 17.3 per cent between five and 10 years. Thus, internal migration, low levels of formal qualifications and a single civil status were all prominent features of the Italian domestic worker.

Despite the pretensions of the ACLI-COLF to convince domestic workers to conceive of their work as not only different but intrinsically better than other work sectors, this did not appear to have permeated the consciousness of domestic workers. Female workers viewed factory work as preferable to paid domestic work. A Neapolitan woman, interviewed for a later ACLI survey in 1989, with experience of both external and internal migration, factory work and paid domestic work stated:

Certainly we were treated better in factories from all points of view, we had more respect, we had more rights. If there is one job which really is not respected it is that of the domestic worker; in factories there is more protection. And also, even it is hard work it is never as gruelling as being a domestic worker (ACLI 1989b, p. 4).[15]

As Dalla Costa (1981) has argued, in the 1970s, the severe disadvantages of live-in work for Italian nationals led them to prefer both factory work and the production of goods in the informal economy. The 1974 ACLI survey revealed that an overwhelming number of interviewees (70.2 per cent) considered domestic work to be poorly perceived by society at large. Nevertheless, 66.1 per cent were not ashamed of working as domestics, although only 14 per cent stated that they would continue to work as domestics if they had a family and husband who earned an adequate wage. In a random sample of 20 questionnaires from a 1967 ACLI-COLF survey, the response to the question 'do you like working as a domestic worker' indicated a range of opinions, but these were more negative than positive. Comments ranged from 'it is disgusting', to 'so so', to 'it is a recognised and high profession just as any other'. The insufficient consideration afforded to domestic work was thus acknowledged by domestic workers themselves, but not necessarily internalised.[16] In the Italian case, the invisibility of paid domestic work, the low status accorded to it, and its differential treatment even compared to other employment sectors traditionally associated with women,[17] contributed to Italian women's rejection of such work and the demand for overseas domestic labour. More specifically, Italian domestic workers had become increasingly reluctant to be employed as live-in workers.[18]

Recruitment, Demand and Regulation

As discussed in chapter 2, national legislation regarding migrant workers was introduced in Italy in 1986. The regulation of overseas domestic workers prior to this occurred via government circulars issued by both the Ministry of Labour and Social Welfare and the Foreign Ministry. In this section, I shall demonstrate that these circulars indicated both a desire to protect the position of current and potential Italian domestic workers and sought to construct the labour function of migrant women as their pre-eminent role. Indeed, the manner in which the migration of women was conceptualised and regulated indicates that from an early stage, migrant women's labour function was given prominence.

In 1972, the opening preamble to circular n. 37/106/III painted a picture similar to that of De Paz:

> This Ministry has verified the growing tendency, in recent months, to employ foreign labour, coming principally from developing countries, to work as domestic workers.
>
> The phenomenon, which is of a considerable size, can probably be attributed not just to the limited supply and growing cost of national workers in the same sector, but also to the mistaken assumption that the employment of foreign domestic workers will allow one to entirely or partly exempt oneself from a duty to pay insurance contributions.[19]

Those involved in the drafting of these government circulars were certainly alert to the prospect of competition between migrant labour and Italian labour and unequivocally prioritised the employment of Italian nationals over that of foreign nationals. Employment contracts for foreign nationals were only possible once the unavailability of Italian nationals in the locality had been verified.[20] Indeed, a ministerial circular issued in 1973, applicable to migrant workers in general and not just to the sphere of domestic work, showed the reluctance on the part of those regulating employment to employ foreign nationals in preference to Italian nationals:

> In many cases we have noted that work authorisations have been issued, to the aforementioned foreign citizens, in cases where the labour market shows the availability of large numbers of Italian workers ... Employment offices are reminded of the need to conform their actions to former directives with the aim of attaining, as a matter of priority, the full employment of available Italian workers. They must bear in mind that the issuing of 'work authorisations' *must be rigorously controlled* to avoid an excessive recourse to foreign workers, often not justifiable given objective circumstances.[21]

In an attempt to account for the use of migrant labour in the domestic work sector, a subsequent circular, issued in 1973, chose to focus on the propensity of employers to engage foreign domestic workers rather than on the reluctance of Italian women to enter the profession.[22] Continuing in this train, Circular 7/122/II issued in 1975, was intended to prevent the illegal employment of foreign domestic workers. The Ministry of Labour believed that employers were purposefully finding ways to avoid utilising the correct recruitment channels as delineated in ministerial dispositions. It stated:

It has been noted ... that interested employers (some of them presumably acting on advice from organisations operating illegally in the sector) are providing declarations which even if they appear to be formally in line with existing legislation regarding the placing of domestic staff, nonetheless raise doubts as to the truthfulness of these same declarations.[23]

What this latter point proves unequivocally, is that despite a ministerial concern to restrict the employment of foreign nationals and encourage the employment of Italian nationals, a specific demand for migrant women's labour was apparent. By attempting to ensure that there were no legal economic advantages to the engagement of foreign nationals by Italian employers, the Ministry of Labour was attempting to stem the increasing numbers of Italian employers who appeared to prefer the services of foreign nationals. However, it is probable that ministerial regulation of overseas domestic labour in part contributed to the attractiveness of migrant women's labour for the Italian family, *even* within the legal sphere. Lower wages than those commanded by Italian nationals were stipulated in contracts and migrant women were additionally tied to employers in a way that would have been unthinkable for Italian women.

At government level, the desire to restrict the incoming migration of foreign domestic workers was clearly discernable. Circular n.140/90/79 issued in 1979 first noted the extent of the demand for foreign domestic workers: 'As is known, the phenomenon of employing non-EC foreign workers for domestic work has become quite significant'.[24] The ministry was patently unhappy with this situation and an inter-ministerial group was established which intended to: 'eliminate, or at least to contain, the uncontrolled presence of foreign workers, regulating their flows based on the real needs of the national market for domestic work ...'.[25] The ministry's position seemed to be conditioned by a belief that a potential pool of Italian nationals could be mobilised to engage in domestic work and thus eliminate the necessity for migrant workers. However, as I will show below, this official position did not correspond to reality.

Again, this 1979 circular stressed the need to ascertain the availability of Italian workers before authorising permits for foreign nationals. The facsimile of bureaucratic forms for domestic service included in this particular circular confirmed that the regulation of foreign domestic workers was envisaged in such a way as to construct the labour function of migrant women as a pre-eminent role. Already, in 1972, Circular 37/106/III had stipulated that migrant domestic workers could only be employed for full-time work: 'A work authorisation cannot be issued for more than one work contract, nor for work on an hourly paid basis'. Thus at this stage the possibility of part-time work on an hourly paid basis was a legal impossibility for potential recruits. In reality, only the latter possibility could facilitate the family organisation of migrant women. The fact that this was not legally permissible emphasised that it was the labour function, and not the general conditions of these women, which was conceptualised as useful and beneficial to Italian society.

Not surprisingly, application forms for prospective foreign domestic workers showed a concern with migrant women's ability to perform their labour function properly. The prospective worker had to produce medical evidence endorsed by the Italian consulate's doctor which demonstrated her good health. She was also expected to be of good civic and moral integrity. This concern with her health and her potential to infect the healthy Italian family is reminiscent of an early historical attitude to domestic workers (see chapter 4). The prospective worker could indicate her preference in terms of location and in terms of the size of family that she was prepared to work for. She was also required to indicate her anticipated length of stay in the country but was obliged to remain for a minimum of one year.[26] Prospective domestic workers' presence in Italy was irrevocably tied to their employment function. The application for domestic work included the following statement:

> ... in the event of the work contract being terminated early by the worker, the latter must immediately return to their country of origin and must wait three years before seeking further work in Italy.[27]

This reflected a clear vision of foreign domestic workers as migrant contractual labour. As was observed in chapter 2, the organisation of migrant labour in this way is particularly beneficial to the receiving country given that it minimalises the reproductory costs of that labour. However, for the migrant domestic worker in Italy, it implied a vulnerable location in relation to employers, particularly in situations of exploitation or abuse. In those instances where the foreign domestic worker would be inclined to change employer, this would have to be weighed up against the prospect of an effective three year repatriation period. At the time, a spokesperson for the Cape Verdean community was highly critical of this restriction and argued that greater flexibility should be incorporated into the legislation to facilitate a change of employer without automatically losing residence status.[28]

The Italian employer was also obliged to enter into a contract.[29] The employer was responsible for providing air tickets for foreign domestic workers both for their arrival and departure.[30] In the event of an earlier than anticipated return, the employer was still obliged to pay for the return ticket regardless of the circumstances which had led to the breakdown of the contract. The contract further reiterated that migrant domestic workers were entitled to treatment comparable to Italian domestic workers. In other words, migrant workers' conditions of work were to be governed by the legislation pertaining to the domestic work sector. Nevertheless, their status as *migrant* workers meant that their employment relationship had been differentially constructed from that of Italian nationals. The employer was undoubtedly placed in a stronger position since the extension of an employment contract or the formulation of a new and different contract remained a decision in the hands of the employer.

The 1979 circular additionally regulated the contract between prospective employers and domestic workers. Diplomatic or consular bodies in the sending countries would receive the applications of prospective domestic workers. These applications would be sent by these bodies to the Department for the placement of workers (*Direzione Generale del Collocamento della Manodopera*). The provincial offices (*Ufficio provinciale del lavoro*) would indicate to this department their anticipated need for overseas domestic workers, based on their local context and taking the availability of Italian nationals into consideration. The department would then distribute the requests for employment to the various provincial offices. In turn, these provincial offices would provide the prospective employer with a choice of workers.[31] However, in those cases where the provincial offices could not provide migrant domestic workers, the employer could also present an official request indicating their preferences in terms of the country of origin. This request would be forwarded to the consulate in the appropriate country.

By the early 1980s guidelines issued by the Ministry of Labour in 1981,[32] regarding the employment of migrant workers, indicated that the ministry had begun to accept the categorical demand for their labour given the absence of a national pool of labour: 'as a rule foreign workers are employed in jobs for which Italian workers are no longer available (typical examples are domestic workers and agricultural labourers)'.[33]

Nonetheless, the proposals outlined in this document continued to demonstrate adherence both to the concept of migrants as contractual migrant labour and to the necessity to protect the national labour force from competition. It was envisaged that authorisations for work for foreign nationals would be forthcoming subsequent to verification of the unavailability not only of Italians but also of European community citizens.[34] The preference for European community labour was viewed as a means of offsetting potentially negative consequences within the internal labour market. This clearly implied that external European community labour was preferable to the labour of African and Asian migrants. While the reasons for this are not articulated, it is to be surmised that the ministry envisaged a more positive context of reception for European community nationals.

The Employment of Migrant Women as Domestic Workers

Data from the INPS (*Istituto Nazionale della Previdenza Sociale*)[35] for the 10-year period between 1972–82 show that 1,060,339 people engaged in domestic work nationally. Of these, 1,004,302 were Italian workers and 56,037 were foreign. African women constituted the largest group of foreign domestic workers (38.2 per cent) with Lazio accounting for 78.3 per cent of domestic workers in the central[36] region of Italy.[37] These figures, however, do not offer an exhaustive picture of the situation as they present an overview only of the legally operating domestic service sphere. During this 10-year period 141,834 Italian women in the Lazio region paid insurance contributions as domestic workers, compared to a figure of 6,965 for African domestic workers in the region. As has already been ascertained, establishing an accurate numerical picture of the presence of migrants during this stage of the immigration process is virtually impossible. Nonetheless, even working with the unreliable estimates of the 1970s,[38] these figures indicate that only a limited proportion of African domestic workers were employed with a legal contract. INPS data for the year 1979[39] showed that the majority of foreign female domestic workers in Italy worked in Lazio (5,778 out of a total of 8,586). At this stage, the developing countries which provided most of the foreign labour were Ethiopia, the Philippines and the Cape Verde Islands (Korsieporn 1991).

It is worth highlighting the extent of female migrant labour force participation at this stage. In fact, during the 1970s, certainly within the legal sphere of employment, domestic work was a dominant category of employment for migrant workers. Between 1969 and 1975, there was a significant growth in the number of work permits issued by the Home Office to foreign nationals in the region. In 1969, 8,598 were issued, 10,922 in 1972 and 13,515 in 1975. Employment authorisations issued by another government body indicated a more gradual rise in trends. The Roman provincial employment office (UPLMO – *Ufficio Provinciale di Lavoro*) issued 3,625 employment authorisations in 1976, 4,056 in 1977 and 4,266 in 1978. The majority of employment authorisations in 1978 were issued to people from developing countries (65.2 per cent). What is particularly interesting about these statistics however, is the dominance of domestic work as an employment sector for foreign workers. In 1978, 90 per cent of the work authorisations issued by the Rome UPLMO to nationals from the developing world were for domestic work.[40]

In this section, I will discuss the early experiences of Black women migrating to Italy. The focus is largely on the nature of their migration to Italy, their biographical profiles and their initial experiences of domestic work. A more detailed discussion of their working conditions appears in chapter 6.

Interview narratives indicate that many African migrant women travelled alone at relatively young ages. Cape Verdean women in particular travelled as contractual migrant labour. Their initial migratory flows were a direct consequence of informal recruitment carried out by Capuchin friars based in the islands. Via contacts with Roman parishes they initiated the first migratory flows to Rome. The ensuing characteristics of Cape Verdean migration, however, confirm Monica Boyd's (1989) thesis concerning the importance of family, friendship and community networks in influencing the recent migration to industrial nations. Typically these women arrived in their late teens and early twenties, beginning in the late 1960s and continuing throughout the 1970s, 1980s and 1990s. Lucila (interview 2) for example, arrived in 1975, aged 19. She migrated alone but her sister was already working in Italy. Maria Joanna (interview 5) also migrated alone. She was 22 when she arrived in 1969. She had previously been working in a bakery in Portugal,[41] but moved to Italy where her cousin was employed as a domestic worker. Although most of the women migrated alone, some had already formed families in Cape Verde. This was the case of Clara (interview 6) who had migrated alone to Italy at the age of 22 in 1971. Her three young children (aged 5, 2 and 1) were left in Cape Verde and cared for by her mother. Margarita (interview 8) similarly left two children to be cared for by relatives in Cape Verde. Elena (interview 23) migrated to Rome in 1976, aged 21 to replace her sister who was getting married and returning to Cape Verde. She came 'for the experience and out of curiosity'. Gabriele (interview 25) came to Rome in 1972, aged 26. She was married and left her four children in Cape Verde to be cared for by her husband and other relatives. Cape Verdean women thus overwhelmingly migrated autonomously and even in those instances where they already had their own families, they were usually compelled to leave them behind in the country of origin. Cape Verdean migration was fundamentally an economic migration, made possible by existing demand within the receiving country:

> I must say that Cape Verdean immigration to Italy has been a typically economic migration ... Our problem has been to look for work to find a solution to our

situation where colonialism did not create ... opportunities, structures for the Cape Verdean people.[42]

The migration of Eritreans and Ethiopians was influenced both by the earlier colonial relationship with Italy and, in the case of Eritreans, by the political situation in Ethiopia. Some migration from Eritrea was therefore a consequence of political factors. As one Eritrean woman stated: 'I came away in '77, it was the situation which pushed me to leave my country; as you know, the war has been ongoing for 23 years'.[43] Abebech (interview 11) migrated from Ethiopia in 1979, aged 16. She had other relatives living in Rome and chose Italy as a destination country because she knew she could obtain work easily. Abeba (interview 17), an Eritrean, migrated to Italy in 1970 when she was 28, leaving behind two children aged 10 and six. In contrast to the migratory characteristics of Cape Verdean women in the 1970s, there also seemed to be evidence of an older generation of Ethiopian/Eritrean women migrating to Italy. This may have been attributable to men's involvement in the armed struggle in Eritrea and women's greater economic responsibility for the family unit. Emma (interview 27), for example, migrated to Rome in 1975 aged 46. At that stage she already had two grown-up children, but left Eritrea because of the war. Elsa (interview 19) migrated in 1980, aged 40. She had also migrated to Italy because of the war and because she had relatives living in Rome.

Previous colonial ties had created certain expectations amongst some East Africans. As one Eritrean woman stated:

> ... but then this life in Italy, back home you do not think that it is like this; if you migrate you imagine you will live well because back home the Italians live very well, they are the richest; the Italians are the most powerful.[44]

The reality of the Italian situation and the combination of a political refugee background and a clandestine status immediately put paid to this woman's aspirations to study in Italy:

> ... coming here I was not able to study; I did not know the language, I had studied in English, I did not have any documents as I came away illegally; I had no qualifications, nothing, it was not easy to find a school and I began working as a live-in domestic.[45]

The political background of Eritreans was a contributory factor to their migration. Their testimonies revealed an acute interest in the political situation at home and this was confirmed by a representative from the Eritrean women's association, the UDE:

> The majority are also politically active. They work, all the domestics have meetings ... they listen ... they follow politics. Because we have suffered because of the war. It is not just those who are fighting who have suffered (interview, UDE).

Lemlem (interview 10), for example, stated that she always followed what was happening in Eritrea, even though she did not understand politics very well. However, some of her very close relatives were still in Eritrea and it was therefore important for her to know what was going on.

Thus, a combination of political and economic motives characterised the migration of some Eritreans. Lemlem (interview 10) had migrated in the context of a partial family migration. She migrated to Italy when she was 18 with her brother who was 14. Their father was already working in Rome as a domestic worker. They had left Eritrea because of the war. However, their mother and four other siblings remained there. Their mother did not want to migrate and did not think it would be good for the whole family to move. On their arrival in Italy, the father could not afford to look after both the children. As a live-in domestic worker himself he could not provide accommodation for his children. Lemlem started working straight away as a domestic worker along with her brother. Her brother only did this for a short time and then went to stay in a residential home. Her father also wanted her to study but she was acutely aware of the need to contribute economically to the family and felt it was more important for her brother to study: 'Because he is a boy and later he will take the place of my father'.[46] Although Lemlem maintained that she had never been very interested in studying, it seems clear that the importance of educational achievement for her brother was considered within the context of a family migrational strategy linked to future economic and cultural prospects.

The nature of the demand for female migrant labour exemplifies the tension discussed above regarding the state's attempt to regulate the employment of migrant women's domestic labour and the desire of employers to exploit this migrant labour to the full. This can be seen in the conditions of employment offered to migrant women. Many of the Cape Verdean women who migrated in the early 1970s had their contracts arranged before entering Italy.[47] These had often been arranged by a relative already based in Italy. Matilde (interview 1), for example, arriving in 1978 at the age of 18, had her contract arranged for her by her sister. Elena (interview 23) and Gianna (interview 24) both had contracts arranged for them. However, employment was also available within the undocumented sector of domestic work.[48] When Lucila (interview 2) arrived in 1975 at the age of 19, she worked for three years and six months as an undocumented migrant. Antonia (interview 16) changed jobs frequently to try to secure a proper employment contract. Maria Joanna (interview 5) also worked for three years illegally, having entered Italy on a tourist visa. Evidence of collusion on the part of employers regarding illegal work is discernible. In the case of Maria Joanna (interview 5), for example, despite the fact that she entered on a tourist visa, her employment had already been arranged while she was resident in Portugal. Indeed, her employer came to collect her at the airport but did not subsequently legalise her position.[49]

The quest to legalise their status often lay behind the employment mobility of migrant women. The possibility for such mobility indicates that there was substantial demand within the domestic service sector. Maria Joanna worked for a total of six years as an illegal worker. During this period she changed families three times, each time with the expectation that they would legalise her status. Clandestinity did not necessarily entail bad treatment on the part of the employer. In describing her illegal situation with her first family, Maria Joanna maintained 'I was happy there'. However, the implications of clandestinity meant that for six years she could not return to Cape Verde. More seriously, clandestinity meant no access to public health care. Still working illegally for a third family, Maria Joanna acquired a serious infection which was eventually treated with penicillin. Her employer had not assisted her and eventually, with the help of her cousin, she was forced to seek private medical treatment.

Clandestinity was not the only motive for precipitating a change in employment. Migrant women might also change employers for more personal reasons. For example, Rosa (interview 3), worked for nine months in a provincial town in Lazio. She left because her employers gave her a day off on Wednesday. This meant that she could not meet with other members of her family resident in the region who, like most domestics, were free on Thursday afternoon and Sundays. Her employers had argued that it was not stipulated in her contract when her day off would be. Clara (interview 6) also changed her first job so that she could be nearer her sister. This, despite the fact that she described the family for whom she then worked as 'an excellent family'. Antonia (interview 16) initially migrated to Palermo in 1977 but after a year she moved to Rome because her mother was working there as a live-in worker. She found a family in Palermo who were moving to Rome and she moved with them. The willingness of migrant women to change employer in order to facilitate family contact and proximity points to the development of strategies to combat the subordination of their multiple identities to a dominant work identity.

At this stage of their employment histories, all of the women interviewed were engaged as live-in domestic workers and uniformly stressed the difficulties of such work. The principal problems, as it had been for Italian live-in workers before them, concerned the long hours, abuse by employers, lack of free time and lack of privacy. These were structural problems endemic to the live-in work relationship. Migrant women were however subject to greater exploitation because of their migrant status, which meant that their presence in Italy was precarious. Moreover, clandestinity undoubtedly gave employers the upper hand within the domestic work relationship.

One of the women interviewed did however consider the economic benefits of the organisation of this type of work. Maria Joanna (interview 5) maintained that her move to Italy had been partially influenced by her dissatisfaction with her situation in Portugal where, as she stated, 'I was working to maintain the house'. However, her uncritical view of live-in domestic work may have been conditioned by the fact that she was liberated from this type of work via marriage to an Italian national at a relatively early stage.

Lower wages for overseas domestic workers when compared to Italian domestic workers suggests that Italian employers did not necessarily have to employ migrant women illegally to gain some advantage. This can be deduced from the salaries stipulated for Cape Verdean women in their contracts during the 1970s. For Cape Verdean women migrating in 1970, the average contractual wage was L40,000.[50] Already in 1967, advertisements requesting domestic staff in the Rome newspaper *Il Messaggero* indicated that Italian domestic workers could earn L70,000 to L80,000 for live-in work.[51] This suggests a clear salary differential between the two groups which cannot be attributed to the undocumented status of migrant workers. Rather these were women migrating on a regular contract, where their salaries were stipulated at a rate below that of Italian domestic workers. When Elena (interview 16) migrated to Rome in 1976, her salary was stipulated at L80,000. Again, a comparison with advertisements in *Il Messaggero* in 1977 suggest blatant financial discrimination. Advertisements placed by Italian employers offer salaries of between L200,000 to L250,000 for live-in domestic work. There were two inserts from Filipina women offering their labour in the supply section for domestic work. They were still based in the Philippines and were offering their labour at L108,000.[52] In 1977, the adverts still appeared to be targeting the domestic market, and some employers were explicit about this in their specific inserts.[53] Nonetheless, for Italian employers, there were a number of advantages in employing foreign nationals. Employment within the undocumented sphere facilitated exploitative working conditions and low wages. Although the employment of foreign nationals via legally regulated contracts meant that Italian employers would incur the expense of an airline ticket, they could, nevertheless, stipulate low wages in these contracts.[54]

Live-in work entailed a wide variety of tasks. A number of women stated that they had to do 'everything'. Essentially the work consisted of cooking, cleaning and general housework in those instances where families had no young children. Child-care was also a task for some women. In some cases, the employers had engaged more than one worker and consequently job specification would be more clearly delineated. Maria Joanna's (interview 5) employers had engaged two home helps, one of whom was an Italian. Lucila's (interview 2) employers had also hired a nursemaid. Nonetheless, working conditions could be transformed as a consequence of the internal reorganisation of employed staff. For example, Lucila's family discontinued the employment of the nursemaid and Lucila was obliged to assume these additional responsibilities.

African women were employed both in cases where the mother of the employing family was engaged in paid work and where her function was that of a full-time housewife. Many of the working female employers were professionals. For example, Matilde worked for a psychologist, Lucila for a magistrate, Rosa for a primary school teacher, Maria Joanna for a dentist. Margarita (interview 8), on the other hand, worked for a widow/housewife who had a young son. However, a number of the female employers were housewives. Elena (interview 23) was employed by a family where the father was a lawyer and the mother was a housewife, with two children aged one and four. Interestingly, even when the children had grown up, these particular employers retained her services as a live-in worker.

The taxing nature of live-in domestic work was constantly stressed by interviewees. Matilde (interview 1) described the work as 'very difficult'. She stated that she felt particularly exploited when she arrived because she was not familiar with her working rights and therefore worked many more hours than she should have. She highlighted the difficulty of being on call for virtually 24 hours a day. A degree of resignation was evident in her acceptance of domestic work as the principal employment opportunity for migrant women. Commenting on domestic work, she stated: '... it does not give you any satisfaction but if you do not have any qualifications ...'. Francesca (interview

9) also described domestic work as: 'heavy work … but you cannot find other kinds of work, it is very difficult'.[55] Lemlem (interview 10), in describing a typical working day with the first family that she worked for, stated that she would wake at 6.30 to 7.00 in the morning and not finish working until 10.00 in the evening. Her female employer was a housewife whose husband was a lawyer. They frequently entertained and on these occasions Lemlem would not finish working until 2.00am in the morning. She was granted her two hours rest period in the afternoon in accordance with the collectively bargained national contract. However, it is important to highlight that her two hour daily rest period had to take place within the confines of the employers' home. In effect, this meant that she was virtually imprisoned in the home for extensive periods of time. Lemlems' free time on a Thursday afternoon and Sunday afternoon would be from 4.00pm in the afternoon to 9.00pm or 10.00pm in the evening. She did not find the work in itself difficult as she had been used to doing housework in Eritrea, but she highlighted linguistic difficulties, the amount of work, and the fact that she was constantly closed up within the house as three of her principal initial problems. Not only were the working hours long, but her employers'[56] primary interest in her labour meant that they attempted mentally, if not practically, to restrict other aspects of her identity. Her female employer did not want her to have a boyfriend and frequently told her that she should not get married. The power of the employer extended to control over free time. Thus even if Lemlem had finished all her work on a particular evening and asked to go out, the response would frequently be: 'At this time? It's too late'. This again indicated the employers' concern over her labour. Their reluctance to give permission for her to go out late in the evenings was motivated by their concern about her employment performance on the following day. As Lemlem stated: 'I was always scared to ask permission. If I go out today, then tomorrow I really have to work hard'. No wonder then, that when Lemlem started to work for this family she stated that she cried continually. She worked for this family for nine years and despite their constant criticism of her ability to work: 'you can't do anything, you're always making mistakes', when she eventually left them to work for two families on an hourly paid basis, they pleaded with her to stay.

Another Eritrean domestic worker additionally stated that employers would often ask their employee to do things which were clearly beyond the remit of their contract:

… where I am now, every now and again he [the employer] tries it on by asking me to do things which are just not on, I mean to say, the days of slavery are over

... Sometimes he asks me to put his socks on ... to cut his nails ....[57]

Interviews with representatives of the ethnic minority communities included in this case study confirmed that during the early stage of Black women's presence, long hours, low pay and an undocumented status were some of the characteristics which typified their experiences.

The Trade Union Response

During the early years of settlement, female migrant domestic workers found only limited support from the trade unions. In 1982, a conference was organised by the regional federated trade-union body CGIL-CISL-UIL. This gave an important platform to migrant representatives while simultaneously providing the unified trade union body with an opportunity to recognise the specific difficulties of migrant workers.

The power of the employer is repeatedly cited as problematic by a variety of ethnic minority representatives.[58] This was stated quite emphatically by Isaias, the representative from Tigray, Ethiopia:

> The first issue to deal with in terms of legislation is the work contract and residence permit. The way in which the current work contract has been formulated must be heavily criticised ... where all privileges are granted to the employer, whilst the worker is deprived of minimum trade union rights and is left to the mercy of abuse, blackmail and intimidation by the employer. [This legislation] allows the employer to break the contract by bringing its end date forward, while this is categorically denied to the worker, as the penalty would be repatriation or similar (CGIL-CISL-UIL di Roma e del Lazio 1982, p. 58).

Moreover, the desire for work on a part-time basis was already clearly in evidence. As Isaias argued:

> The worker who is forced to work on a full-time basis is forced to live with the employer, subjecting themselves to outrageous exploitation. In such situations working hours are not at all respected. The worker is always subjected to being called outside of their regular hours of service (ibid., p. 58).

Isaias proceeded to connect the potential for transforming the organisation of domestic work to the importance of resolving wider issues, such as housing for migrant workers.

The intervention of the Cape Verdean representative Maria Crescencia Mola, at a round table discussion held a month later, and again organised by the regional CGIL-CISL-UIL federation reiterated these views concerning the absolute domination of employers over their employees. Mola had worked for ten years as a live-in worker. She called for an enquiry into employers' treatment of migrant workers and into the offers of work encouraging domestic workers to come to Italy. She was evidently accentuating an important link between the demand for domestic workers within Italy, which had led to active recruitment policies overseas, and the contradiction inherent in the subsequent poor treatment of these workers. This poor treatment was graphically described by Mola: 'I have to say that very often our employers' dogs in Italy are treated exquisitely in comparison to a worker, to a domestic worker' (ibid., p. 80).[59]

Mola's intervention emphasised that there was a general lack of knowledge regarding migrants' treatment in Italy and she called on the regional CGIL-CISL-UIL federation for support. While she recognised the growing concern being shown towards domestic workers in terms of discussions taking place about schools and nursery places, Mola was adamant that 'the struggle here is to make people understand how we are treated in Italy ... to really know what it means to work from morning to evening with these employers' (ibid., pp. 80–81). She considered the proposal to enforce a limit of eight hours to the working day, as suggested by the CGIL, as impossible to implement within the live-in domestic work relationship. Mola additionally perceived tangible difference between the experiences of Italian domestic workers and migrant domestic workers. In her view, Italians' ability to find part-time work and have independent accommodation was an important difference. But their status as nationals of Italy was also seen to be significant. Indeed, Mola repudiated the concept of parity of treatment extended towards migrant domestic workers as contained in the ministerial documents which regulated the sector:

> ... we find ourselves in a situation where our rights in Italy, our documents are tied to the Employment inspectorate, to Alitalia, to the Police Headquarters in Rome, to the Hygiene Office so, you can just imagine if the question of our equal treatment in Italy will ever be resolved (ibid., p. 81).

The interventions of migrant representatives at both the conference and round table discussion indicated deep dissatisfaction with their working conditions in Rome during the 1970s. Statistics provided by the Federcolf regarding the province of Rome indicated that between 1976 and 1982, the number of disputes involving migrant domestic workers progressively increased. In 1976, 47 per cent of disputes for the province of Rome involved migrant women. By 1980 this had increased to 66.4 per cent and by 1982 to 81.6 per cent.[60] These figures not only suggested that the numbers of migrant women engaged in domestic work were growing, but also indicated that compared to Italian nationals working in the sector, they encountered a greater degree of exploitation.

The arrival of migrant workers during a period of trade union strength did not seem to have facilitated the development of strategies to protect them from exploitation. A trade union sponsored conference held in Rome in 1982 was seen as important precisely because of this belated attention. One intervention described it as: '… the occasion – and I'm being rightly self-critical when I say this – to overcome our delay. Our delay in recognising your problems. Our delay in defining how we are going to intervene. We are here to fill this gap with you.[61] An executive member of the Lazio CGIL-CISL-UIL federation, Erminio Chioffi, attributed this neglect in part to the employment sectors available to migrant workers:

> It is important to stress that foreign workers' occupation has a peculiar 'hidden' character which is not simply a result of their undocumented status but also coincides with their very employment location (in private houses, behind the scenes in hotels and restaurants, isolated in the countryside, on beaches, …). This contributes to their presence being 'ignored'.
> Finally, what must also be said is that ahead of the very clandestinity in which this group of immigrant workers operate in is the limited organised and political presence of the trade union forces in these employment sectors, which have always been characterised by an important presence of irregular labour (ibid., p. 62).

The limited response from the trade unions was thus attributed to the historical invisibility and characteristics of migrant workers' chosen employment sectors. Certainly, the women I interviewed did not indicate the trade unions as a source to which they felt they had recourse in the event of work-related problems. For example, Matilde (interview 1) stated that she did not rely on any particular organisation or association for help but tried to solve her problems by herself. Rosa (interview 3) approached the Portuguese consulate for advice about her employment conditions. More frequently, these women turned to other family members for assistance.

As the representative body of Italian workers, the trade unions' interpretation of the phenomenon of immigration was of some importance. Had they viewed the inception of migratory flows as a result of push rather than pull factors, then their predisposition to defend the rights of migrant workers may have been limited or at any rate subordinated to the necessity to primarily protect the Italian worker. The interventions at this 1982 conference, however, indicated an unequivocal acceptance of a demand for migrant labour as a consequence of Italian nationals' repudiation of particular types of employment. According to Chioffi:

> This work force is not at all comparable with the Italian work force, and in particular with young people looking for their first job. Rather, within our labour market, it occupies those areas which have deliberately been left vacant and are rejected by our workers (CGIL-CSIL-UIL di Roma e del Lazio 1982, p. 62).

This perspective was reiterated by another executive member, Santino Picchetti, during the course of the conference:

> ... we really have a lot of work to do in Rome regarding the protection of foreign workers' social and employment rights. We should show solidarity towards them knowing, as we do, that their presence is not an alternative to Italian workers. The characteristics of the labour market are such that it would be difficult to find Italian workers for the areas in which these foreign workers work (ibid., p. 64).

Thus the acceptance of pull factors within Rome and the regional context of Lazio was considered an irrefutable fact by several trade union representatives. This view, articulated by a sector which by its very nature has an informed understanding of the labour market, clearly challenges the interpretation of the situation given by the policy makers of the region in the late 1980s and early 1990s. As we saw in chapter 3, legislation drawn up by the region in the mid-1980s was still responding to a presumed surplus of migrant workers.

In the early 1980s, trade unionists appeared to consider a migrant status as integral to migrants' experience as workers. In other words, the working situation of migrants could not be divorced from their status as migrants. It was also noted that there had been a negative construction of migrants' relationship with the institutions. This was accurately described by Mario Baldassarri, secretary of the Rome CGIL-CSIL-UIL federation:

> ... unfortunately up until now there has been no organic relationship between employed workers and the democratic institutions, a relationship has only existed between migrant workers and the police where the blackmailing powers of the employers play a natural part (If you don't behave as I want, if you ask for a rise

too insistently, I will report you to the police and you will be deported immediately) (ibid., p. 84).[62]

This description presented a graphic portrayal of how the essential duality of migrant workers' status combined to place them in a particularly disadvantaged position in the labour market.

The proceedings of these trade union discussions nevertheless pointed to a significant gap between the working experiences of migrant workers and trade union mobilisation. At this stage of the migratory process to the region, there still appeared to be a dominance of female workers. This can be gleaned by the nationality of the migrant representatives who contributed to these trade union initiatives. In the main they represented those ethnic groups whose communities consisted of substantial components of women.[63] Photographs of migrants participating in a public meeting on immigration in Piazza Navona portray an almost all-female audience.[64] Photographic representation of a substantial delegation of female migrant workers at the 1982 1 May procession in Rome suggested that there was a degree of interaction between female migrants and the trade unions. Nonetheless, a reading of the proceedings of these trade union initiatives suggested that the conditions of this female migrant labour force in the 1970s had essentially escaped the attention of the trade unions. Progressive forces were thus failing this section of the migrant community at a crucial time. In fact, during the 1970s, it was the Catholic sector which gave sustained attention to the predicament of female migrant labour. Religious organisations such as the Caritas and ACLI-COLF were the prominent associations in the early period of women migrants' presence. For example, it had been a Catholic organisation which had acknowledged Cape Verdean women's desire to have a meeting place, and on the initiative of a social worker and a priest from the religious association 'Tra Noi', a place was provided for this purpose.[65]

As stated earlier, despite a recognition of the incidence of migrant women domestic workers, the now more radical ACLI-COLF did not incorporate migrant women into their 1974 national survey. The ecclesiastical API-COLF, on the other hand, carried out a specific study of migrant women. The research was published in book form in 1979, authored by Erminio Crippa and entitled 'Bitter Work: Female Migrants in Italy'. Crippa's publication represents one of the first published studies of the condition of female migrant domestic labour,[66] and was based on research carried out by the API-COLF from 1976 onwards. As we have seen in chapter 4, Erminio Crippa had been a prominent figure within the arena of domestic work and had defected from the ACLI-

COLF in 1971 to pursue a more clerical line within the API-COLF. The API-COLF's observation that there existed an 'enormous demand for live-in workers' (Crippa 1979, p. 25) seems a valid assessment of the state of the domestic service market.[67] The API-COLF survey brought to light a number of common problems articulated by female migrant workers in the 1970s. These included long working hours, insufficient food, clandestinity, sequestration of passports and a general lack of free time.[68] The API-COLF proposed a number of strategies as a response to this new group of domestic workers. These included the creation of residential centres for migrant women in large cities and establishing offices to be managed by migrant women. There seemed to be some recognition that migrant women might face different problems from Italian women working in this sector. One of the proposals thus aimed to develop a network of services specifically designed for migrant women as well as extending to them those services already available. The association did not, however, obscure its religious objectives in relation to migrant workers, and certainly did not plan to condone extreme reactions to their situation:

> The religious issue cannot be ignored either. We must not forget these 'lands of mission' which have approached the thresholds of our Churches and our homes. While some might want to prepare them for an armed and revolutionary struggle in Europe, we can help them to prefer a patient cultural revolution (ibid., p. 48).

Conclusion

African women's presence in Rome during the 1970s indicated a growing demand for their labour as live-in domestic workers, with their employment, when structured through legal channels, premised on the unavailability of Italian labour. Nonetheless the existence of a parallel recruitment channel in the undocumented sector exposed these women to highly exploitative working conditions. The power of the employer reigned supreme and the weakness of the trade unions in relation to domestic workers certainly did not help. In short, a combination of variables conspired to perpetuate their disadvantaged situation. Firstly, a conceptualisation of their presence as contractual migrant labour accentuated their primary labour function. Secondly, their location within an employment sector which was peripheral to the concerns of the trade union movement. Thirdly, the cultural development of the sector had been overly influenced by the prevalent ideology of Italy's Catholic subculture.

It was an ideology which encouraged domestic workers to internalise their roles as akin to motherhood, thus minimalising their status as workers. Finally, but certainly more difficult to quantify, was the racialised inferiorisation of migrant women which contributed to their poor treatment by employers.

Predictably, the greater attention paid to the general issue of migration in the 1980s would have implications for African women. The new awareness about immigration provided an opportunity to resolve migrant women's social invisibility and the problems connected to this. As Francesca (interview 9) stated: 'In the 1970s, we worked day and night, we were like slaves'. To what extent then, would greater awareness as well as improvements in the domestic work sector transform the conditions of African women's presence in Rome?

Notes

1   A national study published by ECAP-CGIL in collaboration with Rome University in 1979 epitomised how difficult it was to define the phenomenon during this period. The statistics provided appear impossibly contradictory and inaccurate. An example is the study's estimation of the size of the major ethnic groups present in Italy. The table produced presents the figures in terms of minimum and maximum estimations. Thus, the Cape Verdean community was estimated to be at a minimum of 6,000 and a maximum of 22,000. Likewise the Ethiopian community was estimated at between approximately 12,000 and 43,000. See Figure 2 of ECAP-CGIL (1979, p. 15).

2   For some more journalistic reports on immigration to the region, see *L'Unità*, 2 September 1977; *Il Messaggero*, 4 September 1977; *Paese Sera*, 13 September 1977.

3   See Bakan and Stasiulis (1995) for an excellent article demonstrating how the construction of ethnic hierarchies within the domestic work sector is frequently mediated by domestic placement agencies. This means that these agencies do not only control the employment of minority women but also have an influential role in determining the inception of migratory movements from specific countries.

4   See Orsi's (1987) paper on the stereotypical media representations of Black women in Italy.

5   Unione Sindacale Italiana lavoratori Domestici.

6   Cited in De Paz (1976b).

7   Ibid.

8   This view of domestic work as a temporary occupation has long historical roots. In her paper on domestic workers in Rome in the mid-nineteenth century, Margherita Pelaja (1988, p. 498) demonstrates how domestic workers perceived their work as 'a transitory solution, the first stage of a career ... a bit of work as a servant and then marriage ...'. However, although this vision of domestic work was also present in the post-war period, there were Italian women who would continue working as live-in domestics until retirement.

9   See De Paz (1976a) and (1978) for examples of recruitment via clerical channels.

10 For a more detailed discussion of this see Beccalli (1985); Del Boca (1988) and Bettio (1988c).

11 'Le Colf nella società e nel Movimento Operaio', VIII Assemblea congressuale nazionale, Siena 1973, p. 2.

12 'Le Colf nella società e nel Movimento Operaio', VIII Assemblea congressuale nazionale, Siena 1973, p. 2.

13 Although the association had committed itself to this national survey at its important 1973 congress precisely because it had begun to recognise the presence of overseas domestic labour, in the event, these women were excluded from the study. This omission is accounted for in the introduction to the survey: 'Our study has not taken into account a phenomenon which is of growing significance: that of coloured [sic] domestic workers. We are fully aware of this limitation; nevertheless, we preferred to postpone the analysis of an issue which presents very specific aspects to a subsequent study ...' (Turrini 1977, p. 34).

14 The results of this survey were presented in an edited report by the sociologist Olga Turrini in 1977. The publication was entitled 'Reserve Housewives'.

15 Even during the inter-war years, an inferior ranking was ascribed to domestic service. In explaining the lure of the city for rural Italian women, De Grazia (1992, p. 184) states 'At worst, they could hire out as maids'. Willson's (1993) study of female factory workers before and during the second world war also showed that domestic service was seen as an inferior option to the principal employment opportunities available to women in the area at the time – factory work and dressmaking. The inferior status conferred on domestic work is replicated in studies dealing with other national contexts. For example, in the case of African-American Southern migrants, Hine (1990, p. 293) states: 'A factory worker, even one whose work was dirty and low status, could and did imagine herself better off than domestic servants who endured the unrelenting scrutiny, interference, and complaints of household mistresses and the untoward advances of male family members.

16 This also emerges in other studies of domestic work carried out in the United States. The psycho-sociological study of African-American domestic workers by Judith Rollins (1985) revealed that workers managed to retain a sense of self-worth despite their employment as domestic workers. Hine (1990, p. 294) goes so far as to state that Black women developed a culture of dissemblance to protect the 'sanctity of inner aspects of their lives' by creating the appearance of disclosure.

17 For example, despite evidence of consistent migration from the South to the Centre and North for domestic work, Cutrufelli's analysis of women's working situation in the South failed to consider paid domestic work. In her section dealing with Southern migration and women, the emphasis is on migration to other European countries, and the employment niche discussed focuses on factory work. Similarly, the section on domestic work concentrates on the unpaid domestic work of women. See Cutrufelli (1975).

18 See the opening speech of Carla Faccincani on this point at the 1970 national congress. 'La condizione della categoria e dell'organizzazione sulla soglia degli anni 70'. Relazione organizzativa: delle realizzazioni e delle lacune dei Gruppi ACLI-COLF, tenuta al VII Congresso Nazionale dalla Segretaria Nazionale Carla Faccincani.

19 Ministero del Lavoro, Circolare n. 37/106/III, Rome 30 December 1972 'Nuova procedura per la concessione della autorizzazione al lavoro in favore dei lavoratori stranieri addetti ai servizi domestici'.

20 Ibid.

21 Ministero del Lavoro, Circolare n. 38/107/III, Rome, 25 June 1973 'Impiego in Italia dei lavoratori subordinati stranieri. Disposizioni integrative'.

22 See Ministero degli Affari Esteri, Circolare n. 22, Rome, 8 May 1973 'Nuove procedure per l'autorizzazione al lavoro di stranieri, non cittadini di Paesi C.E.E., addetti ai servizi domestici'.

23 Ministero del Lavoro, Circolare n. 7/122/II, Rome, 21 July 1975 'Mediazione abusiva di mano d'opera straniera addetta ai servizi domestici (Art. 2 legge 2 April 1958, n. 339)'.

24 Ministero del Lavoro e della Previdenza Sociale, Circolare n. 140/90/79 del 7–12–1979, 'Ingresso ed impiego in Italia di cittadini stranieri extracomunitari da adibire ai servizi domestici'.

25 Ibid.

26 See facsimile of application forms included with circular n. 140/90/79 (allegato 1).

27 Ibid.

28 See CGIL-CISL-UIL di Roma e del Lazio (1982).

29 See Circular 140/90/79, Allegato 4.

30 However, a number of testimonies reveal that employers would subsequently deduct this money from the salaries of migrant domestic workers. See De Lourdes and Pimental (1989) and the testimony of Mota in Caritas Diocesana di Roma (1989) for two examples.

31 Margarita (interview 8), from Cape Verde, found employment in this way. She reported that her documents were placed at police headquarters, an Italian family saw a picture of her and selected her for employment.

32 These guidelines were motivated by the urgent necessity to introduce legislation which would regulate immigration comprehensively. See Ministero del Lavoro e della Previdenza Sociale, Documento di Lavoro, Rome, 9 February 1981, 'L'impiego dei lavoratori stranieri in Italia'.

33 Ibid.

34 Ibid.

35 The INPS collates data regarding workers registered for social security purposes.

36 Tuscany, Umbria, the Marche, Abruzzi and Molise.

37 These statistics are cited in Sacconi (1984).

38 See for example Perotta (1988, p. 64), for his comparison of the different estimates of the size of the Cape Verdean community in Rome. Although the average estimate hovered around 5,000, other sources put forward quite different estimates.

39 This data is cited in Korsieporn (1991).

40 These statistics are cited in ECAP-CGIL (1980).

41 Portugal had been an important outlet for migrants from Cape Verde because of the colonial relationship which existed between the two countries until 1975, when Cape Verde gained its independence.

42 Testimony of Cape Verdean female worker, reproduced *ad verbatim* in Caritas diocesana di Roma (1989), pp. 179–80.

43 Testimony of Eritrean female worker, reproduced *ad verbatim* in Caritas diocesana di Roma (1989), p. 123.

44 Ibid., p. 125. An Eritrean intervention at a round table discussion on immigration, held in Rome in 1990, demonstrated exasperation at Italians' ignorance of its ex-colonies: 'It is disgraceful that [Italians] don't know where Eritrea is, where Somalia is. It is disgraceful for Italians, 70 years of colonialism, 100 years of life together and they don't know geographically where Eritrea is. We are not from Sri Lanka, with all due respect, nor from Nigeria, or from the Ivory Coast. These people have, with all due respect, ... just arrived in Italy. But ... our grandfathers, our great grandfathers paid with their lives for Italy, in its

dirty colonial wars, when they went to fight to occupy Libya, Somalia and Ethiopia. Our grandfathers died wearing Italian uniforms, not Eritrean ones (Tavola Rotonda 1990).

45 Testimony of Eritrean female worker, reproduced *ad verbatim* in Caritas diocesana di Roma (1989), p. 125.

46 This family strategy was seen to have been successful by both Lemlem and her brother. When I interviewed him, he was studying for a first degree at the University of Rome and working part-time at a residential home.

47 This would mean that the Italian employer would undertake to provide the air ticket for the domestic worker to come to Italy.

48 The ECAP-CGIL (1980) study claimed that 50 per cent of the Cape Verdeans present in Lazio (essentially Rome) had entered Italy without a proper employment contract. However it is not clear on what basis they make this calculation.

49 The ECAP-CGIL (1980) study noted that in approximately 50 per cent of cases, employment contracts were not renewed. This could mean that even in those cases where the employment contract was initially properly regulated, employers could refuse to renew it, and facing repatriation (see circular 140/90.79) foreign workers would agree to work without a contract.

50 Salaries appeared to be much higher in Milan. One of the Cape Verdean women interviewed in Rotterdam had migrated to Milan in 1971 with a contract. She started on L190,000, which rose to L100,000 after six months and L110,000 after nine months. Her cousin working in Rome at the same time, was earning L50,000. She eventually found a job for her in Milan where her salary more than doubled to L120,000.

51 See Appendix 3, *Il Messaggero*, 2 February 1967.

52 See Appendix 3, *Il Messaggero*, 3 February 1977.

53 Ibid.

54 Italian employers recruiting from Cape Verde would send money for the airline ticket and for the young women to obtain a passport via the Italian consulate. One of the women I interviewed in Rotterdam had a contract which stipulated her salary at L50,000 in 1972. However, her employers did not subsequently pay her for three months, because of their expenditure for the air ticket. They did eventually start to pay her but only paid half the agreed amount (L25,000 monthly).

55 It should be noted that when I asked interviewees what work they did in Italy, their response frequently indicated that there could only be one response to such a question. In other words, the women themselves saw their work as being uniformly organised.

56 Even when domestic workers were employed by a married couple it was normally the female employer who structured and managed their work. Domestic workers therefore had a more direct relationship with the female employer. See also testimony of another Eritrean domestic worker who stated: '... in the interviews which we did [on a language course] we were asked: with whom did you have more difficulty, men or women. Many replied: the woman, because she is always with you ... while the man is never at home'. See *ad verbatim* interview published in Caritas Diocesana di Roma (1989, p. 131).

57 *Ad verbatim* interview reproduced in Caritas Diocesana di Roma (1989:, p. 130).

58 Although the experiences of Filipina domestic workers lie beyond the scope of this study, it is worth highlighting that abuse of the national contract in terms of pay and working hours was cited as a feature of their conditions.

59 It would seem comparisons between employers' treatment of their dogs and their treatment of domestic workers has historically been used as a benchmark of the status of domestic workers. In the early twentieth century one parlourmaid stated: 'I think in our days dogs

are far better treated than human beings as we are not allowed to use the bath, but in my last situation four dogs were bathed weekly and my share of the bath was to keep it clean after them', (*The Guardian*, 28 May 1913). The housemaid Lavinia Swainbank, however, was fastidious enough to prefer to have a hip bath in her room when she discovered that the dogs were bathed in the family bath. See her autobiography in Burnett (1977, p. 223).

60   17.5 per cent of these disputes involved Cape Verdeans, 6 per cent involved Ethiopians. The majority involved Filipina women (47 per cent). See 'La Federcolf e le Colf estere' in *Le Colf*, February 1983, p. 7.

61   The intervention was that of Prof. Alberto Benzoni, responsible for civil rights within the Italian Socialist Party (ibid., p. 60).

62   A similar perspective was expounded by Alfredo Zolla, a representative of the CGIL. See CGIL-CISL-UIL di Roma e del Lazio (1982), pp. 85–7.

63   At the first conference held on 4 march 1982, the migrant representatives were from Eritrea, Tigray (Ethiopia), the Philippines and Cape Verde. At the second round table discussion held on 29 April 1982, the only intervention from migrants was from the Cape Verdean community.

64   See CGIL-CISL-UIL di Roma e del Lazio (1982).

65   See OMCVI (1989).

66   The methodology used by the API-COLF for the survey referred to by Crippa is not presented, thus the scale of the survey cannot be ascertained. The survey was, however, based on interviews carried out throughout the national territory.

67   In this publication Crippa (1979, p. 27) interprets the presence of migrant labour as a combination of push and pull factors: '… it's a fact that 'the hunger for domestic workers' which is apparent in Italy in Employment offices, at least when it comes to the unobtainable live-in workers, coincides with a hunger for jobs and a means to survive for thousands of migrant girls'.

68   See ibid., pp. 33–7.

6   Transformation and Change

The previous chapter addressed the situation of African women in Rome at a time when immigration had yet to acquire social and political visibility at the national level. In the 1970s, both an unofficial laissez-faire approach and a particular construction of migrant women's roles contained in government circulars could be identified. Both constructions gave weight to migrant women's labour function. The 1980s provided an opportunity to challenge this construction and to facilitate the establishment of a model for migrant women which would not simply approximate existing national gender models but which could accommodate the specificity of Black female migrants' interlocking social identities.

In the first section of this chapter, I demonstrate that the demand for migrant women's labour continued into the 1980s and early 1990s. This demand can be attributed principally to Italy's changing family structure. This did not mean that Italian family cohesiveness, as discussed in chapter 1, was lost. Rather, it began to assume new and different forms. Further insight into the domestic work relationship is also provided in the first section of this chapter, through a discussion of the working experiences of African women in Rome. I address the contractual regulation of the domestic work sphere to highlight the enduring structural problems of the sector and to examine the specific impact these had on migrant women. My argument here, is that during the 1980s and early 1990s, domestic work remained the principal employment sector for migrant women and that the particular difficulties of live-in work encouraged some African women to aspire to, and in some cases actually accomplish, further onward migration to other industrially advanced countries. In the second half of the chapter I examine the voluntary and institutional response to migrant women's conditions in Rome. Here, it is argued that these organisations concurred with the segmentation of the Italian labour market in relation to migrant women. The nature of their attempts to open up new avenues of employment to migrant women were influenced by a general awareness of strong demand in the domestic work sector. These attempts were further hampered by the logistic difficulties of employment training for single migrant women whose need to earn an income is essential.

143

Supply And Demand

In the 1980s and early 1990s, although some women were able to make the transition to hourly paid work, the demand for Black women's labour remained strong in the live-in sector of domestic work. Several of my key informants attributed this demand for live-in labour to the absence of adequate social services provision:

> [Live-in employment] covered a series of needs which the state had never been in a position to cover and was increasingly unable to, such as the care of the elderly and children. These were things which Italian women, who, at this stage were participating fully in the labour market, were no longer able to do (interview, ACLI-COLF).

The CELSI-CGIL[1] key informant echoed these sentiments:

> I must keep coming back to my view that the domestic work situation in Italy and above all in Rome derives from the poor management ... of social services. Often an Italian woman or family, if they have elderly parents, cannot look after them alone. They have to turn to a domestic worker. Then, however, the worker is no longer a domestic but a care assistant for the elderly.

While, in the 1970s, African women were mainly working for families with young children or simply wealthy families, in the 1980s, their employment as live-in workers to care for the elderly appeared to be on the increase. The key informant at the YWCA women migrants' project (see below) confirmed that employers' requests at her office were largely to organise care for the elderly:

> We function a little like an employment office, in the sense that the families know us, call us and ask for domestic help. Essentially the demand is for elderly people, thus live-in assistance, including nocturnal assistance (interview, YWCA).

This demand is consistent with contemporary demographic trends in Italy. According to Dell'Orto and Taccani (1993, p. 113):

> Whereas the old [65+] overall have doubled in absolute numbers, and almost doubled as a percentage of the whole during the last forty years, the old-old [75+] have tripled both in absolute numbers and in percentage terms during the same period.

The question of care is closely related to these demographic changes. In their research on aging in Italy, Zanatta and Mirabile (1993) do not consider the use of paid domestic workers to care for the elderly. They do note, however, that the number of old people living in residential homes is very low[2] and argue that the tendency to live alone and independently is becoming widespread amongst Italy's elderly population. However, where elderly people need care, the responsibility normally falls to daughters. These women can be described as epitomising the 'sandwich generation' of women: '... who are busy on both fronts caring for their growing children and their aging parents' (p. 56).[3] With the decline in the number of full-time housewives available to provide full-time care to elderly family members, the domestic worker can theoretically function as a surrogate family member. Family members can pool resources as an expression of shared responsibility for elderly relatives and to neutralise the financial implications of providing such assistance. Sara (interview 26) for example, was employed by four sisters to care for their elderly mother. The ACLI-COLF key informant, in citing her own personal circumstances, indicated a similar family arrangement:

> ... we were forced ... we have a very elderly grandmother. So, I, my sister, my cousin together we managed to do it, even though the cost is not low if you employ someone properly ... however, perhaps in two or three, ... it can be done.

Despite the demand for their labour, migrant women were unable to radically transform the structural organisation of the domestic work sector. Despite some of the objective advantages of live-in work, evidence from interviewees suggests that African women would have preferred hourly paid work had it been easily available and once the problems contingent to hourly paid work could be resolved. The YWCA representative confirmed this:

> Usually they find live-in work. I must say that they would all prefer to work on an hourly paid basis, because live-in work clearly brings a series of problems with it, such as a lack of free time ... Unfortunately however, the demand is higher for live-in work.

The UDE key informant depicted a similar scenario in relation to Eritrean women:

> The work for female domestics is very heavy because they work every day, especially if they are live-in ... it's not that they work for eight hours. They are

also tired of living in the house, of sleeping and working in the same place, because they have no free time. They would also like to work on an hourly paid basis, but they cannot find accommodation, so they are forced to work as live-in workers.

Hourly paid work constituted a feasible option only for those migrants who had been working in Rome for a considerable amount of time. Thus, an established group such as the Cape Verdean community was eventually able to penetrate the hourly paid market. Many of the Cape Verdean women interviewed had made the transition to hourly paid work. In fact, the OMCVI key informant described the contemporary working situation of the Cape Verdean community as being overwhelmingly on an hourly paid basis:

> It is now extremely difficult to find Cape Verdean women employed as live-in workers. They want their independence. It's obvious, because the needs of a Cape Verdian women are the same as those of an Italian woman, there's absolutely no difference. They want a family, children, a husband, etc.

This did not entirely correlate with my own evidence, where I encountered Cape Verdean women who, despite migrating in the 1970s, were still working as live-in domestic workers in the 1990s. Indeed, even those Cape Verdean women working on an hourly paid basis, made reference to friends or relatives who were still employed within the live-in sector. Moreover, recent arrivals would always commence within the live-in sphere. Maria (interview 4), for example, migrated to Rome in the late 1980s and immediately found work as a live-in worker. The job had been organised by her brother who was already living in Rome. She liked the family who treated her 'like a daughter' and she was regularly employed by this family for two years. She left only because of the arrival of her partner to Italy. Again, she found new employment immediately. She remembered that she left the first family on the 19 May and found a new job on the 27 May working as a live-in couple with her partner. Thus within only eight days she had secured subsequent employment. As she herself stated: 'it is easy for Cape Verdian women to find domestic work'.

The shift to the hourly paid sector exposed African women to employment vulnerability. This sector is characterised by greater competition as Italian nationals also engage in domestic work on an hourly paid basis. Indeed, migrant women were considered to be at a disadvantage within this sector:

> It's more likely that an Italian woman will have her home and her family etc. ...
> She can recycle herself, organising work with two or three families, and knows

the appropriate rates. These things are much more difficult for a migrant domestic worker … (interview, ACLI-COLF).

In addition to the advantages that Italian nationals appeared to enjoy within the hourly paid sector of domestic work, migrant women were further disadvantaged by any economic instability in the country. This is because an economic crisis not only affects the sector in terms of lessening demand for domestic workers, but it also swells the number of women who offer their labour as domestic workers. Referring to the economic crisis of the early 1990s, the ACLI-COLF representative stated 'at present [domestic workers] are going through a considerable crisis, because right now there is a general employment crisis, so they are the first to lose their jobs'. This was also highlighted by the AS, CDR representative: '… especially now that Italy is going through a period of economic difficulty, there are many people who are giving up their hourly paid domestic worker'. These assertions were borne out by the testimony of Rosa (interview 3) who had been working in Italy since 1973. Having worked on a live-in basis for eight years, she had subsequently continued to do domestic work, but on an hourly paid basis. She stated that she had never encountered any difficulty in finding work. However, she noted that more recently several Italian families had begun to dispense with the services of their domestic employees, and she expressed some concern about her own future economic stability. Abeba (interview 17) also felt that in recent years it had become more difficult to find hourly paid work but she attributed this to the higher number of migrants living in the city.

Evidence from interviewees indicate that a range of factors affected women's ability to make the shift from live-in to hourly paid work. The desire to live as a family unit with their children was frequently a decisive factor. This was easier if women's partners were also working in Rome, but was difficult for women who were actually or effectively single parents while in Rome.[4] Affordable accommodation was a major impediment in managing this transition. Aster (interview 13) wanted to do hourly paid work, because although she had a 'normal' relationship with her employer, she did not like living in the same house with her. However, she saw the provision of accommodation as the crucial advantage of live-in work. Even where women had moved to independent living accommodation, the accommodation was rarely considered to be satisfactory. If women had wider obligations, the decision to shift to hourly paid work had to be made very carefully because of the implicit insecurity of such work. The financial implications of doing hourly paid work did not relate simply to women's domestic situation in Italy. Often external family obligations imposed major burdens of expenditure. When I asked Filomena (interview 22) why she did not try to do hourly paid work she responded: 'I won't be able to make ends meet. Rents are too high and we also have to help our relatives in Cape Verde'. Hourly paid work, moreover, lends itself well to casual employment and this may have contributed to migrant women's difficulties in obtaining or choosing to work in this sector.

Unpublished data from the INPS reproduced in the tables below indicate that Rome had the highest number of both Italian and migrant domestic workers. These figures only represent a partial view of the phenomenon as they concern only those employees for whom employers pay insurance contributions. Thus comparative figures for different towns (Table 6.1) may also be an indication of the extent to which domestic workers are employed in the undocumented sphere. The low figures for Bologna may suggest that good service provision can lead to a different organisation of reproductive care. The data disaggregated by age (Table 6.2) suggests quite convincingly that the trend has been towards a greater involvement of migrant women in the sector. The older cohorts show a dominance of Italian women, while new and younger entrants to the sector are predominantly migrant women. Table 6.3 indicates the numbers of hours worked by domestic workers. Given that more migrant women work in the live-in sector, one would expect a higher proportion of them to be represented in the higher categories of hours worked. Two interpretations can be offered for this. Firstly, this may again be an indication of migrant women's presence in the undocumented sphere. Alternatively, it may reflect a practice current amongst some employers to pay contributions for a minimum number of hours to reduce their costs. This works to the disadvantage of migrant women in terms of the eventual pension they will receive, but is sometimes accepted by women to secure employment in the legal sphere and to earn higher wages in the short-term.

Table 6.1   Number of domestic workers registered at the INPS in four cities

	Italians	Migrants
Rome	17,593	17,565
Milan	11,229	9,062
Naples	7,534	3,031
Bologna	3,397	1,474

Table 6.2   Number of domestic workers registered at the INPS in Rome by age

Age	Italians	Migrants
Up to 20	47	37
21–25	485	982
26–30	1,107	2,851
31–40	2,924	7,543
41–50	5,287	4,512
51–60	6,602	1,424
61–65	872	149
Above 65	269	67

Table 6.3   Number of domestic workers registered at the INPS in Rome by hours worked per week

Hours	Italians	Migrants
Up to 10	6,081	5,975
11–20	5,053	5,067
21–30	3,701	3,700
31–40	1,305	1,236
41–50	1,033	1,084
Above 50	420	503

Source: unpublished data, *Osservatorio sul lavoro domestic*, INPS 1993.

Circular 156/91

The most telling evidence of the national demand for migrant domestic workers is contained in a circular issued by the Ministry of Labour in 1991. The ministerial circulars discussed in the previous chapter were issued at a time when popular and state attention to the issue of immigration was limited and when there was no obvious national strategy regarding the regulation of immigration. By 1991, the sociopolitical situation was radically different. The two legislative acts of 1986 and 1990 symbolised the restrictive direction of the Italian state in relation to immigration (see chapter 2). It is therefore of some significance that only one year after the 1990 Martelli law, a government circular created special provisions for new entries to Italy for domestic work.[5]

The growing attention paid to the issue of immigration from the mid to late 1980s had affected the domestic work sector. In view of the amnesties included in both the 1986 and 1990 legislation, the Ministry of Labour had suspended new authorisations for domestic workers from outside the country. On the 3 March 1990, circular n. 31/90 had confirmed this bar on new authorisations. However, the 1991 circular indicated that the live-in domestic service sector was buoyant:

> ... the need to remove the abovementioned block and to permit new entries of non-Ec migrants who want to work in the domestic work sector has been a request from several quarters (Public Administration, public and private bodies, trade union bodies, including those participating in the consultative body addressing the problem of non-Ec workers). This is also because currently there seems to be a real lack of Italian workers, Ec workers and non-Ec workers legally resident in Italy, who are prepared to work in this sector (Circular 156/91).

The 1991 circular thus permitted the authorisation of new entries from abroad. The provision was exclusively for live-in work. Overseas workers could not be employed for less than 40 hours a week and the employer was under an obligation to provide appropriate accommodation. The provision tied both employer and employee together for a period of two years. It was the employer's responsibility to ensure that the domestic worker did not engage in employment other than that for which a permit had been granted. Home Office data for the period to September 1992 showed that in this nine-month period there were 22,800 authorisations for such work.[6]

There are several important points to be drawn from the issuing of circular 156 in 1991. Firstly, this circular can be seen as irrefutable evidence of a very real demand for migrant women's labour. Secondly, the emerging consensus towards restrictive policies which had begun to permeate national legislation was clearly not applicable to the specific constituency of domestic workers.[7] Domestic workers did not seem to embody either an economic or a cultural threat. Finally, the organisation of migrant women's labour as contractual migrant labour constituted an explicit construction of the employer/employee relationship as one approximating a form of unfree labour.

Working Conditions in The 1980s and 1990s

Network migration continued to have an important recruitment function in the 1980s and 1990s. Virtually all of the women interviewed had migrated to

Rome because of the prior presence of a relative or friend. In most cases, these friends or relatives organised their employment. This contributed to Black women's restriction to the domestic work sphere as women's contacts would naturally be within this sphere of employment. The motives for women's migration remained similar. In the case of Cape Verdean women, economic factors were the principal motivating cause. In the case of East African women, war and its contingent economic problems frequently forced women to consider migration.

In the 1980s and 1990s, women were still migrating to Rome because of the security of finding work or to be near other relatives. Alex (interview 20) had first migrated to Athens from Eritrea. She had worked in Greece as a domestic worker and found her employment experience in Rome and Athens to be quite similar. However, she moved to Rome in 1987 because she had more relatives living there. Filomena (interview 22) migrated to Rome in 1987, having lived in Portugal for 10 years. She had been working in a clothing factory in Lisbon, but the salary was extremely low. A friend of hers in Lisbon had migrated to Italy and organised a job for her. She had heard that jobs for women were easily available in Rome and thus considered this to be a good move.

However the demand for migrant women's labour did not guarantee a favourable working environment. Where employment conditions were favourable, Black women exhibited remarkably high levels of employment stability.[8] Elena (interview 23) had been employed by the same family since migrating to Italy in 1976 when she was 21 years old. Her stable employment background was indicative of the correct treatment she had received in this family. Her employers (a lawyer and a housewife) had two children. The work had become less onerous as the children in the family had grown up and her employers had taken on additional help which lightened her work load: 'Before the work was heavier. Now a man comes to help with the cleaning. Also, previously I used to always have to serve at the table, whilst now often they eat from the trolley'. Despite the fact that Elena described her employers as being like a family to her, she still articulated a desire to live by herself: 'I would like to get a little house and live by myself and maybe work as a seamstress. But when I say that I want to go off and live by myself, they just don't want to hear it'. Strong reciprocal emotional ties had clearly been established, but the live-in aspect of the work still made Elena dream of moving out. Gabriele (interview 25) who migrated in 1972 had been employed by her current employers for 18 years and had in fact only changed employers twice since coming to Rome. Women seemed to judge good treatment as being related to employers' observation of contractual obligations and the treatment of their workers as human beings. Thus Filomena (interview 22), who had a particularly bad initial employment experience, expressed her satisfaction with her current employers for whom she had been working for the last five years:

> Where I am now it is completely different. I cannot find fault with them [my employers]. I have been really happy in the last five years. I can go out during my daily rest period. I can go to the cinema. I am free on a Thursday afternoon and on Sundays. They even let me out in the afternoon because I'm learning how to drive.

Women sometimes changed employers not necessarily because of poor treatment but because the job was particularly onerous. Gabriele (interview 25) stayed with her first family for six years. Her employers had seven children and were both employed. This meant that her workload was especially heavy: 'I left because I was tired. In the end there were 12 of us and I was doing everything. But for me it was like being in a family. I still have a very good relationship with them'. Sara (interview 26) worked for an elderly woman of ninety who was completely dependent on her. She couldn't walk by herself and had to be fed. Sara worked extremely long hours. She was up at 7.00am and didn't finish working until 11.00 at night. On her day off she would be replaced by a nurse who also assisted her in the mornings. Nonetheless, her workload was substantial because of the incapacity of the woman she was employed to care for. These examples indicate the circumstantial factors which exacerbate Black women's working conditions. However there were many instances where difficult working conditions were a direct result of the employers' own volition.

Some employers attempted to impose quite unacceptable demands on their employees. These did not relate simply to their employment tasks. There were other means by which employers sought to control domestic workers. Naturally, women would normally seek to change employer in these circumstances, but this was not always a straightforward process, especially if they were undocumented workers. Some women endured extreme forms of exploitation and abuse. When Filomena (interview 22) moved from Lisbon to Rome she encountered severe problems with her 62 year old employer – a housewife in a wealthy family:

> I had a lot of difficulties in the early days because the *signora* treated me so badly. She used to play spiteful tricks on me. She treated me so badly. She used to make me kneel down to clean. She treated me as if I were a thing, an animal.

The family employed three gardeners but they only paid me L500,000 per month whilst all other domestics were earning L900,000. She used to make me work until 5.00pm on a Thursday. I wasn't allowed to eat until 3.30 in the afternoon – once I almost fainted. I did not have my daily rest hours, they did not let me out of the house. When cleaning the floor I had to change the water every two metres. In the end I had a nervous breakdown. I only just managed not to go completely mad.

Alex (interview 20) also eventually changed from her first employer: '... because the work was heavy and my employers were horrible and the salary was low'. Almaz's case (interview 15) represented an extreme example of exploitation. An Ethiopian, she had previously migrated to Sudan where she had been employed as a domestic worker. She had moved to Italy with her Sudanese employers, having worked for them in the Sudan for three and a half years. At the time of interview, she had only been in Rome for 10 months and did not have proper documents. She recounted how hard she was being made to work, looking after two children and doing all the cooking and cleaning. She was not given a day off or any holidays and generally worked from 7.30am to 9.30pm. The level of exploitation could be seen in the salary that was paid to her. This was L250,000 monthly at a time when other women I interviewed were earning between L1,000,000 and L1,200,000. Her employers additionally attempted to confine her to the house. This, she felt, was to prevent her from having access to other people and making comparisons with other people's employment conditions. It was clear that she was tolerating her situation only because of her undocumented status. She felt that she would not find alternative employment because of this.[9] Undocumented employment and the threat of expulsion could thus be used to impose excessive forms of exploitation. One evening at the Tra Noi association, several women spoke to me of the case of a young woman.[10] She had migrated to Rome two years earlier, leaving two young children behind in Cape Verde. She was irregularly employed as a live-in worker. The family for whom she worked had not paid her for the last seven months. As one woman said to me: 'They really are treating her like a slave'. This young woman was terrified of the implications of her undocumented status. She was continuing to work and live with this family hoping that they would eventually pay her. Undocumented work was thus clearly a means through which employers could easily exploit domestic workers. As one of the Cape Verdean interviewees stated:

You do not have a life in Italy because you are always dependent on others. These things should be exposed. There are those working illegally, those who do not have enough to eat, those who are not being paid their wages. This is a crime. As soon as they know that you don't have any documents the exploitation is worse (Filomena, interview 22).

Women would in fact frequently change jobs to acquire or ensure legal status. Antonia (interview 16) for example, could not remember how many times she had changed employers. Her longest period of employment stability had been for four years and her shortest had been for two days. Her principal motivation for changing jobs was in order to be regularised, however employment conditions even where she was regularly employed would also inform her decision as to whether to change employer. She had found the family with whom she stayed for only two days unacceptable because her room was very small to the point that it made her feel claustrophobic. She also did not like the attitude of her employers and sensed their desire to impose a rigid and exploitative work schedule. She walked out after two days without being paid. On another occasion, potential employers (two doctors) had offered to pay her a salary of L1,200,000 but they did not want to pay any insurance contributions. She refused and eventually they agreed to pay the minimum contributions (i.e. as if she were only employed for 25 hours weekly). However, once she had moved in they stopped paying her contributions. On top of this, she was expected to do everything in the house. Her working day would start when their little girl awoke at dawn. She had no rest period because she had to look after the little girl all day. She found this very tiring as she was on her feet all day and consequently left this employment after a relatively short period. She stayed at a friend's house temporarily, doing some hourly paid work until she could find another live-in job. It is clear that Antonia was only able to 'walk out' of jobs in this way because she had access to a network of friends who were living independently. Their homes could thus constitute a temporary base while she secured better employment. For those women who did not have such networks, it was clearly more difficult to change employer.

Employers' control was also imposed in other ways. Their establishment of certain general rules impacted on women's lives in specific ways. At the time of interview Antonia (interview 16) was employed by a 66 year-old semi-retired female professional. Her employer had never married and had no children. On the whole, Antonia was quite happy there, as she found it easier to work for just one person. One problem that she did articulate was her employer's requirement that she return home by midnight on her days off. As Antonia said: 'Either I take no notice or else it really gets on my nerves because I don't see why I can't come home when I want. I'm 38 years old and have a

21 year-old son but you always remain a child here'. Emma (interview 27), who had migrated to Rome when she was 46 confirmed this attitude saying that employers always spoke to you as if you were a child.

I gained some insight into the nature of employers' control as a result of the qualitative methodological approach adopted for this study. Apart from the general tendency among the women I interviewed to project a commonality of experience for domestic workers, women were also reluctant to give me friends' phone numbers because they were normally not permitted to receive many phone calls. When phone numbers were passed to me, I was frequently given very clear indications as to when to phone. This was not normally related to when I would find the domestic worker at home, but rather to when the phone call would give the least disturbance to their employers.

The question of employers' control is of course intrinsically connected to the question of migrant women's autonomy. The interview process shed some light on this. Although live-in workers have their own room, it was clear that even on their days off they normally could not bring people 'home'.[11] As well as interviewing women at the various meeting places of their communities, I also interviewed live-in workers in cafés near their places of work. On one occasion, Tanha (interview 18), who appeared to have a wide degree of autonomy in running the home, invited me to the house when the employers were out. She was free enough to show me around her employers' apartment in Parioli and to offer me coffee and a croissant.[12] In stark contrast to this, when I went to meet another interviewee she was accompanied by her employer. I want to recount this encounter as it reveals much about the types of relationship that can be established between employers and their employees.

I was given Elsa's (interview 19) telephone number by a contact, with strict instructions not to phone at an inappropriate time. Thus I was advised to phone at around ten in the morning or around six in the evening. Elsa seemed very happy to do the interview and we arranged that on the day of the appointment I would go to the main square near her place of employment and call her from there. When I did call, her employer (male) answered the phone. He seemed to know that she had been expecting my call and said 'she will come down shortly'. It was to my great surprise then, when he appeared with her, stating: 'I am her employer. I am a magistrate'.[13]

The interview was conducted entirely in his presence. In fact he took us to a spacious bar where we were able to sit together and where he offered us tea. I must stress that this was a Sunday afternoon, a time when all regularly employed domestic workers are supposed to be free. The employer's presence at this interview was undoubtedly intrusive. I initially focused my questions on Elsa's reasons for migrating and addressed her earlier employment experiences. She seemed quite prepared to fully answer questions regarding these earlier experiences, informing me of how much she earned, how she was treated and how much she had to pay for her son to stay in a residential home. For example, she told me that she earned L300,000 monthly in her first job in 1980. However, when I asked her what her current salary was, there was an embarrassed silence and her employer intervened saying: 'She does not want to reply to this question'. There were other occasions where her employer would 'summarise' what he thought Elsa was trying to express to me as he felt that she was not being linguistically concise. Although I will be dealing with the issue of domestic work and family life in the next chapter, I want to highlight Elsa's family situation to indicate how the different positioning of employer and employee leads to dual and contrasting perspectives over the same issues.

Since arriving in 1980 with a son aged one, Elsa has been consistently employed as a live-in worker. During this time her son has lived almost exclusively in residential homes. For the first eight months of her stay in Italy, she paid a private Italian family to care for him. This was organised by her cousin who was already working in Rome. However, the cost of this child-care in relation to her salary was prohibitive. Her employer put her in touch with the Caritas who found her a residential home, situated just outside Rome. The cost was L100,000 monthly. She contributed L30,000 and the Caritas contributed L70,000. The crucial input of the voluntary sector is thus clear. Elsa had been an undocumented worker but she was able to take advantage of the 1986 amnesty to regularise her position. Subsequently, the *Comune* of Rome took on some of the expense for her son's place in a residential home. She was asked to pay L50,000 and after a year this was increased to L100,000. When he was 13, she paid the total expense of L350,000.[14] The response of Elsa and her employer to the situation of her son reveal two quite different perspectives. Elsa, for example focused on the fact that her son had 'practically grown up in residential homes'. Given her financial commitments to other relatives in Eritrea, she did not feel that hourly paid work and independent accommodation were financially viable. Her employer on the other hand, did not attribute importance to the separation of his employee from her son, rather he was concerned to demonstrate the generosity and benevolence of the Italian State/voluntary sector with regard to Elsa, and indeed it was clear that he saw her as privileged in comparison to other migrant workers: 'Let's say that she [Elsa] is the lucky one amongst her compatriots. She is in quite a good position. She is a non-Ec migrant who is happy in Italy. She has been helped in so many ways, Caritas etc.'. With regard to her son he stated: 'Her son has practically grown up in our house. When Elsa went to Eritrea he stayed with us at home'. Unfortunately I was unable to verify this statement with either the son or Elsa herself. Given that the son had stressed the importance of not disturbing the employers when giving his mother's phone number to my contact, the employer's assertion seemed questionable. Also, it was not clear whether the son had been asked to go and *work* for them, while his mother temporarily returned to the country of origin, in order to maintain her job. Despite the contractual obligations of a holiday, one interviewee told me that when she returned from holiday in Cape Verde she had been permanently replaced by someone else.

The encounter with Elsa indicated an excessive amount of intrusion on the part of the employer. Her employer informed me during the interview that Elsa had only agreed to talk to me because she thought I was a journalist and I would therefore constitute a means through which greater publicity could be given to the problems of Eritrea. Elsa did in fact talk at length about Eritrea and the problems of reconstruction after the end of the war. But if this was the case, why was the presence of the employer necessary? In this particular case, the relationship between employer and employee appeared to be marked by deference and paternalism. To what extent Elsa's deference represented an example of Hine's concept of Black women's culture of dissemblance (see chapter 5) is impossible to determine.

Paternalism and benevolence did clearly feature in the relationships between employers and employees. Antonia (interview 16) described this as a false benevolence: 'They tell you that you are one of the family but you should never kid yourself about this. I've worked for many families. I know what they are like. They give you presents and then a few weeks later it will be thrown back into your face'. She recounted that only in one family had she been treated 'normally' and allowed to eat together with them at the table. On the whole, domestic workers would eat separately from their employers. Lemlem (interview 10) told me that she always left her portion in the kitchen before serving the meal, otherwise they would finish the food without thinking that she had to eat too.

Aspects of employers' behaviour could be seen to reflect a vision of employees as dehumanised labour. A clear example of this can be seen in the case of Filomena (interview 22). While her employers were away on holiday in America, her mother died and three days later her sister. Her employers returned from America a week later and subsequently threw a large dinner party (15 people). As Filomena stated:

I just cannot understand the mentality of some Italians. There is no sensitivity … I was crying while serving at the table for that dinner while they were enjoying themselves. Plus, on top of that, they did not even want people to call me at home to offer their condolences'.[15]

This was clearly an example of complete insensitivity on the part of the employers which corroborates the view of those women who felt that employers had a singular interest in their labour function. This implicitly constrained women to a labour identity, negating the expression of a multiplicity of identities.

Women did find ways of rebelling against their subordination. The principal means by which women rejected exploitation was through securing alternative employment. Interestingly, while many were not happy with their employers, their employers were perfectly happy with them. Thus, when Antonia (interview 16) left her employers because she felt the work was too hard, they called the agency which had initially arranged the job to beg her to come back. Although she did not immediately find alternative employment, she preferred temporary insecurity rather than being subjected to exploitation. When Lemlem (interview 10) left the family for whom she had worked for ten years, they also pleaded with her to stay. In fact, they subsequently asked her back to 'train' her successors. Lemlem noted that since she had left they had had a number of different workers, tending to confirm the difficult working conditions that existed in that specific family. As I have argued above, where domestic workers found congenial working conditions they demonstrated a high level of employment stability.

Apart from leaving their employers, Black women would find other ways of circumventing the control of employers. One evening Antonia (interview 16) slipped out at 11.30 at night to go to a club and sneaked back home at six in the morning: 'Every now and again you just have to do this, otherwise you would be really unhappy'. Tanha (interview 18) deflected control by asserting her autonomy: 'I am autonomous, I run things, just because you have fairer skin it does not mean you can boss me around'. With this confidence, it was not surprising that she argued frequently with her male employer: 'He has said that he has never had to argue so much with a maid'. Despite these difficulties, women were still able to construct meaningful relationships with specific members of the family. Thus, although Lemlem had had difficulties with her employers, she spoke very positively about her relationship with their daughter. Others frequently spoke of the fact that they had brought up their employers' children. Gabriele (interview 25) for example said: 'I practically brought them [the children] up'. Lucila (interview 2) spoke of having been practically a mother to the child she was employed to care for.

What emerged from my interviews and the questionnaires completed by Somali women was that no uniformity of behaviour could be attributed to employers. Although the women were extremely critical of those employers who instituted exploitative working schedules, they never failed to recognise and give credit to the genuinely good employers. In resigning themselves to the fact that it would be extremely difficult to move out of the domestic work sphere, they aspired to an improvement in their working conditions. In fact, many of them saw domestic work as an honest profession like any other. Although this seemed to be a fairly consistent view with the Cape Verdeans, there were noticeable generational differences amongst East African women, as we shall now see.

Domestic workers' view of domestic work has some influence on their willingness to seek employment in this sector. As we saw in chapter 5, Italian women's gradual disengagement from the sphere was partly linked to their belief that the sector had a poor reputation. This was frequently internalised by the workers themselves who generally sought to do other work and remained in the domestic work sector only when there were no other available opportunities. It has already been established that Black women have few options outside the domestic work arena, but to what degree did Black women consider domestic work to be humiliating employment?

Antonia (interview 16) indicated a pragmatic response:

> You have to resign yourself to domestic work, they are not going to give you a job in a factory or even to do cleaning in hospitals or nursing. Domestic work is, however, clean and honest work. Italian women do not want to do it so they cannot say that we're stealing work from them. You've got absolutely no chance of getting office work.

Tanha articulated a quite different view, undoubtedly reinforced by her personal circumstances where she had been able to make the transition from live-in work to hourly paid work, but due to unfortunate circumstances was forced back into live in work (see below): 'It is a horrible situation, the work is horrible, you're called for everything – Tanha I want a glass of water, Tanha make me a coffee ...'. Many interviewees in fact referred to being continually 'on call' to provide service for their employers. A frequently cited case was that of being woken in the early hours of the morning to make coffee or tea for the employers' guests. Filomena (interview 22), who had previously worked in Lisbon for ten years, was able to pinpoint the oppressive nature of live-in work. In fact she felt that this type of work had diminished both her internal spirit and external beauty:

> When I arrived in Italy, people used to say to me 'you're like a flower'. But after one year of work, I was in a really bad way. In Portugal, I did not earn much money but I had tranquillity, integration, friends. I have only now understood that money is no substitute for all of that.

Profound dissatisfaction was pronounced by younger East African women, who had migrated to Italy more recently. This dissatisfaction was exacerbated particularly if they had had an office job in their country of origin. The following assertions from two Ethiopian friends exemplifies this. Abebech (interview 11), who had migrated in 1979, stated that she had always worked as a domestic. She was not ashamed of this work, in fact she maintained that domestic work or factory work was the same – simply a job. She herself noted the difference between herself and those of her friends who had migrated to Rome more recently. Hanna (interview 12) was a case in point. In her late 20s, she had had an office based job in Ethiopia, but in Italy had always worked as a domestic worker: 'It is awful work and I hate it, but in Italy you can't find anything else'. The questionnaires completed by Somali women also indicated that domestic work was viewed as menial and humiliating.

The Collectively Bargained National Contracts

As was briefly mentioned in chapter 4, the problems for those working within the domestic work sector stemmed historically from its legal categorisation as atypical work.[16] In this section I shall discuss the development of the collectively bargained domestic work contracts. These contracts have validity if employers adopt a formal contract with their employees and are therefore meaningless for undocumented workers. The contents of these contracts can be read as an indication of what interested parties consider to be appropriate contemporary employment conditions for the paid domestic work sphere. While these contracts were applicable to all domestic workers – nationals and non-nationals – certain stipulations had different implications for the two groups. Moreover, some migrant women are governed by contracts which have been specifically drawn up for overseas domestics workers (see circular 156/91 above).

Three principal areas can be identified as constituting enduring problematic structural aspects of the domestic work sector: working hours, maternity and sickness benefit and insurance payments.[17] In effect, the latter refers to employers' propensity to employ domestic workers within the official labour market thus obliging them to pay insurance contributions to the INPS.[18] These insurance contributions are important for domestic workers because they confer the right to invalidity and unemployment benefits, disability pensions, normal pensions and maternity benefits. Clearly this mode of employment is more costly to the employer. The reluctance of employers to pay the appropriate insurance contributions should be seen as a problem of the sector, but one which exacerbates quite specifically the situation of migrant women, as it contributes to their undocumented status in Italy.

One of the principal tasks of the category unions in other employment sectors has been their involvement in obtaining collectively bargained national contracts. These are industry/sector-wide agreements which establish wage levels and general working conditions for specific sectors.[19] The negotiation of these three-yearly national contracts became the 'focal point of industrial bargaining' from the 1960s to the mid-1970s (Bedani 1995, p. 209). As we saw in chapter 4, prior to 1973, the domestic work sector could hardly be described as a hotbed of radical activity. The impossibility of stipulating a national contract before 1969 undoubtedly contributed to the levels of exploitation perpetrated against the domestic worker by her employer. No doubt encouraged by gains made by workers in other sectors, the ACLI-COLF imagined that the conditions of domestic workers would be dramatically improved via the collectively bargained national contracts. National contracts established since 1974 have certainly modified working conditions. However, these contracts have achieved only limited success. This is partly a consequence of the retrograde starting point of domestic workers when compared to other sectors. But it is also reflective of an inherent competing tension within the personalised one to one employer/employee relationship. A tension which, to my mind, continues to be resolved to the benefit of the employer.

The ACLI-COLF has been very vocal regarding the national contracts. The API-COLF has also supported the national contracts but has rejected radical demands. At the national congress held in 1970, just prior to the ACLI-COLF's split, Erminio Crippa (subsequently API-COLF) had stated:

One should curse a contract, if it takes away or endangers the collaboration between domestic workers and families; if it obscures the possibility of experiencing the human and cordial aspects that this type of work allows, demands and develops'.[20]

National contracts were seen as having negative revolutionary potential: 'Insisting on contracts, without maturing the culture, would mean throwing dynamite into the hearts of domestic workers; planting seeds of revolution, not of spring'.[21] At the API-COLF's X national congress held in 1979, the president of the association, Giovanna Ardigò unequivocally prioritised the needs of the family above that of possible contractual gains for the domestic worker:

> It might seem urgent to discuss what we still do not have, such as sickness benefit; but we need to resolve the basic problem: to re-discover the importance of the home, of the family and of a job which allows contact with life and the human being (Il X Congresso API-COLF 1979, p. 61).

Conversely, a number of the interventions at the ACLI-COLF national congresses stressed the importance of improving the national contracts. Awareness of the difficulties of collective bargaining for the sector was particularly in evidence during the 1982 congress as there were problems regarding the renewal of the contract.[22] Giovanni Bergami, the national secretary of the FISACAT-CISL trade union indicated quite clearly that there was a limit to what could be incorporated into the national contract because of the intransigence of the employers:

> ... we had better not delude ourselves about modifying this platform, which might be judged insufficient or moderate, but the reality is that, to date, it has been rejected by the employers because it is seen to be too demanding. We know that the bosses are wrong ... but we know that we are in a sector in which it is difficult to develop 'industrial platforms', which do not even work in industrial sectors (ACLI-COLF 1982, p. 22).

Collectively bargained national contracts stipulate wage minimums for different industrial sectors. In the case of the domestic work sector, the point at which minimum wage levels were fixed was normally one *below* actual wages. This gives some indication of the strength of the employers. National agreements could only be achieved if wage levels were set at a low level despite the fact that it was widely recognised that domestic workers could command higher wages. Indeed, in the individual contract drawn up between employer and employee on the basis of the national contract, a higher wage could be stipulated (*superminimo*).

One area where the national contract has improved the working conditions of domestic workers relates to the stipulation of working hours. By 1988, the national contract had reduced the working week of the live-in domestic worker to 56 hours.[23] The first national contract in 1974 had settled the working hours at 66 hours. This suggests that domestic workers' working hours *before* the establishment of a national contract must have been particularly onerous. Several women who had begun working in Italy in the 1970s commented on the fact that their free time had been particularly limited in the early 1970s. As Isabella (interview 36) said: 'In those days we were only free on Sundays. Thursdays is modern'! Since this time however, working hours stipulated by national contracts have been progressively reduced. In 1978 working hours were limited by six hours to 60 hours. The 1984 contract reduced this to 58 hours and the subsequent 1988 national contract modified this by two hours to 56 hours. In 1992, the working hours of a live-in domestic was reduced to 55 hours. While this should be viewed as a considerable achievement for the sector, this should not detract from the fact that domestic workers are still expected to work extremely long hours. Until the 1992 contract their weekly rest period was 24 hours. This would normally be taken on Sundays or on two half days including Sundays. Article 10 of the 1992 contract provided domestic workers with an additional 12 hour rest period, extending the previous provision to 36 hours.[24]

Domestic workers enjoy only a very tenuous protection in case of illness. As a result, this aspect continued to constitute a mobilising issue for both the API-COLF and the ACLI-COLF.[25] Extended periods of illness corresponded to unemployment for domestic workers. This is because the national contract offered only minimal protection in this regard. Article 19 of the 1988 contract for example stipulated the length of time that employers were legally obliged to keep their employees' jobs open. After three to six months of employment there would be 10 days protection, six months to two years employment offered one month's protection and after two years employment the employee would be protected from dismissal for three months. The 1992 contract significantly improved domestic workers' position. Article 20 stipulated that up to six months of employment would guarantee protection for 10 days; six months to two years employment offered 45 days protection and after two years employment, the employee would be protected for 180 days. There was no change in the contract for part-time workers (i.e. those who worked less than 24 hours for one employer). Both the 1988 and 1992 contracts stipulated that their jobs would be kept open for eight days after three to six months of service, 10 days after six months to two years of service, and fifteen days after two years of service. During periods of illness, domestic workers would be entitled to 50 per cent of their normal salaries for a maximum of eight, 10 and 15 days respectively. Domestic workers are thus only partially protected in the event of illness.

The 1988 contract also confirmed that domestic workers were not comprehensively protected by national legislation governing working mothers (law n. 1204, 1971).[26] In effect they could not be employed two months prior or three months subsequent to the birth. Article 18 stipulated that the presentation of a certificate of pregnancy protected them from dismissal until they began maternity leave. However this was effectively nullified by Article 28 which regulates the termination of a contract between employer and employee. The warning period for either party wishing to terminate the contract was stipulated at 15 days for up to five years of service with the same employer, and otherwise a month after five years of service. The 1992 contract did however differentiate between the employer and employee with regard to the termination of a contract. Article 29 stipulated that employees would have to give half as much notice to terminate a contract. Nonetheless, domestic workers were protected only to the degree that the correct payment of insurance contributions in the two years prior to their pregnancy would entitle them to maternity benefits. In reality, the consequences of pregnancy are not governed by the articles pertaining to maternity but rather by the articles governing the termination of a contract. In any case, the personalised nature of the relationship between employer and employee means that pregnancy is highly inconvenient for the employer and particularly problematic for live-in domestic workers. The situation was accurately described by my key informant from the CELSI-CGIL:

> When a woman becomes pregnant while working for a family she will be given the sack and be unemployed. Even if there is legal protection for pregnancy, this protection is not fully applied to domestic workers, because, above all, the employment relationship is different to the employment relationship in a company. The protection is only for a few months and even then, given that it is a very personal work relationship, there is no full protection. The trade union can intervene if they are sacked but once a relationship like that has broken down, it cannot be reconstructed (interview, CELSI-CGIL).

And as one the Eritrean interviewees stated in discussing the relevance of a contract, if employers want you to go, contract or otherwise, they simply say, 'I don't want you, go' (Lemlem, interview 10).

This conflict between maternity and employment as a live-in domestic worker has been rationalised by some activists within the ACLI-COLF. In the following quotation, the 'other' victim is represented in the form of an elderly person, but the logic of the perspective articulated is clearly also applicable to female employers:

> ...as I said before, the job has changed and the families have changed. So, if you imagine, let's say an elderly man for example, who has problems and in order to be more or less self-sufficient has a live-in domestic to help him out. If the domestic worker becomes pregnant, he would have to pay for two of them and obviously this would not be possible. So, it's an issue which affects the weakest, because on the one hand it affects the elderly person who, without the domestic worker, is forced to have a very difficult life and on the other hand it affects the domestic worker who, in this case, finds herself without a job, thus without possibilities, and in the end unable to remain in this country (interview, ACLI-COLF).

This interpretation highlights quite effectively a very fundamental aspect of the domestic work sector. The historical roots of this profession are grounded in servitude and the expectation that the needs of the domestic worker are subservient to those of the employer. The desire to offer domestic workers more protection in the labour market continues to rest upon a difficult tension. This tension concerns the establishment of a hierarchy of competing needs within the relationship between employer and employee. The consequences of the imbalance in the resolution of this tension are heightened for migrant women. The areas that have been accentuated as problematic entirely embody this point. Working hours, sick leave and maternity benefit are all areas in which the national contracts agreed upon in Italy have subordinated the needs of the domestic worker to the needs of the employer. The employer's needs are for a healthy person with no dependants, who is contractually obliged to attend to the family's needs for extended periods of time. The ineffectual protection of the employee in crucial areas such as illness, maternity and working hours automatically offers greater security to the employer. In short, the resolution of areas where the tension surrounding the notion of competing needs is most acute, reveals a structural inequality between the employer and employee.

For migrants, the implications of limited sickness and maternity protection[27] in terms of loss of employment are formidable. The lack of an infrastructure to assist in situations of temporary unemployment coupled with the possibility of repatriation contextualises their working conditions and the type of treatment they accept from their employers. The testimony of an Eritrean representative encapsulates this:

... I know that we don't have many rights, but we have got some, for example, in the contract it states that we [live-in] must work 10 hours, but all of us working as domestics don't only work 10 hours, there are many that I know who get up at 7.00 in the morning and go to bed at 11.00; and then, even if you wanted to leave, it's not easy, you think, you don't know where to go, ... with your suitcases, you can't find accommodation, the hotels are expensive, so you don't say anything ...[28]

More recently, the national contracts have recognised that both foreign women and Italian nationals work as domestic workers. Article 4 of the 1992 contract included a work permit as one of the documents that prospective migrant domestic workers had to provide for their employers. Article 14 of the 1992 contract indicated some sensitivity towards the circumstances of migrant domestic workers. This article regulated domestic workers' holiday period. Regardless of whether they were live-in or part time workers, domestic workers were entitled to 25 days holiday. However, a special provision was available for women migrants, whereby they could accumulate their holidays over two years to facilitate a long holiday in their country of origin (Art. 14).

However, although Article 1 of the 1992 contract stated categorically that the provisions were applicable to both Italian and overseas domestic workers, in practice this was only partially true. This was because migrant women domestic workers were first and foremost governed by immigration legislation. From a legislative perspective, this ensured that migrant women's ethnicity/ nationality was privileged as the dominant identity. This had implications for their conditions in the domestic work sphere. As was discussed above, special provisions enacted for migrant women entering Italy after 1991 meant that they were tied to the employer in a way that the Italian national was not. Thus, national immigration regulations perpetrated a distinction between Italian and migrant domestic workers. In fact, in addition to the differential regulation of new female migrants, a further ethnically based distinction was apparent regarding insurance payments for domestic workers. Until 1986, minimal contributions were expected for foreign workers. Thus, in 1972, for an Italian worker being paid up to L700 an hour, the employer's contribution would be L118 per hour. For a migrant worker the contribution would be L61. In this way, migrant workers would have been cheaper to employ. In 1987 however this situation changed and the insurance contributions for migrant workers were set at a fractionally higher rate than those for Italian workers. Thus, for an Italian worker being paid up to L4.260 an hour, the employer's contribution would be L1.003 an hour. For the migrant worker the contribution would be

L1.018. The higher contribution for migrant workers was inclusive of a quota to provide for their eventual return fare to their country of origin. This modification, established subsequent to national legislation governing immigration in 1986, may well have been partially influenced by the national and regional tendency (see chapter 3) to develop strategies to assist migrants in their eventual return home. What this meant for female migrant domestic workers was that they were legally more expensive to employ than Italian workers. However, given that, since the 1970s, the supply of live-in Italian workers has been substantially reduced, this situation was unlikely to lead to Italian employers reverting to Italian workers. What it was more likely to lead to was a preference amongst employers to employ migrant women within the undocumented sphere of labour.

Domestic Work, Security and Status

The enduring demand for live-in workers has functioned as a reliable safety net for some African women. Two of the women I interviewed were forced to return to live-in domestic work and a third woman was contemplating this. Tanha (interview 18) had worked as a live-in domestic for 14 years after which time she found hourly paid work. At a later stage she met and married an Italian man with whom she had children. They lived as a family unit, and she continued doing hourly paid work. A combination of serious misfortunes propelled her back into live-in work. Firstly, her husband died of cancer. Subsequent to this, there was a fire in her home where she lost most of her possessions. She was forced to put her children in a home and recommence work as a live-in domestic. At the time of interview, she had been doing this for almost a year and did not foresee a change of circumstances. Having lived independently and in a happy family unit she was, understandably, finding it quite difficult to adjust to her new situation.[29] Gianna (interview 24), on the other hand, had first migrated to Italy in 1974. She had been regularly employed as a live-in worker for two years. She left her employment to marry a Cape Verdean man and returned to her country of origin, where they started a family.[30] They had five children (aged 18, 16, 13, 10, 9). At the time of interview she had been working as a live-in domestic for six years. Her return to Rome was a consequence of her husband's unemployment. He had been a sailor but, after two years of unemployment, the family had begun to struggle financially. The possibility of finding secure work in Rome informed her decision to re-migrate. Since returning she had worked for the same family, a retired couple. The family decision for Gianna to re-migrate, instead of her husband, suggests that distinct gendered labour market pull factors exist in Europe.

Some of the women I interviewed were in fact the second generation of women in their families to migrate to Rome. Antonia (interview 16) for example came to Rome when she was 19. Her mother had already been working as a live-in domestic since the early 1960s. As a consequence both her own mother and Antonia herself had been forced to live separately from their children. When Zimzim (interview 21) came in the early 1990s aged 20, she initially stayed with her mother who had been employed as a live-in worker in Rome since 1974. Zimzim subsequently also began work as a live-in domestic. Another Cape Verdean woman that I spoke to informally[31] had been in Italy for four years. She had originally migrated to Ancona. However the family had decided that her 21 year-old daughter would also come to Italy and the daughter wanted to live in the capital city. This woman thus moved to Rome where she found work for both herself and her daughter as live-in workers. In fact, they worked for two generations of the same Italian family, the mother for the older parents and her daughter for the young married couple.

For those women present since the 1970s, there was a feeling that working conditions had improved. Women spoke of domestic workers being freer nowadays. Lemlem confirmed this: 'Before, employers used to say: 'I brought you to Italy and I can also send you back'. Now we decide what we do, before they used to decide for us'. However, what was especially evident was that the 1970s were seen to have presented much greater employment stability:

> In the 1970s they used to ask us if we wanted to work for them. They used to stop you in the street to ask if you had a friend or a sister. Or else, your employers might ask you on behalf of their friends. Now we have to ask for work and we sometimes go through periods of unemployment.[32]

Black women's ethnicity also had some influence on their conditions in Italy. While they spoke quite freely about their experiences as domestic workers, they did not often raise racism as an issue.[33] Their references to racism were related essentially to their exploitation as workers: '[Employers] see the colour of your skin and think that you must work hard' (Lemlem, interview 10). Also Zimzim (interview 21): 'It's really horrible in Italy. I imagine that it's better in England. At least there you're treated as people while here you are like a slave'. Margarita (interview 8): 'There has always been racism, it never ends, we have got used to it. They make you understand that you're not from their country, even in the families for whom you work. You have to be patient'.

Although racism did not permeate their descriptions of their experiences in Italy, when asked specifically about its occurrence, none of them denied its existence: 'They are not openly racist, but it is there' (Lemlem, interview 10). However, it was noticeable that those women who had been in Italy since the 1970s had observed a tangible increase in racism. Abeba (interview 17) for example, present in Italy from 1970, noted that when there were fewer migrants in Rome, people had been more friendly with each other. Gabriele (interview 25) also stated: 'It was much easier to find work in the 1970s and 1980s. We also got on well with Italians ... Up until the 1980s the situation was much calmer. There was more humanity'.

A particular form of racism did impact on Black women's position in Rome. This related to the covert establishment of an ethnic hierarchy within the domestic work sector.[34] A number of studies in Italy have referred to these hierarchies. For example, Hornziel (1990) has argued that Filipina women are consistently located at the top of this hierarchy, because of their ability to speak English, while Favaro and Bordogna (1991, p. 26) attribute this positioning to a perception of them as more 'obliging'.[35] With regard to the Rome area and the groups of my study, there were certainly some differences. On the whole, Cape Verdean women felt they were highly regarded as good and reliable workers. This was confirmed by key informants from voluntary and institutional bodies. Eritreans were also seen as good workers. Lemlem (interview 10), an Eritrean, did not think there was a major earnings differential between Eritreans and Filipinas, rather she argued that Filipinas were willing to be paid less money and that is why some employers preferred them. But it was clear that employers' preferences were influenced by ethnicity. Abebech (interview 11), who often found employment by responding to adverts in the Rome newspaper *Porta Portese*, confirmed that employers were in fact quite concerned with ethnicity. They were normally very explicit about which nationality they did or did not want to employ. A private recruitment agency operating in Rome accepted that employers would normally specify nationality but argued that this was always based on prior experience and not due to racism (interview, ADS). The Somalis are an interesting case because a number of key informants from voluntary sector organisations told me quite explicitly that Somali women were not seen to be good workers. Additionally, Somalis were seen to occupy a privileged location in relation to the majority of other ethnic groups. In 1992, as a result of the political situation in Somalia, special provisions were enacted for Somalis which meant that they could automatically be issued with a temporary permit for employment or for study purposes.[36] This was renewable until such a time that the political situation in Somalia had improved enough to allow their re-entry.[37] In comparison to other Black workers then, this afforded Somalis some advantages as Ethiopians and Eritreans were only entitled to a permit if they were employed or studying. But as one voluntary worker stated: 'Somali women do not get on well in the labour market. They are considered to be slow and unsuitable' (interview, Caritas 2). Results from the completed questionnaires indicated that only one of the respondents had been employed to do manual labour in the country of origin. The rest had either been students, office or professional workers. In Rome, these women were uniformly working as domestic workers. Without exception they described this work as 'tiring' and 'badly paid'. None of them felt that domestic work reflected their professional capacities. This indicated a high level of dissatisfaction amongst young Somali women who entered Italy in the late 1980s and early 1990s. Examination of their motives for migration sheds some light on this. An overwhelming majority cited either war or political problems as a principal push factor. In a few cases, war was often cited in tandem with unemployment or an insufficient income. The overriding impression was thus that war and its contingent problems had precipitated a wave of Somali migration in the early 1990s. Given that many of these women had previous experience of office or professional work, it may even be likely that they were used to domestic help in the country of origin and this may have accounted for their reluctance to do such work in Italy.

Although frustrated aspirations were much more in evidence amongst young East African women, they were not limited either to this group or to younger generations of women. Dissatisfaction could also be identified through women's verbalisation of the desire to continue their migratory journeys to other countries. This was directly related to the difficult circumstances prevalent in Italy for female migrant workers. The results from the questionnaires indicated that only one of the Somalis intended to settle in Italy. The majority hoped to return to Somalia in the short and medium term, while a few hoped to migrate to another country. Canada has been a major destination country for Ethiopians and Eritreans,[38] but it has recently become more difficult to enter unless backed by a major sponsor. Zimzim (interview 21), however, still hoped to migrate to either Canada or America: 'I have already applied. I am waiting for the outcome. If I can't find another life, I want to go back to my country. It really is horrible in Italy'. Sara (interview 26) noted that Italy was a particularly bad place to be a migrant because of the difficulties of acquiring independent living accommodation. She named Canada, Britain, Holland and Sweden as much better destination countries because you could have access to council housing and benefits. Ardah (interview 28) reiterated this point:

> The work in Italy is really horrible. I am not a graduate, I only completed middle school, but in Rome, even if you have a degree, if you are a foreigner, all you will find is domestic work. Somali women who have managed to go to other countries are better off. In Canada and England they help refugees. They give you a home and money if you are unemployed.

Clearly there was widespread awareness of different and better conditions in other countries. The presence of established communities of Cape Verdeans, Eritreans, Ethiopians and Somalis in other national contexts facilitated comparisons. However, it was not only very young women who were contemplating further migration to improve their situation. Two Eritrean women in their 50s whom I interviewed informally at Rome's Central Station, had been working in Italy for over 20 years. Both of them asked me whether I was in a position to help them to come to England to look for work. These views indicate that while Black women recognised that Italy could offer secure employment, it was the nature of that employment and the near impossibility of any social mobility out of this employment which contributed to their desire to migrate elsewhere. There were high levels of dissatisfaction about the opportunities for Black women in Rome and Italy was seen as a retrograde country in relation to other European countries because of this. As Filomena stated: 'We live our problems on a daily basis. People should know what goes on in Italy. We've hardly found America here. We've found the Third World'.

From Rome to Rotterdam

In order to investigate whether migrant women's perception of other countries offering greater opportunities was correct, I conducted interviews with 10 Cape Verdean women who had continued their migration from Italy to the Netherlands. Whereas Italy had attracted single-sex female migration from Cape Verde in the 1970s, the Netherlands had attracted single-sex male migration from Cape Verde, mainly as sailors. The women interviewed had migrated to Italy between the years 1969 and 1977. Some had migrated directly to Italy from Cape Verde, others had migrated first to Lisbon, where the largest Cape Verdean community in Europe currently resides. The women had worked in Italy for differing lengths of time. The shortest time period was two years, the longest 16 years, with an average working time of six years. Six of the women had moved to Rotterdam through marriage to a Cape Verdean who was based there. They had met their husbands in a variety of situations, but normally in either Lisbon, Rotterdam or Rome while they or their future husband had been on holiday. Four of the women had been able to move to Rotterdam because their sisters or other family members were living there. After marriage, some of the women became housewives in Rotterdam or did part-time work. However, all of the women had subsequently had labour market experience in Rotterdam. At the time of interview, eight were still employed, one was a housewife and one was on social security benefits. The most obvious disparity with their working experiences in Italy concerned employment location. Without exception, they had all worked as live-in domestic workers in Italy. Although their employment location in the Netherlands was still predominantly in the manual service sector, their employment experiences were more diverse. In Rotterdam, their main employment occupations were as chambermaids in hotels, ancillary workers in hospitals, cleaners of offices and private homes and behind the scenes work in Italian restaurants. One of the women worked in the post room at the city council and another was a deputy supervisor for cleaning services at a school. A number had been able to pursue some form of study in the Netherlands. One had taken a diploma as a home help but was currently on social security benefits because the working hours available were not compatible with her obligations as a single parent.

A principal difference in women's experiences of Italy and the Netherlands concerned the management of maternity. It was generally felt to be much easier to have a family in the Netherlands: 'In Holland, as the mother of a family, it is better. You go to work, you come home and your child is there waiting for you' (Marta, interview 30).

Access to social security benefits in the Netherlands, in times of need, was very positively evaluated by Cape Verdean women, even when they themselves had not had to seek recourse to it. Single parenthood was clearly less problematic because of this. The only woman not employed at the time of interview was a single parent. Although she had worked previously in Rotterdam and was actively seeking work she stated: 'I am not obliged to work here because I have children and I am a single mother. I thank God that you have everything here, the government helps me. In Italy this could not happen' (Jacintha, interview 33). Djina (interview 35) reiterated this perspective: 'It is better in Holland because the government helps you with your children. Here there are so many people who do not work, but they can eat and clothe themselves. In Italy if you don't work, you don't eat'. Isabella (interview 36), who had worked in Italy for 16 years, cited the absence of state support or alternative employment opportunities in Italy as forcing one to accept the difficulties of live-in work:

> Life in Italy is very distressing. Your employers treat you as if you don't count for anything. Your female employer attacks you, and her daughter and even her husband because you haven't cleaned their shoes properly. Every day of the year you have to do that work. You need to have enormous strength to carry on, as you need that salary because the Italian government doesn't give you any other opportunity. They tell you, this is the work that we have here.

For those women who did not migrate to Rotterdam through marriage, the presence of relatives in Rotterdam facilitated their migration. Transnational networks and the relative proximity of Italy to the Netherlands encouraged interaction and family visits. This exposure allowed some women to envisage alternative working and living conditions. As Maria Silva (interview 31) stated:

> I really liked Italy but I did not want to live there for the rest of my life. I had visited Rotterdam several times on holiday and I could see that I could have a better life there. My life is better in Rotterdam, in Rome you can't have your own house, you always have to live with your bosses.

On the whole, these women felt that their situation was better in The Netherlands:

> You have more opportunities in Holland. If you are a legal [migrant] you are supported by the government, you can have your own home. Life is very different to life in Italy. There is no comparison. You have your home, you have your job. And there is another thing, you always have money, because the government will support you if you are unemployed, so you are always protected by the government (Isabella, interview 35).

Despite this widespread recognition that their situation was better in the Netherlands, many of the women professed to feeling nostalgia for Italy. Moreover, in spite of their experiences, nearly all of them preferred Italy as a country, partly because of the climate but also because they felt people were more open there: 'In Rome, if you went into a shop, people used to have a joke with you. In Holland, they don't like to joke with foreigners. But we're better off here, because we can have a home, we can study ...' (Jacintha, interview 33). Furthermore, the life style in the Netherlands meant that even if they lived relatively near to each other, they did not see their friends as frequently as they did in Italy. In fact, the uniformity of their lives as live-in domestic workers in Rome had signified a fairly regimented social life organised around their free time on Thursday afternoons and Sundays. The nature of such work meant that they were all keen to 'escape' from their employers' houses to meet up with friends. As Jacintha stated 'Friendships in Rome were much closer, here they are more distant'. Despite some nostalgia for Italy, there was little if any nostalgia for the employment sector they had left behind. As Marta (interview 30) stated: 'At the beginning, when I first came to Holland, I missed Italy – the weather, my friends, the language – but I didn't miss the house that had to be cleaned at all!'

Diasporic links[39] facilitated Cape Verdean women's onward migration to the Netherlands, where opportunities did indeed appear to be better. While employment opportunities appeared to remain within the realms of the manual service industries, the nature of such work still permitted these women to express their other social identities. Notably, motherhood and family life was facilitated by access to a variety of employment spheres, access to independent accommodation and, in times of need, state financial support.[40]

A Way Out of Domestic Work? The Voluntary and Institutional Response

In this section of the chapter, I will consider the response of the voluntary and institutional sector to migrant women's situation. The focus will centre on training courses and their potential to offer migrant women a feasible alternative to domestic work. I shall be arguing that the success of training courses is contingent on the ability of those organising courses to accommodate the specific circumstances of migrant women's presence in the city.

The Voluntary Sector

Since the late 1980s, an extensive network of associations has developed in Rome as a response to incoming immigration. The voluntary sector has assumed a dominant role since the 1970s,[41] and by the 1980s and 1990s, there was certainly a wide range of voluntary sector organisations providing a valuable network for all migrants.[42] I will briefly discuss the role of the Caritas given its prominence as a national organisation. However, my focus in this section will be on two groups located within the Protestant sphere of voluntary sector activity which developed projects specifically tailored to the needs of migrant women.

The Caritas opened a reception centre for migrants in Rome in 1983. However it had been responsive to migrants' presence before this time (interview, Caritas 1). Its services were well used: in the three year period between 1987 and 1989, for example, 20,955 migrants were registered with the centre. The organisation provided a diversified range of services. These included a mobile medical centre, hostels and refectories. In 1989, the operating budget for the Rome Caritas was almost 14 billion lire, with over half of this operating budget covered by the *Comune* and Province of Rome and the Lazio region.[43] Increasing numbers of migrants availed themselves of Caritas' services throughout the 1980s. For example, while in 1983 1,483 migrants registered at the Caritas reception centre, by 1989 this number had risen to 9,176.[44]

Caritas provided services for both male and female migrants and a Caritas representative claimed that they were particularly attentive to the needs of migrant women in relation to maternity:

> A male migrant with no children is freer ... A woman who has a child does not have and cannot use all of her talents because if she is a good mother, she must also think about her child. So, she is someone whose capacities are halved precisely because she is looking after others. Therefore the female figure warrants more attention, more respect, she must be followed with a lot of attention (interview, Caritas 1).

This approach was evident in relation to accommodation provision for migrants, where migrant women with children were seen as a privileged group.

Within the Caritas network of services, there were thus specific facilities for women. These were particularly useful for undocumented migrant women or migrant women who were temporarily unemployed as a consequence of their pregnancy. For unauthorised migrants these facilities provided important access to prenatal care. For pregnant domestic workers these religious centres provided a crucial safety net during periods of unemployment and homelessness.

There were however other voluntary sector organisations operating within Rome and there was a considerable difference in approach between Protestant and Catholic voluntary sector organisations. One key informant described it as a basic theological difference:

> There is a theological difference because we have a different approach to social work from the Catholic Church. Because the Catholic Church has a hierarchical system because of its theology. We cannot say it is good or bad, that is their teaching and that means they are also a charity system. That means I give to you.

Meanwhile protestant theology is more along the lines of I go together with you and I have an exchange with you. Nobody is higher than the other. So I will also ask you for something if you want something from me (interview, FCEI).[45]

Courses for Women

In the introduction to the book, I argued that the specific location of ethnic minority women can lead to dual exclusion from both the category of gender and the category of 'race'. In the Roman context, most initiatives were generally targeted at migrants as a whole, however a minority of associations did focus specifically on the situation of female migrants. I want to discuss the activities of two of these voluntary sector organisations and in particular the nature of their training courses for migrant women. The two organisations formed part of the Protestant voluntary sector network and worked principally with three of the ethnic communities with which this book is concerned. One was the Female Migrants and Refugees project (*Donne migranti e rifiugiati*)[46] organised by the Young Women's Christian Organisation (YWCA), and a project for migrant women was also organised by the Federation of Protestant Churches in Italy (FCEI).

The YWCA[47] project began in Rome in 1985 and was inspired by the concept of female solidarity. The YWCA organised a variety of activities, including the provision of emergency housing, language courses (in Italian and English for those intending to resettle in Canada), social counselling, health information for women and financial assistance for those women in particularly difficult situations.[48] The project provided initial support for female migrants. Women could remain in the emergency accommodation for differing lengths of time depending on their specific circumstances. One particularly interesting feature of the association's work concerned its provision of a training course on home economics. This course can be seen as an example of the way in which voluntary organisations contribute to a specific structuring of migrant women's role. The rationale for the course was as follows:

> We run a course on domestic science, because, unfortunately or fortunately, the demand for work is principally in the domestic work sector and considering that these are women coming from a different structure they clearly cannot be expected to know how we are organised here in Italy (interview, YWCA).

The duration of the course was six months. Two weekly morning sessions were held from 9.30am until 2.00pm. During the course, East African women would be taught to shop and prepare food for Italians' consumption.[49] Some attempts were made to accommodate these women's cultural difference. Thus, there would be a slight adaptation to this programme during the period of Ramadan, when sewing, ironing and embroidery would be taught. This domestic preparation was additionally used as a channel to improve or teach the Italian language. There was a specific language course which was held three times a week, with each session lasting an hour and a half. These courses were seen as an effective means of facilitating migrant women's entry into the domestic work sphere.[50]

The interpretation of the significance of the home economics course hinges on the YWCA's vision of domestic work as both a misfortune and fortune for migrant women. It seems obvious that the consequences of such a course would naturally lead to the containment of female migrants within the sphere of domestic work. No attempt was being made to challenge the restriction of migrant women to this sphere of work, rather they were trained to perform domestic work more usefully for Italian families. An alternative view would understand the provision of such a course as a practical response to the reality of the Roman labour market for migrant women. In other words, given that the domestic sector was realistically the only sector in which migrant women could envisage employment, why not train them to perform this role more effectively?

In those instances where the YWCA did attempt to expand migrant women's employment opportunities, this was largely unsuccessful. In 1991, the YWCA ran a course for home-helps, open to both male and female migrants, funded by the Lazio region. It was totally unsuccessful. Twenty-seven women from a range of ethnic backgrounds began the course, but only three finished. None of the African women completed the course: 'they dropped out along the way' (interview, YWCA). The problems relating to this course in fact epitomise the intrinsic difficulties of devising suitable training courses for a female migrant target group. The course was structured to last for eight months. Trainees would have to attend on a daily basis, for three hours every afternoon. On completion of the course, a certificate would be issued by the region. Ostensibly, this course offered migrant women the possibility of entering a different sector of work (albeit in another feminised sector of the economy). This sector, however, would permit a degree of autonomy which was difficult to attain within the domestic service sector. In the event, the practical organisation of such a course suppressed this potential. When asked why so few women had completed the course, not surprisingly, logistical problems were cited: '... the course was too long and clearly if they found a job, they could not turn it down' (interview, YWCA).

It seems clear that migrant women's position as primary migrants, and their consequent need to earn an income, undoubtedly conditioned their ability to attend training courses structured in this manner.[51] The philosophy underpinning the home economics course run by the YWCA project can be interpreted in a slightly different fashion if one takes into account the long term project of the Federation of Protestant Churches (FCEI) with regard to migrant women and the close collaboration between the two associations.[52]

The FCEI's Refugees and Migrants Service (SRM) was originally concerned with Italian emigrants living abroad. From 1984 it switched its focus to incoming migrants to Italy. Its three principal activities consisted of sensitising the churches within the FCEI to the issue of immigration, exerting political pressure to obtain appropriate policies for refugees and migrants and providing tangible acts of solidarity to individual refugees or migrants in difficulty.[53] The FCEI's engagement with migrant women's specific situation was a consequence of its commitment to the individual migrant or refugee. This entailed the provision of legal and health advice, linguistic and professional training and accommodation. These services were intended to promote migrants' autonomy.

Specific initiatives were developed for women. In line with its general philosophy, the FCEI prioritised training and development, establishing a tailored service for women in 1986. An integral aspect of this service was the importance of comprehensive self development:

> We try to promote women, not so much in special programmes, but to give them space to develop their capacities. For instance, we try to send them to meetings outside Italy, because we feel that to have travelled twice to an international meeting of Black women is more important than to have followed the management training course in Italy. So we promote them in being linked internationally. We send these women especially on racism and anti-racism programmes, meetings within Europe but also out of Europe as far as we are able to finance it. It is an expensive way to do training but it is rather effective (interview, FCEI).

This emphasis on developing the autonomy of individual migrants contrasts quite noticeably with the philosophy underpinning the voluntary activity of the Catholic sector. The co-ordinator of the FCEI's migratory service, Anne Marie Duprès, reiterated the importance of this at an international convention held in Stuttgart in March 1993 on 'Black/Migrant Women and Health in Europe':

… there is among us still the mentality which wants to become active 'for' the foreigners. In terms of language this suggests that one wants to act in place of the foreigners; of course full of goodwill but still somewhat in the helper-syndrome mode and with the feeling that one can do things better than they. The problem is, though, that often we really *are* more able to do things better, because we have done little or nothing to enable the foreigners, as quickly as possible, to stand their ground within our political and social system. This is what is meant by 'empowerment', the willingness to hand political and social tools over to others so that they can at least represent themselves and do so successfully. [54]

The FCEI had clearly adopted a long term vision of migrants' social integration into Italy and this was applicable also to migrant women. At the root of its vision was a desire to expand migrant women's options. Study and training were viewed as essential components of this strategy:

We try to give study help. We have a study help programme and we always try to give quite a lot of help to women on all kinds of training. It can be language training, it can be vocational training or university training. It depends how useful it is (interview, FCEI).

The association offered small scholarships to assist women in pursuing these objectives. However, it was fully aware of the multiple pressures that migrant women had to contend with, particularly the need to procure employment and wages: 'Most of the women that we are linked to, they ask us for jobs. We do work on this, but we try to push them into understanding that they should learn and study' (interview, FCEI).

Some East African women's[55] reluctance to study and their preference for work was attributed in part to the nature of internal gender relations within some of the communities under discussion:

Some of these women are under pressure by their men and therefore have problems. These men can't understand that the women would like to study, so we have a programme which has always been run by YWCA but which is strongly linked with us, which is a cooking course,[56] but it is the best instrument to promote interest [in women for] studying. Because that is where women accept and men allow them to go, because it is a cooking and housekeeping course which will allow them to find a better job (interview, FCEI).[57]

My key informant described the association's work as frustrating in that it was not always successful in communicating the importance of training to some of the women:

> We have to feel very pleased if those on the cooking courses go on to do reading
> and Italian language courses ... But it happens more than we would like that
> this woman then goes to work, finds a job and after a while after two or three
> years she finds out that it perhaps wouldn't be a bad idea to go and do another
> course. So, although we sometimes feel rather frustrated and have the feeling
> that these people don't understand, that we can't get it over to them, after a
> while it gets to them. At the beginning it is a very small seed but it grows after
> a while. It is difficult to say what comes out of what you plant (interview, FCEI).

Viewed from this perspective, the home economics course could be considered to be more subversive than might appear at first sight. On the other hand, as the FCEI informant herself noted, women pursuing these courses would normally proceed to domestic work. It would seem that the subversive element built into the course was unrealistic, given the economic constraints within which these women operated and the labour market opportunities available to them.

The FCEI's commitment to avoiding dependency can be seen quite clearly in its housing project. Acutely aware of the difficulties migrant women encountered in living together as a family unit (see chapter 7), the housing project run by the FCEI[58] was intended to help migrants acquire access to housing to facilitate family aggregation. The FCEI offered initial financial support for the payment of rent, but the following citation reveals its attachment to its underlying philosophy:

> As soon as a mother comes here and tells us that she will go onto this project
> then we begin work. We can only give two months [rent]. This is also part of the
> way in which we work, we never want to get people dependent on us, so normally
> we only give very short financial support and only if people co-operate. So we
> normally say, we only give if you pay. In other words if you pay with other
> things. You pay by doing this or that. It is never free. It is free economically but
> they have to do something. So we are rather a severe service and also not viewed
> favourably because of this. Not everybody goes on this project, many Somali
> women are angry because they are asked for instance to go on the language
> course or on the cooking course and they refuse. If they don't go then we won't
> pay any more. We will do it once, but let's say for two months she didn't do her
> job, then we say we can't pay any longer, because it's not working because we
> are not useful to you (interview, FCEI).

The 'payment' expected from migrant women varied according to their circumstances:

> If a woman has four children under five, we cannot send her to a language course. But then we would say, you have to go to this office to get your child into kindergarten. If she doesn't even do this, we tell her twice, and then we will not do it for her. For instance we will not go to the office and put the child into the kindergarten (interview, FCEI).

The FCEI additionally sought to develop the political organisation of migrant women. To this end, a group of migrant women mobilised within the FCEI's structures in the late 1980s. They worked within the organisation for approximately two years but the group was eventually dissolved as the FCEI felt that there were too many of these kinds of groups operating in Rome, all composed of the same women.[59] During its two years of existence, the FCEI's migrant women's group had mobilised around specific issues. For example at an FCEI conference in February 1989, it had highlighted the problem of family unification for migrant women.[60] In 1989, it presented a proposal to the Lazio region to gain funding to provide facilities for migrant families to spend time with their children on their days off from domestic work. The group aimed to provide accommodation for Saturday night/Sunday morning so families could physically be together at the weekend.[61]

Although the FCEI can be seen to have been promoting migrant women's development in a broad sense, particularly if compared to initiatives prevalent within the Catholic voluntary sector, it was impotent to challenge the organisation of migrant women's labour as domestic workers. The FCEI's broad interest and support for education as a strategy for self-improvement did however provide some outlet for migrant women's aspirations. Nonetheless, migrant women's financial obligations and wider responsibilities frequently meant that participation in certain projects was difficult, if not impossible.

The Institutional Sector

The problems African women encountered with regard to training courses in the voluntary sector were similarly present at the institutional level. There was growing sensitivity to these problems at the institutional level and the need to form a working group to address the specific problems of female migrant workers was mooted (interview RL2). There was certainly evidence that migrant women were not being catered for in the region's general training packages.[62] For example, in 1991, the areas in which most migrants gained training qualifications were in building, restoration and in computing. In 1992, it was projected that the sectors of plumbing, electrical work and agricultural work should be added to these sectors.[63] A male orientation was clearly present in the nature of these training courses, despite the fact that female migrants represented a substantial proportion of Lazio's migrant community.

Where courses promoted by the region had a potential female audience, the organisation of training courses restricted the full participation of women. For example, the Lazio region encountered similar problems to that of the YWCA regarding a training course it developed for nurses. This project was organised as a response to the national demand for nurses which was identified in the early 1990s:

> There was a need at the national level and there was discussion about bringing in nurses from abroad on contracts. So, we thought that it might be possible to train those people who were already here (interview, RL2).[64]

Migrant women were to be incorporated into the training course for nurses to a maximum of 10 per cent. This was a 10 per cent ceiling, rather than a reservation of 10 per cent of training posts. This meant that migrant women would have to compete for entry on the same basis as Italian nationals. Recognising the disadvantage that this would entail for migrant women, the region's immigration office organised a special pre-training course for those migrant women intending to follow the course. One hundred and fifty expressed an interest in this and the outcome of the pre-training course was described as positive (interview, RL2). The course took place in July and August and required attendance on a daily basis for three hours. It is thus probable that this prevented the attendance of many women. Women employed on an hourly paid basis would have found it easier to attend, particularly as it occurred during the summer months. Nevertheless, the organisation of the training course proper only highlighted the impossibility of these courses succeeding without considering the economic position of female migrants. With regard to the training course for nurses, the key informant from the region's immigration office stated:

> The problem remains one of finding maintenance for those on the course. Because there is a practical and theoretical aspect to these courses, this means that they are involved with the practical side of things during the day, as well as

studying and this means that they cannot work. So, there will be a problem of seeing how to integrate ... their monthly grant of L150,000 for the first year which rises in subsequent years. However this clearly is not sufficient. This is the problem which we need to address in a way which is compatible with available funds (interview, RL2).[65]

In fact, official documentation explicitly recognised the financial difficulties associated with participation in this course.[66]

Age restrictions attached to certain training courses additionally disadvantaged some migrant women. For example, one course advertised at the CELSI-CGIL office was for assistant seamstresses. However the age restriction was set at 25 years. Data available for the province of Rome for the first quarter of 1991 showed that while female migrants under the age of 25 constituted the largest group of women migrants registered at the employment office (78,515), there were substantial numbers of older women migrants. In the 25–29 year age group, 34,803 female migrants were registered and in the over 30 age group, 50,044 women were registered. This indicated that, in fact, the over 25s were a significant percentage of job seekers.

There was undoubtedly a tension between women's participation in courses and their employment as domestic workers. As one trade union activist stated: 'if the woman has to do domestic work, then she cannot do the course' (interview, CELSI-CGIL). The CELSI-CGIL office did promote its own initiatives to increase women's options. Its strategy, akin to that of the YWCA, was a consequence of its recognition that there was strong demand for domestic workers in Rome but that this work was particularly problematic for women in its live-in form. Thus, an attempt was made to restructure the organisation of domestic work:

> We formed a cooperative last December. It is a cooperative formed of migrant domestic workers working on an hourly paid basis and it is a very important project because with this cooperative we are trying, and we have partially succeeded in liberating those migrants involved in the cooperative from the exploitation of live-in work. At the same time, this worker, who is employed by the cooperative will have a pay slip, normal insurance payments ... This is a step forward for freedom (interview, CELSI-CGIL).

In the subsequent year, the same CELSI-CGIL representative indicated that the cooperative was not performing well, attributing this to employers' reluctance to pay the higher costs associated with regularised contractual work. Although this approach sought to minimise the difficulties of domestic work, it did little in terms of offering migrant women any alternative to domestic work.

The above examples suggest that women's migratory status and their principal employment as domestic workers in fact constituted the principal impediments to any attempts to organise their entry into other sectors. Their status as primary migrants meant that work was essential. Certainly, African women migrants in the 1980s and early 1990s did not normally have the luxury of being financially dependent on either their immediate families or on their partners. Moreover, work within the live-in sphere resolved accommodation difficulties. The possibility of attending long training courses clearly stood in conflict with this. In assessing possible options, women did not simply have to consider the implications of an interim loss of financial income, but accommodation also assumed some importance. The training courses established to facilitate migrant women's movement into other employment sectors did not fully take these issues on board. The high drop out rate on these courses, when contrasted with high levels of initial interest for some of them, suggested that a fundamental logistical reorganisation of training courses needed to take place. The FCEI's view of the home economics course as a strategy to encourage migrants to study could constitute a plausible strategy in certain contexts, but in the context of migrant's women positioning within Rome, moulded as it was by the demands of the labour market, this strategy was more likely to encourage migrant women to consider domestic work as their only feasible option. Furthermore, the 'realistic' approach to the opportunities available to African women led to questionable practices, such as the control of African women's fertility. This was evident in the nature of (mainly African) migrant women's orientation when consulting the YWCA's women migrants' project. As the YWCA representative stated:

> As we are a female association, I always try, when they arrive, to speak about and understand if they have any gynaecological problems. At the beginning, they look at me as if to say that it is none of my business. If they are married, I also talk to them about prevention, because clearly in their situation, *they certainly cannot afford to have an additional problem*, i.e. children (my emphasis) (interview, YWCA).

This indicated a rather dangerous, albeit unintentional transition from responding to migrant women's needs to constructing them. Moreover, the presentation of contraceptive advice in the context of their economic function implicitly functioned to marginalise their maternal function.

There is some evidence to suggest that some African women aspired to improve their educational qualifications as a means of self-improvement and to facilitate entry into other sectors of the labour market. As one Eritrean stated: 'It's not that we are asking for a lot, but at least some basic rights ... let them do domestic work if there are no other jobs but at least give them the possibility to do an evening course'.[67] Many Cape Verdean women also exhibited a desire for self-improvement. They were facilitated in this by the establishment, by Jesuit priests, of a Portuguese school in Rome in 1971. The school aimed to assist Portuguese-speaking workers abroad. It provided a range of educational courses, from literacy to the school leaving examination (*maturità*). Throughout the 1970s and 1980s, numbers registering at the school increased. In the academic year 1971/2 there were 54 students registered. The number of registrations peaked in 1980/1 with 358 students registered. 1985/6 began to show a decline in students with 195 registered students. An internal survey conducted in 1983 based on 48 students (75 per cent of whom were Cape Verdeans) indicated that these women attended the school to acquire a level of education that had not been possible for them before.[68] All of them believed that studying would help them in life, and that, more specifically, it would help them to find alternative employment.[69] Attendance at the Portuguese school can therefore be interpreted as a strategy adopted by some Cape Verdean women to modify their structural position in Italy. One Cape Verdean interviewee moved to Rome from Bologna, where she had had a relatively easy domestic work situation in order to attend the Portuguese school in Rome. Attendance at the school entailed some sacrifice, given the organisation of classes over two afternoons which did not entirely coincide with women's free time as domestic workers. As Perrotta (1988, p. 71) has stated:

> Given that 60 per cent of employers refused to allow them another free afternoon, many have reduced their wages or changed families, others have had to reduce their attendance at classes, but without leaving the school.

The testimony of Maria Crescentia Mota clearly indicated the levels of sacrifice and difficulties associated with pursuing this strategy. The question of time again emerged as a principal obstacle to the implementation of strategies intended to offer migrant women new options:

> I think that of the three hundred pupils who enrolled, I have already seen lists of people who have ... abandoned the school, not through any fault of their own, but because employers do not want to grant them the two afternoons per week

to go to school. Lessons for the final year of primary school take place twice a week, on a Wednesday and Sunday. This matches the two afternoons given in the [domestic worker's] contract. But there is the issue of Wednesday instead of Thursday and employers make a fuss about switching from Thursday to Wednesday.[70]

In fact Mota attributed this to the employers' unwillingness to assist domestic workers in their quest for self improvement:

> ... they don't have the slightest interest in our education: they don't let you out of the house until the last cup of coffee has been washed, they don't think about the fact that school starts as 3.30 ...[71]

Mota's personal experience showed evidence of her own tenacity while simultaneously confirming the high level of demand for domestic workers within the region:

> I've changed houses many times, I can't remember how many ... Since I got it into my head that I want to study, I have to find a job where they guarantee me not simply the two half days included in the contract, but where they allow me to work and study ... When this does not happen ... I don't hesitate, I'm off.[72]

In the early 1990s, modes of entry into alternative spheres had been unrealistically structured and as such tended to prohibit migrant women's participation. Awareness of these structural obstacles had begun to germinate amongst the organising bodies, but tangible remedies had yet to be put in place.

Conclusion

The above has shown that throughout the 1980s and early 1990s, the demand for Black women's labour as domestic workers certainly did not disappear. Unfortunately, available data does not allow for a proper overview of trends regarding the employers of domestic workers. My qualitative data has only provided information about employers through the perspectives and work experiences of domestic workers themselves. Here, I found no uniformity, as the interviewees had worked for a mixture of families – single pensioners, housewives, single working women, two parent families with children and two parent families without children. In the 1970s, Black women appeared to be principally employed by housewives and by families with children. By the 1990s, more could be found caring for the elderly. It would however be useful to establish a more accurate regional overview of families who employ live-in workers to care for children, to care for the elderly or simply to perform housework.[73] Qualitative and quantitative research focused specifically on the employers of domestic workers needs to be carried out to provide a more accurate indication of Italian families' structural reorganisation of reproductive labour. The evidence provided does, however, suggest that regardless of internal differentiation amongst employers, family cohesiveness is no longer being comprehensively attained by internal family members.

As well as a reliance on social service provision, external assistance to maintain family cohesiveness is being provided by migrant women. For Black women, this means employment security in the live-in sphere, but vulnerability in the hourly paid sector. Despite the demand for their labour, the structural difficulties of paid domestic work mean that Black women are subject to implicit and explicit exploitation from their employers. Even where employers adhere to contractual regulations, live-in domestic work presents primary female migrants with a range of difficulties. This is related to the primary construction of their identities on the basis of their labour. In reply to my question about the difficulties of female same sex migration, the key informant from the Cape Verdean women's association stated: 'We sometimes feel, in fact most of the time, we feel that we are not real women. This happens to us often. We feel that we are only work instruments' (interview, OMCVI). But Black women also exhibited awareness of their contribution to Italy. As two prominent Cape Verdean activists have written:

> ... we can openly say that we too, with our work, have contributed in a concrete way to the economic development of Italian society. Let's not even talk about the possibilities offered to employers to work outside the home, with the tranquillity of knowing that they have left their children in the arms of trustworthy people (De Lourdes de Jesus and Pimental 1989, p. 90).

I have established that the voluntary and institutional response did not, on the whole, fundamentally challenge migrant women's absorption into the domestic work sphere. In addition, the demand for such labour, confirmed by the provisions of Circular 156, suggests that domestic work will constitute a permanent occupational status for Black women for the foreseeable future. The fact that I encountered women who represented the second generation of women in their families to migrate to Rome as live-in workers, attests to the permanent nature of domestic work as an employment sector for the ethnic groups in my study. In other contexts, the ability of Black women to move out of the domestic work sphere has been contingent on wider factors. Woody (1992) has shown that in the United States, economic restructuring from a production economy to a service economy allowed Black women the possibility of moving into other sectors.

However, domestic work does undeniably constitute a means through which Black women can enter Italy and find secure labour. This exemplifies Glenn's (1992) notion of the hierarchy and interdependence inscribed into the domestic work relationship and increasingly to be found between Black and White women. The 1991 circular tied new entries to their employers for two years, replicating in form the American model of 'sponsorship', which Colen (1986, p. 52) has defined as a 'legally sanctioned indentured servitude'. Noticeably however, although the West Indian domestic workers of her study found that live-in sponsor jobs greatly exacerbated the structural problems of domestic work, they were prepared to 'stick it out' as a means of meeting their specific goals. Black women in Rome appear to have adopted the same attitude, although this has proved to be much more problematic for the younger and better educated generation of East African women.

Notes

1   Centro lavoratori stranieri immigrati. This was established in 1987 and affiliated to the CGIL.
2   According to the 1981 census 2.7 per cent of men and 5.3 per cent of women aged over 75 were living in residential homes.
3   According to a Labos survey published in 1988 and based on a sample group of 1,000 over 75s nationally, 28 per cent were found to live alone and 62 per cent lived with one or more relatives. See Dell'Orto and Taccani (1993).
4   I expand on this in more detail in the following chapter.
5   Circular n. 156/91 of 29/11/1991, 'Lavoratori extracomunitari da adibire ai servizi domestici – nuovi ingressi'.
6   Data cited in AAvv (1994, p. 66).
7   There have been calls for just such a response in other national contexts. For example, when Zoe Baird, the nominee for the post of Attorney General in America was found to be employing two undocumented immigrants in 1993, there were several suggestions that the American Immigration Reform and Control Act of 1986 should be changed to give household workers special visas. For a discussion of these suggestions see Chang (1994).
8   The following discussion refers to the experience of live-in domestics as it is in this sphere that employers can exercise the greatest control and have a significant impact on domestic workers' wider aspirations.

9   In fact, I met and interviewed this woman in the local Caritas office, where she had come to obtain a 'Caritas Card' as a first step to some kind of official registration in Italy.

10   This young woman (aged 24) was actually present but was not prepared to give an interview as she was fearful of possible repercussions.

11   The rooms of domestic workers are normally very small and it is therefore difficult to entertain in them. Nonetheless, despite this spatial prohibition, the underlying constraint was that the employers' home was exclusively a place of employment.

12   The flat was extremely spacious with six rooms. She had her own little room with a bathroom, which was extremely small.

13   His wife had had a stroke eight years ago and was now paralysed in bed. In fact before this time they had employed hourly paid domestic workers. However, since his wife's incapacitation, he had employed Elsa as a full-time live-in worker.

14   It was at this point that I had asked her what her current salary was in order to gauge the relationship between her expenses and her income.

15   Filomena also recounted a similar occurrence with regard to a friend of hers who received a phone call from Cape Verde informing her of her mother's death in the middle of her employer's dinner party. Afterwards, her employer said 'I could kill that friend of yours. She ruined my dinner party.'

16   This is not only relevant to the Italian case. In her study of the South African situation, Cock (1980, p. 72) observed that domestic workers' 'weak bargaining positioning reflects their deprivation of critical rights as workers'.

17   A small survey carried out by ACLI-COLF in 1989 consisted of interviews with 200 domestic workers in 5 major Italian cities. The study showed that protection against illness and dismissal was the problem most universally expressed by domestic workers. See ACLI-COLF (1989b).

18   Contributions are calculated on the basis of the number of hours worked for the employer. At the start of an employment relationship, the employee and the employer fill in form LD09. Contributions are paid on a trimestral basis.

19   In Italy, the metalworkers' federations have traditionally been seen as the most radical sector and in the 1970s, wage settlements for this sector were used to obtain similar agreements in other sectors. (See Golden 1988).

20   The original article was published in *Le Colf*, 1974 and reproduced in Garassini 1992, p. XXIV.

21   The original article was published in *Le Colf*, 1974 and reproduced in Garassini 1992, p. XXV.

22   Indeed there was a delay of several years before its eventual renewal.

23   See full text of the 1988 contract reproduced in *Le Colf*, September 1988. Five migrant women had been involved in this process, a Cape Verdean, an Eritrean, a Latin-American, an Indian and a Filipina.

24   See Anderson (1993, p. 21) for an example of a contract stipulated between a migrant woman and her employer in the Middle East in 1990 where it was stated that the female domestic worker's working hours would be *unlimited.*

25   See *Le Colf*, January 1986, p. 3 for an example of this mobilisation.

26   Article 16 of the 1992 contract gave male domestic workers the possibility of two days paid leave subsequent to the birth of their child.

27   The subsequent chapter will discuss in some detail why the problems of maternity are particularly serious for working migrant women.

28 *Ad verbatim* testimony published in Caritas diocensana di Roma – Siares (1989), p. 130.
29 In fact she showed me many photos of her 'past' life. These consisted of photos of her house, husband and children together.
30 She arranged for her sister to come and replace her. See Interview 23.
31 This was at the Cape Verdeans' public meeting space in Piazza Fiume.
32 Informal discussion at Tra Noi association with a Cape Verdean woman.
33 This may have been attributable to my own Caribbean ethnicity and their assumption that there was no need to expand on this issue because of our partially shared positioning in terms of 'race'.
34 Up to the 1970s, the explicit highlighting of regional Italian 'ethnicities' in newspaper adverts suggested that hierarchies based on regional origin had been integral to the domestic work sector. See Appendix 3.
35 These authors did not question the implications of this stereotype. This seemed to be in part because they viewed these perceived cultural attributes as a guarantor of preferential treatment within the sphere of domestic work.
36 Similar provisions had been enacted for Albanians and Yugoslavians prior to this.
37 'Norme sul rilascio del permesso temporaneo di soggiorno per motivi di lavoro o di studio ai cittadini somali privi del riconoscimento dello status di rifugiato', published in *Gazzetta Ufficiale*, 26 October 1992, n. 252.
38 See Helen Moussa (1993) on the experiences of Ethiopian and Eritrean female refugees in Toronto.
39 For more on the concept of diaspora see Brah (1996) and Cohen (1997).
40 See Andall (1999) for more on the mobility of female migrants in Europe.
41 The proceedings of a conference on immigrants, held in 1978, confirmed that the institutional sphere was almost entirely absent from the regulation of the phenomenon. For the Rome area, the reception centres and organisations offering assistance were almost exclusively religious based. Notably, the only two associations linked to employment sectors were the API-COLF and the ACLI-COLF, indicating the prevalence of domestic work at this stage of the immigration phenomenon. See conference proceedings published in *Servizio Migranti*, n. 9, September 1978.
42 The three trade union confederations all established offices in the 1980s which dealt specifically with the general interests of migrant workers.
43 The exact figures are as follows. Caritas operating budget for 1989: 13,950,689,166. Contribution from Province: 579,760,000; contribution from Lazio region: 1,404,000,000; contribution from *Comune*: 5,213,010,030. Source: Roma Caritas (1990).
44 See Di Liegro and Pittau (1992, pp. 346–7). The involvement of the Caritas was not always viewed in a neutral or favourable light. In fact, there was a feeling from some quarters, that the Caritas was intent on usurping the state's role to validate its own existence. See the Caritas' response to this in Di Liegro and Pittau (1992, p. 380).
45 It was recognised however that compromises were often made within the Protestant sector: 'This is just the theory and at the end you very often have to work with the circumstances and you will do charity like everybody else or do the wrong thing ... it might even be right to do the wrong thing!' (interview, FCEI).
46 This project in Rome was utilised principally by East African women (Somali, Ethiopian and Eritrean), although it was not restricted to these nationalities. This appeared to be a consequence of informal word of mouth networks: 'It doesn't depend on us, we don't choose, they come to us. They know that we exist now, and friends tell friends' (interview,

YWCA). The project was entitled 'Shelter, assistance, advocacy and training for migrant and refugee women'.

47 The YWCA is an international Protestant association concerned with social and economic justice, founded in the late nineteenth century (1877) in England. Eventually it extended its activities to Catholic countries. The first Italian association was founded in Turin in 1894 called *Unione Cristiana delle Giovani*. See information sheet 'Conosciamo L'YWCA-UCDG'.

48 See document prepared for international meeting in Strasbourg in 1988: 'YWCA of Italy: Shelter, assistance, advocacy and training for migrant and refugee women'. The 1988 Strasbourg meeting which took place in April 1988 had as its theme: 'Young migrant and refugee women: a challenge for European YWCA's'. Three delegates from Italy attended, including one female refugee. A number of proposals were recommended to be implemented at the local and European level. These included fighting racism, working with migrant women's groups and young women migrants, publishing personal histories of refugee and migrant women and emphasising the value of a multicultural society. See YWCA-UCDG: 'Progetto "Donne migranti e rifugiate"', May 1988.

49 The utility of the voluntary sector network can be observed in the provision of a kitchen by the Scottish Church to enable those on this course to perfect the practical aspects of the course.

50 This replicates French *state* organisation of migrant women in the post-war period. In 1967, the official agency for state organised migration to France set up a centre in 1967 to offer Caribbean women a 'pretraining' course for domestic work posts. This introduced Caribbean women to 'metropolitan French culture, to modern household equipment, to French cooking ...' (Condon 1995, p. 5).

51 The CELSI-CGIL key informant regarded this as a deficiency implicit within most of the training courses available in the region.

52 The FCEI, formed in Milan in November 1967, united the various sectors of Italian Protestantism. Individual Protestant churches which form part of the federation retain their autonomy while pursuing a common goal regarding the missionary nature of the Church. See 'The Federation of Protestant Churches in Italy', in *nev*, n. 53, 30 September 1991. *nev* is the monthly press service of the FCEI.

53 The FCEI was involved in a number of initiatives related to immigration. It was a member of the National consultative body on immigration within the Ministry of Labour and a founding member of the Italian Council for Refugees (CIR). See 'Il Servizio rifugiati e migranti della FCEI', in *nev*, n. 127, 31 May 1991.

54 See presentation by Anne Marie Duprès at the 'Black/Migrant Women and Health in Europe' conference (3–5 March 1993, Stuttgart, Germany) in the conference report.

55 In the case of the FCEI, this service was widely used by Somalis, Ethiopians and Eritreans.

56 This is the home economics course referred to above.

57 It should be noted that the interviewee herself acknowledged that her perception of internal gender relations within certain African communities was impressionistic.

58 This particular project was financed by the Province of Rome. The FCEI is financed by sister churches in other European countries and by the World Council of Churches. However, it is also subsidised by public institutions in Italy to do work on specific projects for migrants. At the time of interview, the FCEI had two ongoing projects (education and housing). Public financing was notoriously unreliable. In 1993, the FCEI still had not been paid for work carried out in 1990.

59 For example, some of these women would eventually start working within Libere, Insieme (see chapter 9). This suggested that there was an easily identifiable tiny elite of ethnic minority women who were approached by Italian organisations and associations whenever these projects wanted to organise around the issue of minority women.

60 Untitled paper signed by Astier (Ethiopian), Susan (Ghanaian), Joanna (Sudanese), Gabriela (Argentinian) and a Peruvian woman. Convegno FCEI, 22 February 1989.

61 The group was not successful in gaining funding for this project.

62 Some of these courses were financed by the European Social Fund.

63 For more on the professional training of non-EU migrants in Lazio, see Salatto (1992).

64 In some other European countries public sector employment as nurses has been an important option for ethnic minority women. In Britain, particularly after a change in immigration rules in 1962, when potential migrants could only enter for a specific job, Black women found plenty of demand in the lower tier of nursing as auxiliaries and as State Enrolled Nurses (Bryan, Dadzie and Scafe (1985). In France too, Black women from the Caribbean were recruited in the 1960s to work in French public hospitals. (Condon 1995).

65 The monthly incentive was L150,000 for the first year, L200,000 for the second year and L250,000 for the third year. A prize to be awarded on completion of each year was also available. This consisted of one, two and three million respectively. The region was also considering developing a course to train women as home-helps, but this was still at an incipient stage of planning at the time of interview (interview, RL2).

66 'Interventi formativi: ammissione immigrati extracomunitari ai corsi professionali per infermieri', Regione Lazio, assessorato, Rome, 26 March 1992.

67 *Ad verbatim* testimony published in Caritas Diocesana di Roma (1989), p. 199.

68 Under Portuguese colonial rule, it was estimated that 80 per cent of the population was illiterate in the 1960s. See Goutier (1996).

69 For more information on these results, see Perrotta (1988).

70 *Ad verbatim* testimony reproduced in Caritas diocesana di Roma (1989) p. 186.

71 Ibid.

72 Ibid., p. 188.

73 Some indication is given of this at the national level in the results of the most recent ACLI-COLF survey. See chapter 8.

7 Domestic Work and Family Life

In chapter 6, I argued that the tension provoked by the conflicting interests inscribed within the domestic work relationship was resolved at the legislative level to the benefit of the employer. One area where the issue of competing interests is most acute concerns that of maternity. Chapter 4 discussed how the national organisation for domestic workers, the ACLI-COLF, historically viewed domestic work as an important support service to the Italian family. But what importance has been afforded to the family life of live-in domestic workers? The answer to this question raises issues in relation to a number of areas. Firstly, the notion of female solidarity is challenged. Recourse to live-in domestic workers to resolve the difficulties of reproductive care for some women disadvantages other women (in this instance migrant women) disproportionately. Secondly, it reveals the development of new modes of family organisation for some migrant families. These alternative models do not resemble existing Italian models of family organisation and, in some instances, actually reverse previous state strategies relating to families and children. These models also tend to disregard the specific function that migrant families have assumed in migration destination countries. Examples in other countries have demonstrated that ethnic minority families can act both as an important buffer to racism and as a forum for positive self-identity for family members.[1] Finally, as Romero's (1997, p. 152) research as shown in relation to the North American context: 'Exploring domestic service from the perspective of the workers' children provides insights into the hidden costs of maintaining the white, middle-class patriarchal ideal of the American family'.

In previous chapters I have suggested that Black women's social identity was largely constructed around the basis of their labour. This chapter reiterates this supposition by demonstrating the extent to which their maternal identities have been marginalised precisely to enable them to fulfil this labour function. The following discussion should not be interpreted as unqualified support for the nuclear family and women's traditional role within it. In other words, I am not necessarily arguing that migrant women should aspire to the vision of

193

motherhood that became dominant in post-war Italy. Rather, this chapter serves to demonstrate the extent to which the very forces which promoted the dominant model of motherhood in post-war Italy contributed to its subversion by adopting different assumptions in relation to the family relations of migrant women. In the example of migrant women, then, we see the articulation of an inverse trend when compared to Italian women. While the post-1968 period has demonstrated Italian women's desire to reduce the dominance of the maternal role in relation to a paid work role, African women have been engaged in a parallel struggle to reduce the dominance of their paid work role in relation to the maternal role.

The question of motherhood, maternity and the family has represented a core component of feminist debate.[2] As discussed in chapter 1, these discourses were also present in the writings of Italian feminists. The literature on diversity has indicated that, for ethnic minority women, motherhood could be experienced and structured in a manner which differed significantly from the assumed family 'norm'. Referring to the North American context Collins (1994, p. 45) states:

> For Native American, African-American, Hispanic, and Asian-American women, motherhood cannot be analyzed in isolation from its context. Motherhood occurs in specific historical situations framed by interlocking structures of race, class, and gender ... Racial domination and economic exploitation profoundly shape the mothering context, not only for racial ethnic women in the United States, but for all women.

Similarly, Glenn (1994, p. 7) has maintained that 'The concept of mothering as universally women's work disguises the fact that it is further subdivided, so that different aspects of caring labor are assigned to different groups of women'. Her argument that mothering (pregnancy and child-rearing) should no longer be seen as a solely gendered phenomenon, but also as a racialised one has increasing application to the Italian context.[3] My aim in this chapter is to document why and how the family organisation of autonomous female migrants was constructed so differently from the Italian 'norm'. This led to a situation where a superfluous function was sometimes attributed to migrant woman's family role. While this may not have been explicitly articulated as a preferable or alternative model to the normalised arrangement of the mother caring for her child, the development of social structures which perpetuated rather than prevented the separation of the biological mother from her child tended to indicate that the care of migrants' children by their biological mothers was not seen to represent the same social and cultural imperative that it did for Italians. The experiences of Black women therefore, highlighted how the concept and value of motherhood could be differentially constructed for diverse categories of women within Italy.

The focus of this chapter centres on revealing the obstacles that Black women faced in living as a family unit in Rome. I argue that this was particularly problematic where the dominant employment activity of the mother was that of a live-in domestic worker. My focus is additionally intended to counter the direction of academic interest in migrant families living in Italy. In the early 1990s interest in migrant families generally lent support to Morokvasic's (1983a) critique of a pervasive ethnocentric approach towards migrant women which meant they were frequently evaluated in terms of the extent to which they had adopted or were willing to adopt the 'modern' values of western women. Some of the contributions to an academic conference on women migrants held in 1993, in Ancona, were indicative of this trend. For example, papers by Maffioli (1994) and Tognetti Bordogna (1994) indicated a tendency to view the incidence of mixed marriages between migrant women and Italian men as indicative of a step towards modernity.

Tognetti Bordogna's (1994) typology of migrant families in Italy focused on family reunification, joint family migratory projects and mixed marriages. This does not include the typology which I will focus on below. This concerns the separation of families as a direct consequence of the nature of migrant women's labour market participation. This separation was a consequence not only of the gendered labour demand within the region but also the lack of structures to accommodate a relatively new social and cultural phenomenon in Italy – single parent families headed by full-time working women.[4]

Domestic Work and Maternity

As we saw in chapter 4, since the nineteenth century, employment within the domestic work sector was envisaged as a transitional stage. For women, it was considered as a prelude to marriage and, in any case, employers saw marriage as constituting a conflict of interest for their employees. As Coser (1973, p. 35) has written: 'The ideal servant is unmarried, even asexual', and he attributed this to the 'greedy' demands of the employer who seeks to absorb the total personality of their servants. McBride's (1976, p. 56) study of domestic service in nineteenth century Britain and France, showed that 'most servants never married or left service when they married'. Thus, one can identify a historical incompatibility between live-in domestic work and family life.[5] In this section of the chapter, I want to argue that the nature of female migratory movement to Italy, where women were employed as live-in workers, presents particular problems in relation to maternity. In the early post-war period in Italy, one method of combining family life with live-in work was to work as a couple (*coppia*) for a particular family.[6] Generally, however, live-in domestic work for Italian domestic workers was also incompatible with maternity. Nonetheless, the temptation to view the experience of female migrants as a straightforward process of continuity in relation to Italian domestic workers should be avoided. A number of important differences point to a series of diverse constraints for migrant women. Italian live-in domestic workers were undoubtedly subject to the strong Catholic moral doctrine of the 1950s regarding appropriate roles for women. This is likely to have meant that they envisaged domestic work as a temporary occupation until marriage.[7] The importance of Catholic morality at this time also meant that single Italian women were unlikely to embark on single parenthood in the same way that migrant women could in the 1970s. More significantly, for the migrant women of my case study, domestic work did not exist as a transitory stage of employment, but rather constituted a long-term occupation. This would have important ramifications for their ability to express their maternal social identity.

The preceding chapter demonstrated how those provisions of the national contract which ostensibly offer domestic workers some protection in the event of pregnancy, are in practice nullified by the provisions which govern the termination of the contract of employment between employer and employee. Pregnancy has universally had an adverse effect on women's standing in the labour market and it is my contention that the live-in work available to Black women in Italy severely curtailed their options in terms of both having and raising their own families.

In 1989, the then vice-president of the Cape Verdean women's association Carolina Pimental, argued that Cape Verdean women often found themselves in a dilemma concerning maternity:

> A woman who migrates for work, in this case as a domestic worker for Italian families, is always very young. She arrives at a certain age and finds herself in a dilemma: the desire to have a family and the impossibility of having one.[8]

According to a trade union representative working with migrant communities, there were very real difficulties associated with migrant women's maternity:

I have witnessed the problems of women and children myself. Many women come to me and ask me whether I can help them to find a job where they can keep their baby, because otherwise they don't know where or with whom to leave them ... (Tavola Rotonda 1990).

My interviews with African women confirmed the profound difficulties women encountered in negotiating the maternal process. In the majority of cases, pregnancy frequently meant the loss of employment. Rosa (interview 3) had worked for nine years with the same family but was forced to leave when she became pregnant. Francesca (interview 9) was sacked when she was seven months pregnant. Where pregnancy signified a temporary loss of employment, this was, in the vast majority of cases, dependent on migrant women's ability to secure care for their children in other locations. Lucila (interview 2), for example, became pregnant after six years of employment as a live-in domestic worker with the same family. Her employers were prepared to keep her on, but only if she agreed to place her own child in a residential home. She considered this to be very unjust, especially as she had practically been a mother to their child. This disappointment with employers' insensitivity to the problems of maternity is also apparent in the testimony of an Eritrean mother:

> I live with my *signora*; her children have grown up, but she hasn't allowed me to keep my baby girl with me. I collect her on Saturday and Sunday, they don't make a fuss, but they are not happy. However they are not bad people.[9]

This statement reinforces the view held by many interviewees who maintained that employers were essentially concerned with the manner in which peripheral factors could affect their ability to perform their work. In chapter 5, I described the manner in which Lemlem's (interview 10) employers had resented her having or desiring a boyfriend as they felt that this would distract her from her work. The testimony cited above reinforces this. Even where employers may not have explicitly prohibited certain behaviour, their implicit dissastisfaction had a negative impact on the worker. The testimony of the Eritrean woman above demonstrates that although her employers were not bad overall, they nonetheless did not facilitate her desire to exercise a maternal identity, even though this occurred for a very restricted period at the weekend. Gerom (interview 29) also recounted that while living in a residential home, he restricted his visits to his father who was employed as a live-in domestic worker, as the employers did not encourage visiting.

The experience of Antonia (interview 16) highlights the difficulties of organising maternity in the face of employers' reluctance to fully acknowledge their employees maternal social identities. Antonia left her son in Cape Verde when she migrated to Rome in the mid-1970s. He first stayed with his paternal grandmother and then with other relatives. She had always wanted to bring him to Italy but this initially proved too difficult. When he was aged 12, she brought him to Lisbon where he stayed with a friend of hers for three years. At the time, she felt unable to bring him to Italy because she did not have her own home and he could not stay with her at her employers' residence. The arrangement in Portugal did not work out and she had to take him back to Cape Verde for six months. A friend in Italy put her in contact with a social worker who suggested that she foster her son to an Italian family. She was reluctant to do this, because she was not sure how an Italian family would treat a Black child. Eventually it was arranged that he would come to Italy and be placed in a residential home. At the time of interview, she paid L250,000 a month towards his keep out of her salary of L1,000,000. She told me that she had an excellent relationship with her son and that they spoke daily on the telephone. However this was qualified by the statement 'but we can never stay together ... not even in the summer or at Easter'. They once spent a fortnight together in Circeo, on the coast in Lazio, with some other friends. She would have liked to have had another child but she considered this to be impossible in Italy: 'I would like to have another child, but how would I manage, it's already a struggle to live. I would be forced to throw the child into the Tiber'. Antonia also commented on employers' false benevolence in relation to their employees' children. Her current employer had forbidden her to bring anyone to the house. However, after some time she had said that she would like to meet her son, who subsequently visited the house. Some time afterwards, Antonia's son was in the vicinity and popped by to see his mother. When the employer came home and saw him there: '[the female employer] started sulking' and told Antonia off for not informing her that her son would be visiting. As Antonia commented: 'My son just popped in for a second. Even though she is very happy with my work, you can see that my son cannot even come and eat with me sometimes. It's not fair'. Antonia did want to live together with her son in Rome, however, as she stated: 'I've done my sums, to rent somewhere and then survive would be impossible. I'm now resigned to the fact that we will never live together'.

The implications of pregnancy for live-in domestic workers cannot be over-emphasised.[10] Not only does it adversely affect their employment situation but it can often signify homelessness. Lucila (interview 2) stayed with various friends after she had had to leave her family, and subsequently in a *pensione*. The expenditure of living in this type of accommodation and having to eat out dissipated most of her savings. Francesca (interview 9), sacked seven months into her pregnancy, spent two months in a religious institution. Religious establishments were frequently a lifeline for these single pregnant women. In fact, even into the 1990s, religious organisations dominated this sector of provision. Although government institutions had begun to coordinate some of these requests they still relied heavily on the existence of these religious bodies. This was confirmed to me by a local social worker:

> For young mothers, or female migrants about to give birth, the *Comune*, that is we as social workers, look after them. There are institutes which are just for single mothers. Those that we have in Rome are almost entirely run by religious people (interview, AS, RM1).

Despite the existence of the 1971 maternity law, the experiences of these women indicated that they were effectively forced to accept employment conditions which were no longer legally permissible given their status as pregnant workers. For example, Lucila, forced to leave her employers of six years and having used up most of her savings on the *pensione*, was forced to seek employment when she was six months pregnant. She was employed as a live-in worker and worked there for three months until her baby was born. Francesca resumed live-in work when her baby was only 20 days old. It has already been established that live-in domestic work is particularly onerous and these women were working either pregnant or with young babies at a time when only limited structural improvements within the domestic work sector had been achieved.

The difficulties of maternity for these female migrant workers must also be ascertained by the decisions women made about their children left in the country of origin. Clara (interview 6) for example, who had migrated to Italy in 1971 when she was 22, left three children behind in the Cape Verde islands (aged 5, 2 and 1). These children were cared for by her mother. This option was also utilised by Maria (interview 4) who had migrated to Italy in the late 1980s from Cape Verde. She also left her children (aged 7 and 10) to be cared for by their grandmother. She had subsequently been joined in Italy by her husband, but they still did not think it would be feasible to bring their children to Italy. In fact, several of the women I interviewed thought it futile to bring their children to Italy from their respective countries of origin because of the difficulties of caring for them as single parent domestic workers. Hanna (interview 12), for example, did not plan to bring her 9 year-old son to Italy. When I asked Sara (interview 26) whether she would bring her children (aged 16,14, 10) from Eritrea, she responded 'what's the point, where would I put them?'

Decisions about whether to embark on the maternal process were also conditioned by the ensuing logistical problems that this would pose. Lemlem (interview 10), who started live-in work when she was 18, in 1983, considered it almost an act of emotional irresponsibility to have children while working as a live-in domestic. The options that would have been available to her in the event of pregnancy encouraged her to postpone maternity. Commenting on the situation of her Eritrean friends who had chosen to combine maternity with domestic work she stated:

> ... Those that have children have to put them in residential homes, because they don't have the free time to go and pick them up from school etc. I don't want to have a child because I wouldn't want to put him in a residential home. Otherwise when will the child have his parents' affection? When he's grown up?'[11]

The testimony of another Eritrean woman indicated that she had not even considered marriage because of the tangible difficulties of maintaining some semblance of 'normal' married life within the Roman context:

> Some people even get married here, but it's very difficult especially the sexual side; either you have to work together or nothing. If you have a boyfriend, you don't have a home, you don't know where to go. Maybe on a Thursday evening you go the cinema but after the cinema where do you go? You have no home, you can't go back to where you work ... Personally, I have never thought about getting married, especially seeing all these things, I mean, when somebody gets married, at least something must change, like having a home, time ... while instead there are so many who get married and see each other once a week, ... so many problems.[12]

The experience of Filomena (interview 22) equally suggested that live-in domestic work not only logistically created obstacles to maternity but also to women's very ability to establish and maintain relationships:

> When you work as a live-in domestic you don't have personal relationships. You just have crumbs. I haven't been able to establish a relationship because I have become withdrawn, because this type of work also affects you psychologically. I am 39 years old and my greatest sorrow is that of not having

had a child. Many Cape Verdean women have been forced to forego maternity. I hope I do not end up like that. And if I can't have a child, at least a partner.

Representatives from the various communities highlighted the cultural aspect of women having to renege on maternity. The national representative of Eritrean women, for example, stated:

> For you western women, not having children is a choice; a free choice, of emancipation if you want ... For us women from Third World countries, from Africa, where a woman's value correlates to the number of children she has produced, not having children, not getting married is a tremendous thing ... For many women it is like not living! ... I know many women around forty-eight to fifty who are resigned to this life, but they gaze at the children of others in a particular way (Maricos 1990b, p. 89).

In contrast to this, there was evidence from within other communities, that some women positively chose maternity, despite the difficulties this would pose. According to the vice-president of the Cape Verdean women's association, some Cape Verdean women have actually chosen maternity as a refuge from their particular situations. In other words, they minimised the logistical problems that maternity would provoke. Despite the fact that the experience of maternity would be exacerbated by their single parent status, it was nevertheless considered to be important, as it provided them with an alternative to an all consuming work identity. This view did in fact emerge in some of my interviews. Matilde (interview 1) for example maintained that her role as a mother was her most important role and that the biggest sacrifices she had made in Italy had been in order to maintain her three children. Francesca (interview 9) also stated that her maternal role was extremely important. These views tended to contradict Maffioli's (1994, p. 118) hypothesis that pregnancy for an unmarried migrant 'is presumably ... an accident or a misfortune, not a choice'.

The implications of pregnancy for domestic workers may have additionally affected the level of prenatal care that some women received. Favaro's (1994) study of migrant women in Milan and the Emilia-Romagna region showed that female domestic workers often declared their pregnancy at a very late stage to delay the loss of their employment and accommodation. Consequently, they sometimes received reduced prenatal care. It is probable that this was also a problem in Rome, particularly given the dominance of domestic work amongst female migrant workers and the difficulties associated with pregnancy and employment as outlined above. An interview with a key informant at a local health authority (USL RM12), regarding its contact with migrant women via the health centres in the district, indicated that the majority of migrant women came for contraception, or to procure an abortion and sometimes for support during pregnancy (interview, USL RM12).[13] There seemed to be no evidence of repeat abortion amongst migrant women.[14] Normally if these women first came to the health centre for an abortion, they would then remain with the centre for subsequent contraception. The majority of migrant women requesting abortion did so because they were single women or because it was impossible for them to keep their children in the families for whom they worked.[15] Furthermore, for migrant women who sought assistance in relation to pregnancy from within the Catholic voluntary sector, abortion was not presented as an option. In her address to a conference on women and migration, the Somali Saida Ali, a paediatrician and prominent figure in the immigration sector in Rome, highlighted this fact:

> With regard to family planning, many women – those who are undocumented or who don't have any money – cannot even have terminations. Those who are getting health care at religious centres like Caritas cannot have terminations because the doctors working in these centres are conscientious objectors. So they find themselves having to continue an unwanted pregnancy (Ali 1990, p. 100).

As with migrant women's views on whether their employers were good or bad, the women interviewed expressed similar differences with regard to their employers' response to maternity. As Lemlem (interview 10) stated in referring to the experiences of her friends: 'Some [employers], make you leave the house as soon as you get pregnant. Others help you to bring up your child'. The testimony of Lettesgu, however, was somewhat less equivocal: '... the families for whom [domestics] work don't want them [children]. They'd prefer to bring up a dog rather than the children of these women ...'.[16]

An employer's willingness to accommodate mother and children is important for migrant women in terms of their family life. But it paradoxically creates other problems, such as an increased workload or a more vulnerable and potentially more exploitable employment situation. Francesca (interview 9), for example, had worked for the last 13 years in the same family as a live-in domestic. She cared for a couple who were in their early 70s. She described her work as 'doing everything', from the shopping to cooking and cleaning. She had two rooms in the house and lived with her two children aged 11 and 14. While this might ostensibly appear as an optimum arrangement, Francesca cited the difficulties of this type of arrangement as her children approached adolescence. She commented on the fact that because it was not their house, the children were not free to come and go as they wanted because it would 'annoy' the employers. Again, this problem seemed to be inextricably related to the nature of the relationship that is frequently established between employer and employee, where apparently superfluous objects to the labour function of the employee (e.g. children) should be invisible. Domestic workers equally have less flexibility within this type of relationship, as employers are aware that workers would encounter extreme difficulties if they attempted to change jobs with dependants. Alex (interview 20) also lived-in with her baby aged 18 months. Her employer was an 80 year-old pensioner for whom she did everything. She stated that he had not protested too much when she announced that she was pregnant. Although she was now taking her baby to the nursery from 8.00am to 4.00am, she found it extremely difficult to combine live-in domestic work with care for a young baby, as at times the baby started crying precisely when it was the meal-time of her employer. The conflict between the interests of motherhood and employment can be seen to be intensified in this particular instance.

The experience of Gabriele (interview 25) indicates the variety of mothering strategies that migrant domestic workers have adopted. When Gabriele migrated to Rome in 1972, she already had four children who were being cared for by her husband in Cape Verde. After three years she returned to Cape Verde on holiday. When she returned to Italy she found that she was again pregnant. She had this child and continued working for the same family. She was able to keep this child with her. However, the family had seven children of their own and this meant that her workload was particularly heavy. She eventually changed employers because of this but she was unable to take her three year-old daughter with her because her new employers did not have enough space. An informal arrangement was organised with an Italian family that she knew in the neighbourhood.[17] It seemed that a level of solidarity evident in this neighbourhood led to this Italian family offering to care for her daughter. She did not pay this family, they did it out of friendship. Her daughter had lived with them for some 15 years at the time of interview as Gabriele was still a live-in worker. She maintained that she had a very positive relationship with her daughter.[18] Antonia's (interview 16) experience suggests that mothers' separation from their children could be perpetuated across the generations. It has already been established that Antonia was unable to live with her son, who had grown up with a variety of friends and relatives in Cape Verde, Portugal and then in a residential home in Rome. Antonia herself had also not lived with her own mother, who had migrated to Rome as a live-in domestic in the early 1960s.

The above examples indicate the substantial difficulties that maternity presented to live-in domestic workers and the diverse organisational decisions that they made in relation to this. These difficulties contributed to the repression of their interlocking social identities and frequently restricted them to an identity intrinsically linked to the world of labour.

Residential Homes

Thus far we have seen that one possible option for female migrant domestic workers consisted of care for their children by a member of the extended family, not normally resident in the same country. Other women were able to secure employment which provided accommodation for both mother and child. However, two further alternatives have been the institutionalisation of migrants' children and their fostering to Italian families. Both of these options, while resolving the short-term dilemma of child-care, present specific long term problems for migrant domestic workers and their children/families.

The use of residential homes as a strategy for overcoming the logistical difficulties migrant women encountered in attempting to combine motherhood with live-in work can be categorised as a regressive trend, especially if one considers the direction of state policy with regard to the use of residential homes in the care of children. State social service departments refer to articles 30 and 31 of the Italian Constitution as guiding principles in structuring their work. These articles state respectively:

> It is a right and duty of parents to maintain, instruct and educate their children, even if they are born out of wedlock. Where the parents are incapacitated, the law ensures that their duties are carried out. The law ensures that children born out of wedlock have the same legal and social protection as those born within marriage. The law determines the norms and limits to establish paternity (Article 30).

> The republic facilitates, by economic and other means, family formation and the fulfillment of related duties, paying particular attention to large families. It protects maternity, infancy and youth, supporting the necessary institutes to this end (Article 31).

State social services departments, however, normally only intervene in the event of family dysfunctionality. Articles 330–337 of the civil code outlined the instances and procedures to be adopted once parental authority had been revoked. Article 330 stated:

> The loss of parental authority: the judge can declare the removal of parental authority when the parent violates or neglects their duties or abuses their relative powers with serious harm to the child. In such a case, for serious reasons, the judge can order the child to be removed from the family home.

Articles 402 and 403 delineated the duties incumbent on those bodies who assumed responsibility for children removed from their families of origin. Article 403 for example, stipulated the state's duty to care for those minors who have been morally or materially abandoned.

However, what is particularly relevant for our discussion is the legislation introduced in 1983 (law n. 184) which governed the adoption and fostering of minors. Article 1 commenced as follows: 'the minor has a right to be educated in his or her own family'. Article 2 clearly stated that the use of residential homes for the care of children should be adopted only as a last resort and that it was desirable for children to be fostered either by a family or by a single person. Thus the creation of an alternative family context, even if it did not resemble the traditional nuclear family was envisaged for those children who could not be cared for by their biological parents. This was seen to be preferable to an institutional alternative:

> The minor who is temporarily deprived of a suitable family environment can be fostered to another family … either to a single person, or to a family type community, to ensure his/her maintenance, education and instruction. Where a suitable foster family is not possible, the placing of a minor in a public or private residential home is permitted.

At any rate, alternative caring was not intended to replace the biological family but to provide a safe and healthy environment for minors until such time as they could be returned to their biological parents (Art. 4). Foster carers were not only expected to provide a salutary environment for minors but it was also their duty to facilitate the relationship between the child and the biological parents and promote the child's reinsertion into the family of origin (Art. 5). This law emphasised that where the biological parents were unable to fulfil their parental duties, as outlined in Article 30 of the Constitution, alternative provision would be organised by the state. The trend in recent years has therefore been away from institutional arrangements and towards short and long-term fostering and adoption.

As with other areas regarding immigration in the early years, there is scant documentation regarding the numbers of migrants' children who were placed in residential homes during the 1970s. This is largely because these predominantly religious institutions often did not keep proper records. An interview conducted at a small residential home in the centre of Rome revealed that whilst the nuns had consistently cared for migrants' children (mainly from Cape Verde) they also maintained that they had made no distinction between the races (interview, IR). Some official records were collated by the *Comune* of Rome in 1989 and these offer a fairly reliable snapshot picture of the situation in 1989. They also provide some statistics for the period 1985–88, but these are somewhat incomplete and are therefore less precise.[19]

Figures for 1989 indicated that migrants preferred to place their children in residential homes rather than foster them out. Three hundred and seventy-seven foreign children were placed in homes or fostered throughout Rome's 20 districts (*circoscrizioni*) (290 in homes and 87 fostered). The district which dealt with the highest incidence of migrants was the 1st district which is in the centre of Rome. In 1989 this district placed 79 migrants' children in homes which represented some 27 per cent of the total. African children accounted for 38 per cent of the total number of migrants' children in care, and 85.05 per cent of those fostered out to families. Migrants' children represented 20.85 per cent of the overall population of children (i.e. including Italians) who were cared for in residential homes. If we include those minors funded privately, this figure rises to 31 per cent.[20] At this time, migrants constituted only 4.8 per cent of the resident population of Rome,[21] thus these figures pointed to a clear negative trend towards the institutionalisation of migrants' children from specific ethnic groups. The 1983 legislation referred to above emerged out of a growing consensus that institutionalisation was harmful to the child and therefore should only be utilised in emergency situations. Implicit was the assumption that any recourse to residential homes for children would be temporary.

An unpublished report describing social workers' experience of working with migrants' children in the Rome area, prepared for a social work conference in 1991, indicated that the 1983 legislation had been resisted by some of the religious homes as it was seen to depreciate their *raison d'être* (Angius, Gangere, Occhiuto 1991). While the dominance of religious institutions within this sphere should be interpreted as symbolic of the Church's influence in the realm of social charity, their accommodation of migrants' children has certainly permitted a revival of a social practice which, at the theoretical level at least, was increasingly viewed as anachronistic. According to the 1991 report:

> Residential institutes in Rome are almost entirely run by religious bodies. In recent years, as a direct result of the arrival of foreign children, the number of available places have increased. Some of these homes, which had closed down, have recently become active again, precisely because of the influx of foreign children (Angius, Gangere, Occhiuto 1991, p. 1).

Once again Catholic organisations were allowed to wield substantial influence in a specific area of immigration. This was partly a consequence of their existence prior to the inception of the immigration phenomenon. Catholic support agencies were able to respond much more directly to the needs of different categories of women. Halima, a Somali woman applying for refugee status, had the following experience when attempting to enrol her child at a school in Rome:

> The school asked me for my stay and residence permit, and I had neither because I hadn't received a response from the United Nations. I had my Caritas Card, I went to them and asked them to help me find a residential home.[22]

It is in this manner that Catholic voluntary organisations have managed to gain such prominence within the sphere of immigration. In the case of residential homes however, what this meant was that the state was able to subscribe to an organisational system which had been developed for a different purpose and for a quite different target group.

Two interpretations are useful for assessing religious influence in this domain. On a practical level, the influence of religious organisations can be viewed as a valuable and functional response to the demand generated by migrant (women) workers. In this way, it falls in line with what has been said earlier regarding Catholic influence and the immigration issue, particularly in the early stages. The theoretical justification for Catholic mobilisation is clearly in keeping with the Catholic ethos of providing assistance to the needy. But also on the theoretical level, there is some scope for questioning the nature of this mobilisation. Catholicism has consistently accentuated the vital role of the mother in caring for children. This fundamental Catholic premise seems to assume a secondary status when applied to migrants' children. There is thus a clear tension between the theoretical position of Catholicism and the nature of the assistance it provides. It may be that the potential to perpetuate Catholic influence at a social and ultimately a political level may have encouraged assistance organisations to facilitate a regressive strategy rather than attempt to construct alternative models which were more in keeping with their theoretical ideas.

The use of religious homes for the care of Italian children from dysfunctional families has been in decline in Italy for some time. Social workers prefer alternative methods of care such as fostering or adoption. The trend towards the institutionalisation of migrants' children is therefore a particularly retrograde practice, especially since these children are only infrequently placed in homes as a result of a dysfunctional family background. Figures produced for 1989, regarding the reasons for the institutionalisation of migrants' children, clearly support this view. The overwhelming majority of migrants' children were placed in homes because of the logistical (housing and employment) problems that their parents encountered: 56.13 per cent because their families could not provide accommodation for them, 8.55 per cent due to the unsuitable accommodation of their parents, and 12.26 per cent as a consequence of their parents being engaged in full-time work. Only 1.48 per cent were placed in homes because they were considered to be 'at risk'. This picture is replicated in unpublished data from the 1st district of Rome (RM1) for the year 1991. This showed that only a minority of migrants' children were being assisted as a result of a court decision or action. In this year the same number of migrants' children and Italian children were assisted by the social services (44). Of the migrants, only 7 came from a dysfunctional family background; 29 came from 'normal' family backgrounds.[23] Of the Italians, 27 came from a dysfunctional family background and 10 from a 'normal' family background.[24] A third category of children – '*Italiani rimpatriati*'[25] – also exhibited minimal pathological problems.

Figures on the country of origin of these children shed light on the manner in which the articulation of gender and employment in Italy militates against certain forms of family organisation for migrant families. Of the 390 foreign children assisted by the *Comune* of Rome (100 of these had their board paid for by private sources), 109 were born in Italy.[26] The nationalities of the groups with the highest numerical presence in residential homes mirror the ethnic groups of this study: 101 came from Ethiopia, 53 came from Cape Verde, and 31 from Somalia. The figure for Cape Verde is actually higher if one takes into consideration that some Cape Verdeans have Portuguese nationality; 29 children were registered as having Portuguese nationality. Thus, if one excludes the figures for those children born in Italy, we can see that over half of migrants' children in homes in Rome came from African countries. If those born in Rome are included some three quarters may be from African countries.

Domestic work forms the dominant employment niche for these ethnic groups and a direct correlation can therefore be established between this type of employment and the presence of migrants' children in homes. This is confirmed by the statistics cited above on the motives expressed by migrant parents regarding their reasons for placing their children in these homes.

The question of why such a high number of children from Ethiopian (including Eritrean), Somali and Cape Verdean backgrounds are, and have been, present in homes when compared to some other ethnic minority communities should be posed. Moroccans, for example, represent a numerically significant ethnic community in the city of Rome. However, there were very few Moroccan children (4) present in homes within the Rome area. This can be explained by the fact that the characteristics of the Moroccan community differ substantially from the Sub-Saharan African countries under investigation. Primary migration in this community has been undertaken predominantly by men and their employment niche in the Lazio region lies in restoration, hotel work and agricultural work.[27] Nonetheless there are ethnic groups living and working in Rome which exhibit a similar profile to the characteristics of the African groups under discussion and yet appear not to utilise residential homes as a strategy for accommodating maternity. For example, domestic work is a feature of the labour migration of both Filipina and Latin-American women. Yet children from these groups were not represented in high numbers in homes. The key informant from the Latin-American community explained the difference between Latin-American usage and African usage in the following way:

> You know that when a woman is working as a live-in domestic it is because she doesn't have any children. When they have children, Latin-American women do not put them in residential homes. They don't want to do this. They prefer to have a thousand jobs, but they will have a home, maybe there will be twenty of them in a house, but they are together, they have their children with them. They don't put them in residential homes or foster them. Those that are live-in workers don't have children or they have their children back home and send them money (interview, ACLI).

This statement in fact reveals that the difficulties of combining live-in domestic work with maternity are equally present for this community. Thus, this perspective actually confirmed the incompatibility of live-in domestic work with maternity. It also suggested that Latin-American women had been successful in penetrating the hourly-paid market and were consequently able to resolve the organisation of maternity in a different fashion.

Filipino children were equally not present in high numbers in residential homes despite the majority of Filipina women, like many African women, being present as autonomous migrants. The explanation for this can be attributed to the different labour migration strategy of this community.[28] As was stated at a round table discussion[29] by a representative from a Filipino organisation in Rome:

> There is a majority of single mothers. We are not like other communities, like Eritreans or Latin-Americans who keep their children with them. Because there is an issue about how to keep them with you. So the majority of us send our children to the Philippines in order to be able to carry out the work that we do in Italy (Tavola Rotonda 1990).

The option of sending children back to the country of origin or leaving them there in the first place was not an option for all of the African communities studied here. While this option was possible and utilised by the Cape Verdeans it was not feasible for the Eritreans:

> We Eritreans probably have the biggest problem when it comes to children. Because, as you know, the situation is precarious in Eritrea, we have a war that has been ongoing for thirty years ... Our Filipina colleague is lucky to be able to send her children to the Philippines, ... we Eritreans don't have such luck ... (Tavola Rotonda 1990).[30]

The above testimonies and statistics indicate that there were restricted options available to live-in domestic workers who had children. Given that participation in the labour market is integral to the autonomous primary migration of women and that domestic work is the principal means through which they are able to participate in the Italian labour market, the incidence of single women (not necessarily unmarried, but effectively single in Italy) who placed their children in homes clearly demonstrates the difficulty of combining domestic work with maternity. In 1989 data covering the Rome area indicated that some 35 per cent of foreigners' children in homes had only the mother present; 2.3 per cent had only the father present and 30.51 per cent had both parents present.[31] When these figures are broken down by nationality we can see that the experiences of the ethnic groups under discussion do not deviate substantially from the overall figures. Firstly, of those children born in Italy, but of (unspecified) foreign nationality, 48.62 per cent have only the mother present, while 26.6 per cent have both parents present. Of those children of Cape Verdean nationality, 45.28 per cent had only the mother present, while

24.53 per cent had both parents present. For Ethiopians 23.76 per cent had only the mother present while 29.7 per cent had both parents present. Of those children of Somali origin, 25.83 per cent had only the mother present and 45.16 per cent had both parents present. These latter two ethnic groups therefore show a greater balance and this may be partially explained by the presence of political refugees within these ethnic groups. Nevertheless the extremely high figures recorded for the Cape Verdean community, present in Italy as migrant labour and overwhelmingly female, exemplify the problems of combining autonomous female labour migration with maternity in the Italian context.

More detailed data collated by the *Comune* of Rome in 1989 on a selection of migrants' children in homes offers further evidence of the relationship between the employment of migrant mothers and the presence of their children in homes. This data is based on the experiences of 114 children, 66 of whom come from the countries of interest to this study: 21 were born in Ethiopia and seven born to Ethiopian parents in Italy; 16 were born in Cape Verde and 10 born to Cape Verdean parents in Italy; nine were born in Somalia and three born to Somali parents in Italy. The overwhelming majority of these children had adapted well to community life: 78.07 per cent were progressing normally at school, 82.45 per cent had a positive relationship with the other children, 80.71 per cent had a positive relationship with the staff, 80,71 per cent had a high respect for their culture of origin; 84.21 per cent received regular visits. Of interest is the fact that 71.93 per cent received visits only from their mothers, and only 15.79 per cent received visits from both of their parents. A disturbing figure which emerges from this data however, concerns the prospects for the future. For only 10.53 per cent of the children was a return to their families of origin an option for the foreseeable future, while 6.14 per cent were likely to be fostered. However there were no immediate prospects for an overwhelming majority of the children (80.7 per cent). This seemed to indicate that the use of residential homes was not necessarily a strategy embarked upon as an interim stage of family organisation. Rather it was an option selected from a limited range of possibilities and where parents did not necessarily envisage any transformation in the short term. Birth in Italy to migrant parents did not appear to alter this trend. Of the 114 children, 35 were born in Italy to migrant parents. For the majority of these children, the main relationship was with their mothers; 88.58 per cent were visited only by their mothers and a tiny majority by both parents (5.71 per cent); 71.43 per cent of the parents resided with their employers and for the over-whelming majority (91.42 per cent) there were no clear plans for the future.

The difficulties that these migrants' encountered in terms of family organisation, exemplified by these statistics, were confirmed by my own investigation into a large residential home on the outskirts of Rome. There are substantial differences both in the size and modes of organisation of residential homes. As one key informant with extensive knowledge of the situation in Rome stated:

> There are enormous differences. Enormous. The homes are very different. Firstly, the nuns are different, because just as you can meet a good or a bad person, it is the same with nuns, some are good and some are awful. Some residential homes are very old, really horrible, others, even if they are old, are quite nice, they renew them and restructure them. Some nuns are very affectionate, they work very well. For others, they are more like a warehouse for these children, as if they were keeping a suitcase at left luggage for a period of time. Some nuns are interested in the mothers, others are not (interview, AS, RM1).

The testimony of a Somali woman, present in Italy for political motives, indicates both dissatisfaction with the residential home that her daughter was placed in and the emotional problems inherent in this system of family organisation:

> When I used to go and pick up my daughter they used to give her to me all dirty, with her hair uncombed ... I said to the nun, 'listen, I brought you clothes and you said they weren't necessary so I brought them back and now I'm amazed to find my daughter in these conditions!' ... And then my daughter kept telling me that she wasn't happy there that they didn't pay her any attention ... So I said to her 'you'll have to put up with it, I can't do anything'. She stayed there for 15 days, but the last time I went to get her she said 'You don't love me any more'. I couldn't take it any more and I took her away.[32]

The single sex boys residential home where I conducted my research could unquestionably be categorised as a nice institution. Situated in pleasant grounds on the outskirts of Rome, it was conceptualised almost as a town within itself, with extensive sports and recreational facilities for the children. It had its own internal school and the boys were supported by a network of medical, psychological and family experts. The Irish founder of this national network intended that the community should recreate a family atmosphere for the children. It was run by the Congregation of Christian Brothers, a community of religious people who work specifically with young people. Since 1987 the 'Boy's Town' in Rome has additionally promoted an important annual seminar series which addresses issues of importance for community life. These have covered topics such as the child between community and family (1988), violence and abuse (1991) and, of interest to this discussion, ethnicity and community life (1993).[33] A wide variety of representatives from voluntary and institutional bodies have traditionally participated in these seminar proceedings.

Similar to other residential homes, this community did not have any accessible data which would permit an accurate historical overview of the presence of migrants' children in the home. Data for the 1992/3 academic year however showed that of a total of approximately 90 boys, almost half were foreign (43).[34] The majority of these foreign boys were African, principally Eritrean, Ethiopian, Somali, Cape Verdean. The key informant who worked as a social worker at the establishment attributed their presence overwhelmingly to logistical problems: 'The presence of these boys depends exclusively on the fact that they cannot live together with their mothers because she cannot accommodate them in her employer's house' (interview AS, CDR).

Given that the 1983 national legislation governing the adoption and fostering of minors unambiguously categorised the use of residential homes as an inferior option to fostering in families, the presence of migrants' children for long periods of time clearly contradicts the spirit of the said legislation. The experience of the Rome Boy's Town indicates that extensive periods of domicile in residential homes was not infrequent for migrants' children:

> A long stay is generally anticipated for foreign children. They stay until they are eighteen or until they have finished their education. They stay for a long time as a result of logistical problems which are difficult to resolve (interview, AS, CDR).

Moreover, the network of services available in the Rome area are organised in such a way that residential homes tend to cater for different age groups. As a result, migrants' children frequently had experience of more than one institution.

The fact that migrants' children did not normally come from dysfunctional families seemed to explain their healthier psychological state when compared to that of the Italian children in homes. In fact, some surprise was articulated regarding the manner in which migrants' children seemed able to maintain a healthy relationship with their mothers even if they did not see each other frequently.

In the early 1990s, there had been virtually no comprehensive research conducted into the institutionalisation of migrants' children.[35] In 1993, a regional trade union body (CSIL Lazio) commissioned a study of female migration into the Lazio region by ISCOS.[36] Based on 120 questionnaires administered and completed by field workers of Columbian, Filipino and Angolan nationality, the results might have been a useful resource for observers of this aspect of the immigration phenomenon. However, certain decisions taken as part of the methodological process reduced the utility of the findings of this study. For example, the decision not to distinguish between ethnicities weakened the results of this survey. The multi-ethnic character of immigration to the region was the methodological justification for such a decision. This meant that the criterion for interview was the availability and willingness of any migrant woman to be interviewed. However, what such a criterion led to was a strong bias towards Peruvian women: 56.66 per cent of the respondents were from Peru, 12.50 per cent from Ethiopia, 20.83 per cent from the Cape Verde islands, 8.33 per cent from the Philippines, 8.33 per cent from Romania and 3.33 per cent from Yugoslavia. Thus, while the ISCOS study could offer some very general information about women in the region, the diversity of its sample group meant that its findings had only partial applicability. Nonetheless it did show that 47 per cent of the women interviewed lived with their employer, 34.16 per cent lived with friends and only 10.83 per cent lived with their partners; 40 per cent lived in the same house as their children, 13.33 per cent lived with their spouse and children in the same house, 11.66 per cent of the children lived in the country of origin, 15 per cent lived in residential homes. As we saw above, Latin-Americans did not have recourse to residential homes in the same manner as African women, therefore the picture offered by these statistics on the organisation of family life cannot be seen as representative of the experiences of African women.

Fostering

While recourse to fostering has been the preferred direction of social policy with regard to Italian children, the above discussion has shown that African women's children were more frequently placed in residential homes. In the early 1990s, the use of fostering for migrants' children occurred at two levels within the Rome area. At the institutional level, the practice was organised by social workers at the request of parents. At the voluntary level, it evolved as a consequence of the practical difficulties that the voluntary organisations encountered when attempting to respond to the emergency needs of migrants and their families.

The fostering of children from different ethnic minorities into Italian families raises specific problems. This practice cannot be regarded as the simple extension of a standard procedure to a slightly different target group. Evidence from other countries indicates that a naïve although well-intentioned approach to trans-racial fostering and adoption can be detrimental to the children involved.[37] In Rome, two dominant schools of thought within the social services sector appeared to compete with each other. The perspectives were related to prevailing attitudes towards the use of residential homes and were articulated by a social worker working in this field:

> Regarding their placement in residential homes, we can say that there are certain traditions within social services. One strand demonises residential homes, claiming that they are entirely negative, that children shouldn't be institutionalised and so forth. Another school of thought, however, does not think that residential homes should be demonised because, specifically for migrants' children, it can provide a solution which allows a mother to cope with a period of emergency and does not create a series of problems which emerge when a child is fostered to an Italian family (interview, AS, RM1).

Indeed, this social worker maintained that often the mothers themselves were unclear about which of these two unsatisfactory options was preferable. Fostering was certainly not a straightforward procedure and was considered a complex and delicate strategy to implement. The informal fostering of children within the voluntary sector proved to be even more problematic. In Rome, this procedure evolved under the aegis of a priest (Father Bresciani) and again was a practical response to the tangible difficulties of migrant women's maternity. A key informant from one of the voluntary sector organisations, described him as a very good priest but was critical of the procedure initiated by him. She did emphasise, however, that because voluntary organisations were often working within the confines of a limited range of options, even her organisation had had to make use of this provision:

> Because if in certain moments there is a big arrival, if you have this mother with five or six children on the street what would you do? So you use every channel you have and if there is a family who will take one or two or three of these kids, at least the child is being taken off the streets. And then this became systematic and it became very problematic. In the end it ended up that a mother based in Rome, had a child in Milan and Venice and one in Foggia. Because people became enthusiastic, again through good will. And Catholics are all over Italy so this became natural.[38]

This informal ad hoc mode of operation caused a number of problems. In a few cases the foster parents interpreted the infrequency of family visiting as indicative of migrants' lack of interest in their children:

> People became enthusiastic … and then along came the judge and said look these people don't love their kids, … for a year no relatives have ever come to look for this child, that means these parents are not interested. So this is an abandoned child. So you may adopt it. And this child was lost to his or her natural parents. This did not happen very often because then we, along with other organisations got together and intervened very strongly. And the judges are not criminals, they realised what was going on (interview, FCEI).

An example of this problem can be found in the testimony of Fatouma,[39] during a round table discussion in Rome on migrant women and children:

> There is a young Somali mother here. I have her documents here. She has a six year old son. Until he was five and a half this young woman worked and maintained her son. Then one of these social workers told her 'look, we can help you if we foster your son'. This woman is illiterate. She cannot speak or write Italian. After six months she received 5 sentences from the minors' judge. She cannot see her son, because they no longer want to give him to her. Because the Italian family [has] grown attached to him while the mother who wants her child cannot have him … This is not fair and we will fight against this (Tavola Rotonda, 1990).

The above examples explain why migrant parents often preferred a more informal procedure in terms of fostering. There is certainly some evidence to show that Article 5 of law n. 184 which stipulates that the foster parent must facilitate the relationship between foster child and natural family and encourage their return to their natural families was being contravened. This occurred partly as a consequence of the nature of migrant women's labour, which led to problems in terms of the type of access they could have to their children, but it was additionally fuelled by the foster parents' emotional attachment to these children: 'Some Italians want to adopt a Black child. So if they ask for fostering, in the end they want to have the child' (interview, FCEI). These problems appeared to be replicated even when organised at the institutional level:

> Placing a [migrant's] child into an Italian family creates a series of problems. I personally have seen a number of problematic episodes arise, precisely because the child goes to live in an Italian family and takes on typically Italian ways. So

I am rather on my guard when it comes to fostering children to Italian families. The child stops speaking his parents' language. The child goes to an Italian school, speaks Italian etc. and then has communication problems with his mother. Plus, often these foster families are rich families that offer a life style which the child may not always have had. More so if the child is very little, it is difficult for him to understand why his mother does not have the money to buy him presents whilst his foster family can. Also, it sometimes happens that these families are overly affectionate, and problems arise in the child who can no longer identify who his real parent is and who really loves him (interview, AS, RM1).

Problems such as these have led to greater reflection on the part of the social services regarding the fostering of migrants' children. Nonetheless the decision to allocate children either to a residential home or to an Italian family appeared to be influenced by the philosophy of the social worker dealing with the specific case. A report presented to a social workers' conference maintained that migrant mothers experienced their relationship with residential homes from a position of inferiority (Angius et al. 1991) and one can assume that these feelings of inferiority and inadequacy were further exacerbated in the more private relationship that exists between foster carers and the migrant mother.

Ethnicity, Culture and the Migrant Family

The problems of reconciling maternity with a dominant work role were acutely felt by African women migrants. In 1988,[40] an action-research project[41] was coordinated by the education specialist Francesco Susi. The research project was designed to ascertain the sociocultural and training needs of migrants in the Rome area. In line with the ethos of participation research, the five ethnic communities participating in the study all prepared a final report which identified what they considered to be the main problems facing their respective communities. The Eritrean community cited six general areas: working conditions; housing problems; single parenthood; the use of residential homes; linguistic difficulties; and the inadequate preparation of teaching staff.[42] The Cape Verdean final report cited three main problems – the integration of children and adults in schools, problems of organisation for the community and the loss of culture and language of Cape Verdean children.[43]

Both communities shared a concern about the parent-child relationship in the Italian context. In the Cape Verdean final report it was stated:

The difficult relationship between mothers and their children is accentuated and made worse by the fact that there is no family cohesion. There are few families living together. The majority of parents, because they live with their employers, cannot keep their own children with them and follow their education as in all normal families.[44]

The Eritrean report highlighted a similar difficulty relating to residential homes:

Although the residential homes are seen as an answer, they are only to a certain point. In fact, placing children in residential homes objectively represents the first step of separation; not just physical separation but of emotional separation ... This separation becomes increasingly evident and not even the painful weekly brief visits are able to limit this.[45]

There are additionally cultural implications associated with the use of residential homes and fostering. Much of the care is carried out by religious staff or families with no awareness of appropriate modes of interaction with ethnic minority children. When asked whether prospective foster parents of migrants' children were given any special training, the response of the social worker was unequivocal: 'Not at all. It would be a dream if this could be done' (interview, AS, RM1).

Residential homes were nevertheless seen to be culturally less detrimental to migrants' children as other children from the same ethnic group were likely to be present. Nonetheless, if one considers the testimony of this Eritrean mother, problems of identity were also apparent in residential homes:

... living with all those nuns, the nurses, the other children, when he [the son] saw me, he would be crying and I would be crying. Seeing how dark I was, he was frightened and did not realise that he was dark as well. He used to cry terribly. On top of that he could not speak my language and I had to speak to him in Italian. I was embarrassed to speak to my son in Italian; it seemed an impossible thing.[46]

Certainly in the residential community where I conducted research, the practitioners had become attentive to the concept of cultural difference and were attempting to develop new educational strategies which could encompass this difference. The decision to dedicate their annual conference to the theme of ethnicity and community life in 1993, while indicative of this community's attentiveness to the issue, also indicated that theoretical and practical attention to this whole question had been largely absent. Moreover, this conference was an initiative of the voluntary and not the state sector.

The discussions that emerged from this conference indicated that the educationalists were unclear as to how to proceed with migrants' children. There was no discussion about developing alternative structures to accommodate the organisational implications of maternity for migrant domestic workers. The focus was on establishing a more tailored response to the specific needs of migrants' children within residential homes.

In the introduction to this chapter, I argued that migrant families have constituted an important arena for positive cultural self-identity in other sociopolitical contexts. In this manner, migrant families, particularly those that have experienced hostile contexts of reception, can equip their children to deal with racism. Working groups were established at the conference to consider specific problems related to ethnicity and community life. What emerged from the ensuing discussions, confirmed by my own informal discussions with adolescent and ex-residents of this particular community, was that community life had failed to prepare Black children adequately for the outside world and the racism they would face. In other words, the desire to replicate a family environment within the institution naturally based its family model on the Italian family. Ironically, the pleasant academic and social environment of this particular community had shielded these children from the harsh reality of racism. As a consequence, Black children were unprepared for the hostility they encountered outside the protection of the community walls. For example, during an informal discussion with some Eritreans and Somalis, the boys expressed their shock to me at the abuse they received outside the confines of the home. This is one example of the manner in which a well-intentioned 'colour-blind' approach can be detrimental for migrants' children. It also confirms that the physical and cultural separation that occurs between parent and child can entail the loss of an important aspect of the type of social education that ethnic minority parents can pass on to their children.

Family Unity

Evidence from interviews and from the practitioners involved in placing or caring for migrants' children confirmed the difficulties of finding an alternative solution to these arrangements in the short term. It seemed clear that any feasible remedy had to centre on resolving the work/housing dilemma. This reference to work does not refer solely to the organisation of domestic work in Rome, but also refers to the gendered labour market opportunities available to these communities. Male employment in the African communities discussed in this book was not marked by the same degree of stability that women enjoyed in the labour market. This further diminished the prospect of 'normal' family life for these migrants. Angius, Gangere and Occhiuto (1991) observed that over a five year period, those children with both parents present in Italy remained in homes for a maximum of two years. Children of single parents, however, remained there for considerably longer periods. Thus, the presence of both parents on Italian territory appeared to facilitate the resolution of difficulties associated with family organisation. In some cases, however, the effective single parent status of some families was due not to the emotional break-up of couples but to their physical separation as a consequence of diverse labour demands at both regional and European levels.[47] In the late 1970s, the then president of the Cape Verdean association in Rome had already highlighted how male migration from Cape Verde had been directed to Germany and the Netherlands (ECAP-CGIL 1979).[48] Data presented in chapter 3, regarding the employment situation of migrants in the Lazio region indicated that gender impacts in a significant way on the ethnic groups with which this study is concerned.[49] A number of the Cape Verdean women I interviewed confirmed this in relation to their partners. Matilde's (interview 1) husband worked in a restaurant but she stated that it was very difficult for him to find regular work in Rome. Maria's (interview 4) husband worked as a builder. However, he was working clandestinely, having entered Italy in 1991. This more precarious employment situation for men reduced the possibility for migrant families to live together as a family unit particularly where the primary occupation of the mother was domestic work. Family unity became possible where the husband and wife were employed as a couple, or where the woman was able to make the transition to hourly paid work. Alex (interview 20), was a live-in worker with an eighteen-month year old baby. The father of the baby was also in Rome but lived in the suburbs and worked irregularly. They saw each other whenever they could. I interviewed her on a Sunday, her day off, but her partner was working on that day so they were unable to meet up. They were planning to meet briefly during the following week. Political conditions in Eritrea and Somalia also explained the single parent status of some African families in Italy, with male members often involved in the war or imprisoned (Ali 1990; Maricos 1990b).

Although some African men also worked as domestic workers, this was not viewed either by them or by the women in their communities as appropriate employment. Gerom (interview 29), who worked briefly as a domestic worker in Rome, aged 14, had found it especially problematic. It was equally difficult for him to accept his father working as a live-in domestic. When he eventually went to live and study in a residential home he restricted his visits to his father partly because he could not tolerate seeing him in such a servile role.[50] His sister Lemlem (interview 10) also saw problems in the employment of men as domestic workers: 'It is easier for women to find work because they accept everything. Men, on the other hand, because many of them have studied, are not prepared to accept domestic work'. She cited the case of her brother and argued that someone in his position (then an undergraduate student) should never have to do domestic work.

Housing

We have seen above that the reason most frequently given to explain the presence of migrants' children in residential homes was linked to Black women's employment as live-in workers and thus to the lack of independent living space. The availability of housing (plus hourly paid work) was therefore critical to the possibility of living as a family unit. Where suitable initiatives have been taken, this has been seen to have an impact on the family lives of migrants. Milan began allocating council housing to Eritrean families in the 1980s and this allowed families to keep their children with them (Maricos 1990). In the early 1990s the Lazio region had not generally been pro-active in resolving the housing dilemma of migrants.[51] Indeed, as late as 1993, the region had not established any reception centres which could function as emergency housing. This meant that this domain was still organised overwhelmingly by the voluntary sector.[52]

Interestingly, virtually all of the Cape Verdean women that I interviewed who had made the transition to hourly paid work and independent living accommodation frequently commented on the inadequacy of their living space.[53] Indeed, several referred to their homes as 'a hole' and all complained about the difficulties in acquiring better and larger living accommodation. Nonetheless, the establishment of an autonomous family base was clearly an important goal for some migrants and could be undertaken as part of a wider family strategy. For example, Lemlem (interview 10), Gerom (interview 29) and their father all contributed to the rent on a flat so that they could have a family base even though they could not live together on a permanent basis in the said flat. Only Lemlem lived there permanently as she had been able to make the transition to hourly-paid domestic work after nine years of live-in work. However, her father continued to work as a live-in domestic worker while her brother worked part-time in the residential home in which he had grown up.

Where migrant women have been living in unsuitable emergency accommodation, they have been active in attempting to procure decent accommodation for their families. In the early 1990s, Somali political refugees (many of them women with small children) were housed primarily in hotels in Rome, notably the Hotel Ward and the Hotel Giotto. Here they lived in unhygienic and overcrowded conditions. A health inspection carried out by the local health authority found mice droppings, damp rooms, fleas and unusable sanitary facilities. At one stage the Hotel Ward, designed to sleep 78 was accommodating 500 people. An evacuation of the building was ordered which became a police operation.[54] The Somalis were transported to a Country club in Castelfusano some distance from Rome. They subsequently returned to the city and initiated an all-night protest, calling for a more viable solution to their accommodation problems. Women were particularly prominent during this protest. Their demonstration disrupted Roman traffic and there was eventually a violent confrontation, with 11 people wounded (six Somalis and five police officers) and a number of arrests.[55]

These accommodation difficulties go some way in explaining why some mothers preferred to leave their children in their countries of origin, not as a temporary measure, but as preferable to bringing them to Italy and placing them in residential homes. Clara's (interview 6) story is a case in point. She arrived in Rome in 1971 leaving three young children (aged 5, 2 and 1) in Cape Verde to be cared for by her mother. It was some eleven years later in 1982 that she managed to bring one of these children to Italy.[56] This child, then aged 13, went straight into a residential home and remained there for four years.[57] Similar to the other interviewees, Clara described their current dwelling as 'a small house'. As a single parent, Clara's ability to bring only one of her children to Italy indicates the problems of combining domestic work with maternity in Rome. Maria Crescentia Mota had left her daughter in Cape Verde when she was 18 months old. She also expounded on the problematic decision of whether to leave or bring her child to Rome:

> ... I tried ... Many people tell me that in their view the best solution would be to bring her here to Italy. But I don't think that this would be a good solution, because I would only bring my daughter to Italy if I had the possibility of ... not controlling her, I don't want to control her but I want to support her and give her the opportunity of living in a city or a country like Italy where everything is different with respect to my own country. However the life I lead in Italy does not allow me to ... not just maintain her but to be close to her, because if I bring her here where do I keep her? There are no houses ... To bring her here would

mean sending her to a residential home and she would lose the affection of my mother and my sister ... [58]

Two of the women I interviewed were married to Italians and lived as family units with their partners and children. Maria Joanna, had worked illegally in Italy for six years since her arrival in 1969. Subsequent to her marriage to an Italian, she had been able to regularise her position. She lived with her husband and their two children.[59] Maria Joanna recounted to me the experience of one of her Cape Verdean friends who had encountered real difficulty in caring for her three children as a single parent. The first child, although born in Italy had been sent to Portugal to live with its grandparents. Her second child grew up with her in Italy in what Maria Joanna described as 'a horrible damp house'. When she had a third child she was unable to cope and the child was informally adopted by an Italian family. Margarita (interview 8) had also left two children behind in Cape Verde when she migrated to Italy at the age of 22. However, subsequent to her marriage to an Italian and the birth of their child, she was able to bring one of her son's to live with her and her husband in Rome.

Family Reunification

The possibility for family reunification (i.e. the secondary migration of family members) is not necessarily a straightforward process.[60] The first piece of national legislation introduced to regulate immigration in 1986 explicitly protected migrants' rights to family reunification. Article 4 of law 946 stated that non-EC national workers had a right to family reunion. The worker had to show that he or she could provide the family with 'normal living conditions'. Parents were only allowed entry as dependants and could not seek employment once settled in Italy. Spouses had to wait for a period of a year before they could legally seek employment and for the duration of the year they were financially dependent on their partners. Commenting on this provision the head of the Cape Verdean women's association, De Lourdes Jesus (1989, p. 80) stated:

> ... migrant families are organising around law 943, which promotes family reunification. But when the children arrive, what does this society reserve for them? The majority of children end up in a residential home and are educated by people who are not familiar with their cultures. On top of this, the work

carried out by their parents (domestic work) does not allow normal family life
....

A document prepared by a group of migrant women under the aegis of the Federation of Protestant Churches was particularly critical of the manner in which the provision was being granted: 'What is meant by "normal living conditions"? Does this mean a monthly salary of L700,000 ... how much do we have to earn to be joined by our loved ones?' (Gruppo di donne migranti 1989, p. 73).

Moreover, the bureaucracy implicit in this legislation functioned to delay procedures. Not only did this provision permit a substantial degree of discretion and potential discrimination, but it also failed to acknowledge the economic and social niche which migrants occupied in Italy. The legal provision stipulated that the migrant resident in Italy must be legally employed in order to process a family reunification request. However, as was argued in chapter 2, the informal economy is integral to Italy's economic system and there is a propensity for migrants to be absorbed within this sector. In the same vein, the manner in which property is rented in Italy also militated against a straightforward implementation of this provision:

> Let us just think for a moment about resident Italian citizens. Do they all have an employer willing to provide written proof of how much they earn? Do they all have a job? And accommodation? From what we know and what we hear daily, unemployment, lack of housing and exploitation are all widely present in Italy (Gruppo di donne migranti 1989).

Thus the employment position of migrant women might have been in the informal sector and their living accommodation may have been in rented housing where the owner refused to issue a formal contract. In such a situation, the worker would be unable to provide the necessary legal documents to demonstrate that he or she was in a position to cater for incoming family members. In female single sex communities, the legal constraint which prohibited migrant spouses from obtaining a work permit during their first year of stay either forced men into a position of dependency or into the informal labour market.[61]

Conclusion

This chapter has demonstrated that live-in domestic work had a negative impact on the family lives of the migrant communities under discussion and the difficulties that pregnancy posed for live-in workers functioned as a restrictive mechanism to their fertility. In other words the logistical implications of pregnancy could, in some instances, force migrant women to postpone either indefinitely, or in the short term, their decision to procreate.

Residential homes, fostering, leaving or sending children to the country of origin, acquiring hourly paid work and independent living accommodation represented the main options available to migrant women domestic workers. Hourly paid work coupled with decent living accommodation clearly constituted a preferable mode of family organisation, one which, moreover, bore some resemblance to the model of contemporary family organisation within Italy. Nonetheless, as was shown in chapter 6, the transition to hourly paid work can lead to a different set of problems, the most serious of which is increased competition from Italian domestic workers and subsequent vulnerability in the labour market.[62] Given the single parent status of a substantial number of women migrants, labour market instability was not an option that they could easily countenance. Earlier chapters have additionally indicated that the dominance of domestic work as a sector of economic activity for female migrants within the Rome area limits opportunities for penetrating different spheres of labour activity.

It is my view that the Roman context was unable to accommodate what was a relatively novel form of family organisation within Italy – single parent families headed by women. A report on Italian families published in 1988 showed that single-parent families accounted for no more than 1 per cent of all families and that only a quarter of such families included children under 15 (Bimbi 1992).[63] Thus there has clearly been no established precedent for single parent mothers with young children. Moreover, migrant women have not been able to exploit a nationally established precedent regarding family organisation where the mother is employed in the labour market. This precedent concerns the existence of extended family networks. The decline of the extended family network in Italy has been noted and has engendered substantial structural problems in relation to the care of the elderly and children (Ferrera 1986). Nonetheless, extended family networks and especially the input of the mother or mother-in-law of the married woman, continue to facilitate Italian women's participation in the labour market (see Paci 1983; Saraceno 1987; Del Boca 1988).

In other social contexts ethnic minority communities have also been able to rely on networks developed by friends and family to care for children.[64] For the migrant groups of this study however, the problem lay in the uniformity of their employment opportunities. This greatly reduced the possibility of informal or family assistance in the care of children:

> The people in her [the migrant woman] group, her co-nationals, are also trying to survive. It's obvious that there isn't the option, as there is for Italians, to get help from that sister who doesn't work, or your mother who isn't working any more and so they turn to public bodies (interview, AS, CDR).

In this sense, institutional and voluntary bodies functioned as a substitute extended family network for some migrant women. However these bodies organised this care in a particular way. Indeed, they assumed a dominant parenting function in relation to the biological parent. The acceptability of this differentiated construction of maternity runs counter to established ideological discourses regarding maternity and Italian women. These bodies have tended to accommodate rather than challenge this construction. The conclusions drawn by the American sociologist Bonnie Dill in relation to nineteenth century America appear pertinent:

> Racial-ethnics were brought to this country to meet the need for a cheap and exploitable labor force. Little attention was given to their family and community life except as it related to their economic productivity. Labor, and not the existence or maintenance of families, was the critical aspect of their role in building the nation (Dill 1988, p. 418).

Evidence produced in this chapter corroborates one of the main arguments of this book regarding the construction of African women's identity as fundamentally labour related. The marginalisation of a gendered aspect of their interlocking identities – as mothers – has contributed to this. In the early 1990s, the Lazio region had yet to seriously address the implications of how the combination of an autonomous female migratory journey and the specific employment category available to migrant women impacted on family organisation. Moreover, contrary to the direction of social policy in Italy which, in recent years, has attempted to accommodate Italian women's desire to engage in the paid labour market, the example of African women in Rome indicated the necessity for an opposing strategy. In other words, African women migrants required policies which would provide greater equilibrium between their maternal and work roles, but from a reversed perspective. This chapter has shown that specific constituencies of women may encounter the imposition of quite different ideological and practical constructions of their gender roles. The example of African women in Rome thus stands as an anomalous example of the tension that exists between women's maternal and paid work function in Italy.

Notes

1   For a discussion of this see Amos and Parmar (1984) and Collins (1994, p. 57).
2   For a discussion of some feminist perspectives on mothering see Nancy Chodorow with Susan Contratto (1989), 'The Fantasy of the Perfect Mother' and Okin (1997).
3   The ongoing debate generated by ethnic minority feminist theorists on this issue has served a dual function. Firstly, it has sought to legitimise existing models of family organisation within minority communities which do not conform to a preferred universal norm (Collins 1990; Glenn 1994). This has been used to counter the dysfunctionality argument frequently ascribed to ethnic minority family organisation. Secondly it has sought to expose how family lives are constructed differently according to the inter-related concepts of gender, race and class. Collins (1994) has in fact argued that the experiences of 'women of color' should be located at the centre of feminist debates about mothering precisely because work and the family have not normally existed as two separate spheres for women from these communities.
4   In Cape Verde, for example, single parenthood is not uncommon. The high rate of male outmigration has contributed to this. See Finan and Henderson (1988).
5   Condon's (1995) study of French Caribbean women's migration to France in the post-war period also showed that live-in domestic work was incompatible with motherhood. One of her interviewees, who had migrated to Paris in 1958, was forced to send her baby back to her mother in Martinique after only a few months since in her words: 'I couldn't have kept her with me, while I was working as a maid' (p. 16). In Singapore, we find a more contemporary example of this incompatibility. Here, work permits issued to foreign domestic workers are contingent on their fulfilling a contractual obligation not to get pregnant or marry Singaporeans. See Tan and Devashayam (1987) and Yeoh and Huang (1999). See also Romero (1997) on the perspectives of the children of domestic workers.
6   Couples would frequently seek domestic work together. See Appendix 3.
7   This may have been a popularly held notion judging from a male character in Moravia's short story 'La Serva Padrona', who says to the domestic worker: 'But wouldn't you prefer to get married and have a husband and stay in your own home?' (Moravia 1959, p. 108).
8   *Ad verbatim* testimony, reproduced in Perrotta (1991, p. 89).
9   *Ad verbatim* testimony of Eritrean mother, reproduced in Perrotta (1991, p. 80).
10 One of the Cape Verdean women interviewed in Rotterdam informed me that some Cape Verdean women had been forced to make use of back street abortion facilities in Rome prior to the introduction of the abortion law in 1978.
11 It is worth noting that many of her Eritrean friends thought she was crazy to adopt such an attitude and felt she should go ahead with maternity regardless of the logistical problems that this would pose.
12 *Ad verbatim* testimony of an Eritrean national reproduced in Caritas diocesana di Roma (1989, p. 132).
13 This was an informed but impressionistic overview, since the key informant could not provide a precise statistical breakdown.

14　The incidence of repeat abortions amongst Italian female users has often been cited as a negative characteristic of abortion usage in Italy. In 1986, 28.1 per cent of Italian women undergoing a termination of pregnancy had already had a previous termination. See Camera dei Deputati (1987).

15　An unpublished study on the characteristics of newborn babies of migrants in Rome confirmed the lack of accurate quantitative data on the health conditions of migrants. The study found that the risk of death in the first year of life was twice as high for migrants' children when compared to newborn Italian babies. See Bertollini R et al. (n.d.) 'Caratteristiche neonatali dei figli di immigrati a Roma negli anni 1982–1988'.

16　*Ad verbatim* testimony of Lettesgu, reproduced in Caritas diocesana di Roma (1989, p. 140).

17　The neighbourhood was *Testaccio* which she described as 'a nice area where everyone knew each other'.

18　Two of her other four children now lived in America with their father who had remarried, one lived in Paris and another with her grandmother in Cape Verde.

19　This phenomenon had not been monitored and recorded by official state bodies. Some data became available in the late 1980s. Even so, these figures were still likely to be incomplete, given that some fostering took place informally amongst friends or was organised by religious voluntary groups. The figures refer to those children of foreign residents who were subsidised by the *Comune* of Rome and do not include those funded by other means.

20　This data is taken from the report 'Minori stranieri istituzionalizzati' produced for the *Comune* of Rome.

21　See Caritas di Roma (1992).

22　*Ad verbatim* testimony, reproduced in Perrotta (1991, p. 87).

23　Data was missing for eight of the migrants' children.

24　Data was missing for five of the Italian children.

25　This category is used to refer to children of Italian nationality who had returned from East Africa.

26　This category is not differentiated by nationality, but it refers in the main either to children born to foreign nationals or to children born from relationships between migrants (mainly women) and Italian citizens.

27　See Altieri and Carchedi (1992); Strozza (1991).

28　See Korsieporn 1991.

29　This round table was part of the Lazio region's '*Festa del popolo*' held in 1990. This month-long festival aimed to promote the presence of ethnic minorities in the region. One evening was dedicated to the particular situation of migrant women and children.

30　This perhaps explains why there were higher numbers of Eritrean and Ethiopian children in homes.

31　Data was unavailable for a relatively large percentage of these children (26.93) and it is not clear how this might impact on the percentages cited for the other categories.

32　*Ad verbatim* testimony of Halima, reproduced in Perrotta (1991, p. 87).

33　I attended this three day seminar in September 1993 and participated in the workshops.

34　The term approximate is used because during the same academic year some children left the home while there were also new arrivals.

35　A few undergraduate theses have been conducted. Alessandro Becagli's (1990) *tesi di diploma* looked at the services available in the Rome area for migrant mothers and their children. Gloria Bianco's (1992) *tesi di laurea* assesses how migrants' children placed either in residential homes or fostered construct their identity. See also D'Ottavi's (1990) article on problems of cultural identity for migrants' children.

36 ISCOS is a body which promotes the international politics of the CISL trade union body. It works on international cooperation and development.

37 See Biri Yaya with reference to the British context. 'Transracial Fostering': A Black Perspective', Norwich: Social Work Monographs, 1994.

38 Saida Ali, a Somali doctor and activist, confirmed this in a separate intervention. See (Ali 1990, p. 99).

39 She spoke on behalf of another Somali national who could not speak Italian.

40 References are to the 1991 second edition.

41 As part of the methodology five 'reflection groups' were established – Cape Verdeans, Eritreans, Filipinos, Iranians and Moroccans. Four hundred and twenty questionnaires were also distributed to these ethnic minority groups.

42 See the final report prepared by Gerom Keflay and Ogbe Beyene in Susi (1991).

43 See the final report prepared by Maria de Lourdes Jesus and Antonia Vitorina Goomes in Susi (1991).

44 Cited in Susi (1991, p. 172).

45 Ibid., p. 176.

46 Cited in Favaro (1994, pp. 152–3).

47 Extended families were often widely dispersed. For example, Antonia's (interview 16) mother had retired back to Cape Verde having worked in Italy since the 1960s; Antonia's father lived in Holland. Her brother in Portugal and her sister was still in Cape Verde hoping to migrate to Europe.

48 See the article by Antonio Pastore in *Il Manifesto* (9 February 1992) regarding a Somali woman and pregnancy. There is reference to the woman's husband moving on to Germany with their two children 'where he found stable employment'. See also Ziglio's (1988) study of the Eritrean community in Milan which showed that men joined their partners in Italy only when better employment opportunities had not presented themselves elsewhere.

49 A trade union document (CGIL, CISL, UIL 1992)) on supply and demand for migrant workers in Rome confirmed this trend. The study was based on interviews with 1,019 migrants (68 per cent male; 32 per cent female). As the study did not distinguish between ethnic groups it is not possible to extrapolate specific data relevant to the communities under discussion here. Nonetheless, the employment categorisation utilised to present the data did indicate strictly gendered labour markets for male and female migrants. Male work largely consisted of 'invented work' (windscreen cleaners, flower sellers, street hawkers) while female work consisted of 'domestic work'.

50 For example, he despised the fact that his father's employers used a bell at the table when they wanted their glasses filled with water or wine.

51 One obvious example of the housing emergency for migrants in Rome was the occupation of a disused pasta factory called the Pantanella by a large number of mainly Arab and North African men. For a more detailed discussion of this see Ter Wal (1996).

52 The Roman branch of Caritas, for example, had a network of emergency housing.

53 I visited a private residential development where many Cape Verdean families lived. Many of these families lived in minimal living space. One of the mothers sent her children outside prior to the interview to create some space.

54 A few months earlier Azzaro, councillor for social services, had organised a similar evacuation of the Pantanella. See footnote 51.

55 For newspaper reports of these events see 'Il giorno dei somali', *Corriere della Sera*, 16 May 1991 and 'La Pantanella dei Somali', *Il Manifesto*, 16 May 1991.

56 When I asked her why she had not brought over the other two, she stated that they were studying and she thought it would be better to leave them there with her mother. However, given that she brought over the middle child whose situation could not have been much different from her younger sibling of one year, it is probable that logistic and economic problems also weighed heavily on this decision.

57 Her daughter spoke quite positively about her experiences in this residential home: 'it gave me some protection at a difficult time' (Dosci, interview 7).

58 *Ad verbatim* interview reproduced in Caritas diocesana di Roma (1989, pp. 180–81).

59 While the children were at primary school she had been able to continue working because their school operated a long day (*lungo orario*). However she had to give up work and became a housewife when her children began middle school. This was because school ended at 12.30pm. She was the only one of the women I interviewed who was a housewife and this was apparent in the time she could spend with me. In fact she was so keen to meet me that she came to pick me up for the interview!

60 In France, for example, the temporary suspension of this provision in the 1970s was used as a deliberate means of restricting the entry of more migrants.

61 In later legislation, family reunification was extended to a wider range of relatives. To be eligible, the migrant worker was required to have an annual income equivalent to an annual welfare income (see law n. 40, 1998).

62 Ziglio's (1988) study of the situation in Milan noted a distinct correlation between hourly paid work and periods of unemployment amongst Eritrean domestic workers.

63 See also Zanatta and Mirabile (1993) on this point who argue that the low level of single parent families with young children indicates that single parent status in Italy is indicative of more traditional forms of single parent status such as widowhood rather than newer forms which can be linked to marital instability.

64 See for example, Collins (1990) who refers to the practice of othermothering amongst African-Americans as a strategy of child care. Romero's (1992) study also found that for those Chicana domestic workers whose extended families lived in the city, female relatives constituted a valuable source for child-care.

8 Gender, Ethnicity and Class: the Evolution of the ACLI-COLF Organisation

In chapters 8 and 9, my focus is on the response of two women's associations to the presence of ethnic minority women and thus to a new and racialised constituency of gender. My main argument here is that both organisations, in different ways, were unable to totally relinquish their primary roles as representatives of indigenous Italian women. Moreover, their inability to be fully inclusive of migrant women's interests was partially determined by the conflict of interest implicit within the employer/employee domestic work relationship which characterised relationships between Italian women and migrant women. This chapter will consider the evolution of the ACLI-COLF organisation from the 1970s to the early 1990s. In the 1970s, both the delegitimisation of Catholic ideology[1] and the strength of the trade unions were particularly pertinent for associations representing domestic workers. As discussed in chapter 4, in the face of these new trends, the API-COLF remained committed to the pre-1971 strategy, reinforcing its links with Catholicism,[2] while the ACLI-COLF anticipated a fruitful relationship with the workers' movement. I shall focus here on the ACLI-COLF association, as it is this latter association which embarked on a radical new policy direction to challenge the organisation of the domestic work sector.

The ACLI-COLF's central positioning within the domestic work sphere signified that it had an early awareness of class and ethnic stratification amongst women. Thus, here was an organisation which experienced tangible proximity to notions of privilege, subordination and exploitation within the category of gender. This, at a time when the Italian women's movement tended towards a marginalisation of these differences through its validation of the concept of women's commonality (Caldwell 1991). Although in the 1970s, the ACLI-COLF was primarily concerned with positioning itself within the trade union movement, it did additionally seek to respond to the emergence of the Italian women's movement. To some extent, the visible social profile of the feminist

231

movement forced the issue of class differences between women onto the ACLI-COLF's agenda. Who would be its natural ally – working class workers (men and women) or (largely) middle class women? A discussion of the association's relationship with the women's movement serves as a useful frame of reference for assessing changes in the association's ideology and strategy as the presence of migrant women in the sector became more prominent.

Between Italian Women: the ACLI-COLF and the Women's Movement

The prominence of the women's movement in the 1970s, with its early emphasis on the value of domestic work (unpaid), as well as the ACLI-COLF's involvement with domestic workers (paid), might lead one to anticipate a natural relationship between these two spheres. However, it had been the Catholic (conservative) sector, and not the progressive sphere of women's political activism, which had established and maintained a privileged relationship with domestic workers in the post-war period. Margherita Repetto, a prominent figure within the national women's organisation UDI, acknowledged this in her speech to the IX ACLI-COLF national congress held in 1976:[3] 'The work carried out by the ACLI towards a sector like the domestic work sector is extremely significant ... because it has bridged a gap left open by other social forces; and this is a reason for self-criticism for all of us, even for an association like the UDI' (ACLI-COLF 1976, p. 7).[4] Repetto did however argue that domestic workers should be incorporated into the wider battle regarding women's situation and envisaged that there could be some co-operation between the two associations. The prospect of transforming domestic workers into 'family assistants' was interpreted as an important sign of female solidarity, necessary for improving women's general situation.

By 1979, when the ACLI-COLF held its tenth national congress in Assisi, the social presence of the feminist movement was much stronger. This could be seen in the address given by the national secretary of the ACLI-COLF, Clorinda Turri. She felt that the association should prioritise connecting the specific problems of domestic work with the women's liberation movement. Despite this objective, the nature of domestic work accentuated a problem implicit within the concept of female solidarity. This was aptly summarised by Turri:

> ... what has become increasingly apparent in these years is that the domestic work relationship and the unjust conditions that it imposes on hundreds of

thousands of women is not a sectoral or marginal problem; it can be seen increasingly as a phenomenon which is closely tied to a number of social processes; in particular as a consequence of the refusal, on the part of women, to continue to accept a sexual division of labour which confines the housewife ... to do domestic work even when this represents a double work burden; however this legitimate instance of women's liberation is causing a new contradiction because domestic work ... is being off-loaded onto other women who find themselves confined to a role of 'reserve housewife'... (ACLI-COLF 1979, p. 7).[5]

A very basic contradiction between different constituencies of women was thus registered. It is, however, crucial to note that in recognising that both the workers' movement and the ACLI-COLF were calling for the development of social services to deal with the issue of reproductive care and domestic labour, Turri warned of the danger of seeing these services as simply beneficial to women. She argued that the tendency to do this was a direct consequence of men's refusal to engage in a transformation of gender roles and maintained that it was imperative for the workers' movement to engage with this issue as an integral component of its general strategy. I emphasise this point here, since, as will be argued below, the 1980s and early 1990s witnessed a gradual shift away from such a position. The notion of greater male participation with regard to domestic work was submerged and female solidarity was increasingly called upon to resolve the difficulties Italian women encountered in reconciling family and work roles. Such a shift in fact entailed a buttressing of the traditional division of labour within the home, through the employment of one woman, normally supervised by the female employer, to execute domestic tasks. This situation did not therefore call into question the necessity for a transformation of men's roles but rather reinforced the notion of women's traditional responsibility for reproductive care.[6]

By 1979, although the importance of the women's liberation movement had been acknowledged, the ACLI-COLF was nevertheless critical of its neglect of the domestic work sphere:

If we are placing at the centre of our strategy ... our refusal to be 'reserve housewives' it is partly because we believe that the problem of domestic workers as women and of the contradiction that the domestic work relationship increasingly creates between women has not been properly addressed even by women's movements ... Addressing this problem means placing at the centre of the debate on the woman question, the structural aspect of domestic work, of a different qualitative and organisational form for it, as a central issue for any process of emancipation or liberation for women (Turri, ACLI-COLF 1979, p. 8).

Furthermore, there was a forthright rejection of the domestic work sector functioning to facilitate gender privilege: 'our sector [knows] that the price of female emancipation for certain sectors of the middle class cannot be paid by other women who still endure material hardship' (Turri, ACLI-COLF 1979, p. 8). This perspective would inform the association's strategy in relation to the organisation of the sector. Already, the debates of the 1973 and 1976 national congresses indicated that the association was keen to implement a radical transformation of both the working conditions of employees and the status conditions of employers. In particular, the association sought to overcome the private nature of the employer-employee relationship, envisaging a new figure of 'family collaborator' or 'family assistant'. The proposal was for such assistance to be organised as a social service rather than as a private one, with direct links to public bodies. In terms of the service users, the ACLI-COLF anticipated that these family assistants would be employed in response to social exclusion rather than social privilege. Thus 'family collaborators' would provide care in the community for groups such as the elderly, hospitalised and disabled people.[7] The ACLI-COLF, therefore, was, unequivocally focused on improving conditions for working class female domestic workers (and increasingly ethnic minority women) and in assisting marginalised families rather than privileged families. This was reflected in their new philosophy guiding the association's training courses for domestic workers. Domestic workers would no longer be trained to graciously accept their subservient position in relation to the employer. As the then national secretary, Pina Brustolin had stated at the 1973 congress:

> Everyone will understand how our approach to training and professionalism is quite different to the past where we prepared workers for bourgeois families, while today we are called to respond to the needs of working-class families.[8]

Nevertheless, support for the underlying ethos of the women's movement led to a belief that the relationship between the female employer and the female employee could be transformed:

> ... let us here relaunch the proposal to re-establish ... - amongst domestic workers and female employers open to this message -, that solidarity between women which is at the root of the feminist movement. Not in order to mystify, with a form of left-wing paternalism, the nature of the domestic work relationship, but to understand that it is the source of common subjection and that together it is possible to take the initiative to change it, to overcome its current characteristics.

It is a proposal which we already put forward at the last congress but which has still not had a concrete reply. There is thus a risk that amongst domestic workers ... feminism could be seen as an elite phenomenon, which is only relevant to women belonging to socially privileged classes (Turri, ACLI-COLF 1979, p. 9).

A number of the delegates however, were, if not explicitly critical of aspects of feminist ideology, certainly particularly sensitive to the issue of gender privilege and exploitation in the struggle for liberation from men. Carla Lazagna, a delegate from La Spezia, was overtly critical of the feminist movement:

...the women's movement cannot grow on the backs of domestic workers. Behind every woman who is able to embark on a process of emancipation is a mother or a domestic worker. In other words, there is a woman who carries out the role of the housewife. This means that the housewife role in our society is indispensable and this also explains why amongst domestic workers there is clear contempt for that feminism which constructs its liberation on the backs of other women black or white (ACLI-COLF 1979, p. 16).[9]

Judging from the experiences articulated by women delegates during the national congresses throughout the 1970s, it would have been difficult for the concept of sisterhood and female solidarity, as espoused by the Italian feminist movement in the 1970s, to be uncritically accepted by domestic workers. Many of the women who participated in these congresses were likely to be materially experiencing something quite antithetical to the concept of female solidarity in the private context of their employers' homes.

By the time of the 1982 ACLI-COLF congress, specific awareness of gender, as opposed to a reductive focus on class, had begun to affect the ACLI-COLF analyses. Nonetheless, the organisation's intrinsic involvement in the domestic work sector meant that the question of exploitation between women remained a central and difficult contradiction which would constantly resurface. The views of Rosalba Dessì, a provincial delegate for Rome were indicative:

But we professional (or reserve) housewives who experience personally the contradiction of the double day, what should we say? ... When women, through employment, find the means to escape from the ghetto of the family in order to affirm themselves, they force the domestic workers who substitute them to pay for this emancipation. This is then the contradiction: women liberate themselves 'using' other women (ACLI-COLF 1982, p. 40).[10]

The notion not only of privilege between women, but also the exploitation of this privilege, was therefore repeatedly articulated by activists within the association throughout the 1970s and early 1980s. A decade later a quite different picture had emerged. The overt recognition of exploitation between women in the 1970s may be attributable to the fact that during this period, it was the workers' movement rather than the feminist movement with whom the ACLI-COLF sought a closer relationship. This implied a vision of their disadvantage as workers rather than as women and indicated that they saw class differentials as the basis of their exploitation. Despite some attention to the issue of gender, class stratification continued to dominate their analyses. Their emphasis on class and their desire to form alignments with the workers' movement was not unproblematic however, and the marginalisation of domestic workers by the trade union bodies continued into the 1980s.

Between Italian Women and Migrant Women: the ACLI-COLF and Ethnicity

But what of the ACLI-COLF's relationship to ethnic minority women and hence to the position of subjects that were both racialised and gendered? In the 1970s, the ACLI-COLF evolved into an association with a clear class perspective, enabling it to see through the pious mystifications of its former conservative ideology and to focus on the structural dimensions of exploitation. For this reason, it is perhaps no accident that it was during the 1973 congress that the question of migrant domestic workers was raised for the first time. Consonant with the association's new class perspective, the presence and employment of migrant women was viewed essentially as a weapon of the employers to fracture working class mobilisation and strength. As Pina Brustolin stated:

> In terms of recruitment, we cannot help but be worried by the spread of the phenomenon of 'importing' coloured [sic] domestic workers which certainly represents an unscrupulous response from employers to their obligations, which today are a result of legislation and in the future will be guided by contractual duties. In fact many of these workers are employed without a regular work permit ... and therefore any obligation to pay insurance contributions is avoided. This is an obvious attempt to use these workers, available to work under any conditions, as a 'reserve army of labour', just when there is a more mature combatant mood within the sector to take forward its battle for emancipation.[11]

Ianniello Rosetta, a delegate from Rome, graphically described the nature and extent of the exploitation perpetrated against migrant domestic workers:

> ... our comrades who come to our country to work are not protected in any way, they work like animals, they are treated like dirt and they earn just enough to survive ... The problems of foreign female workers is a hot issue which affects all of us, and we must all take on board their difficulties and the obstacles that they encounter to carry out their work.[12]

Generally, it was recognised that the association had little knowledge of the true dimensions of the phenomenon of migrant domestic workers and the ACLI-COLF committed itself to a detailed national survey of the general conditions of domestic workers.[13] On the whole however, this lack of knowledge and the enormous changes which were occurring both within the ACLI-COLF and the workers' movement meant that migrant women's conditions would, in this period, remain largely peripheral to the practical and theoretical concerns of the association. In 1976, the question of ethnic minority women still appeared to be relatively marginal to the principal concerns of the association. As the theme of the ninth congress in 1976 indicated,[14] the association remained centrally concerned with its relationship to the workers' movement. Thus, at this stage, both gender and ethnicity were subordinated to issues of class. In her address to the 1976 congress, the national secretary Pina Brustolin did not include migrant women into her analysis and the concluding motion to the congress prioritised the renewal of the national contract. This is not of course to argue that migrant women were to be excluded from any gains made by the sector but rather to suggest that their specific positioning within the sector had yet to be properly addressed. By 1979 however, and probably as a consequence of the growing numbers of migrant women entering Italy for domestic work, the ACLI-COLF began to adopt a more inclusive conceptual and practical approach towards migrant women. The new national secretary, Clorinda Turri, suggested that the presence of migrant women and the rejection of domestic work by Italian women constituted two important new processes within the sector. The employment of migrant women continued to be viewed as a means for employers to avoid the contractual gains achieved by Italian women workers. There was also an explicit acknowledgement of migrant women's weaker position in comparison to Italian domestic workers – they were generally paid less, were frequently irregularly employed and worked longer hours. Not only their employers appeared to have reverted to an outmoded formulation of the employer/

employee relationship. According to Turri (ACLI-COLF 1979, p. 5):

> [they are forced] into almost total subjection at the hands of private agencies and employers. A type of subjection which recreates real conditions of servitude which we thought we had overcome forever in our country.

In the face of this, it was argued that a paternalistic attitude was not an appropriate response to migrant women's situation but rather 'a clear and militant solidarity' was called for (ACLI-COLF 1979, p. 5). Turri suggested that the association should liaise with the organisations of migrant workers. Underpinning her calls for solidarity with migrant women was an understanding of a common exploitation based on class. Turri expressed some concern that the economic crisis of the 1970s had led to more Italian women offering their labour as domestic workers. It was felt that this might lead to a 'war amongst the poor' between Italian and migrant domestic workers.

In some ways, this latter consideration marked the beginning of a flawed interpretation of migrant women's positioning within the domestic work sector. It assumed a similarity of structural conditions dictating Italian women's and migrant women's participation in the sector. Such an interpretation in fact diminished evidence of a racialised structural segmentation within the sector, where migrant women would work only as live-in workers and Italian women were beginning to work principally on an hourly paid basis.[15]

Reference to a war among the poor implied a similarity of circumstances which did not in fact exist. Certainly, some competition might have existed with the older live-in Italian workers. However, judging by the ease with which migrant women could find alternative employing families, it seemed that during the 1970s, the demand for live-in workers began to outstrip the supply. Migrant women, however, appeared to be sensitive to the accusation that they were taking jobs away from Italian women. In her address to the national congress in 1979, Brito Tiago, a representative of the Cape Verdean association in Italy, emphasised both that Cape Verdeans did not want to compete with Italian workers and also presented the Cape Verdean presence as a temporary one.[16]

By the end of the 1970s, the ACLI-COLF had begun to interpret the increased demand for domestic workers as a replacement for the housewife figure. The employment of a domestic worker was seen as a functional solution to the rigidity of working hours in Italy, the lack of free time and the poor quality of social services. Issues of ethnicity, gender and class were all considered relevant to the domestic work situation. This could clearly be seen in the association's identification of groups with which it should establish alliances – female migrant workers, women's movements and marginalised workers. With regard to female migrants it was stated:

> We must get used to considering domestic workers from other countries as an integral part of our sector. Not only, we must also not forget that our choice to be part of the workers' movement obliges us to show fraternal solidarity with workers and exploited peoples all over the world (Turri, ACLI-COLF 1979, p. 14).

In contrast to migrant women's absence in the concluding motion of the 1976 congress, in 1979, the concluding motion recognised the grievances presented by migrant delegates at the congress and aimed to publicise and respond to them. Throughout the 1980s, increasing attention was paid to the issue of migrant workers. At the 1982 congress, a number of the interventions referred to the general situation of migrant domestic workers[17] and delegations of migrant workers participated in the national congresses.[18] Concern continued to be expressed by Italian activists over whether the recently acquired gains of the sector would be undermined by the presence of migrant workers. As one of the members of the national executive argued:

> … employers prefer migrant domestic workers precisely because they can pay them less, speculating on their dramatic situation and on their disinformation with respect to rights which should be guaranteed within the employment relationship.[19]

In her introductory speech to the congress, Clorinda Turri, still acting as national secretary, argued that it was important to formulate legislation which was inclusive of the specific situation of migrant domestic workers to counter their exploitation by employers. This position in fact encouraged the ACLI-COLF to support wider state legislation to regulate the position of migrant workers in general. The association's approach was thus unequivocally inclusive of migrant workers, dictated by the value of class unity: 'We need to break the natural hold of the bosses by uniting the sector and overcoming the temptation for opposition between the two groups' (Turri, ACLI-COLF 1982, p. 7). To this end there was strong support for legislative gains within the domestic work sector to be applicable to migrant domestic workers and the association argued for the inclusion of an explicit reference to migrant women in the collectively bargained national contracts.

By the early 1980s then, the question of ethnicity with regard to the domestic work sector had unquestionably entered the vocabulary of the ACLI-COLF. This attention would increase in intensity as the issue of immigration attracted sustained consideration at the wider national level. This can clearly be seen in the proceedings of the 1985 ACLI-COLF conference which occurred a year before the promulgation of law 943, the first comprehensive piece of government legislation on immigration. During this congress, a special round table discussion was held on the question of migrant domestic workers. It should be noted that this did not signify that the issue of migrant domestic workers was subsequently excluded from the rest of the proceedings. In fact, a number of migrant representatives spoke during the main proceedings[20] and Italian delegates continued to make reference to the situation of migrant domestic workers in their speeches. It was the round table discussion, however, which provided the forum in which the ACLI-COLF could spell out its position regarding female migrant domestic workers.[21] The opening speech by Clorinda Turri (now deputy national secretary) indicated that the condition of migrant domestic workers was seen to be closely intertwined with their general situation as migrants.[22] This seemed to imply that although class location was seen as fundamental, ethnicity and a migrant status were privileged over gender as causes of disadvantage. It was for this reason that the ACLI-COLF called for the implementation of appropriate national legislation governing migrants as a whole. The association reiterated its opposition to special employment norms for migrant domestic workers as it was felt that these would be abused by employers hoping to find docility in their overseas domestic workers. To a large extent, the ACLI-COLF perspective emulated the Christian solidarity position of its parenting structure, the ACLI. Aldo De Matteo, for example, then vice president of the ACLI, unequivocally stated: 'foreign workers ... are not stealing jobs, but are pioneers. They have accepted heavy jobs, often rejected by Italians and it is unfair to accuse them of competing when this is not the case' (ACLI-COLF 1985a, p. 56).

Given that in the 1970s and early 1980s migrant women were employed almost exclusively as live-in domestic workers, it would have been virtually impossible for an association such as the ACLI-COLF to ignore their presence. This proximity meant that the ACLI-COLF pre-empted both national government and the more progressive arena of women's politics in responding to the specific situation of migrant women. It would ultimately adopt an inclusive stance, paying sustained attention to migrant women's specific difficulties at its national congresses. Inclusiveness in itself would not necessarily improve their situation. Rather, the nature of the general strategy of the association into which migrant women were being integrated would be the critical factor in instigating change. Given the ACLI-COLF's development of a radical position during the 1970s and early 1980s, to what degree would it have the potential to transform the position of migrant workers through its wider understanding of and strategy for the domestic work sphere? I want to argue that by the mid 1980s, the association had reverted to promoting an ideal of sacrifice for the domestic worker (albeit to a lesser extent than the conservative API-COLF), but this time in the name of female solidarity. In the following subsection, I shall engage with the ACLI-COLF's contemporary conceptual interpretation of domestic work. I argue that while in the early 1970s the relationship between (largely Italian) female domestic workers and their employers was initially seen to be marked by an exploitative class relationship, by the late 1980s this position had been modified. The ACLI-COLF now emphasised the intrinsic value of the female relationship between employer and employee. This emphasis minimised emerging evidence which indicated that the relationship between women in the domestic work sector could not simply be reduced to a gender relationship as it was being increasingly structured by the inter-relationship of gender, class and ethnicity.

The ACLI-COLF and its New Interpretation of Domestic Work

In the early 1990s, a series of articles were commissioned by the ACLI-COLF with the express purpose of contributing to the creation of a new theoretical framework with which to analyse domestic work.[23] It is my contention that the analyses put forward in these articles revealed the association's tendency to obscure class and ethnicity as important factors inscribed within the domestic work relationship. This was evident from the nature of the debate which centred principally on explaining and interpreting *Italian women's* need for domestic workers. This focus functioned to minimise the interests of the domestic worker, thus producing a reductive account of supply and demand factors operating within the sector.

In discussing the relationship between Italian families and the demand for domestic workers, Alemani (1992), maintained that it was the emerging diversity of existing family relationships (one-parent families, single people, etc.) which had not only modified the type of demand for domestic work but had also affected the employer/employee relationship. She argued that the increasing propensity for the female employer to work outside the home had led to a greater willingness on the part of the employer to delegate rather than to supervise, thus permitting the possibility of autonomous management for the domestic worker. She did attempt to interpret the new demand for live-in work but failed to fully engage with the racialised dimension of the new labour supply. In her analysis, demand was attributable to a series of factors. These included the insufficient number of nursery places, the limited number of schools operating an extended day and the increase in the number of pensioners who frequently require company as well as assistance. She maintained that women often had no option but to utilise private organisations or live-in domestic workers as strategies to facilitate family life. Livraghi's (1992) contribution replicated some of these ideas, as she too focused on how the transformation of Italian families had led to a new plurality of service demands. Marina Piazza (1992) similarly sought to highlight the Italian employers' perspective by stressing the multiple pressures inherent in their 'double presence' (in the home and at work) and the rigidity of city times which caused specific difficulties for women. Di Nicola's[24] article centred on analysing the reasons for Italian women's postponement of maternity. In her view, for Italian women to combine motherhood with both paid employment and a social life, they must have support from parents, in-laws, other relatives or 'be able to afford the luxury of a domestic worker who today represents the last hope not only for bourgeois families, but for all those middle class families who have specific caring needs' (Di Nicola 1994, p. 176).

As I have demonstrated above, in the 1970s, the ACLI-COLF explicitly recognised the contradiction of women exploiting other women for reproductive work. In the early 1990s, none of the contributors sought to explore this. Alemani (1992) touched on this issue, maintaining that one of the fundamental contradictions which women's movements have consistently been unable to resolve is that of women achieving their liberation/emancipation through the sacrifices of other women. During the 1970s and early 1980s, the ACLI-COLF had acknowledged that ethnicity or a migrant status had caused greater and specific disadvantage for migrant women, but by the 1990s this perspective had quietly faded from view. The series of commissioned articles in the early 1990s focused on the female (Italian) employer and this prohibited the development of any framework which could accommodate the complexity of women's interaction within this relationship. By emphasising the difficulties that Italian women encountered in reconciling their family and work roles, these articles served only to validate Italian women's increasing propensity to employ domestic workers.

This new ACLI-COLF interpretive model can be situated within Romero's (1992) typology of the relationship between domestic workers and their employers. Her description of employers in the North American context identified several categories but it is the Common Victim proposition which best accommodates the ACLI-COLF perspective. The Common Victim view maintains that the sexist structuring of society signifies that whilst professional women have to compete in a man's world, it is still assumed that they will take responsibility for housework and child-care. The female employer thus views herself as no less a victim than the domestic worker.[25] One problem with this typology is that it replicates the notion that it is other women (often privileged by class and ethnicity) who gain from the work of domestic workers. This occurs because the work executed by the paid domestic worker is assumed to be the work of the wife/mother, thus it is she, and not other members of the family, who is expected to supervise the fulfillment of household tasks. These patriarchal assumptions do not however mean that women can totally distance themselves from their own responsibility within the employment relationship. As Romero (1992, p. 169) has argued:

> Feminist analysis should consider not only the privilege and benefits that husbands obtain at the expense of their wives but also those that one group of women obtain at the expense of another. Certainly, as employees, professional women are sometimes victims of sexism, but they still make decisions that ultimately result in shifting the burden of sexism. Hiring household workers to take the place of wives or mothers maintains male privilege at home.[26]

The propensity to conceptualise the issue of domestic service in terms of the Common Victim proposition has a repressive function in that it diminishes the weaker position of the (migrant) domestic worker. In other words, the Common Victim perspective somehow fails to encapsulate the extent of the power disparity inscribed within this relationship.

It would seem that the ACLI-COLF gradually began to assimilate and promote this notion in the mid 1980s and this was likely to have consequences for its conceptual and strategical development in the future. A clear example of this can be found in the Charter of Responsibilities and Rights drawn up for domestic workers for the occasion of its twelfth national congress in the mid 1980s. Here, the Common Victim syndrome is explicitly acknowledged:

> We suffer particularly as a result of the contradiction that is created in this relationship between women; many of them [female employers] can improve their own quality of life and minimise the discrimination that affects them in the current division of roles in society by utilising our work to free themselves from domestic work. We domestic workers, on the other hand, cannot use for ourselves or for our families the services which we offer to other women (ACLI-COLF 1985b, pp. 2/3).

Nevertheless, and quite significantly I would argue, one finds contained within the section outlining the responsibilities of a domestic worker, approval for the domestic worker to view her relationship with her female employer as an act of solidarity between women:

> The domestic worker, as a woman, sees the importance of valorising the fact that she is in an employment relationship with other women, whether they are traditional employers of domestic workers or women who use a home-help service. The domestic worker feels, as a woman and as a female worker, that this relationship between women must be solid for a journey of personal liberation and to promote a common battle for social services which all women can use (ACLI-COLF 1985b, pp. 2/3).

This document does note the contradiction 'between women' in its preamble, however, the onus of sacrifice and solidarity is placed on the disadvantaged domestic worker. It is she who must make sacrifices in order to promote a battle which will ultimately be beneficial for all women. Notably absent from the section dealing with the domestic workers' rights is any suggestion that female employers should also make sacrifices as a contribution to women's struggle, let alone encourage their partners to make some.

This mode of analysis had begun to prevail by the late 1980s and was readily applied to the specific situation of migrant women. The acceptance of Italian women's need for female migrant labour to perform a live-in function and the concurrent emphasis on the perceived advantages of this for migrant women were used to validate this perspective (interview, ACLI-COLF). The position adopted by the association suggests that ascribing a victim label to domestic workers may have been applicable when employers emanated essentially from the upper classes, but the emergence of employers from within middle income categories has tended to invalidate this notion conferring instead a Common Victim status on both service user and provider. As Sacconi (1984, pp. 40–41) has written in relation to this structural change in the background of the employers of domestic workers: 'far from being a luxury ... it is becoming a real necessity in all those families with young children or elderly members'.

By the early 1990s, the drift towards a narrow gender analysis was consolidated and utilised to interpret the findings of a major survey of domestic workers undertaken by the ACLI-COLF in the early 1990s:[27]

> ... the hypothesis which informs our work is that the tensions [and] imbalances ... which we find in the domestic workers' conditions are to be found in the tensions and imbalances which characterise women's condition ... the conditions

of the domestic worker then as a mirror of women's condition ... (IREF/ACLI-COLF 1994, p. 9).

Although the ACLI-COLF argued that the presence of migrant women constituted the most important new feature within the sector, and acknowledged that their insertion into the live-in sphere had exacerbated their working conditions, its overriding perspective stressed the useful reconciliation of migrant women's needs and Italian women's needs: 'The type of supply that the migrant domestic worker is prepared to offer reconciles itself well with the needs exhibited by a part of the service users' (IREF/ACLI-COLF 1994, p. 11). Thus, the perceived advantages of live-in domestic work for migrant women (provision of accommodation, food, greater savings potential and therefore the possibility of larger remittances) have been utilised by the organisation to present migrant women's location within the live-in sphere as a preferred choice. Evidence from different national and historical contexts indicates that domestic workers will abandon live-in work for day work or other employment sectors as soon as this becomes available.[28]

The analysis used to account for the fact that Italian women have largely rejected employment as live-in workers, confirms that a reductive gender focus is not sufficient to understand migrant women's and Italian women's position: '... Italian domestic workers prefer to be employed on an hourly paid basis rather than on a live-in basis as this would mean them having to give up an autonomous lifestyle or the impossibility of looking after their own nuclear family' (IREF/ACLI-COLF 1994, p. 13). Remarkably, the pertinence of this statement for migrant women is totally overlooked. The ACLI-COLF additionally asserted that young (Italian) women avoid the domestic work sphere because they view it as anachronistic in view of women's changed circumstances (AAvv 1994, p. 42). Again, there is no indication that such a view might be equally pertinent to many of the young and professional migrant women who cannot exercise such a choice. This view may be conditioned by what Morokvasic (1991) refers to as pervasive ethnocentric assumptions about migrant women's backwardness. In other words, their conditions in Italy are acceptable given that it is assumed that they are not only an improvement on conditions in their country of origin, but also provide escape from oppressive cultural traditions. To this end, the ACLI-COLF failed to engage with the reasons why migrant women work as live-in domestics, and in so doing evaded the issue of ethnicity. This omission was determined by a paternalistic approach to migrant women which focused on the advantages of live-in work for migrant workers and perceived the disadvantages as being largely related to problems of the sector as opposed to their structural location as female migrants confined to a specific area of the economy. In this way, the severe social consequences of live-in work for migrant women could be marginalised. This perspective was also used to privilege the gendered ethnicity of Italian women against that of migrant women. The importance of Italian women's family role was explicitly acknowledged as a valid reason for their repudiation of live-in work. The family role of migrant women, on the other hand, was entirely overlooked. This conceptual omission suggested that although the association had ostensibly adopted an inclusive approach to migrant women, in reality, it continued to be principally concerned with representing the interests of Italian women, not only as domestic workers but increasingly as employers of domestic workers.

The foregrounding of gender for the analysis of the IREF/ACLI-COLF study can thus be said to have led to some debatable conclusions. One of the questions included in the survey regarded the relationship between female employers and their employees. This was used to assess the extent to which gender could constitute an element of cohesion between women. The results indicated that a greater degree of familiarity was apparent between women within the employer/employee relationship.[29] This led to a very positive assessment of the potential for increased collaboration between women. By the 1990s then, the belief that the relationship between female employer and female employee was no longer conflictual led to an apparent resolution of the old and familiar dilemma regarding privileged women's exploitation of disadvantaged women. The new position was decidedly different from that described above with reference to the 1970s:

> Is the affirmation still valid that the emancipation of women necessarily negates the same emancipation of other women forced into a domestic role? The responses relating to this seem to indicate that this antagonistic vision has been overcome and is allowing space for comparison and dialogue from which a new relationship between women can develop (IREF/ACLI-COLF 1994, p. 14).

Indeed, even the presence of migrant men in the sector was promoted as positive:

> It is indicative ... that male [migrants] ... are willing to carry out tasks which have typically been assigned to women and that families are accepting men to fulfill certain tasks. A step forward perhaps for a different and more equal re-distribution of reproductive care work within the family ...? (IREF/ACLI-COLF 1994, p. 13).

It is, I think, extremely pertinent that migrant men are here lauded for standing at the vanguard of a transformation of gender role stratification within Italy.[30] At the same time, an unspoken compliance with Italian men's reluctance to participate in this transformation is evident in the apparent acceptability of hiring migrant women and men to do domestic labour.

The unmistakable prominence of gender and the value attributed to the domestic work relationship between women has had important implications for the nature of migrant women's inclusion into the ACLI-COLF's analysis. Privileging migrant women's gender over their ethnicity has functioned to obscure the ongoing racialisation process within the sector, leading to false assumptions regarding women's solidarity. Indeed, this focus on solidarity, while not totally negating the existence of exploitative relationships, has effectively marginalised themes of exploitation. A number of hypotheses could be put forward to explain the ACLI-COLF's gradual change of emphasis. Firstly, there had been changes in the political climate. The progressive collective action of the 1970s had led to a retreat into private life in the 1980s, culminating in more moderate forms of activism and analysis. Secondly, there had been some improvement in domestic workers' situation via the collectively bargained national contracts. Thirdly, the ALCI-COLF's most recent survey had indicated an improved relationship between employer and employee. Finally, and perhaps most significantly, is the relevance of the structural change in the status of employers. The blatant class exploitation between upper class leisured female employers and working class women had become much less apparent in Italy. Now middle class women, with new aspirations and roles, were seen to have a functional necessity rather than a superfluous desire for domestic workers. This undoubtedly contributed to the new focus on gender. Nevertheless, the marginalisation of ethnicity by the ACLI-COLF meant that Italian women's needs, both as employers and domestic workers were implicitly seen as more important than those of migrant women.

Conclusion

The continued demand for live-in domestic workers by Italian families has accentuated the unresolved tension between productive and reproductive care in Italy. As previous chapters have shown, this led to the coexistence of a flexible hourly-paid domestic work sphere (dominated by Italian women) and the persistent rigidity of the live-in sphere (dominated by migrant women). This duality suggested that migrant women's situation could not simply be explained by reference to gender stratification alone. Rather, attention also needed to be paid to their migrant status and the rigid structural constraints of live-in work. Recent trends within the ACLI-COLF indicate a privileging of Italian women's gendered ethnicity as middle class employers and as (largely) hourly paid working-class domestic employees. In the 1970s, when the ACLI-COLF abandoned its clerical response to the domestic work sector and moved towards a class and gendered interpretation, it was able to explicitly articulate those factors responsible for domestic workers' subordination. More recently, however, it has been loath to explicitly verbalise the manner in which a migrant status functions to subordinate ethnic minority women within the domestic work sphere. At its fourteenth congress in 1994, it did recognise migrant women's need for more political space and autonomous representation within the association and also pledged to support them in their need for housing (ACLI-COLF 1994). Generally, however, the 1990s saw a shift towards the acceptance of the *utility* for Italian female employers to have access to live-in domestic workers, seeming to typify Frankenberg's (1993) concept of power evasion as discussed in the introduction to this book. This evasion could be observed when the ACLI-COLF asserted Italian domestic workers' preference for hourly paid work to facilitate their family roles but failed to fully investigate the implications of live-in work for the family life of migrant women. The ACLI-COLF's focus on women as a disadvantaged group not only avoided acknowledging the weaker position of migrant domestic workers but it equally masked class differences between Italian women by validating the choices of those middle class families financially able to employ live-in domestic workers, without engaging in a corresponding discussion of working-class women's inability to do so. Interestingly then, it would seem that the potential for an inclusivity which acknowledged the specific structural location of migrant women was more prevalent in the 1970s than in the 1990s. In the 1970s, there was no attempt to fuse the interests of middle/upper class women with those of working class women. Rather the exploitation seen to be inherent within the domestic work relationship was something to be challenged and, indeed, radically altered. By the 1990s such a fusion of interests had become an integral component of the ACLI-COLF's strategy and it is precisely the attractiveness of interpreting migrant women's presence in the live-in sphere as a straightforward and useful reconciliation of supply and demand which in fact suggests that the contradiction at the basis of the domestic work relationship remains unresolved.

Notes

1 The results of the divorce referendum in 1974 are frequently cited as indicative of a secularising trend in Italy. See Clark, Hine and Irving (1974).

2 The API-COLF did integrate the issue of migrant women into its broader strategy. In 1978, it dedicated its XI National Day to the issue of female migrant workers and at its XI National Congress in 1982, it anticipated that the 1980s would be the decade in which more attention would be paid to migrant women. Its congress documents throughout the 1980s did indeed indicate that the association paid attention to migrant domestic workers and at its 1985 congress it committed itself to training leaders for the organisation from ethnic minorities. Nonetheless, migrant domestic workers were essentially being integrated into an organisation which continued to subordinate domestic workers to the employer. Domestic workers were discouraged from seeking high salaries and their work was still promoted as a vocation to be carried out with love: 'Don't forget "the smile" which no code or no institution ... can order, but we can and must "give"' (API-COLF 1985, p. 15). This perspective was not conceptualised as servitude but rather as a Christian expression of service and this distinction between service and servitude continued to be emphasised into the 1990s. For some more examples of the API-COLF's ideological stance and its involvement with migrant domestic workers see API-COLF 1991; Garassini 1992 and its periodical *Le Colf* (July 1982, June 1985, January 1987, July 1988).

3 The UDI's participation in this congress was indicative of the new Left-leaning direction of the ACLI-COLF.

4 This is an abbreviated reference as the congress proceedings were published in a special addition of *Acli-Oggi*, the ACLI's periodical.

5 This is an abbreviated reference as congress proceedings were reproduced in a special issue of *Acli-Oggi*.

6 Vaiou (1995, p. 43), in her study of Southern European women argues that 'male identities in the south do not include in their definition caring and domestic labour'.

7 The national secretary of the UDI, Costanza Fanelli, saw cooperatives as the way forward in overcoming the individual work relationship of the domestic worker. See her intervention at the 1979 national congress (ACLI-COLF 1979).

8 See 'Relazione Organizzativa dell'incaricata nazionale: Pina Brustolin', Assemblea Nazionale Congressuale, Siena 1973, p. 7.

9 See also the interventions of Bianca Buri from Milan and the trade union representative Gianna Bitto on this point at the 1979 congress.

10 This delegate would become the national secretary by the time of the 1985 congress, at which time she called for greater links with the women's movement. See ACLI-COLF (1985a, p. 19).

11 Relazione Organizzativa dell'incaricata nazionale: Pina Brustolin', Assemblea Nazionale Congressuale, Siena 1973, p. 10.

12 Intervention published in *La Casa e La Vita*, May/June/July 1973, p. 4.

13 In the event, they were excluded from the survey carried out in 1974.

14 'Le Colf nel movimento operaio per lo sviluppo dei servizi sociali per un nuovo modello di vita'.

15 This structural differentiation had in fact already been observed by Turri at the 1979 congress. See (ACLI-COLF 1979, p. 5).

16 See her intervention in (ACLI-COLF 1979, p. 16).

17 Even the contributions by the representatives of the main political parties referred to the question of migrant workers. See interventions by the Christian Democrat member of parliament Giuseppe Costamagna and that of Mariangela Rosolen, a member of the Italian Communist Party's national women's committee (ACLI-COLF 1982).

18 This in itself was significant as it suggested that the ACLI-COLF did attempt to integrate migrant women into its organisational structures at an early stage.

19 See intervention by Rita di Maio (ACLI-COLF 1982, p. 33).

20 See interventions by Yeshi Habits, the Filipino representative Corazon Sim, and an Eritrean representative Alì Moussa.

21 'Le Colf immigrate in Italia: linee d'impegno dell'associazionismo'.

22 In fact the congress sent a telegram to the Home Secretary regarding the urgency of an immigration law and asked to hold a meeting with him to present the specific case of domestic workers. The original telegram is reproduced in the proceedings of the 1985 ACLI-COLF congress.

23 These were published in 1992 and 1993 in a journal, *Quaderni di Azione Sociale* – a debating forum for Italian associationism. Claudia Alemani, an ACLI-COLF representative, opened and closed the debate with two articles entitled: 'Le Colf: un'identità molteplice tra persistenza e mutamento' and 'Le Colf: emblema del femminile'. The intervening articles consisted of Marina Piazza: 'Le implicazioni attuali del concetto di doppia presenza'; Renata Livraghi: 'Le famiglie e la produzione di servizi'; Giulia Paola Di Nicola: 'Le sfide sociali della maternità'. Some of these articles were reproduced in the ACLI series 'Transizioni' in 1994 in a publication reporting the results of a survey into the conditions of domestic workers. See AAvv (1994).

24 This article was also originally published in *Quaderni di Azione Sociale* but references here are to the reproduction of this article in AAvv (1994).

25 Jacklyn Cock (1980) presented a similar thesis regarding the situation of Black domestic workers and their employers in South Africa which she describes as a politics of mutual dependence.

26 See also Ramazanoglu (1989) on this point.

27 The interpretative framework adopted for the survey was established during the course of a seminar organised by the ACLI-COLF and IREF in Rome in February 1991. The research took place between 1991 and 1993. This survey currently constitutes the largest and most up-to-date national survey of the domestic work sector. It was based on interviews with 717 domestic workers, 92.7 per cent of whom were women and 34 per cent of whom were migrants.

28 See Hine (1990) on the case of African American southern domestic workers and De Grazia (1992) on Italian women in the inter-war period.

29 36.5 per cent of workers considered their relationship with their employers to be 'friendly', with a slightly lower figure for migrant women (32.8 per cent) and a higher figure for Italian women (38.5 per cent).

30 This view was reiterated by the national secretary Maria Solinas in her speech to the 1994 congress. See ACLI-COLF, *Le Colf tra nuovi modelli familiari e crisi dello stato sociale*, XIV Assemblea Nazionale ACLI-COLF, Rome, 24–26 February 1994.

9 Crossing Boundaries: the Libere, Insieme Association

Previous chapters have discussed Black women's experiences in Italy and considered their position in relation to the wider gender debate within Italy. This chapter is concerned with the development of political relationships between Italian women and ethnic minority women and the ways in which this represented an attempt to establish a more inclusive gender politics in the country. The chapter begins by briefly examining the recent history of political feminists' relationship to questions of 'race and ethnicity' and then proceeds to a discussion of a major initiative promoted by women activists within the Pds. This stands as one of the first attempts, in the early 1990s, to incorporate the question of ethnicity into the gendered political practice of progressive women activists and it took the form of a mixed women's association called *Libere, Insieme*.[1] I shall be arguing that the attempt to address ethnicity within the framework of progressive feminist thought exposed some weaknesses in the theoretical underpinnings of the practice of a gendered politics.

Progressive Women's Activism and Ethnicity

In the 1970s, when Italian second-wave feminism was at its peak, 'race' and ethnicity were seen as parallel but separate issues. There were several instances where Italian feminists, in attempting to theorise the inferior status of Italian women, drew parallels between women's inferior status and the inferior status of Black people, in particular African-Americans. Writing in 1976, the feminist Dacia Maraini equated women's self-denigration to African-Americans' self-denigration and Dalla Costa (1978) argued that there were similarities in the acts of sexual violence perpetrated by men towards women and the violence of slave masters towards their slaves. In another feminist text, while the close similarity between women, Black people and Jews was asserted, women's situation was nevertheless seen to be qualitatively different and it was argued that racism could only be resolved once the question of women had been addressed (see Abbà et al. 1972, p. 60). Ethnicity then, was conceptually utilised as an analogous case to gender stratification, but the relationship between these two constructs was not considered.

In the early 1970s, Italian feminism had initially focused on women's unity and thus on the affirmation of the self as woman (Caldwell 1991b). One clear example of this can be found in a feminist text by Pia Bruzzichelli (1976, p. 11):

> In a word, being a woman is common to all women and the problems of every woman, as women, are the same for all women. Becoming aware of this means, or should mean acquiring an attitude of solidarity and establishing a network of relationships, intentions and information ... which allow and develop such solidarity (p. 11).

As Cammarota (1984) has noted, the movement initially established itself in opposition to the male sphere and this encouraged it to overlook existing differences between women. It was at a later stage, that an important shift in emphasis occurred whereby emphasis on the biological identity of women was replaced by greater recognition of internal differences among women (Pasquinelli 1984). Migrant women living in Italy would nevertheless remain an 'invisible' group into the mid-1980s.[2] This invisibility can undoubtedly be partially attributed to the absence of 'race' as an aspect of political formation within Italy.[3] Writing about racism in Italy in the late 1980s, Laura Balbo, a Left-wing political activist, confirmed that in the period of her life in which she had been most politically active, the question of 'race' had been almost totally absent:

> For a long time I, ... the Italian Left, were convinced that ... the oppression of Black Americans would, sooner or later, be overcome by a politics of integration. Issues of racism were not our responsibility, our struggle. We offered indignation and solidarity and occasional attention ... But I think you could say that racism was not central to the political agenda of the Left.
>
> We have behind us therefore, empty decades of cultural elaboration and daily experiences concerning 'racism'. This is how we have arrived at the present (Balbo 1989, p. 14).

Although one might argue that feminists did not initially notice migrant women because they were such a small presence, some awareness of their existence was apparent in a number of progressive sociological texts written by women. However, even where migrant women were mentioned, there was limited, if any, evaluation of the material conditions of their presence. Indeed, these early writings seemed to set a precedent for the manner in which migrant women would be discussed in the future, in that the presence of migrant women was typically used to elucidate Italian women's situation. For example, Cammarota (1984), in her discussion of domestic work, highlights the issue of women doing other women's domestic labour:

> It almost seems as though a woman's emancipation can only occur by off-loading a part of her own domestic duties onto another woman. It is not by chance that the number of domestic workers has risen noticeably over the last few years. The reasons behind this growth in the domestic work sector can be ... attributed to the organisational needs of a working woman and the fact that she cannot ... reconcile her double presence so she prefers or is forced to delegate part of the domestic labour to another woman if she wants to have a minimum amount of space for herself (Cammarota 1984, p. 61).

Migrant women, however, are referred to only in parenthesis. Cammarota (1984, p. 62) continues: 'On the other hand, there are increasing numbers of women prepared to work on an hourly paid basis (without taking into account the numerous domestic workers from the Third World), to balance their family budgets ...'. Because Cammarota focuses on the use of hourly paid domestic work by Italian women as a means of reconciling family and work roles, the problems that migrant women encountered in reconciling these two roles, within the live-in domestic sphere, is simply not addressed. Similarly, Rita Randazzo's (1986) study of the transformation of women's roles in the south of Italy notes the apparent contradiction between the widespread unemployment of Italian women and the presence of domestic workers from Third World countries. Randazzo attributes this to the fact that Italian women living in marginalised families can only accept work where remuneration is not too low and the working hours are not too long. No attempt is made to account for why these same factors did not similarly impede migrant women from employment in the domestic work sphere. In contrast to Cammarota's (1984) parenthesised reference to African and Asian domestic workers, Rita Sacconi (1984) presented a more inclusive and critical account of domestic workers' situation in Italy:

> But how can we interpret this lack of interest by those who for years have been fighting for equal dignity and equality for women with respect to men in the labour market? Is it a lacuna, or is there perhaps a tendency to obscure the fact

that the domestic worker represents an uncomfortable contradiction: that of the emancipation of women through other women (Sacconi 1984, p. 40).

Dalla Costa (1981, p. 126) also acknowledged the presence of migrant domestic workers in the early 1980s. She argued that Italian women's reluctance to work as live-in domestic workers not only paralleled Italian women's increasing reluctance to do unpaid domestic work 'out of love', but was also indicative, of their new 'threshold of unavailability'. Indeed, live-in domestic work was the principal type of salaried employment rejected by Italian women, which, in her mind, explained why this sphere of domestic work was being taken over by migrant women. Nonetheless, Dalla Costa did not consider the significance of migrant women's availability to work as live-in workers in relation to the wider gender debate. In fact, she located migrant women alongside migrant men as exploited workers and optimistically predicted that they would develop relationships with the local Italian proletariat as a means of challenging their lack of power.

Even into the 1990s, when widespread attention was being paid to the issue of migration, overviews of women's situation in Italian society continued to exclude migrant women. Franca Bimbi, writing on the theme of women's citizenship, juxtaposed the position of Italian women to the *general* position of migrants: '... the increase in social stratification brought about by non EC immigration may well have the effect of strengthening the position of women within the system of social guarantees' (Bimbi 1992, p. 94). She thus seemed to be anticipating that the presence of a more marginalised group would present Italian women with greater access to citizenship rights. Here then, was an explicit separation of gender and ethnicity even though Bimbi did go on to raise the question of whether civil citizenship and social security guarantees would also be extended to migrant women. Beccalli (1994), in her overview of the women's movement in Italy, failed to consider migrant women at all.

In 1991, an article published by the noted feminist academic Anna Rossi Doria, did attempt to explore this unknown territory. She herself acknowledged feminism's absence in this sphere:

> ... Italian research on the immigration phenomenon does not generally pay attention to the specific situation of women... It should be highlighted that even feminist culture did not pay any attention to these issues (Rossi Doria 1991a, p. 80).

The generally exploitative working conditions of migrant women were in Rossi Doria's view symptomatic of their dislocation from the achievements of Italian feminism, particularly in terms of maternity legislation. In an address to the national conference of female parliamentarians (a Left-wing grouping) in May of 1991, Rossi Doria presented a frank assessment of the problems involved in constructing relationships between women from different ethnic groups:

> ... I think it is obvious that the construction of multi-ethnic cities, and in our case, of a correct relationship between ourselves and migrant women, are arduous tasks. We certainly can't get away with nice words about our being united as women, nor with generical statements such as: we're fighting inequality, we respect difference. The contradiction between universalism and respect for difference is articulated in a very difficult way between western women and women from the Third World. We will only be able to develop, if not multi-ethnic cities, at least something more dignified, if we are able to establish a loyal relationship with migrant women – including a serious analysis of our differences – and if we respect their possible desire not to have any relationship with us (Rossi Doria 1991b, p. 8).

It would be difficult to contest the assertion that Italian women activists on the left of the political spectrum generally failed to recognise the specific, marginalised position of migrant women. In an interview published in *Il Manifesto* in the early 1990s, the Eritrean activist Maricos articulated her disappointment at this neglect: 'I expected more ... at least from women in the trade unions and the Left-wing parties ... but nothing'.[4] When asked to account for this lack of attention from the progressive sphere, my key informant attributed it to migrant women's insertion into the domestic work sector and the close relationship of this sector to Catholic associationism.[5]

New Directions

From the early 1990s, a number of political initiatives began to emerge within the Left regarding migrant women. An (untitled) document produced by women within the Communist Party was the precursor for the mixed association which was formed in 1991. This early document indicated both Communist women's desire to get to know migrant women and their desire to incorporate the issues articulated by these women into their continually evolving political practice: 'European women together with female migrants and our [Italian] female emigrants ... to write another page of the Communist Women's Charter'. In a subsequent document, delineating a provisional Female Migrants' Charter, the contribution of Communist women to wider European issues on migration was highlighted.[6] The issue of migrant women was approached in terms of a double invisibility – as women and as migrants. Inscribed within their proposals for a Female Migrants' Charter were calls for an immediate right to work for those women entering Italy under the family reunification ruling; specific projects for women with regard to training and professional requalification; the right to housing and family unity and the right to maternity benefits even for unemployed women migrants (Le donne comuniste 1989).

The political desire to establish a Female Migrants' Charter indicated continuity in the strategy of the Pci's women's section. As discussed in chapter 1, their own 1986 Women's Charter was seen as an important theoretical and practical landmark in the evolution of women's mobilisation within the party. At that time, the question of ethnicity had been totally marginalised from their project.[7] The discussions in 1989 were thus an attempt to rectify this omission. Moreover, it was envisaged that a relationship with migrant women would ultimately contribute to a more useful political Charter for women as a whole.[8]

A sustained response to the presence of migrant women by Italian women activists emerged from within the Left in the early 1990s. In this period, there was a proliferation of mixed (by nationality and gender) organisations responding to the general issue of immigration in Italy.[9] Two innovative associations based in Rome emerged in the spring of 1991.[10] They represented the first concrete attempt to create an arena for common action between women of different ethnicities. The two organisations were *Donne senza frontiere* (Women without Borders) and *Libere, Insieme* (Free Women Together). Although the two associations shared some common objectives, there were differences in their positions. In the following sections, my focus is on the manner in which these associations sought to approach this new constituency of women and, in particular, the manner in which they attempted to foster collaboration between progressive female activism and ethnic minority women. The public visibility and greater mobilisation of the *Libere, Insieme* association contributed to its prominence. This chapter will therefore pay sustained attention to the latter's organisation and strategy, although I begin by a brief discussion of the *Donne senza frontiere* association.

Donne Senza Frontiere

The objectives of this association centred on facilitating meetings and an exchange of information between women from different cultures. Its initial document stated that the association would be composed of women (Italian and foreign) who wanted to contribute to the construction of a multi-cultural society. It also planned to provide an information service for migrant women, undertake research, compile documentation and develop training initiatives.[11] It was anticipated that Italian and migrant women members would be attracted to the association for different reasons:

> *Donne senza frontiere* is aimed at Italian women who want to get to know other cultures and different ways of being women and to foreign women who want to understand better the reality of the country in which they are living and to participate in the establishment of a different and more just society (Donne senza frontiere 1991, p. 1).

In an article published in the Socialist newspaper *Avanti!* and written by the president of the association Marta Ajò, further insights into the goals of the association could be gleaned. Ajò (1991) viewed the association as marking an important departure from the tradition hitherto established in Rome, where migrant women had historically organised on the basis of their ethnicity. One could detect, therefore, implicit support for aggregation on the basis of gender rather than ethnicity.

Assistance for working mothers and their children, the valorisation of female identity, and respect for equal rights were cited as problems common to both Italian and foreign women. This notion of commonality was reiterated by Ajò in an interview with Bianca Maria Pomeranzi, published in *Noi Donne*. She argued that all cultures saw women as 'different' and that it was precisely this diversity which made women similar to each other, despite coming from different cultures (Pomeranzi 1991). The association did, however, hope to achieve common objectives based on the respect and valorisation of diversity (Ajò 1991). Indeed, the aim was that of an equal (*paritario*) relationship between women of different races and cultures (Pomeranzi 1991). Of some importance was Ajò's argument that women had a special role to play in promoting a culture of tolerance with regard to racism. Indeed she maintained that women could become 'strategic agents' in this role, given their function as transmitters of culture. There was thus an assumption that women would naturally be more tolerant than men with regard to the issue of racism and that they could use this natural tolerance to promote improved relations between different ethnicities.

Although Ajò claimed political neutrality for the organisation (interview,

DSF), it was based within the Left.[12] The association's membership did not simply include Italian women as representatives of Europe and the diverse range of ethnicities present in Rome as representatives of the developing world. Rather, its members also included French and Australian nationals (interview, DSF). Although the association clearly aimed to constitute a broad cultural association, some ethnic groups were notably absent. For example, there were no Cape Verdean women members. This was attributed to the existence of an established Cape Verdean women's association in Rome rather than to the aims and objectives of the association itself. Indeed, Ajò adamantly asserted that she refused to become paranoid about how many migrant women were present within the association (interview, DSF). This seemed to contradict the fundamental objectives of the association and precluded debate regarding the relevance of the association's agenda for the variety of ethnic minority women present in Rome. Although the association had a Latin American co-president,[13] Ajò was its visible public representative.

This association attained limited visibility in the Roman context. Its broad cultural base was unlikely to render it attractive to migrant women and its refusal to evaluate whether ethnic minority women might or might not find the association attractive negated a critical aspect of its own cultural objectives. *Donne senza frontiere* would ultimately be obscured by another mixed women's association, *Libere, Insieme*.

The Libere, Insieme Association

The political document for the *Libere, Insieme* association was produced in the spring of 1991, although the association was not formally launched until December of that year. It was initially temporarily based at *Botteghe Oscure*, the headquarters of the Pds, indicating the primary involvement of Pds women.[14] However, it defined itself as an autonomous association and was composed of women from the Pds, the non-governmental organisations, the trade union movement and the Left generally.[15] In April 1993, Teresa Savini, a principal activist within the organisation stated that there were approximately 100 members, over half of whom were ethnic minority women. These were mainly African, Filipina and South American with a small presence of East Europeans.[16]

The founding political document of *Libere, Insieme* clearly asserted areas of difference and areas of commonality between women: 'We are women who have *different* languages, countries, personal histories and life conditions but have *equal* rights, needs, desire for liberty and affirmation' (*Libere, Insieme* 1991, p. 1). In comparison to *Donne senza frontiere*, the association *Libere, Insieme* embraced a broader perspective regarding the relationship between Italian and ethnic minority women. The organisation was clearly conceived not simply as a broad cultural grouping but rather as integral to the development of progressive female political practice in Italy. Indeed, the fact that migrant women had been excluded from earlier gender discourse was implicitly acknowledged by the assertion that Italian female activists should no longer ignore their presence:

> *We Italian women* on the Left, from the PDS, from the non-governmental organisations, from the trade union movement, are aware that it is no longer possible to establish a political project of female strength and of social transformation without taking on board the great subjective strength which has pushed so many women from Africa, Latin America, Asia, the Middle East and the East, to leave their own countries and their own certainties to face a new country with different customs, a different culture and language; to live in our cities, to work, almost always without rights, in our homes.
>
> This presence questions the quality of our project, the possibility that it can really become a useful instrument of change in the lives of so many women (*Libere, Insieme* 1991, p. 1).

Thus, establishing and pursuing the objectives of *Libere, Insieme* was intended to contribute to the validation of a broader political project. This was not to be a prescriptive venture. Rather, a common elaboration of how this new relationship between Italian women and ethnic minority women would evolve was envisaged. Furthermore, it was not assumed that defining such a relationship would be straightforward. In fact, the document refers to the need to create a new language to engage in this project: '... it is necessary to work our a common language to explore the multiple worlds of women and the different paths to emancipation and liberation' (p. 1). Combating social inequality between women and providing support for those women who experienced hardship was seen as a prerequisite for liberating all women.

While the Italian women involved in the association were engaged in an expansion of their broader political project, the priorities of ethnic minority women were somewhat different: '*We women from different countries* want to live as protagonists' (*Libere, Insieme*, 1991, p. 2). The question of culture had not been highlighted by the Italian women, however it predictably assumed some importance for ethnic minority women, who articulated the desire to retain their respective cultures and language.

Sections four and five of the document outlined the different priorities of Italian and ethnic minority women respectively and the final section focused on the common programme of all the women participating in this project. These common objectives replicated, in some cases, those advocated by the association *Donne senza frontiere*. For example, *Libere, Insieme* also intended to undertake research and to compile documentation. However there were some notable differences in approach between the two associations. While *Donne senza frontiere* presented its new mixed association as an important departure from the tendency of migrant women to aggregate on the basis of ethnicity,[17] *Libere, Insieme*, did not preclude a relationship with those ethnic minority women who opted to organise also on the basis of ethnicity. In fact the development of such a relationship was cited as an important objective. It was envisaged that it would be possible for women within the association to: 'relate to everything that women were doing in other associations, organisations and political groups' (*Libere, Insieme* 1991, p. 2). This approach was undoubtedly reflective of the internal ideological evolution of Pds women activists who had begun to place great value on the importance of establishing autonomous (i.e. not mediated by their parenting party) relationships with diverse constituencies of women.[18]

The links between bondage and liberation were encapsulated in the final statement of the political document:

> We are convinced that it will not be possible to construct a really humane and just world, a world for women and men, if each of us does not have the opportunity to become the 'mistress' of her own life (*Libere, Insieme* 1991, p. 2).

The reference to a world for women and men mirrored the political vocabulary of Pds women and reflected their adherence to the concept of sexual difference (see chapter 1).[19] Nonetheless the significance of this final assertion lay in the association's desire for all women in the Italian context to establish full control over their own lives. As we saw in previous chapters, the power of the Italian employer, particularly within the live-in domestic work relationship, was likely to ensure that the concept of 'mistress' for ethnic minority women would signify power of and exploitation by other women rather than the expression of their own female autonomy. It was of some importance that the political document had not attempted to disregard this fundamental conflict between Italian women and migrant women. Under the section delineating the objectives of the Italian women within the association it was stated:

This presence of [female migrants] calls into question a big contradiction for us: in order 'to exist' and affirm ourselves in society we delegate to them the family and care work that we cannot or do not want to do. Often our choice for maternity means that it is impossible for them to have or keep a child with them (*Libere, Insieme* 1991, p. 2).

It was not clear how this contradiction would be addressed, but its very articulation suggested a realistic approach to constructing a useful dialogue between different constituencies of women. Indeed, the very structure of the political document reflected a recognition of the different perspectives that women involved in the organisation would have. The first three sections were all expressed in the first person plural: 'We are different women ... We want to have a relationship ... We feel we have a common destiny'. The fourth and fifth sections presented the respective priorities of Italian women (We Italian women ...) and ethnic minority women (We foreign women ...) while the final section described their common objectives (We want ...).

Two major political initiatives were organised by the association in 1992 and 1993. These initiatives consisted of a week-long programme of political and cultural events held at the *Palazzo delle Esposizioni* in Rome. *Libere, Insieme* attained some public prominence through this mobilisation and there was widespread coverage in the press. For the purposes of this discussion, I will focus on the political aspect of these initiatives, although it does not appear that there was any decision to privilege either the cultural or the political activities of the association. The general theme of the 1992 mobilisation was 'Women between Modernity and Tradition' and in May of 1992, two round table discussions were held. The first was entitled: 'The Cultural Identity of Migrant Women' (9 May 1992) and the second: 'Migrant Women: Conditions, Rights, Expectations (14 May 1992). I shall discuss these round table discussions in a fairly schematic fashion.[20] My purpose here is not only to provide information regarding a new cultural and political formation, but also to highlight the issues that were emerging as important for the organisation's participants.

The Cultural Identity of Migrant Women

The subject choice for this first round table discussion demonstrated the association's receptiveness to the notion of interconnected social identities. Nevertheless, the introductory address of the chairperson still privileged gender:

...There are many identities, even for us ... Identity is not a total belonging, but a plurality of belongings, whereby all of us, I repeat both foreign women and Italian women, are firstly single women, with an individual history and who, alongside and within this individual history, have a series of collective belongings including that of ethnicity (Rossi Doria, ALI 1992a, p. 2).[21]

The participants at this round table discussion consisted of an equal number of Italian and ethnic minority women discussants. The ethnic minority participants reflected the ethnic diversity of Italy's female migratory population, while the Italian participants' experience of immigration had been formed in different regional contexts.[22] It seemed clear that the discussion was conceptualised as a means of providing greater knowledge about the particular experiences of migrant women. Thus, Favaro's contribution focused on Egyptian women in Milan[23] while Amelia Crisantino, provided an account of the situation of primarily Filipina women in Palermo.[24]

The interventions of Maher, Maricos, Rochas and Saravia all fostered an alternative approach to the issue of cultural identity. Their arguments not only refuted the tradition/modernity perspective but simultaneously reversed the direction of cultural/ethnic evaluation. With regard to the former point, both Maher and Maricos exposed the contradiction in assuming that migration to Italy would signify emancipation: 'They arrive in Italy and instead of finding a situation in which they can achieve emancipation, they find work in the house of another woman' (Maher, ALI 1992a, p. 32) and '...our desire for emancipation as women, ... ends the moment that we end up in the homes of Italian families' (Maricos, ALI 1992a, p. 36). While emancipation is frequently interpreted as signifying greater choice for (migrant) women, the process of emancipation in the Italian context was to a large extent unduly conditioned by migrant women's pre-eminent identity as domestic workers.

As was argued in the introduction, intrinsic to the tradition/modernity debate is an assumption that whatever form this modernity takes it will be positive. It is for this reason that 'traditional' women are expected to embrace modernity as an emancipatory strategy. The Eritrean participant, Maricos, argued for an acknowledgement amongst all ethnicities (i.e. including Italian) of the limits and problems of their respective cultures:

> If I have to trade my culture and my identity for that of the host society, it must have something extra ... I have worked with Italian women for years. Today I know what is not right in my culture for women, but I also know what I don't like in Italian culture; if I have to put my culture aside, as Italian society often asks me to do, I need to find something which substitutes my ideals, my values,

my rites, my symbols, something which offers me more that what I am leaving behind (Maricos, ALI 1992a, p. 40).

Migrant Women: Conditions, Rights, Expectations

Similar themes emerged during the second round table discussion dedicated to migrant women's conditions. Margherita Boniver, the then Minister for Immigration opened the debate and focused entirely on development issues. Remarkably, she made no reference to the specificity of the Italian case, despite the potential of her political role. Conversely, the introductory speech given by the secretary of *Libere, Insieme*, Teresa Savini, touched on areas which were crucial to any successful progression for the association (Savini, ALI 1992b, p. 4). Savini focused on the difficulties involved in establishing both a multi-ethnic society and an equal relationship between people of different cultures. Her vision did not anticipate homogenisation, but rather the establishment of a framework which could not only guarantee citizenship rights for ethnic minority women but which could also accommodate cultural difference.

The contributions of both Charito Basa, a representative of the Philippine Women Council and Giovanna Zaldini from the Italian Association of African Women offered a historical appraisal of Filipina and Somali women respectively. With regard to the Italian context, Basa maintained that the principal problems for Filipina women were clandestinity, lack of housing, long working hours, separation from their families and their humiliation at being offered only domestic work despite their professional qualifications (Basa, ALI 1992b, pp. 6–13). Similarly Zaldini described the history of Somali migration and cited a lack of housing, the difficulties of domestic work, linguistic problems, Italian bureaucracy and the problems of maternity as the community's principal problems (Zaldini, ALI 1992b, pp. 26–33).

The contribution of Anna Focà, a representative from a non-governmental organisation dealing with women and development (*Coordinamento ONG Donne e Sviluppo*), was the first to raise the question of nomenclature. She rejected the terminology of 'immigrants' and chose instead to talk about 'Women from the South' and 'Women from the North'. Like, Boniver, Focà's argument derived from a development perspective, but she was emphatic about the importance of recognising difference between women, accentuating, for example, the emphasis women from the North have placed on the value of the body. Her position regarding difference between women was centred on a belief that because women's conditions were not identical, women's struggle for emancipation and liberation likewise could not be the same. Thus she argued that it was more appropriate for women's struggles to be rooted in their own traditions and backgrounds. Contextualising this to a tradition/ modernity framework she stated: 'Every woman starts from her own tradition in order to arrive at her own modernity' (Focà, ALI 1992b, p. 23).

The above discussions indicate that the audience present at this round table discussion were exposed to a number of new perspectives regarding women and migration. Members of the audience were able to contribute to the debate after the official speakers. Their contributions reinforced some of the arguments articulated by Focà regarding the different priorities of Italian women and African and Asian women. For example, some of the interventions by Italian women reflected their interest in different cultural practices. Thus, Maria Luisa Forenza called for more discussion on the question of infibulation and Somali women. Elvira Panotti's intervention was reflective of her self-asserted claim to being a founder of (Italian) feminism and she criticised the limited attention that had been paid to the question of women's bodies and in particular the exploitation of migrant women's bodies as prostitutes, magazine brides and more generally within the sex tourist industry.

Most of the contributions from the migrant women present at the debate highlighted specific aspects of their working or general conditions within Italy. Maité called for the protection of migrant women's rights.[25] Salua Dridi, a Tunisian migrant, raised an issue which had not really been addressed by the main participants of the round table discussion – the specific problems of live-in domestic work.[26] Dridi did not deny that migrant women faced problems related to their respective cultures but it was clear that she did not consider such problems as central, prioritising instead problems relating to their working conditions:

> I would like to speak about a very delicate subject, that is of migrant women who work as live-in domestic workers. They really are victims, on the one hand because of the problems that they have in the country of origin ...; on the other hand because of their employment conditions in the country of immigration – inside a house working 24 hours like a slave ... You cannot make a woman work day and night. That woman has the right to go out, to talk, to meet other people ... It is no shame to work as a domestic worker because it is a job through which one can earn money, one should therefore work without being embarrassed, but on the other hand a lot of care should be taken and women should not be considered slaves (Dridi, ALI 1992b, p. 38).

Panotti's comment on this assertion is revealing:

Salua Dridi's protest should be extended to the lives of all women because a 24 hour day is a normal day for all women and all housewives. So, we can say that what is being reproposed for domestic workers is relevant for all women (Panotti, ALI 1992b, p. 39).

Panotti's collapsing of the 'specific' features of migrant women's 24-hour servility into the 'universal' features of the feminine condition was symptomatic of a tendency to evade both the reality of migrant women's working conditions and the fact that some Italian women were involved in their exploitation. The concept of all women being on call 24 hours a day certainly did not do justice to live-in domestic workers. The women whom I interviewed where the female employer was a housewife certainly would not have equated their position with that of their female employer. After describing to me a typically onerous day at work (see chapter 5) I asked Lemlem (interview, 10) what her female employer (a housewife) did during the day. Her reply was a monosyllabic 'she sleeps'. When I asked her to expand she did so with derision: 'she doesn't do anything'. Although there is a connection to be made regarding paid domestic work and Italian women's unpaid work within the home, some recognition of the weaker position of the live-in domestic worker is warranted. Panotti's attempts to ascribe a Common Victim situation to all women is not supported by the evidence and it tended to trivialise the exploitative relationship that can exist between some Italian women and migrant women.

The final two interventions at the round table discussion did focus more attention on the issue of domestic work. Rosalba Dessì, an ACLI-COLF representative, discussed the contractual problems that migrant women encountered within this sector of work and argued for a wider network of social services to prevent women exploiting other women. However, it was only in the final intervention by Anna Rossi Doria that an attempt was made by an Italian participant to explore the fundamental contradiction referred to in the *Libere, Insieme* founding document:

> ... we need to begin to find a way of working around the issue which has [just] emerged, ... to find a solution where neither good intentions nor a trade union perspective will be enough ... It requires the commitment of all of us women to find a way of coming together, all of us, foreign women and Italian women, to face this issue as a real internal contradiction. It is a contradiction for us western women, and we cannot off-load responsibility onto the government, nor onto the State (Rossi Doria, ALI 1992b, pp. 43–4).

Rossi Doria thus unequivocally emphasised the personal responsibility of Italian women with regard to this contradiction. She raised a crucial area of work for the association, although it is clear that she did not foresee any immediate and obvious answers to this dilemma. Rather this issue was presented as requiring a strategy to be developed. Her position stands in contrast to some of the other contributors, since she explicitly highlighted this as a major and fundamental question for the advancement of the association.

To a large extent, this round table discussion displayed that Italian and ethnic minority women had different priorities. Both the official speeches and the informal interventions of migrant women were comprehensively more focused on their material conditions within Italy, indicating areas on which they envisaged improvement. While the Italian contributors were attentive to the material conditions of migrant women, their content revealed a much more focused interest in the value of a mixed association and on general issues to do with culture. This implied that while migrant women saw the association as a vehicle through which their specific problems could be resolved, the Italian women were more interested in the significance of having a mixed women's association. A racialised dichotomy of goals could thus be identified. In this first major mobilisation for the *Libere, Insieme* association, a critical issue – the contradiction of migrant women's work liberating Italian women – was not given due attention. Despite the organisation's political document intimating that this issue should be explored, no mechanism was adopted to facilitate this. Rossi Doria had drawn attention to the question but was herself unable to push the debate forward.

Press Reports

The activities organised by *Libere, Insieme* from the 9–14 May 1992 were widely reported in the press. Some of the articles simply provided information about the events, such as the one published in *Trovaroma* on the 6 May entitled 'Women travelling between modernity and tradition'.[27] Subsequent reports however paid more attention to the cultural aspects of the initiative.[28] Indeed, some reports made no mention of the round table discussions.[29] An article in the *Corriere della Sera*, referred to the members of the association as being engaged in a cultural project. An article published in *Il Paese delle donne* (28 May 1992) did give a proper summary of the issues raised and similarly, a piece in *ASPE* (28 May 1992) paid minimal attention to the cultural aspects of the initiative and quoted extensively from the speakers of the round table.

A rather more personal piece written by the feminist Anna Del Bo Boffino was the only article which attempted to look more closely at some of the issues involved in attempting to cross boundaries in terms of women's associationism. Her piece was entitled 'We and those women from other cultures' and was published in *L'Unità* (12 May 1992). Del Bo Boffino immediately acknowledged a shared female condition: 'They are women like us, and we know perfectly well that they share with us the female condition'. But she additionally acknowledged the degree of separateness between Italian and ethnic minority women: 'They seem closed in their own world, and very few of us want to break down their defences. In fact, it's easier this way: for us, who feel the difficulty of their presence, and for them, who have a difficult existence'. Del Bo Boffino did however pinpoint channels for communication. These involved migrant women's proximity to Italian women as neighbours, as parents, and in their relationship with Italian women as domestic workers. Her perspective once again proposed a universal female experience. Moreover, in comparing ethnic minority women's culture with that of Italian women, Del Bo Boffino sustained the tradition/emancipation polarity by comprehensively locating migrant women within the traditional unemancipated sphere. Having stated that channels of communication existed in the domestic sphere, she then used this domain to exemplify migrant women's 'tradition':

> … paradoxically, it is precisely in the domestic arena that initial suspicions can be noted: her way of treating men and children is the result of a female culture which has not yet been broken by emancipation. And their quiet adaptation to a patriarchal order provokes rebellion in us. In some ways we feel threatened by a past that we have partially left behind, and which today seems to be coming back and is so liked by men within the home (and outside of it).

The patriarchal system is here interpreted as assisting men and children, but Del Bo Boffino failed to consider how this patriarchal system in combination with the privileged gendered ethnicity of Italian women militated against migrant women to the benefit of both Italian women and men. She attributes a feeling of 'unease' to Italian women in their contemplation of migrant women, but it is to be noted that this unease is provoked by the visibility of migrant women's presumed *tradition* rather than from any contemplation of the benefits that migrant women's labour have delivered for Italian women.

Press reports covering the 1992 *Libere, Insieme* initiative presented the organisation as a cultural association – a means through which Italian women could understand or have access to ethnic minority women's cultures. Only one article (*ASPE*, 28 May 1992) cited Maricos's observation that migrant women's emancipation was confined to the four walls of the Italian family. None of the reports attempted an analysis of migrant women's economic and social standing within Italy, suggesting that the debate about migrant women was being framed in cultural relativist terms.

In 1993, the *Libere, Insieme* association repeated the format of the 1992 initiative.[30] Two of the round table discussions focused on areas where there is considerable tension for female migrants – domestic work and maternity. Would the association be able to offer any new perspectives regarding this fundamental tension?

Domestic Workers: the Relationship between Necessity and Liberty: the Desire for Emancipation

This round table discussion was chaired by the president of the Cape Verdean women's organisation, Maria Lourdes De Jesus. Rather predictably, given our discussion in chapter 8, the ACLI-COLF representative Alemani, promoted a Common Victim interpretation of domestic work:

> ... it is no longer so much bourgeois families, or even families from more diversified social classes who request live-in domestic workers, but it is women who need other women, it is they who find themselves crushed between the labour market, their family of origin, their current family, their children and their elderly parents. I believe that this is a different stage with respect to previous years from which a different level of solidarity may emerge – a greater solidarity given that both domestic workers and women face the same problems (Alemani, ALI 1993a, pp. 8–9).

Thus, although one can detect partial acknowledgement of the different positioning of the two categories of women, this does not modify Alemani's fundamental argument that women essentially encounter the same problems. This stance was indirectly questioned by an Italian woman attending the debate, although her intervention was a more focused criticism of feminism, rather than the Common Victim proposition. Bocca Rossa was particularly critical of the historic feminists:

> Italian women can now afford a domestic worker instead of fighting for social services: they have resolved their problems on the backs of domestic workers ... I know that many old feminists have a domestic worker at home and they think they are doing this woman a favour. They completely forget that this

woman has the right to a private life, they think: 'As a white emancipated woman, I am doing you a favour as without me you would die of hunger'. There is a risk of us going backwards with such a view and immigrant women should confront Italian women to demand their right to a life (Bocca Rossa, ALI 1993a, pp. 30–31).

In addition, when Renata Bagatin, the national secretary for a trade union body (FILCAM CGIL), argued that domestic work should be given its due dignity, Bocca Rossa, again formulated a pertinent response, stressing that all domestic workers should have their own homes in order to achieve this dignity and to avoid exploitation. However, it was on the question of female solidarity that Bocca Rossa perhaps made the most incisive observation:

> I think that the issue of domestic workers is especially central because it reveals a series of other problems and contradictions for Italians. Recourse to a domestic worker to resolve so many problems has now passed into collective consciousness because some problems cannot be resolved by social services and it is much easier and more realistic to resolve them with a domestic worker, for example, help for the elderly which is a dramatic and extremely widespread problem (Bocca Rossa, ALI 1993a, p. 32).

Jacqueline Kawere, one of the ethnic minority participants, raised a different issue with regard to domestic work.[31] Her contribution focused on the difficulties migrant women encountered in expressing their multiple identities. She stressed the dehumanising experience of domestic work and proposed not only a modernisation of the domestic work sector but also the importance of allowing migrant women to penetrate other sectors. This proposal stands in contrast to the perspective articulated by Alemani whose interpretation of live-in domestic work as *necessary* for Italian women failed to promote any organisational modification of domestic work. Indeed, Alemani's argument is centred on the increasing necessity for live-in domestic work given the inadequacy of social services and the multiple roles and duties of Italian women. As we have seen in previous chapters, only a reorganisation of the domestic work relationship would facilitate the expression of migrant women's interlocking social identities. The preceding chapters also demonstrated how the nature of courses organised for migrant women often functioned to restrict them to the domestic work sphere and there was further evidence of this during the *Libere, Insieme* initiative. Anna Burgio, a representative from a Roman cultural association (La Maggiolina), informed the forum of her organisation's intention to organise a baby-sitters' training course for migrant women. Although she acknowledged that ethnic minority women frequently had a much higher cultural level than that being catered for by the proposed course, she argued that proper training to care for Italian children might be beneficial. Once again, this indicated the manner in which a well-intentioned response to the specific problems of ethnic minority women in fact concealed a desire to respond to the specific needs of Italian women. A downgrading of ethnic minority women's capabilities was acceptable given its utility in providing Italian women with the type of care they envisaged for their children.

'Maternity' (Pds Women) and 'Maternity in a Foreign Country' (*Libere, Insieme*)

The above discussion has attempted to document incipient attempts to incorporate the concept of ethnicity into a gendered framework. The Pds women's section only began to engage with the notion of ethnicity in the late 1980s/early 1990s. This meant that important political documents such as the Women's Charter (1986) and their legislative proposal on time (1990) excluded the specific conditions of ethnic minority women. Although the establishment of the *Libere, Insieme* organisation was an attempt to rectify this, this seemed to lead to a separation of migrant women's issues from the 'mainstream' concerns of Pds women. Indeed an analogy can be drawn with the difficulties Pds women had originally encountered when trying to affect the dominant values of the party in general. In a similar vein, the activities and debates occurring within the framework of the *Libere, Insieme* organisation did not seem to penetrate the activities of the Pds women's section. I will use the issue of maternity to illustrate this point, discussing a Pds women's conference held on the subject in January 1992 and a *Libere, Insieme* conference held on the topic in May 1993.

In light of what has been said earlier regarding the relationship between Pds women and the intellectual perspectives of Italian feminism (see chapter 1), the treatment of the issue of maternity was reflective of the shift that had occurred within Italian feminism in relation to motherhood. As Passerini (1994, p. 237) has argued, the 1970s feminists 'lived through a profound rebellion against the traditional ideas of the mother and rejected them, often rejecting motherhood themselves altogether'. However, the ideological evolution of Italian feminism has led to sustained attention to the question of 'symbolic' motherhood.[32] What is important for the purposes of this discussion, is that the issue of maternity in relation to migrant women was effectively marginalised from the proceedings of the Pds conference. Instead attention to the question of migrant women and maternity was broached in a subsequent *Libere, Insieme* forum. As discussed in chapter 1, Communist women's experiences within the Pci/Pds indicated that separate spheres were important and useful spaces for women activists but that their validity was diminished if an appropriate channel of communication between the respective spheres was not established. The absence of this channel precludes reciprocal influence and leads to the ghettoisation of what the mainstream perceives to be marginal.

The proceedings of the 1992 Pds women's conference[33] indicated that a significant theoretical shift was occurring amongst women activists in relation to gender and maternity.[34] The proceedings also suggest that these new discourses were based on the specific experiences of Italian women. For example, ethnic minority women did not make any contribution to the conference. Livia Turco, then head of the women's area of Pds politics argued that maternity was an enriching experience for women, but one that was also fraught with ambivalence. The question to be posed then was: 'How can we ensure that female liberty and the experience of maternity are not in conflict?' (Turco 1993, p. 3). An important role was ascribed to the importance of maternity in women's ideological and creative development and the relationship with the mother was seen to be critical. This positional shift, when compared to some of the prevailing ideologies in the 1970s, was high-lighted by a number of the conference participants. Gaiotti de Biase[35] (1993), for example, argued that the women's movement's of the 1970s and 1980s had been focused on abortion and had thus paid less attention to maternity. The link to abortion is perhaps predictable. In the 1970s, abortion did in fact constitute a crucial mobilising issue for the Italian feminist movement[36] and the possibility of rejecting maternity was seen to be intrinsic to women's liberation and self-determination.[37] A number of the conference participants were now arguing that it was time to revisit their views on abortion.[38] Claudia Mancina (1993), for example, proposed that greater reflection on the ethics of abortion was necessary given the developments that had occurred in the field of bio-ethics.

What was patently clear was that these new discourses did not explicitly include ethnic minority women. Their exclusion was clearly reflected in the language used by the conference participants. A number of the speakers referred specifically to 'Italian women' in their general discussions on maternity.[39] In the few cases where ethnic minority women were mentioned, it was to highlight the difficulties of maternity for *Italian women*. Thus, Elisabetta Addis (1993, p. 47) stated that recourse to domestic help for Italian women normally meant recourse to another woman and in parenthesis she stated that this other woman was '... very often, a non-EC migrant'. Gaiotti de Biase (1993, p. 100) suggested tax reductions so that (Italian) women could obtain domestic help without having to resort to the undocumented sphere. The only paper to specifically raise the question of migrant women was the one which outlined the situation of a sector of Italian society which has itself been socially and politically marginalised. In addressing the issue of maternity in Sicily, Finocchiaro and Rizza (1993) highlighted the huge gap which existed between the demands of Sicilian women and the institutional culture and structures prevalent in the region. Nonetheless, the conclusions to their paper indicated a clear commitment to incorporating the needs of ethnic minority women into these existing inadequate structures. This solitary example of inclusiveness with regard to a racialised category of gender emphasised the extent of migrant women's marginalisation from mainstream gender discourse. Notably, there was some inclusion of ethnicity in a broader sense; some of the speakers framed their arguments within a global perspective. Thus, Livia Turco (1993, p. 11) argued that autonomy and female liberty in relation to maternity united women throughout the world. Similarly, Riviello (1993, p. 19) argued that female freedom and procreation would constitute a bond of solidarity between women all over the world. At the conceptual level therefore, one could observe some attention to ethnicity in global terms, however, the significance of a racialised gender category within Italy remained conceptually on the periphery.

Migrant women's effective exclusion from these discourses is striking. Although the major initiatives of the *Libere, Insieme* association had not yet occurred, the association did formally exist. Nonetheless it appeared that the political and cultural objectives of the association were being locked into a separate sphere of gendered political activity and were not expected to penetrate the analyses being developed within the 'mainstream' political sphere regarding gender. Yet, there were numerous instances throughout the 1992 Pds conference on maternity where the generation of ideas with regard to maternity were transferable and pertinent to the situation of migrant women. Certainly, those proposals which argued for a different organisation of work and leisure times to facilitate maternity assumed some resonance for migrant women. Riviello's (1993, p. 22) assertion is indicative:

> The Left, women, cannot accept that this model is unmodifiable and they suggest quite a different view, a society in which the theme of human and social reproduction has full citizenship. What is needed primarily is a different organisation of work, of times, of cities.

It was clear that a new value and emphasis on maternity was being developed by Italian women activists. Of significance is the fact that similar reflections failed to find a voice in the conference on migrant women and maternity which occurred within the framework of the *Libere, Insieme* association. In fact, the *Libere, Insieme* debate failed to investigate the construction of new forms of family organisation for migrant women as outlined in chapter 7. The negation of migrant women's maternal role was raised by only a minority of the round table discussants and was, in any case, never developed as a central issue. Given the nature of the attention that had been afforded to the question of maternity by the progressive female political sphere, there were essentially two ways in which this omission could be interpreted. Firstly, it suggested greater interest and support for indigenous women's maternal role. Secondly, it indicated evasion of an inescapable and unpalatable fact – that migrant women's labour is used to facilitate Italian women's reproductive role at the expense of their own. Evasion of these problematic issues was possible even within the *Libere, Insieme* debate as the organisers chose to conceptualise it from a socio-sanitary perspective. While such a focus was useful in providing empirical information about migrant women's experience of pregnancy and birth, it completely marginalised ethnic minority women's *postnatal* experiences of maternity. This focus was a natural consequence of the dominance of medical practitioners invited to participate in the debate.[40]

The debate was presided over by the Pds representative Mariangela Grainer, who framed the discussion in terms of whether the Italian social and health system was in a position to accommodate the cultural differences, traditions and pathologies of different ethnicities. She argued that Italian women had challenged the view that maternity was women's only destiny, transforming it into a question of choice. Given the context of the discussion, it might have been appropriate if this notion of choice had been applied to the specific situation of ethnic minority women. Instead, links between ethnic minority women's fertility and demography were established and the question of genital mutilation was also raised. Reference was made to the universality of aspects of women's experience with some acknowledgement that migrant women's experience was more problematic.

> ... this issue of maternity for the migrant woman is much harsher than for an Italian woman because it conflicts much more with economic and employment issues. The juxtaposition between choosing to have a child or working, which is still present for Italian women who fear going backwards in relation to certain achievements, is for migrant women even more lacerating (Grainer, ALI 1993b, pp. 8–9).

Subsequent contributions all focused on the socio-sanitary aspects of maternity. Thus, the contribution of the gynaecologist Cristina Damiani, reflective of her own interest in innovative gynaecological methods, described different cultural attitudes to maternity based on her working experience in a variety of African countries. Another gynaecologist, Elizabetta Canitano, highlighted the problems of undocumented female migrants in terms of the difficulties they encountered in having access to health care. This is undoubtedly one area where the experience of maternity, in its health aspects, affected migrant and Italian women in quite different ways and Canitano (ALI 1993b, p. 37) emphasised the fact that migrant women had access to restricted health care within the Catholic voluntary sector because of the ideology underpinning its service. The Zairean gynaecologist, Susanna Diku made a much more forceful link between migrant women's difficulties with maternity and their employment niche:

> In our centre we know of women who have terminated pregnancies so as not to lose their jobs or of those who have continued their pregnancies and now have to find somewhere to sleep, because what was needed was an efficient person and not a pregnant person. These women face labour in an extremely anxious way in terms of 'where shall I go; who will take me to hospital; what if the baby arrives at night …
>
> When they come out, they either find themselves alone or at any rate in a difficult situation … Once this woman has left hospital, she must start work as soon as possible and show her boss that despite the baby she can do what she was doing before and thus prevent her boss from employing somebody else (Diku, ALI 1993b, pp. 47–8).

While Diku's contribution formulated an explicit link between maternity and paid domestic work, the final contribution to the round table discussion by Vittoria Tola, a Pds councillor, formulated an explicit link between Italian women and migrant women:

> Italian women who are interested in these issues should not think that these issues have been resolved. They must also involve foreign and migrant women and try to address the sense and meaning of this important event for all of us together.
>
> I know perfectly well that in different parts of Italy, there are initiatives to create structures for migrant women. I think it is a mistake to isolate migrant women from the Italian context (Tola, ALI, 1993b, pp. 62–3).

Of note then, is the fact that while migrant women were consistently excluded from the Pds conference on maternity, several of the Italian contributors to the *Libere, Insieme* debate invariably made a connection between Italian women's experience and migrant women's experience. Gender was thus privileged as a common marker of disadvantage in both the *Libere, Insieme* and the Pds debates on maternity. The omission of ethnicity in the Pds conference and the tendency to focus on a common female experience in the *Libere, Insieme* debate again signified that ethnicity would remain on the margins of the conceptual arguments, obscuring the significance of a racialised gender category.[41]

It is probable that the absence of migrant women's voices during this debate led to the subordination of issues related to their tangible difficulties in organising family life. Despite the fact that the Pds conference on maternity was on a much grander scale than the *Libere, Insieme* round table discussion, the contributions to the Pds conference focused both on the socio-sanitary and the sociocultural aspects of maternity. The fact that the sociocultural aspects of migrant women's experiences was not addressed is particularly significant because, without it, the question of a parallel but fundamentally diverse construction of the maternal role was simply not addressed. The *Libere, Insieme* debates comprehensively displaced responsibility for migrant women's experience of maternity to inadequate health facilities for women *in general* and to the unfamiliarity of Italian medical staff with different cultures. This avoided discussion of some Italian women's collusion in perpetuating a system of quasi bonded labour which *logistically* negated migrant women's aspirations for maternity. Although Italian women's collusion in this domain can be attributed to a patriarchal system which assumes their responsibility for reproductive care, their own participation in accepting this model of welfare organisation does warrant questioning. One of the principal contentions of this book is that the use of migrant domestic workers has functioned to perpetuate the traditional family structure in Italy. The information presented in this chapter offers some insight into the political response to an evolving Italian society. The activities of the *Libere, Insieme* association suggest that even the progressive sphere of women's politics was unable to fully confront the basic gender dilemma at the root of the domestic work relationship. This implied that the political sphere was acquiescing to a social solution to the challenges facing the Italian family which was acceptable to both Italian men and women.

Pds Women's Politics and Ethnic Minority Women

The manner in which some Pds women attempted to embrace ethnicity should not however be limited to a discussion of the ideas being mooted within the *Libere, Insieme* association. Indeed, the extent to which the wider Pds women's sphere responded to the question of migrant women gives some indication of the extent to which two different political projects could be integrated. I have already demonstrated how migrant women's experiences remained on the periphery of the important Pds women's conference on maternity. But how did Pds women activists outside of the *Libere, Insieme* forum perceive the relationship between gender and ethnicity and more specifically how would this new reality impact on their broader political project?

In 1992, the first national edition of the diary *Agenda ottomarzo* was produced,[42] dedicated to women from different cultures. The Diary validated the direction of the political practice of Pds women and explicitly acknowledged the inspiration of feminism.[43] In fact Pds women felt that their promotion of the theory of sexual difference placed them in a good position from which to contend with different markers of social stratification such as ethnicity and religion.[44] The Diary aimed to give migrant women not simply a voice, but their own voice. [45]

I have emphasised that the founding document of the *Libere, Insieme* association recognised that the exclusion of migrant women from the political practice of Pds women constituted a weakness. This view was reiterated by one of the editors of the Diary, Monica Lanfranco:

> The weak point of the 'Women's Charter' developed by Communist women in 1986, was the relationship with women from other countries who were guests in our country. Communist women at that time noted that foreign women were by then visible in large and small cities; that they almost always came in through the service door, in many of our homes ... But politics, even women's politics, remained distant.[46]

Not only was the inclusion of ethnic minority women seen as necessary for the credibility of progressive women's politics but it was envisaged by some as offering a means to put into practice aspects of the Women's Charter. With reference to those mobilising within *Libere, Insieme*, Monica Lanfranco stated:

> The female promoters have in mind an agile association working on concrete projects and which can once again put in motion the energies of those Italian

women who are disillusioned with the old ways of doing politics but still want to respond to reality.[47]

This suggested that the presence of migrant women may actually have been seen as providing an opportunity for Pds women to fulfill one of their objectives of the 1986 Women's Charter, which was that of increasing their contact with 'ordinary women'. The desire to construct a dialogue with ethnic minority women undoubtedly fitted quite neatly into this overall strategy. In their 1992 political document, which outlined the future strategy of women activists within the party, alliances with different sectors of the female population were seen to be very important:

> We are committed to try and construct an alliance between women; those that are active in parties, in trade unions, in associations, in institutions, in the voluntary sector, in women's autonomous spaces. We think that it is important to reconstruct, starting with the specificity of each experience, a collective force … (Donne del Pds 1992, p. 1).

The importance of recognising both women from the Southern hemisphere and ethnic minority women living in Italy was ranked as one of four key issues for Pds:

> We realise that it is no longer possible to construct a project of female strength and social transformation without taking on board the great subjective strength of so many women from Africa, Latin America, Asia, the Middle East, East Europe (Donne del Pds 1992, p. 16).

Despite these assertions, there were several instances where, once again, migrant women remained on the periphery of the political programme of Pds women. The most obvious example of this can be found in the proceedings of the first national congress of Pds women, held in Rome in December 1993. A long opening speech was delivered by Livia Turco, covering a broad range of issues seen to be integral to future political strategy.[48] What I want to focus on here is the manner in which migrant women were incorporated in or excluded from her vision of the future direction of Pds women's activism.

The first mention of immigration occured within the context of the emergence of the Right-wing parties in Italy. There is a subsequent section dedicated to interdependence between women around the world but this is clearly focused on the question of ethnicity in a global, rather than a domestic context. The question of women and work did however receive substantial attention in Turco's address. Paid employment for (Italian) women was viewed as critical for their self-determination, confirming the importance attributed to women's access to paid work by the progressive female sphere. Italian women's demand for paid employment was viewed as an indication of their desire for autonomy. As has been demonstrated in relation to the Black women in my case study, the paid work to which they had access may have offered a degree of financial autonomy, but it severely restricted their autonomy in other spheres.

Turco linked her analysis of the general issue of immigration to the increasing hierarchisation and inequality of the labour market, which, in her view, was a means to fracture worker solidarity. Of significance however, is that her one specific mention of the working conditions of migrant women is utilised to highlight the problems of Italian women workers. Once again, we find the conditions of migrant women subordinated to the concerns of Italian women, suggesting a fairly direct privileging of an Italian gendered ethnicity over the gendered ethnicity of female migrants.

Turco argued that high levels of unemployment amongst Italian women had led to their availability for service work both within the family and the informal economy. To validate this, she presented data on the number of women engaged in irregular paid domestic work (although not stated, her reference is clearly to hourly paid domestic workers). But, yet again, it is the manner in which migrant women were included into her analysis which is revealing: 'Recently, a labour supply offering full-time service has reappeared (with availability to live with their employers) from female migrants from non-European countries' (Prima conferenza delle donne del Pds 199, p. 36). Firstly, as has been established in earlier chapters, migrant women's employment as live-in workers was not recent, nor could it simply be attributed to the existence of a supply of labour. The demand for such labour was also an important contributory factor to this 'reappearance' of live-in domestic work which was in fact a replacement for work previously carried out by working class Italian women. Turco's reference to migrant women's 'availability' to work as live-in workers also negated their desire to restructure their employment to hourly paid work. Although Turco acknowledged that Italian women's ability to participate on the labour market was still principally due to other women's labour – unemployed young women, students, migrant women, unqualified Italian women (adults) and grandparents – this broad categorisation failed to explore the specificity of these diverse groups. In the case of migrant women, it negated the significance of ethnicity as a particular form of social stratification. Conceptualising women's assistance to other women in the labour market in this way can be accommodated within the Common Victim argument. However, this once again privileges gender as an axis of social stratification, subordinating other markers of disadvantage. Migrant women and their Italian female employers could appropriately be described as Common Victims if it was made clear that they were victims of different processes. Capitalism, patriarchy and racism are three broad categories which can be used to account for their 'victim' status. However, these processes are not always separate, discrete categories. They may be interwoven and they may intersect with each other in different ways leading to a differentiated impact for diverse groups of women. Turco's tendency to adopt a 'shared victimisation' approach, rooted in a gender based analysis, did not encourage the visibility of class and ethnicity as analytical categories to explain the complexity of both migrant women's subordination and middle class Italian women's privilege.

Turco's speech did envisage support for migrants in general, arguing as she did that new strategies of inclusion were necessary. However, on the whole, migrant women were excluded from the broad category of gender and included in the broad category of 'race'/ethnicity. For example, in the section dedicated to family policy, the question of migrant women and the family was totally invisible. The final section of Turco's speech, dedicated to increasing the effectiveness of the political practice of Pds women, did envisage the inclusion of ethnic minority women: 'We can still embark on new paths. Define institutional instruments which give power to the different perspectives of women. We must also avail ourselves of foreign experiences' (Prima conferenza delle donne del Pds 1993, p. 58). However, this projection for inclusion was not apparent in the proceedings of the rest of the conference. Certainly, the debate which had taken place within the separate structures of the *Libere, Insieme* association appeared to have had limited impact on its immediate parenting structure – the Pds women's area of politics.

Conclusion

In her work on the American women's movement, Barbara Ryan (1992, p. 132) has stated: 'Including the diversity of women into feminist analysis and activist commitments is a fundamental goal of the women's movement today'. As was argued in the introduction, this debate is present in a variety of national contexts. It is a relatively recent debate in Italy, which I have sought to highlight using the case of the *Libere, Insieme* organisation. In other national contexts, some of the problems which have emerged have centred around what ethnic minority female activists perceive as white women's reluctance to acknowledge their privileged ethnicity (see Ryan 1992; Amos and Parmar 1984). In the Italian case, it is unlikely that in the immediate future the debate between women of different ethnicities will be formulated in 'racial' terms particularly since this language has not yet permeated the mainstream as a tool with which to understand migrants' disadvantage. Given the specific situation of migrant women within Italy however, it may be that this debate will be formulated in 'exploitative employment' terms. This is because these two constituencies of women frequently interact within a largely unmediated relationship as employer and employee.

The following honest reflection by my key informant offered some insight into why conflict amongst women did not appear to have emerged within the *Libere, Insieme* projects. Her reflections also indicated the potential for a more problematic encounter in the future:

> Look, we still have very little experience of this issue [differences between women within the association], because there have not been many opportunities. Up to now, there have not been many difficulties, because we have been getting to know each other and collaborating on a project, a project where each of us has been working in her own sphere. It hasn't been that women of different nationalities and cultures have worked together to produce a show or a common reflection. Each of us has produced in our own spheres. So, there haven't even been opportunities for great conflict and it is clear for anyone who has experience of relationships between women, that it should be taken into account that there will, undoubtedly, be conflicts … for example, even I notice that I can have a much more immediate relationship with people if I don't have to put myself into another logic, while on the other hand, whoever is obliged to continually adopt our logic, then I exploit this, in other words, I engage in a relationship with someone and it is she who puts herself into my logic. So I think that the biggest effort is on the part of the other person and not on me. However, I have not had any difficulties with those people who are used to doing it. On the other hand I have encountered real problems of code and behaviour with some people, for example, when some Somali women who had been in Italy for a short time came. I had difficulty in understanding and interpreting some of their requests (interview, LI).

The political scientist Zincone (1993) has described *Libere, Insieme* as a 'successful' association, but it is not clear what parameters she adopted to justify this assertion.[49] While there were a few Italian participants who attempted to broach the association's 'fundamental contradiction' regarding the relationship between Italian women and migrant women in the wider society and thus as *employers* of migrant women, these voices were not especially dominant, and in any case did not seem to carry any more weight than those who subscribed to the Common Victim theory. Pds women's reluctance to explore the 'distorted' emancipation of Italian women is indicative of the importance of the issue at stake. Any thorough analysis of migrant women's employment location can only reveal a negative aspect of the 'progress' achieved by feminism and Italian women's emancipation. The choice to evade a full discussion of this or to adhere to the Common Victim approach is clearly less divisive, but ultimately an obstacle for a more inclusive gender practice within Italy.

We cannot ignore the fact that Pds women's involvement in the *Libere, Insieme* association signified that it was a quasi-political association. The nature of the association's mobilisation, as discussed here, did not promote a single unified view of the way forward. Rather, it provided a platform for interested parties to present analyses and to suggest strategies for the future. This facilitates a critique of the respective perspectives of individual contributors but makes the task of evaluating the association itself more problematic. Nevertheless, Pds women's political objective of representing (Italian) women would undoubtedly prove problematic if the use of live-in domestic labour was fully explored and explicitly criticised. This suggests that while, at the cultural level, there was a receptiveness to migrant women, at the political level, Italian activists were still primarily representatives of a national constituency of gender.

The intersection between gender and ethnicity is still at an embryonic stage in Italy. The *Libere, Insieme* association offered a professional élite of ethnic minority women the opportunity to collaborate with Italian women activists. However the parallel existence of migrant women's associations whose agenda was more clearly focused on the actual conditions of migrant women, rather than on the significance of a mixed women's project ,was likely to mean that the majority of ethnic minority women would continue to aggregate on the basis of ethnicity or even a gendered ethnicity rather than on the basis of gender.

Notes

1   I am here using the activities of Pds women activists as one example of female progressive activism in Italy. See chapter 1 for a discussion of their role within this sphere.

2   Work published on Italian feminism by foreign authors shaped by political contexts in which ethnicity did feature, similarly did not highlight either the exclusion of migrant women by Italian feminists or the conditions of migrant women. See for example the work of two American authors, Birnbaum (1986) and Hellman (1987).

3   Although of course the (inferior) racialisation of southerners has long and historic roots. See Dickie (1994) and Gribaudi (1996).

4   See Pajetta, G (1990a), 'Nere, emancipate, invisibili', in *Il Manifesto*, 15 November 1990.

5   This is not to argue that female political activists from within the Catholic sector were more responsive. It was the Catholic voluntary sector rather than the Catholic political sphere which initiated the response to migrant women. Indeed, when the women's section of the Christian Democrat Party were approached in 1992, they had not mobilised at all around the issue of migrant women and instead directed me to the Christian Democrat organisation which dealt with Italian *emigrants*. This was ANFE – Associazione nazionale degli emigrati.

6   For example, Communist women had contributed to initiatives calling for the extension of political refugee status to non Europeans in Italy. They had also called for the European institutions to make a declaration against racism and xenophobia in Europe (see Le donne comuniste 1989).

7   The Charter had stated: 'We have learnt that in politics choices are marked by class and by gender' (Sezione femminile della direzione del Pci 1986, p. 9).

8   This omission would subsequently be referred to as the weak point of the 1986 Charter (see below). For information on the social policy proposals of the Pci on migrant women, see the document prepared by Romana Bianchi and Silvia Barbieri, two female parliamentarians responsible for equal opportunities – Governo Ombra (1990) *Donne Immigrate. Proposte di iniziativa su politiche sociali*. April, Rome. Some earlier Pci legislative proposals had been inclusive of migrant women: Gramaglia-Rodotà ed altri 'Riconoscimento del valore sociale della maternità ed estensione della indennità relativa alle cittadine non ancora protette e alle donne straniere che abbiano eletto il proprio domicilio in Italia da almeno 12 mesi' (17 June 1988). See Montecchi (1993). More specific attention had also begun to be paid towards migrant women by the CGIL in the early 1990s. A specific group was established to examine the position of female migrant workers. It was noted that the number of women migrants involved in the immigrants' trade union grouping (*Coordinamento nazionale immigrati*) was minimal and objective difficulties also prevented them from an active participation in the women's trade union grouping (*Coordinamento donne Cgil*). It was proposed that the question of female migrant workers should be taken up as a political issue by the trade union organisation as a whole. See 'Scaletta gruppo di lavoro lavoratrici extracomunitarie', Rome, 16 October 1990.

9   See Campani (1994b) for a description of some of these groups.

10   Initiatives developed in other cities too. See Battaglino (1991) with regard to the Turinese experience and for information on initiatives in Milan and Bologna see Rossi Doria (1991b). See also directory in *L'Agenda ottomarzo 92/93* regarding mixed groups nationally.

11   These objectives were outlined in the association's introductory pamphlet, *Donne senza frontiere* (1991).

12   Her own political background was in the Socialist Party.

13   This was the anthropologist Pilar Saravia, a prominent activist within the Latin American community in Rome.

14 Indeed, writing in 1993, the political scientist Zincone described the association as a Pds organisation devoted to migrant women.

15 The association did eventually move to a different location with the help of European Union funding (interview, LI,).

16 See interview with Savini in *Il Manifesto*, 15 April 1993.

17 The fact that Italian women activists had ostensibly aggregated on the basis of political and ideological difference meant that their own aggregation on the basis of ethnicity tended to be overlooked.

18 See Women's Charter of 1986.

19 The party had also accepted aspects of their new political vocabulary. Article 2 of the Pds Statute referred to a 'party of women and of men' (Partito Democratico della Sinistra (1991)).

20 Clearly the round table discussions only give insight into the more formal areas of the association's activities. Some participant observation in planning meetings would undoubtedly have offered a different perspective and may have indicated areas of greatest tension. The issue of internal tensions was broached via my key informant (see below).

21 References for the contributors to the round table discussions are given in abbreviated form. I have given their surname followed by the letters ALI (Associazione *Libere, Insieme*) and the date to refer to their verbatim speeches.

22 Ainom Maricos, an Eritrean social worker and the national representative for Eritrean women, based in Milan; Lucia Rochas, a Chilean social worker, based in Milan; Pilar Saravia, a Peruvian anthropologist based in Rome; Vanessa Maher, an anthropologist, born in Kenya and based in Turin; Amelia Cristiana, a teacher and sociologist from Palermo; Graziella Favaro, the director of the Immigration Project for Milan City Council.

23 Her focus on an ethnic group where the women have largely migrated to Italy as secondary migrants was indicative of her interest in what she saw as 'traditional' women's adaptation to Italy and her intervention fitted squarely into the tradition/modernity framework.

24 Crisantino produced a rather naive account of this migration. For example: 'I think that this is the first time in the history of the world that there has been a female migration' (Crisantino, ALI 1992a, p. 8). She also asserted that there was no racism in Palermo towards migrant women contradicting her own description of the creation of an ethnic hierarchy in the town.

25 Her position with regard to the goals of the association indicated that there was no absolute consensus about the organisational validity of *Libere, Insieme*. In fact she was quite critical of its explicit focus on diversity: 'I would prefer it if migrant women were not seen, if there was strong integration so that everyone is equal. As far as I'm concerned, this distinction between Italian women and migrant women within the association is annoying' (Maité, ALI 1992b, p. 36).

26 Indeed, it could even be argued that the very organisation of the initiatives prevented live-in domestic workers from participating in the round table discussions. Although one of these was scheduled at an accessible time (Thursday afternoon), the second one took place on a Saturday.

27 For more examples of articles which sought to provide schematic information about the events see 'Colf sulla scena e immagini dal mondo', in *L'Unità* 8 May 1992 and 'Le italiane e le altre. Video, foto e poesia a Roma', in *Il Manifesto*, 9 May 1992.

28 See for example, an interview with one of the artists displaying her work: 'L'Africa al femminile', in *L'Unità*, 10 May 1992. See also 'Conoscere per capire', in *Paese Sera*, 10 May 1992.

29 See for examples, '*Libere, Insieme*, femminile plurale', in *Paese Sera* 9 May 1992 and 'Storie per capirsi', in *Corriere della Sera*, 10 May 1992.

30 Although once again there was a full cultural programme, my focus is, once again, on the round table discussions. Three of these were held in Rome in May 1993: 'Colf: Rapporto tra necessità e libertà: Voglia di emancipazione; 'Il tempo della maternità' in un paese straniero'; Stereotipi culturali ed esperienza migratoria. I have not addressed the contents of the latter discussion as it focused on the issue of migration and cultural stereotyping in a general sense and did not relate very closely to the actual conditions of African and Asian women living in Italy. See Associazione *Libere, Insieme* (1993c).

31 Kawere represented a cooperative called Maboko na Maboko based in Rome.

32 For a discussion of this see Giorgio, A (1997).

33 The proceedings were published in 1993 as 'Il Tempo della maternità'.

34 Miriam Mafai (1992) reflected on this in an article published in *La Repubblica* with a provocative title describing the 'somersault' of Pds women ('Mamma è più bello ...' La capriola delle donne pds).

35 Gaiotti de Biase's background had originally been within the Catholic women's sphere. The disintegration of the Italian political system in the early 1990s led to the Pds's attempt to inhabit the centre-Left ground and to attract left Catholics to its party (the notion of the *sinistra diffusa*). Gaiotti de Biase's move to the Pds women's sphere was reflective of this. Her move was in fact highlighted during the first conference of Pds women held in 1993 (see Prima Conferenza delle donne del Pds (1993, p. 18).

36 See Andall (1994).

37 This was also true of French feminists. Duchen (1986, p. 51) writes 'From 1970 to 1975 the analysis of motherhood was almost exclusively tied to the campaign for free, legal abortion on demand and contraception'. See her chapter on 'French Feminists and Motherhood: Destiny or Slavery?'

38 See, for some examples, the contributions of Sanna (1993), Mancina (1993) and Gramaglia (1993). Other participants, while recognising the necessity for change, also clearly felt it was important to reiterate their support for certain basic premises regarding legal abortion provision.

39 For example, Labate (1993, p. 126) argued that solutions should be found which were 'consistent with maternity as it is today experienced by Italian women'. Similarly, Riviello (1993, p. 24) maintained that the potential of maternity would depend on an ability to 'communicate to Italian women that our proposals are relevant to them, to their daily lives'. For further examples, see Gaiotti de Biase (1993, p. 80) and Turco (1993, p. 8).

40 The speakers included three gynaecologists (Cristina Damiani; Elisabetta Canitano and the Zairean Susanna Diku), one obstetrician (Annamaria Gioacchini), a paediatrician (Maria Edoarda Trillò), a health visitor (Olga Scorretti) and a medical anthropologist (Nicoletta Diasio). The two non medical speakers were Mariangela Grainer from the Pds and Vittoria Tola, a regional councillor for the Pds. The medical practitioners were all working in the Lazio region and principally in Rome.

41 Once again there was substantial journalistic reporting regarding the 1993 initiative but as with the 1992 events, most articles simply gave information about the general cultural programme with a few summarising the arguments of the main speakers. See, for some examples, 'Esistenza, amore e guerra. Parla la città delle donne', *Paese Sera*, 14 April 1993; '"Libere Insieme', una settimana al Palaexpò', *Il Manifesto*, 15 April 1993.

42 This Diary was promoted by Pds women and the association Eletta which had been established in October 1991 as a forum for women elected to political office at a range of levels (e.g. provincial and regional).

43 See introduction by Livio Turco in *L'Agenda Ottomarzo 92/93* p. 6.

44 See statement 'Dalle donne del Partito Democratico della Sinistra a tutte le donne' in *L'Agenda Ottomarzo 92/93*, pp. 9–12. The Diary took the form of a series of interviews, poetry and prose related to the experiences of migrant women in Italy. The Diary was distributed nationally as a supplement to the Pds newspaper, *L'Unità*.

45 See the 'Chiavi di lettura' section by Monica Lanfranco e Silvia Neonato in *L'Agenda Ottomarzo 92/93*, pp. 13–15.

46 See Monica Lanfranco's contribution to *L'Agenda Ottomarzo 92/93* entitled 'Libere Insieme per gestire l'esilio', pp. 16–17.

47 Ibid., p. 16. Lanfranco did remark on the fact that within the *Libere, Insieme* association Pds women were engaging with a particular political class of foreign women, whom she described as the strong ones. This point was also made to me by another key informant who described the *Libere, Insieme* organisation as an association for women of a certain educational level (interview, FCEI). Writing in *Paese Sera*, the journalist Emanuela Morolo similarly stated that it was the intelligentsia of female migrants who had joined together with women on the Left, trade unionists and academics to form the association. See the article 'Culture intrecciate', *Paese Sera*, 15 May 1993.

48 Topics addressed included employment, welfare reforms, the South, tax reform, family policy, the rise of the Right in Italian politics, the end of Catholic political unity in Italy and women's presence in the political world (see Turco in Prima Conferenza delle donne del Pds, pp. 11–61).

49 One of the key informants from the Lazio immigration office had also cited women's associations like *Libere, Insieme* and *Donne senza frontiere* as the protagonists of change within the Lazio region (interview, RL2).

Conclusion

I hope that one day Italian women will be more sensitive to the presence of foreign women within their homes. These women look after their families and children, giving them the peace of mind to go out to work. But above all they must realise that the freedom they assert by abusing another woman's freedom is not true freedom (Lourdes, ALI, 1993, p. 350) (Cape Verdean activist and journalist).

There is no other European country where ... there is a comparable demand for live-in domestic workers. This is a sign of Italian women's high level of emancipation (which is riven with contradiction and which perhaps partly explains our current silence regarding female migrants) ... (Rossi Doria 1991a, p. 80) (Italian feminist and academic).

This book has examined the circumstances of Black female migrants in Rome. It has shown that their experiences were inextricably connected to prevailing conditions within the domestic work sector. I have sought to document how domestic work, and particularly its organisation as live-in work, creates specific constraints for migrant women and suggested that this use of female migrant labour is being adopted as an adjustment mechanism for the new requirements of the Italian family. It is clear that the domestic work sector remains a marginalised sector of employment and this, together with the specific employment conditions under which migrant women have been hired, has contributed to their social marginality and invisibility.

The live-in organisation of domestic work is particularly incompatible with migrant women's desire for maternity. In chapter 1, I suggested that maternity has constituted a 'protected' aspect of Italian women's social identities and that, in the post-war period, maternity was ideologically constructed as their dominant and principal function. In contrast to this, I have maintained that a quite different definition of womanhood has been applied to Black women. This definition has centred on their dominant constructed role as workers, a role which was expected to assume precedence over other social roles such as mothering.

These contrasting trends in part arise from Black women's employment location. However, they also stem from their absorption into a classically male migration framework, where a labour function is paramount. This book has shown that existing structures within Italy were not responsive to the specific needs of primary female migrants, and especially their needs as single parent working mothers. This was partly a consequence of the relative scarcity of single parent households in Italy, as well as the sheer novelty of this type of migratory flow to Italy.

Despite the fact that my case study is limited to Rome, it seems probable that many of its findings are generalisable to other cities and regions where autonomous female migrants are employed principally as domestic workers. Although some evidence has recently emerged regarding the availability of factory work for Moroccan women in the Veneto region, this has not replaced demand for their labour in the domestic work sphere (Schmidt di Friedberg and Saint-Blancat 1998). The experiences of African women has shown that, structurally, migrant women are restricted to the same employment niche. However, their ability to respond to these restrictions can be conditioned by their motives for migration. Thus, in the case of East African women, where migration has been partly determined by political factors, conditions in the country of origin could limit their options within Italy. Ethnic origin, in terms of the specific characteristics of the sending countries, may thus provide different results for diverse groups. Furthermore, the arrival of new migratory groups, engaged in different labour migration strategies, may well affect the ethnic communities of this case study. De Filippo (1994), for example, has shown that East European women in Naples are being employed as domestic workers on a rotating basis[1] and Decimo (1996) has noted how their presence has adversely affected Somali women's situation. Only time will tell how the changing contours of incoming migration to Italy will further impact on the employment opportunities and experiences of settled communities. Indeed, as the immigration situation changes, so too have the characteristics of female migration to Italy. In addition to the continuing flow of primary female migrants, women are also migrating as part of family reunification processes. Studies of Moroccan women in Italy show evidence of both types of migration within the same ethnic group (Schmidt di Friedberg and Saint-Blancat 1998).

In contrast to several studies on migrant women in Italy, the focus of this study has not centred on migration processes or the transformation of gender relations within ethnic minority communities. Rather, I have sought to stress the determinacy of structure in affecting migrant women's conditions, recognising a specifically Italian sociocultural and political context. I have shown that Italy's post-war political polarisation led to the dominance of the Catholic subculture in the domestic work sector. Catholic ideology regarding women's role and Catholic conceptions on the resolution of labour conflict thus had substantial influence over the sector. It is tempting to predict that a quite different picture may have emerged had the domestic work sector fallen under the influence of the Communist subculture, but even the radical class perspective adopted by the ACLI-COLF in the 1970s was unable to fully identify the interlocking paradigm of domination to which Black women were subjected. The ACLI-COLF's involvement in the domestic work sector offered it a privileged vantage point from which to view the interactive processes of gender, 'race' and class. Its adoption of a rigorous class analysis in the 1970s, meant that both Italian women and migrant women were categorised as gendered and racialised class fractions. From the mid-1980s, however, the adoption of a narrow gender analysis ultimately functioned to marginalise ethnicity both as a contributory factor in migrant women's disadvantage and as evidence of racialised transformations within the sector.

Any conclusions to be drawn, however, must focus on the parallel but intertwined narratives of this book. The significance of the Italian sociocultural context in shaping migrant women's experiences is attributable to what Ginsborg (1995) has termed the enduring familism of Italy. Amongst others,[2] Ginsborg has pointed to the existence of strong kinship ties in Italy, which are seen to contrast significantly with emerging trends in Northern European countries. In the 1970s, changes in Italian women's aspirations led to increasing numbers of women seeking a social identity beyond the domestic sphere. The growth of this trend in the 1970s and 1980s led to a conflict between Italian women's productive and reproductive roles. The live-in domestic worker route was already in place and middle class women were to make use of it as a strategy for combining employment with family work. Thus, the use of live-in domestic workers can be linked to a strong family-based culture, which, despite Italian women's greater presence in the labour market, has sought to preserve the family in traditional terms. Menniti et al. (1997, pp. 225–6) have argued that there have in fact been profound changes to the Italian family but suggest that this new family behaviour is not particularly visible. They attribute this to 'Italians' capacity to change without breaking with their history and their convictions, and to adapt to new demands of social life in a very gentle way'. If we relate this notion to the employment of migrant domestic workers, we see the crux of the tension between Italian women and their families and migrant women and their families. Employing a live-in worker may indeed constitute a gentle means of accommodating transformations within the Italian family. However, seen from a different perspective, this choice is anything but gentle. As the experiences of African women has shown, employment conditions and the implications of live-in domestic work can be extremely harsh.

It is clear that structural conditions in Italy severely restricted migrant women's agency. Structural constraints consisted of demand within the live-in sphere of domestic work, the effects of the ACLI-COLF's location within a Catholic subculture, the absence of alternative employment opportunities, labour contracts which tied migrant women to their employers, the cultural familism of Italy and the prevalent family support system to assist working mothers. In the face of this, migrant women's agency was restricted to their ability to transform their work relationship from a live-in relationship to an hourly paid relationship and their ability to acquire independent living accommodation. For those unable to achieve this, a degree of autonomy could be attained through securing alternative and better live-in employment situations. As I have shown, some women were even able to achieve further onward migration and the experiences of Cape Verdean women who continued their migration from Rome to Rotterdam epitomised the restrictive nature of Italian structural constraints. The same women who found themselves confined to the live-in sector in Italy, were able to work, have families, and live in their own homes in the Netherlands. Nevertheless, what Italy did provide for these female migrants was a fairly secure and constant source of employment. This fact should not be dismissed lightly. As autonomous labour migrants, they needed this employment security both to support themselves and to discharge transnational household responsibilities. Moreover, in some cases, although some interviewees ultimately failed to acquire independent accommodation in Italy, money saved from live-in work was sometimes invested in housing outside of Italy.

Given the significance of domestic work in shaping Black women's experience in Rome, an important question to emerge from this book is *why* live-in domestic workers virtually disappeared in countries such as Britain and France, but prevailed in Italy. Economic and cultural factors have been put forward as explanations. The economic factors relate to the existence of areas of endemic poverty in Italy which persisted into the post-war period. Ginsborg (1990), for example, has argued that Italy was still an underdeveloped country in the mid-1950s. Thus while live-in domestic work was becoming obsolete in other West European countries, particularly as alternative employment opportunities became available for working-class women, a supply of indigenous domestic workers could still be found in Italy. From the 1960s onwards, cultural factors began to mesh with economic factors. Italy's economic boom (1958–63) and the subsequent development of a cult of domesticity for Italian women contributed to the reduced supply of live-in domestic workers within Italy. From the 1960s onwards, potential employers of domestic workers would have to look to regions of poverty not within the national context but within the global context. At this stage, it is probable that most of the demand was generated by upper class families, but subsequently more middle class women would opt to hire paid domestic labour.[3] Employers of domestic workers were able to gain some advantage in the transition from a domestic labour force to a migrant labour force. As the case study has shown, even where Black women were legally employed on contracts in the 1970s, their salaries were lower than those commanded by Italian workers.

But there are additional factors which have contributed to the growing reliance on migrant domestic workers, factors which are likely to perpetuate the live-in domestic sphere in Italy. Firstly, while Menniti et al. (1997) rightly attest to new forms of family behaviour in Italy, some areas have been resistant to change. In particular, the limited participation of Italian men in housework has led to Italy being described as 'the European country in which the work of the family is least well-shared between spouses' (Trifiletti 1995, p. 180). If this situation does not change substantially, it is likely to encourage more families to seek recourse to migrant domestic workers. A second area which is likely to fuel the demand for live-in workers concerns the growing elderly profile of Italian citizens. In the early 1980s, an ISTAT survey showed that the main source of help for the care of Italian children under ten were grandparents.[4] However, Italy's aging population will increasingly need, rather than be able to offer care. Moreover, the care of the elderly is an area 'in which the state transfers the burden of responsibility most explicitly and almost totally onto extended family members' (Trifiletti 1995, p. 192). Families are thus increasingly likely to employ live-in carers to enable them to fulfil their family obligations in a culturally acceptable manner.

Domestic service has long been associated with the concept of modernity. In the 19th century, in both Britain and France, domestic service was seen to have a modernising capacity through its ability to facilitate urban acculturation and subsequent employment mobility (McBride 1976). Then, the domestic servant reflected the growth of a new middle class and by the middle of the century, some three-quarters of such households had at least one live-in servant (Davidoff and Hall 1987). By the middle of the twentieth century, domestic service was no longer seen to be consonant with modernity, representing as it did, a 'pre-modern' relationship. Rather, free labour was seen to typify modern society and the structural characteristics of domestic service were thought to typify a pre-industrial world (Coser 1973). At the end of the twentieth century, the retention of live-in domestic service in Italy can be seen as indicative of a particular model of modernisation. Italy's rapid modernisation and the state's deficiency in providing a supporting infrastructure, in part explain families' reliance on domestic workers. However, this has perpetuated a form of unfree labour into the 1990s. In the 1980s, the actions of the political class suggested that this was an entirely appropriate strategy to pursue. Oscar Luigi Scalfaro,[5] for example, maintained that unless the domestic work sector was supported, old people would end up in public institutions (Scalfaro 1988, p. 3) and Bettino Craxi[6] considered migrant women's ability to 'sacrifice their own interests and personal ambitions' to look after other families to be laudable (Craxi 1988, p. 6). Most accounts of migrant women's involvement in the domestic work sector fail to recognise that, while some families do have a functional necessity for domestic labour, others essentially employ domestic workers as status symbols. This use of domestic workers is emblematic of Italy's modernisation and new wealth and has contributed to the establishment of pernicious ethnic hierarchies which adversely affect specific ethnic groups.

There are clear class implications to these new trends. The use of migrant domestic workers to reconcile family and work roles suggests that the needs of Italian middle class women are being prioritised over those of working-class women. Employing live-in workers is not a valid option for working-class women, who earn lower wages and whose homes are not architecturally designed to accommodate domestic personnel. While in the early 1970s Italian women activists had originally sought collective solutions to issues of child-care, the growing use of migrant domestic labour suggests acceptance of individualised solutions based on personal income criteria. This clearly disadvantages working-class or poorer women for whom adequate collective structures have yet to be uniformly put in place.

One of the aims of this book has been to explore and evaluate the impact of migrant women's presence on the Italian gender debate. The use of domestic workers points to an obvious dualism between women, where some Italian women accept and are complicit in a system which protects their reproductive roles while simultaneously negating those of other women. However, the presence of migrant women, and their use as live-in domestic workers, clearly also questions the perceived 'success' of the Italian model of female emancipation.

The importance of recognising the interactive nature of gender, 'race' and class processes in Black women's lives was stressed in the introduction. Italian women's associations, discussed in previous chapters, have all shown awareness of migrant women's disadvantage, but their increasing propensity to utilise gender as an analytical framework, effectively negates migrant women's interlocking social identities. As I have argued, the tendency to extrapolate one process from this interlocking system of domination and promote it as the dominant marker of disadvantage, produces a reductive account of Black women's situation. This book has shown that it is migrant women's insertion into a marginalised and feminised working-class employment sector as well as their status as migrants which has contributed to a specific locus of disadvantage.

Cock's (1980, p. 227) assertion that 'Domestic service is a social institution which reflects changing patterns of domination' appears particularly apt in the Italian case. Arguably, it is the process of social standardisation within Italy which has facilitated acceptance of this distorted model of Italian women's emancipation. There has been a failure to transform women's role as the prime givers of reproductive care. The new aspirations of Italian women have fundamentally affected the Italian family but the traditional organisation of reproductive work has been largely unchallenged. The use of migrant domestic workers has led to new forms of organisation for reproductive work, but while freeing some middle class Italian women *and men* from the laborious aspects of this work, it has concurrently contributed to the continuation and expansion of the archaic and oppressive institution of live-in domestic work, restricting female migrants to a narrow labour function. Moreover, the continuing tendency to treat gender and immigration as separate categories means that Black women's labour as domestic workers continues to have reduced visibility. Even recent overviews of Italian women's attempts to reconcile work and family life fail to take migrant women's contribution into account (Trifiletti 1995; Menniti et al. 1997; Bimbi 1997; Del Boca 1998; Del Re 2000).

The issues facing Italian women exemplify an unresolved issue for women in advanced industrial societies. Labour market participation is integral to their new social identities, but they continue to assume responsibility for reproductive care and this constitutes an enduring area of conflict. Nonetheless, as this book has shown, the decision to discharge this function onto other women, in the form of live-in service, is a regressive strategy for all groups of women. The findings presented in this book suggest that the inclusive feminism project will prove problematic within Italy precisely because the use of migrant women's labour has provided some Italian women with possibilities for increased autonomy while simultaneously reproducing inequality for Black women. The domestic work sector can be seen as a site of entrenched hierarchies of power which mask the interdependence characterising the relationship between Italian women and migrant women. More generally, the experiences of African women reflect Castles' (1995) model of differential exclusion. While there is clear support for their labour market integration, there is a concurrent disregard for their social or political citizenship. It would appear that Italians are reluctant to completely relinquish their attachment to the old family structure. What this book has unequivocally established however, is that the social value attributed to the family is limited to the *Italian* family. Indeed, its very protection rests on the negation of other women's family lives.

Notes

1 Morokvasic's (1991) research on East–West European migration has shown that Polish women have set up these rotating systems to enable them to return home at regular intervals.
2 See also Barbagli (1997).
3 A focused study on the employers of domestic workers is necessary. Further research in this area could provide much useful information regarding structural change in the Italian family.
4 Data cited in Menniti et al. (1997). See also Tobias (1997) on the situation in Spain, where a 1993 survey showed that almost half of Spanish women between the ages of 65 and 79 help their children with domestic tasks and particularly child-care.
5 Scalfaro was president of the Italian Republic from 1992–99.
6 Craxi, the former leader of the Italian Socialist party, was prime minister of Italy from 1983–87.

APPENDICES

APPENDICES

Appendix 1: Interview Profiles[1]

Interview 1: Matilde (Cape Verde). Migrated to Italy in 1978, aged 18. Hourly paid worker, living as a family unit with her partner and three children.

Interview 2: Lucila (Cape Verde). Migrated to Italy in 1975, aged 19. Hourly paid worker. She had one child, who lived with her.

Interview 3: Rosa (Cape Verde). Migrated to Italy in 1973, aged 19. Hourly paid worker. She lived with her two children.

Interview 4: Maria (Cape Verde). Migrated to Italy in 1989, aged 32. At time of interview, working on an hourly paid basis. She had left her two children (aged 7 and 10) in Cape Verde to be cared for by her mother.

Interview 5: Maria Joanna (Cape Verde). Migrated to Italy in 1969, aged 22. At time of interview, she was a housewife. Married to an Italian man and living as a family unit with their two children.

Interview 6: Clara (Cape Verde). Migrated to Italy in 1971, aged 22. Hourly paid worker. She had originally left three children behind in Cape Verde, one of whom she eventually brought to Rome.

Interview 7: Dosci (Cape Verde). She was brought to Italy by her mother (interview 6) in 1982, aged 13. At time of interview, she was a student.

Interview 8: Margarita (Cape Verde). Migrated to Italy in 1982, aged 22. Hourly paid worker. She had left two children behind in Cape Verde. She married an Italian man, had another child and brought one of her children from Cape Verde to Italy.

Interview 9: Francesca (Cape Verde). Migrated to Italy in 1975, aged 18. Live-in worker. She had two children (7 and 14), both born in Rome, who lived with her at her employers' residence.

Interview 10: Lemlem (Eritrea). Migrated to Italy in 1983, aged 18. Hourly paid worker, with no children.

Interview 11: Abebech (Ethiopia). Migrated to Italy in 1979, aged 16. Hourly paid worker. Her son lived with her husband, from whom she was separated, in Rome.

Interview 12: Hanna (Ethiopia). Migrated to Italy in 1992, aged 27. Hourly paid worker. Had one son (aged 5) in Ethiopia, being cared for by her mother.

Interview 13: Aster (Ethiopia). Migrated to Italy in 1991, aged 24. Live-in worker, with no children.

Interview 14: Allam (Eritrea) Migrated to Italy in 1992, aged 27. Live-in worker. She had 3 children aged between 7 and 11, all living in a residential home in Rome.

Interview 15: Almaz (Ethiopia). Migrated to Italy in 1992, aged 25. Live-in worker. She was married with no children.

Interview 16: Antonia (Cape Verde). Migrated to Italy in 1977, aged 19. Live-in worker. At time of migration, she had left her only son in Cape Verde. She subsequently brought him to Italy and placed him in a residential home.

Interview 17: Abeba (Eritrea). Migrated to Italy in 1970, aged 28. Hourly paid worker. She had two children born in Eritrea and one born in Italy. At time of interview, two of her children were living with her while one remained in Eritrea.

Interview 18: Tanha (Cape Verde). Migrated to Italy in 1969, aged 21. Live-in worker. She had three children. One born in Cape Verde and two born in Rome. Two of the latter were sent back to Cape Verde temporarily (for four years and six months respectively) to be cared for by her mother. At time of interview, two of her children were living in a residential home in Rome.

Interview 19: Elsa (Eritrea). Migrated to Italy in 1980, aged 40, with her baby. Live-in worker. Her son had lived in a variety of residential homes throughout his childhood and adolescence.

Interview 20: Alex (Eritrea). Migrated to Italy in 1987, aged 24. Live-in worker. She had one child (18 months), born in Rome and living with her at her employer's residence.

Interview 21: Zimzim (Eritrea). Migrated to Italy in 1992, aged 20. Live-in worker. Single, with no children.

Interview 22: Filomena (Cape Verde). Migrated to Italy in 1987, aged 30. Live-in worker. Single, with no children.

Interview 23: Elena (Cape Verde). Migrated to Italy in 1976, aged 21. Live-in worker. Single, with no children.

Interview 24: Gianna (Cape Verde). Migrated to Italy in 1974, aged 24 and remained for two years. Re-migrated to Italy in 1988. At time of interview, she was a live-in worker. She had five children all living in Cape Verde and being cared for by her husband and mother.

Interview 25: Gabriele (Cape Verde). Migrated to Italy in 1972, aged 26. Live-in worker. She had four children born in Cape Verde and one born in Rome. The latter child was informally adopted by an Italian family. None of her other children lived in Italy.

Interview 26: Sara (Eritrea). Migrated to Italy in 1990, aged 39. Live-in worker. She left her three children in Eritrea to be cared for by her mother.

Interview 27: Emma (Eritrea). Migrated to Italy in 1975, aged 45. At time of interview, she was retired but had spent her entire working life in Italy as a live-in domestic. Her children were adults at the time of her migration.

Interview 28: Ardah (Somalia). Migrated to Italy in 1990, aged 23. Live-in worker. Single, with no children.

Interview 29: Gerom (Eritrea). The brother of Interview 10. At time of interview, he was a student.

Interview Profiles of Cape Verdean Women in Rotterdam[2]

Interview 30: Marta. Migrated to Italy in 1972, aged 16. Left Italy in 1978.

Interview 31: Maria Silva. Migrated to Italy in 1970, aged 18. Left Italy in 1976.

Interview 32: Joanna. Migrated to Italy in 1970, aged 27. Three year-old child left in Cape Verde with her mother at time of migration. She subsequently had two children in Italy. They were cared for by relatives and friends in Cape Verde and Portugal. She left Italy definitively in 1978.

Interview 33: Jacintha. Migrated to Italy in 1971, aged 17. Left Italy in 1982. Married a Cape Verdian man based in Rotterdam, but had their first child while still working as a live-in domestic in Rome.

Interview 34: Tanha. Migrated to Italy in 1977, aged 18. Left Italy in 1979.

Interview 35: Djina. Migrated to Italy in 1973, aged 30, leaving three children under the age of 5 in Cape Verde. Left Italy in 1975.

Interview 36: Isabella. Migrated to Italy in 1973, aged 23. Left Italy in 1989. Single, with no children.

Interview 37: Otaldina. Migrated to Italy in 1979, aged 33. Left Italy in 1989.

Interview 38: Ana. Migrated to Italy in 1969, leaving her 18 month toddler with her mother in Cape Verde. Left Italy in 1979.

Interview 39: Margarida. Migrated to Italy in 1971, aged 23. Left Italy in 1975.

Interviews with Key Informants

ACLA (*Associazione dei cittadini latinoamericani*): a Latin-American migrants' association in Rome.

ACLI-COLF: a national organisation for domestic workers, active throughout the post-war period.

ADS (*Agenzia di servizi*): a private recruitment agency in central Rome, operative since the early 1990s.

AIDA (*Associazione Italiana di Donne Africane*): this association was formed in 1990. Its founding members were four women of Somali origin.

API-COLF: a splinter group from the ACLI-COLF formed in 1971.

AS, CDR: social worker, *Città dei ragazzi*. A large residential home for boys situated on the outskirts of Rome.

AS, RM1: social worker, *Comune di Roma* (RM1). A high percentage of migrants in Rome were resident in this district.

Caritas 1: an influential Catholic voluntary sector organisation.

Caritas 2: an influential Catholic voluntary sector organisation.

CELSI-CGIL (*Centro lavoratori stranieri immigrati*): a trade union office dealing with migrant workers. The centre was established in Rome in 1987.

DSF (*Donne senza frontiere*): this association was formed in 1991. It was a mixed forum for Italian and migrant women.

FCEI (*Federazione delle Chiese Evangeliche in Italia*): a Protestant voluntary sector organisation.

IR (*Istituto Religioso*): a small residential home situated in the centre of Rome.

LI (*Associazione Libere, Insieme*): this association was formed in December 1991. It was promoted by Pds women as a forum for Italian and migrant women.

OMCVI (*Organização das Mulheres Caboverdeanas em Italia*): an organisation for Cape Verdean women formed in 1988. An association for Cape Verdean men and women has existed since the mid-1970s.

Pci: women's section of the Italian Communist Party.

Pds: women's section of the Democratic Party of the Left.

RL1 (*Regione Lazio*): Immigration Office.

RL2 (*Regione Lazio*): Immigration Office.

UDE (*Unione di donne eritree*): this was an international association of Eritrean women which had been active in Italy since 1978.

USL RM12: Health Assistant, USL RM12.

YWCA – Women and Migrants Project: this was a Protestant voluntary sector organisation. The project for migrant women had been operative in Rome since 1985.

Addtional sources

Questionnaires completed by Somali women.

Transcription of a round table discussion held in 1990 on migrant women and children organised by the Lazio Region's Immigration Office. Migrant women, trade unionists and voluntary workers participated in this debate: 'La Condizione Femminile', Festa del Popolo, Regione Lazio, Rome, September 1990. This is unpublished data and is referred to in the text as Tavola Rotonda (1990).

Participant observation at the YWCA Women and Migrants project.

Informal conversations with African women at *Piazza Fiume*, the 'Tra Noi' organisation, *Ristorante Africa* and Rome's central station, *Stazione Termini*.

Notes

1   All of the female migrants had originally worked as live-in domestic workers, but some had made the transition to hourly paid work.
2   All of the women interviewed in Rotterdam had worked exclusively as live-in domestic workers in Italy. Unless otherwise indicated, they did not have children whilst in Italy.

Appendix 2: Country Profiles

Cape Verde

Cape Verde is an archipelago situated in the Atlantic 385 miles west of Senegal, West Africa. A former Portuguese colony, it achieved independence in 1975. The climate of this island state is subject to long periods of drought and immigration has long constituted an important economic option for its inhabitants. In 1993, it had a population of 398,000,[1] but more Cape Verdians live abroad than in the islands. Its largest emigré communities, outside Africa, live in America and Portugal.[2]

Ethiopia

Ethiopia is an East African state. Apart from the Italian occupation between 1936–41, Ethiopia has constituted an independent nation. In 1993, it had a population of 53,297,000.[3] In 1974, the imperial rule of Emperor Haile Selassie was deposed and a socialist state was established. Ethiopia's long history of inter-regional and inter-ethnic conflict led to a war economy. This, as well as drought, led to serious famine in the 1980s. Both national liberation struggles and revolutionary struggles have produced large numbers of Ethiopian refugees.[4]

Eritrea

Eritrea is an East African State. Eritrea was colonised by Italy in the late 19th century and remained under Italian control until 1941. It was subsequently administered by the British until 1952. It was then federated to Ethiopia until 1962, after which it was fully integrated as a northern province of Ethiopia. The Eritrean Liberation Front was formed in 1961 to pursue independence from Ethiopia and Eritrea became an independent republic in 1991. In 1992, it had a population of 3.5 million.[5]

Somalia

Somalia is an East African state. In 1993, it had a population of 8,543,000.[6] In the late nineteenth century Somalia was subject to French, British and Italian colonialisation. Italian Somalia in the South and British Somaliland in the North became an independent Somali republic in 1960. In 1969 Siad Barre became the leader of this new Socialist state. In 1991, civil war broke out in Somalia and in 1992, a United Nations peace keeping mission was sent in, led by America, but was withdrawn in 1995. This situation produced many Somali refugees in the early 1990s.[7]

Notes

1   World Bank Atlas (1994).
2   For more on Cape Verde's sociopolitical history see Carreira (1982), Foy (1988) and Lobban (1998).
3   World Bank Atlas (1994).
4   For more on Ethiopia's socio-political history see Wubneh and Abate (1988) and Zewde (1991).
5   Iyob (1995). See also for more on Eritrea's socio-political history.
6   World Bank Atlas (1994).
7   For more on Somalia's socio-political history see Laitin and Samatar (1987) and Samatar (1994).

Appendix 3: Some Evidence of Supply and Demand within the Domestic Work Sector in Rome: Advertisements Placed in the Roman Newspaper *Il Messaggero* 1967–87

Il Messaggero, **2 February 1967**

Demand

55,000 monthly small family needs full service.
Live-in service urgently needed 70,000, part-time service 55,000. Piazza Vittorio.
Actress urgently requires live-in woman, L80,000 monthly.

Supply

Tuscan woman requires part-time work.
General maid from Belluno, excellent references, looking for part-time work (8–16).
Very good general maid from Padova, excellent references, looking for part-time work (8–17).

Il Messaggero, 27 February 1972

Demand

Married woman on her own needs a live-in general maid.
Sixty year old man on his own seeks a live-in woman, under 37.
Live-in domestic worker required with references. Salary L100,000 negotiable.
Live-in domestic worker required, 20–35, excellent salary, should be prepared to re-locate to Terni.
General maid needed, Mondays, Wednesdays, Fridays 8.30–17.00. L4000 daily.
General maid with references needed four times a week, 10.00–15.00, L3000 including lunch. Parioli.

Supply

Male domestic worker available, cooking, ironing, driving licence, references.
Excellent worker from Perugia, with references, seeking part-time work.
Woman from Padova, with references, seeking live-in work or part-time work.
31 year old general maid from the Abruzzi region, with excellent references, seeking full-time work (8.00–18.00).
Couple from the Abruzzi region with excellent references, wife – general maid, husband – driver, waiter.

Il Messaggero, 3 February 1977

Demand

Live-in domestic worker and baby-sitter required for three people, L200,000.
Live-in Italian general maid required, with references, 3 adults, Parioli.
Domestic workers required, board, lodging and salary provided.
Live-in domestic worker required with references. Salary L200,000.
Childless couple in a refined house in the centre of Rome seek general maid with excellent references.
Industrialist, alone with 13 yr old son requires a babysitter L250,000, live-in domestic worker or full-time worker.

Supply

Foreign domestic worker with excellent references, available immediately for live-in work.
Filipina domestic worker with excellent references, ready to migrate. Salary L108,000.
Domestic worker in Manila, excellent references, ready to migrate. Salary L108,000.
Capable live-in foreign domestic workers available immediately.
Woman from Perugia, excellent references, available for full or part-time work.
30 year old woman from the Abruzzi region, very punctual, with references, available for part-time work.
Domestic worker with references available to work 4 hours in the afternoon, alternate days considered.
Live-in general maid from the Marche region, excellent references, available for a small family.

Il Messaggero, **28 February 1982**

Demand

Live-in domestic worker required, L350,000 monthly, capable, reliable.
Live-in general maid with excellent references required for a female pensioner, excellent salary, no agencies.
Live-in domestic worker required, aged 45, reliable.
Single man seeks general maid, able to give injections, L350,000 monthly.

Supply

Very able domestic worker from Perugia, excellent references, available for part-time work.
Couple from Perugia available, excellent references, experienced, willing.
Live-in domestic worker from the Abruzzi region available, willing and with references.
Woman from Umbria, with references, available for part-time work.

Il Messaggero, 20, 21 and 22 February 1987

Demand

Italian or Filipina live-in domestic worker with excellent references required for family of three, Parioli.
Husband and wife require Italian couple with references or live-in domestic worker.
Educated general maid required, live-in or full-time work.
Live-in domestic worker, under 40, who speaks Italian, required with references. Excellent conditions.
Couple required, preferably from the Marche region and with excellent references. Should be prepared to re-locate to Cavitanova Marche.

Supply

Foreign girl available for domestic work, excluding live-in work.

Advertised salaries for live-in workers

1967: L55.000-L80,000.
1972: L100,000.
1977: L200,000–L250,000.
1982: L350,000.

Bibliography

AAvv (1994), *Donne in frontiera. Le colf nella transizione*, Transizioni 17, Milan: Editrice Nuova Stampa.

Abbà, L., Ferri, G., Lazzaretto, E., Medi, E. and Motta, S. (1972), *La coscienza di sfruttata*, Milan: Mazzotta.

ACLI (1960), *I gruppi ACLI domestiche*, Rome: Edizioni ACLI.

ACLI (1967), *Professioniste nella famiglia moderna: Le collaboratrici familiari*, Rome: Edizioni ACLI.

ACLI-COLF (1976), *Le Colf nel movimento operaio per lo sviluppo dei servizi sociali per un nuovo modello di vita*, IX Assemblea congressuale ACLI-COLF, 3–4 April, in *Acli-Oggi*, Edizione speciale, anno XIV, no. 103–4, 12–13 April.

ACLI-COLF (1979), *Le Colf: Da casalinghe di riserva a protagoniste di una nuova qualità del lavoro*, X assemblea nazionale ACLI-COLF, 12–13 May, in *Acli-Oggi*, anno XVII, no. 164–5, 13–14 June.

ACLI-COLF (1982), *Cooperare per la solidarietà, l'autotutela, la partecipazione*, Atti dell'XI Assemblea Nazionale, 20–21 November.

ACLI-COLF (1985a), *Le Acli Colf per il lavoro associato per nuove forme di solidarietà*. Atti della XII Assemblea Nazionale ACLI-COLF, 7–8 December.

ACLI-COLF (1985b), *Carta delle responsabilità e dei diritti delle Colf*.

ACLI-COLF (1989a), *Professionalità e diritti per una nuova cittadinanza sociale*, Atti della XIII Assemblea Nazionale ACLI-COLF, 10–12 March.

ACLI-COLF (1989b), *Ricerca condotta dalle ACLI-COLF sulle condizioni di vita e di lavoro delle colf in Italia*, ACLI.

ACLI-COLF (1994), *Le Colf tra nuovi modelli familiari e crisi dello stato sociale*, *XIV Assemblea nazionale ACLI-COLF*, Rome, 24–26 February.

Addis, E. (1993), 'Le risorse per scegliere un figlio', in *Il tempo della maternità*, Relazioni al convegno organizzato da Area Politiche Femminili Direzione Pds, Rome, 9–10 January 1992, pp. 39–50.

Ajò, M. (1991), '"Donne senza frontiere" un solo linguaggio per straniere e italiane', *Avanti!*, 14/15 April, p. 19.

Alberoni, F. (1970), 'Aspects of Internal Migration Related to Other Types of Italian Migration', in Jansen, C. (ed.), *Readings in the Sociology of Migration*, Oxford: Pergamon Press, pp. 285–316.

Alemani, C. (1992), 'Le Colf: un'identità molteplice tra persistenza e mutamento', *Quaderni di Azione Sociale*, May–June, no. 87, pp. 59–69.

Alì, S. (1990), untitled conference intervention, pp. 99–101, in Regione Emilia-Romagna, *L'emigrazione al femminile*, Atti del Convegno, Bologna, 12–13 January, pp. 99–101.

Alternativa Donna – Atti della VII Conferenza delle comuniste (1986), Rome: Editori Riuniti.

Altieri G. and Carchedi F. (1992), 'L'immigrazione straniera nel Lazio', *Inchiesta*, January–March, pp. 29–39.

Altieri, G. (1993), *Presenti ed escluse. Le donne nel mercato del lavoro: Un universo frammentato*, Rome: Ediesse.

Amaturo, E. and Morlicchio, E. (1990), 'Problemi di metodo nell'indagine empirica sull'immigrazione straniera in Italia', in Cocchi, G. (ed.), *Stranieri in Italia*, Bologna: Istituto Cattaneo, pp. 227–38.

Ambrosini, M. (1995), 'Immigrati e lavoro in Lombardia. Verso il superamento di un doppio pregiudizio', *Studi Emigrazione*, vol. 32, no. 119, pp. 491–503.

Amos, V. and Parmar, P. (1984), 'Challenging Imperial Feminism', *Feminist Review*, 17, pp. 3–19.

Amott, T. and Matthaei, J. (1991), *Race, Gender and Work: A Multi-Cultural Economic History of Women in the United States*, Montreal: Black Rose Books.

Andall, J. (1992), 'Women Migrant Workers in Italy', *Women's Studies International Forum*, vol. 15, no. 1, pp. 41–8.

Andall, J. (1994), 'Abortion, Politics and Gender in Italy', *Parliamentary Affairs*, vol. 47, 2, pp. 238–52.

Andall, J. (1995), 'Migrant Women and Gender Role Redefinitions in the Italian Context', *Journal of Area Studies*, no. 6, pp. 203–15.

Andall, J. (1998), 'Catholic and State Constructions of Domestic Workers: The Case of Cape Verdean Women in Rome in the 1970s', in Koser, K. and Lutz, H. (eds), *New Migration in Europe: Social Constructions and Social Realities*, Basingstoke: Macmillan, pp. 124–42.

Andall, J. (1999), 'Cape Verdean Women on the Move: "Immigration Shopping" in Italy and Europe', *Modern Italy*, 4 (2), pp. 241–57.

Andall, J. (2000), 'Organising Domestic Workers in Italy: The Challenge of Gender, Class and Ethnicity', in Anthias, F and Lazaridis, G. (eds), *Gender and Migration in Southern Europe*, Oxford: Berg, pp. 145–68.

Anderson, B. (1993), *Britain's Secret Slaves*, London: Anti-Slavery International, Human Rights Series, no. 5.

Angius, N., Gangere, E. and Occhiuto, M. (1991), 'Esperienza di lavoro con i bambini immigrati, riferita al problema del rapporto del servizio con la tematica dell'accoglienza (istituzionalizzazione)', unpublished conference report.

API-COLF (1985), *Tesi del XII Congresso*.

API-COLF (1991), *Vivere la professione come servizio all'uomo*, Atti del XIV Congresso Nazionale, 12 May.

Arena, G. (1978), 'Il lavoro femminile come fattore d'incidenza geografica', *Geografia*, pp. 158–71.

Arena, G. (1983), 'Lavoro femminile ed. immigrazione dai Paesi Afro-Asiatici a Roma', *Studi Emigrazione*, 70, pp. 177–88.

Asante Molefi, K. (1988), *Afrocentricity*, Trenton, New Jersey: Africa World Press.

Associazione Libere, Insieme (1992a), *Le identità culturali delle donne immigrate*, Rome, 9 May.

Associazione Libere, Insieme (1992b), *Donne migranti, condizioni di vita, diritti, aspettative*, Rome, 14 May.

Associazione Libere, Insieme (1993a), *Colf: Rapporto tra necessità e libertà; Voglia di emancipazione*, Rome, 14–19 May.

Associazione Libere, Insieme (1993b), *'Il tempo della maternità' in un paese straniero*, Rome, 14–19 May.

Associazione Libere, Insieme (1993c), *Stereotipi culturali ed esperienza migratoria*, Rome, 14–19 May.

Atti Parlamentari N.1272 (1988), *Norme di tutela dei cittadini stranieri in Italia*, Disegno di Legge, Senato della Repubblica, X Legislatura.

Bakan, A. and Stasiulis, D.K. (1995), 'Making the Match: Domestic Placement Agencies and the Racialization of Women's Household Work', *Signs*, vol. 20, no. 21, pp. 303–5.

Balbo, L. and May, M.P. (1975), 'Woman's Condition: The Case of Post-war Italy', *International Journal of Sociology*, 5, pp. 79–102.

Balbo, L. (1989), 'Oltre l'antirazzismo facile', *Democrazia e diritto*, November–December, no. 6.

Balbo, L. (1990), in European Parliament Session Documents, *Annex to the report drawn up by Mr. Ford on behalf of the Committee of Inquiry into Racism and Xenophobia*, pp.155–156.

Ballestrero, M.V (1984), 'Women at Work in Italy: Legislation – Evolution and Prospects', in Davidson, M.J. and Cooper, C.L. (eds), *Working Women: An International Survey*, Chichester: Wiley, pp. 103–22.

Barbagli, M. (1997), 'Family and Kinship in Italy', in Gullestad, M. and Segalen, M. (eds), *Family and Kinship in Europe*, London: Pinter, pp. 33–48.

Barile, G. and Zanuso, L. (ed.) (1984), *Lavoro femminile, sviluppo tecnologico e segregazione occupazionale*, Milan: Franco Angeli.

Barkan, J. (1984), *Visions of Emancipation: The Italian Workers' Movement since 1945*, New York: Praeger.

Barrett, M. and Mcintosh, M. (1985), 'Ethnocentrism and Socialist-Feminist Theory', *Feminist Review*, 20, pp. 23–47.

Battaglino, M.T. (1991), 'Fare impresa insieme alle immigrate. L'esperienza di un centro-donna a Torino', *Reti*, no. 4, pp. 20–22.

Battistoni, L. (1986), 'I percorsi lavorativi femminili', in ISTAT (1986), *Atti del Convegno la famiglia in Italia*, Rome, pp. 223–34.

Becagli, A. (1990), *Le relazioni madre-bambino nella realtà dell'immigrazione. I servizi a Roma*, Tesi di Diploma.

Beccalli, B. (1985), 'Italy', in Farley, J. (ed.), *Women Workers in Fifteen Countries*, Cornell University: Industrial and Labor Relations Press, pp. 154–69.

Beccalli, B. (1994), 'The Modern Women's Movement in Italy', *New Left Review*, no. 204, pp. 86–112.

Beckwith, K. (1985), 'Feminism and Leftist Politics in Italy: The Case of UDI-PCI Relations', in Bashevkin, S. (ed.), *Women and Politics in Western Europe*, London: Frank Cass, pp. 19–37.

Bedani, G. (1995), *Politics and Ideology in the Italian Workers' Movement*, Oxford: Berg.

Bedani, G. (1996), 'The *Dossettiani* and the Concept of the Secular State in the Constitutional Debates: 1946–7', *Modern Italy*, no. 2, pp. 3–22.

Belotti, E.G. (1986), 'Cultura delle donne e modificazioni familiari', in Belforte, F., Lemmi, G., Meucci, A. and Bimbi, F. (eds), *Dal dovere all'amore. La donna nella famiglia che cambia*, Livorno: Belforte editore, pp. 93–102.

Berlinguer, E. (1978), 'The Historic Compromise', in Sassoon, D. (ed.), *The Italian Communists Speak for Themselves*, Nottingham: Russell Press, pp. 141–58.

Bertollini, R. et al. (n.d.), 'Caratteristiche neonatali dei figli di immigrati a Roma negli anni 1982–1988', unpublished paper.

Bettio, F. (1988a), *The Sexual Division of Labour: The Italian Case*, Oxford: Clarendon Press.

Bettio, F. (1988b), 'Women, the State and the Family in Italy: Problems of Female Participation in Historical Perspective', in Rubery, J. (ed.), *Women and Recession*, London: Routledge, pp. 191–217.

Bettio, F. (1988c), 'Sex-typing of Occupations, the Cycle and Restructuring in Italy', in Rubery, J. (ed.), *Women and Recession*, London: Routledge, pp. 74–99.

Bhavnani, K. (1993), 'Talking Racism and the Editing of Women's Studies', in Richardson, D. and Robinson, V. (eds), *Introducing Women's Studies: Feminist Theory and Practice*, London: Macmillan, pp.27–48.

Bianchi, M. (1990), 'Le metropoli del nord – un confronto tra modelli sociali e generazioni di donne', *Inchiesta*, April–September, pp. 64–9.

Bianco, G. (1992), *Immigrazione e nucleo familiare "debole" (madre-figlio): questione dei minori in affidamento a Roma*, Tesi di Laurea.

Bimbi, F. (1989), '"The Double Presence": A Complex Model of Italian Women's Labour', *Marriage and Family Review*, no. 1–2, pp. 81–105.

Bimbi, F. (1992), 'La cittadinanza delle donne. Trasformazioni dell'economia del dono e culture del welfare state in Italia', *Inchiesta*, no. 97, pp. 94–111.

Bimbi, F. (1993a), 'Gender, 'Gift Relationship' and Welfare State Cultures in Italy', in Lewis, J. (ed.), *Women and Social policies in Europe*, Aldershot: Edward Elgar, pp. 138–69.

Bimbi, F. (1993b), 'Three Generations of Women: Transformation of Female Identity Models in Italy', in Cicioni, M. and Prunster, N. (eds), *Visions and Revisions. Women in Italian Culture*, Oxford: Berg, pp. 149–166.

Bimbi, F. (1997), 'La debolezza delle politiche familiari in Italia: un caso di federalismo mancato?', in Bimbi, F. and Del Re, A. (eds), *Genere e Democrazia*, Turin: Rosenberg and Sellier, pp. 193–216.

Birindelli, A. (1986), 'L'immigrazione straniera a Roma: problemi ed esperienze della prima fase dell'indagine', *Studi Emigrazione*, Anno XXIII, no. 82–3, pp. 391–402.

Birnbaum, L. (1986), *Liberazione della donna*, Connecticut: Wesleyan University Press.

Bocca, G. (1988), *Gli Italiani sono razzisti?*, Milano: Garzanti.

Boccia, M.L. (1986), 'Interlocutrici forti nei luoghi del potere', *Donne e Politica*, 2–3, pp. 46–9.

Boccia, M.L. (1987), 'La società femminile', *Reti*, September–October, pp. 3–4.

Boccia, M.L. (1989), 'Stare da donne nel Pci', *Reti*, 1, pp. 3–15.

Bolasco, S., Pagliari Pompili, M. and Rella, P. (1985), 'Per una nuova tipologia del lavoro femminile: analisi delle differenze regionali in Italia', *Inchiesta*, October–December, pp. 64–79.

Bonetti, P. (1998), 'La nuova legge italiana sull'immigrazione', *Studi Emigrazione*, XXXV, no. 129, pp. 137–49.

Bonifazi, C. (1992), 'Italian Attitudes and Opinions towards Foreign Migrants and Migration Policies', *Studi Emigrazione*, XXIX, no. 105, pp. 21–41.

Bonini, D. (1987), 'Politica immigratoria e bisogni sociali dell'immigrato. Una prima riflessione', in Sergi, N. (ed.), *L'immigrazione straniera in Italia*, Rome: Edizioni Lavoro, pp. 81–127.

Bonini, D. (1991), 'Le politiche dell'immigrazione. Accoglienza, inserimento, integrazione', in Sergi, N. and Carchedi, F. (eds), *L'immigrazione straniera in Italia. Il tempo dell'integrazione*, Rome: Edizioni Lavoro, pp. 181–202.

Bonnett, A. (1996), 'Anti-racism and the Critique of "White" Identities', *New Community*, 22 (1), pp. 97–110.

Bono, P. and Kemp, S. (1991), *Italian Feminist Thought*, Oxford: Blackwell.

Bordonaro, G. (1991), 'Immigrazione e rientri nel Lazio', *Notizie fatti problemi dell'emigrazione*, anno XLIV, no. 2, April–June, pp. 9–10.

Bossi, U. (with D. Vimerati) (1992), *Vento dal nord. La mia Lega la mia vita*, Milan: Sperling and Kupfer.

Bosworth, R. (1996), *Italy and the Wider World 1860–1960*, London: Routledge.

Bourne, J. (1983), 'Towards an Anti-racist Feminism', *Race and Class*, XXV, 1, pp. 1–22.

Boyd, M. (1989), 'Family and Personal Networks in International Migration: Recent Developments and New Agendas', *International Migration Review*, vol. xxiii, no. 3, pp. 638–70.

Brah, A. (1991), 'Questions of Difference and International Feminism', in Aaron, J. and Walby, S. (eds), *Out of the Margins: Women's Studies in the Nineties*, London: The Falmer Press, pp. 168–176.

Brah, A. (1993), 'Difference, Diversity, Differentiation: Processes of Racialisation and Gender', in Solomos, J. and Wrench, J. (eds), *Racism and Migration in Western Europe*, Oxford: Berg, pp. 195–214.

Brah, A. (1996), *Cartographies of Diaspora*, London: Routledge.

Bruzzichelli, P. (1976), 'Liberare la donna', in Bruzzichelli, P. and Algini, M.L. (eds), *Donna, cultura e tradizione*, Milan: Mazzotta, pp. 7–31.

Bryan, B, Dadzie, S. and Scafe, S. (1985), *The Heart of the Race. Black Women's Lives in Britain*, London: Virago.

Bull, A. (1996), 'Ethnicity, Racism and the Northern League', in Levy, C. (ed.), *Italian Regionalism*, Oxford: Berg, pp.171–88.

Burnett, J. (ed.) (1977), *Useful Toil: Autobiographies of Working People from the 1820s to the 1920s*, Middlesex: Penguin.

Calabrò, A.R. and Grasso, L. (eds) (1985), *Dal movimento femminista al femminismo diffuso*, Milan: Franco Angeli.

Caldwell, L. (1978), 'Church, State and Family: The Women's Movement in Italy', in Kuhn, A. and Wolpe, A. (eds), *Feminism and Materialism*, London: Routledge, pp. 68–95.

Caldwell, L. (1991a), *Italian Family Matters*, London: Macmillan.

Caldwell, L. (1991b), 'Italian Feminism: Some Considerations', in Baranski, Z. and Vinall, S. (eds), *Women and Italy*, London: Macmillan, pp. 95–116.

Calvanese, F. (1993), 'Nuovi modelli migratori: il caso italiano', in Delle Donne, M., Melotti, U. and Petilli, S. (eds), *Immigrazione in Europa*, Rome: CEDISS, pp. 173–84.

Camera dei Deputati (1987), *Relazione sull'attuazione della legge contenente norme per la tutela sociale della maternità e sulla interruzione volontaria della gravidanza (1986)*, Presentata dal ministro della Sanità, Atti Parlamentari, X Legislatura.

Cammarota, A. (1984), *Donna, identità e lavoro. Il movimento femminista di fronte alla complessità sociale*, Milan: Giuffrè.

Campani, G. (1990), 'Donne immigrate in Italia', in Cocchi, G. (ed.), *Stranieri in Italia*, Bologna: Istituto Cattaneo, pp. 3–16.

Campani, G. (1994a), 'Amiche e sorelle', in Vicarelli, G. (ed.), *Le mani invisibili. La vita e il lavoro delle donne immigrate*, Rome: Ediesse, pp. 180–196.

Campani, G. (1994b), 'Ethnic Networks and Associations, Italian Mobilisation and Immigration Issues in Italy', in Rex, J. and Drury, B. (eds), *Ethnic Mobilisation in a Multi-Cultural Europe*, Aldershot: Avebury, pp. 143–7.

Campani, G. (2000), 'Migrant Women in Southern Europe: Social Exclusion, Domestic Work and Prostitution in Italy', in King, R., Lazaridis, G. and Tsardanidis, C. (eds), *Eldorado or Fortress? Migration in Southern Europe*, London: Macmillan, pp. 145–69.

Campus, A. (1994), 'Lavorare "in regola"', in Vicarelli, G. (ed.), *Le mani invisibili. La vita e il lavoro delle donne immigrate*, Rome: Ediesse, pp. 93–108.

Cappiello, A et al. (eds) (1985), *Codice Donna: Norme interne e atti internazionali*, Rome: Istituto poligrafico e zecca dello stato.

Caritas di Roma (1991), *Immigrati in Italia e nel Lazio. Dossier statistico 1991*, Rome: Sinnos editrice.

Caritas di Roma (1992), *Immigrazione. Dossier statistico 1992*, Rome: Sinnos editrice

Caritas di Roma (1993), *Immigrazione. Dossier statistico 1993*, Rome: Sinnos editrice.

Caritas di Roma (1994), *Immigrazione. Dossier statistico 1994*, Rome: Anterem edizioni ricerca.

Caritas Diocesana di Roma (1989), *Stranieri a Roma*, Rome: Siares.

Carreira, A. (1982), *The People of the Cape Verde Islands*, London: Hurst.

Carta di Donne per il partito democratico della sinistra. XX Congresso del Pci.

Castles, S., with Booth, H. and Wallace, T. (1984), *Here for Good. Western Europe's New Ethnic Minorities*, London: Pluto Press.

Castles, S. and Miller, M. (1993), *The Age of Migration. International Population Movements in the Modern World*, London: Macmillan.

Castles, S. (1993), 'Migrations and Minorities in Europe. Perspectives for the 1990s: Eleven Hypotheses', in Solomos, J. and Wrench, J. (eds), *Racism and Migration in Western Europe*, Oxford: Berg, pp. 17–34.

Castles, S. (1995), 'How Nation-states Respond to Immigration and Ethnic Diversity', *New Community*, 21 (3), pp. 293–308.

Cavaliere, L. et al. (1988), 'Comuniste senza commissione', *Noi Donne*, October, pp. 9–10.

Cavarero, A. (1987), 'Per una teoria della differenza sessuale', in Cavarero, A. et al. (eds), *Diotima, Il pensiero della differenza sessuale*, Milan: La Tartaruga, pp. 43–79.

Cavarero, A. (1993), 'Towards a Theory of Sexual Difference', in Kemp, S. and Bono, P. (eds), *The Lonely Mirror. Italian Perspectives on Feminist Theory*, London: Routledge, pp. 189–221.

Censis (1986), *Speciale Emigrazioni. Tra convivenza ed. etnocentrismo*, Quindicinale di Note e commenti, no. 17/18/19, 1–15 September/1 October.

Censis (1988), *Speciale Emigrazioni. Oltre la residualità*. Note e commenti, no. 5, May.

Censis (1991), *Immigrati e società italiana*, Rome: Editalia.

CGIL, CISL, UIL Roma (1992), *Progetto lavoro per gli immigrati a Roma*.

CGIL-CISL-UIL di Roma e del Lazio (1982), *Lavoratori Immigrati (diritti sindacali, sociali, culturali, politici)* Rome.

Chang, G. (1994), 'Undocumented Latinas: The New "Employable" Mothers', in Glenn, E., Chang, G. and Forcey, L. (eds) (1994), *Mothering: Ideology, Experience and Agency*, London: Routledge, pp. 259–85.

Chodorow, N. with Contratto, S. (1989), 'The Fantasy of the Perfect Mother', in Chodorow, N. (ed.), *Feminism and Psychoanalytic Theory*, New Haven: Yale University Press, pp. 79–96.

Clark M., Hine, D and Irving, R.E.M. (1974), 'Divorce, Italian Style', *Parliamentary Affairs*, Summer, pp. 333–58.

Cochrane, A. (1993), 'Looking for a European Welfare State', in Cochrane, A. and Clarke, J. (eds), *Comparing Welfare States. Britain in International Context*, London: Sage, pp. 239–68.

Cock, J. (1980), *Maids and Madams: A Study in the Politics of Exploitation*, Johannesburg: Raven Press.

Cohen, R. (1987), *The New Helots. Migrants in the International Division of Labour*, Hants: Gower.

Cohen, R. (1997), *Global Diasporas*, London: UCL.

Cole, B. (ed.) (1986), *All American Women. Lines that Divide, Ties that Bind*, New York: The Free Press.

Cole, J. (1997), *The New Racism in Europe: A Sicilian Ethnography*, Cambridge: CUP.

Colen, S. (1986), '"With Respect and Feelings": Voices of West Indian Child Care and Domestic Workers in New York City', in Cole, B. (ed.), *All American Women. Lines that Divide, Ties that Bind*, New York: The Free Press, pp. 46–70.

Collicelli, C. (1986), 'Tra convivenza ed etnocentrismo', in *Speciale Emigrazioni. Tra convivenza ed etnocentrismo*, Quindicinale di Note e commenti, no. 17/18/19, 1–15 September/1 October, pp. 3–7.

Collicelli, C. (1988), 'Una nuova centralità', in *Speciale Emigrazioni. Oltre la residualità*, Note e commenti, no. 5, May, pp. 3–7.

Collins, P. (1990), *Black Feminist Thought: Knowledge, Consciousness, and the Politics of Empowerment*, New York: Routledge.

Collins, P. (1994), 'Shifting the Center: Race, Class and Feminist Theorizing about Motherhood', in Glenn, E.N., Chang, G. and Forcey, L.R. (eds), *Mothering: Ideology, Experience and Agency*, London: Routledge, pp. 45–65.

Combahee River Collective (1977), 'A Black Feminist Statement', reproduced in Hull, G., Scott, P. and Smith B. (eds) (1982), *All the Women are White, All the Blacks are Men, But Some of Us are Brave*, New York: The Feminist Press, pp. 13–22.

Commissione nazionale per la parità e le pari opportunità tra uomo e donna/ISTAT (1994), *Tempi diversi. L'uso del tempo di uomini e donne nell'Italia di oggi*, Presidenza del consiglio dei ministri.

Comune di Milano (1990), *Le mille e una donna*, Atti del convegno, 4 March, Milan.

Comune di Roma (1988), *Roma: Immigrazione dai paesi del Terzo Mondo*.

Comune di Roma (1989), 'Minori Stranieri Istituzionalizzati'.

Condon, S. (1995), 'Compromise and Coping Strategies: Gender Issues and Caribbean Migration to France', paper presented to research seminar on 'Caribbean Migration to Europe', Oxford Brookes University, 22–24 September.

Contini, B. (1989), 'The Irregular Economy of Italy: a Survey of Contributions', in Feige, E.L. (ed.), *The Underground Economies*, Cambridge: Cambridge University Press, pp. 237–50.

Contratto Collettivo Nazionale del Lavoro Domestico, 22 May 1974.

Contratto Collettivo Nazionale del Lavoro Domestico, 14 December 1978.

Contratto Collettivo Nazionale del Lavoro Domestico, 8 January 1984.

Contratto Collettivo Nazionale del Lavoro Domestico, 13 July 1988.

Contratto Collettivo Nazionale del Lavoro Domestico, 15 July 1992.

Corti, P. (1990), 'Donne che vanno, donne che restano. Emigrazione e comportamenti femminili', in Corti, P. (ed.), *Società rurale e ruoli femminili in Italia tra ottocento e novecento*, Istituto 'Alcide Cervi' Annali 12/1990, pp. 213–235.

Coser, L. (1973), 'Servants: The Obsolescence of an Occupational Role', *Social Forces*, 52, pp. 31–40.

Craxi, B. (1988), 'Una più giusta valutazione del lavoro domestico', *Le Colf*, May, p. 6.

Crippa, E. (1959), *La tua morale professionale*, Torino: Casa Serena.

Crippa, E. (1961), *Le sante del nostro lavoro*, Torino: Casa Serena.

Crippa, E. (1979), *Lavoro amaro: le estere in Italia*, Rome: API-COLF.

Cutrufelli, M. R. (1975), *Disoccupata con onore*, Milan: Mazzotta.

Cutrufelli, M. R. (1977), *Operaie senza fabbrica*, Milan: Mazzotta.

D'Alessandro, V. (1988), 'Situazione e tendenze dell'occupazione femminile nel Lazio', in ISFOL, *Percorsi femminili. Lavoro, formazione e famiglia nel Lazio*, Milan: Franco Angeli, pp. 239–302.

D'Ottavi, A.M. (1990), 'I bambini e gli adolescenti immigrati da paesi extracomunitari in Italia: condizioni di vita e problemi di identità culturale, ipoteche sul futuro?', in Cocchi, G. (ed.), *Stranieri in Italia*, Bologna: Istituto Cattaneo, pp. 271–76.

Dalla Costa, G. (1978), *Un lavoro d'amore*, Rome: Edizioni delle donne.

Dalla Costa, M. (1981), 'Emigrazione, immigrazione e composizione di classe in Italia negli anni '70', *Economia e Lavoro*, no. 4, pp. 121–31.

Davidoff, L. and Hall, C. (1987), *Family Fortunes. Men and Women of the English Middle Class, 1780–1850*, London: Hutchinson.

Davis, A. (1982), *Women, Race and Class*, London: The Women's Press.

De Filippo, E. (1994), 'Le lavoratrici "giorno e notte"', in Vicarelli, G. (ed.), *Le mani invisibili. La vita e il lavoro delle donne immigrate*, Rome: Ediesse, pp. 65–72.

De Grazia, R. (1984), *Clandestine Employment*, Geneva: International Labour Office.

De Grazia, V. (1992), *How Fascism Ruled Women. Italy, 1922–1945*, California: University of California Press.

De Lauretis, T. (1988), 'The Essence of the Triangle or, Taking the Risk of Essentialism Seriously: Feminist Theory in Italy, the U.S., and Britain', *Differences*, 1 (2), pp. 3–37.

De Lourdes, M. (1989), 'Per un ricongiugimento familiare vero', in Federazione delle chiese evangeliche servizio migranti (ed.), *Casa o fortezza? Italia, L'Europa del 1992 and l'immigrazione*, pp. 79–80.

De Lourdes, M. and Pimental, C. (1989), 'L'emigrazione delle donne capoverdiane in Italia', in Caritas Diocesana di Roma, *Stranieri a Roma*, Rome: Siares, pp. 89–98.

De Paz, I. (1976a), 'Caccia alle "colf" di colore. Mille (300 a Roma) in arrivo', *Il Messaggero*, 20 September.

De Paz, I. (1976b), 'La somala a qualunque prezzo e le nostre "colf" emigrano', *Il Messaggero*, 4 October.

De Paz, I. (1978), 'Per le colf di colore un figlio è un dramma senza soluzione', *Il Messaggero*, 6 April.

Decimo, F. (1996), 'Reti di solidarietà e strategie economiche di donne somale immigrate a Napoli', *Studi Emigrazione*, XXXIII, no. 123, pp. 473–94.

Del Boca, D. (1988), 'Women in a Changing Workplace. The Case of Italy', in Jenson, J., Hagen, E,. and Reddy, C. (eds), *Feminization of the Labour Force. Paradoxes and Promises*, Cambridge: Polity Press, pp. 120–35.

Del Boca, D. (1998), 'Labour Policies, Economic Flexibility and Women's Work', in Drew, E., Emerek, R. and Mahon, E. (eds), *Women, Work and the Family in Europe*, London: Routledge, pp. 124–30.

Del Re, A. (1989), 'Le féminisme italien à l'aube des années quatre-vingt-dix', *Cahiers du Féminisme*, 50, pp. 14–18.

Del Re, A. (2000), 'The Paradoxes of Italian Law and Practice', in Hantrais, L. (ed.), *Gendered Policies in Europe*, London: Macmillan, pp. 108–123.

Delai, N. (1991), 'Flussi di immigrazione, tipologie, percorsi di mobilità e progetti di vita degli immigrati extracomunitari', in Presidenza del consiglio dei ministri (1991), *Atti della conferenza nazionale dell'immigrazione, Rome 4–6 June 1990*, Rome: Editalia, pp. 94–100.

Dell'Orto, F. and Taccani, P. (1993), 'Family Carers and Dependent Elderly People in Italy', in Twigg, J. (ed.), *Informal Care in Europe*, University of York, pp. 109–28.

Di Liegro, L. and Pittau, F. (1992), *Il pianeta immigrazione: dal conflitto alla solidarietà* (2nd edn), Rome: Edizioni Dehoniane.

Di Nicola, G.P. (1994), 'Le sfide sociali della maternità', in AAvv (1994), *Donne in frontiera. Le colf nella transizione*, ACLI series Transizioni no. 17, Milan: Editrice Nuova Stampa, pp. 165–200.

Dickie, J. (1994), 'The South as Other: From Liberal Italy to the Lega Nord', in Cento Bull, A. and Giorgio, A. (eds), *Culture and Society in Southern Italy*, Supplement to the Italianist, no. 14, pp. 124–40.

Dill, B. (1980), 'The Means To Put My Children Through: Childrearing Goals and Strategies Among Black Female Domestics', in La Frances Rodgers-Rose (ed.), *The Black Woman*, London: Sage, pp. 107–23.

Dill, B. (1987), 'The Dialectics of Black Womanhood', in Harding, S. (ed.), *Feminism and Methodology*, Bloomington and Indianapolis: Indiana University Press, pp. 97–108.

Dill, B. (1988), 'Our Mothers' Grief: Racial Ethnic Women and the Maintenance of Families', *Journal of Family History*, vol. 13, no. 4, pp. 415–31.

Donne del Pds (1992), 'I nostri progetti, le nostre battaglie', November.

DuBois, E.C and Ruiz, V.L. (eds) (1990), *Unequal Sisters: A Multicultural Reader in U.S. Women's History*, New York: Routledge.

Duchen, C. (1986), *Feminism in France*, London: Routledge.

Dumon, A. (1981), 'The Situation of Migrant Women Workers', *International Migration*, 19 (1–2), pp. 190–209.

ECAP-CGIL (1979), *I lavoratori stranieri in Italia*, Esperienze e Proposte no. 38.

ECAP-CGIL (1980), 'Considerazioni sul problema dei lavoratori stranieri nella regione Lazio', Rome.

Enloe, C. (1989), *Bananas, Beaches and Bases: Making Feminist sense of International Politics*, London: Pandora.

Ergas, Y. (1982), 'Feminism and the Italian Party System; Women's Politics in a Decade of Turmoil', *Comparative Politics*, 14, 3, pp. 253–79.

Ergas, Y. (1986), *Nelle maglie della politica*, Milan: Frano Angeli.

Escrivà, A. (1996), 'Control, Composition and Character of New Migrations to South-West Europe. The case of Peruvian women in Barcelona', paper presented to conference on 'New Migration in Europe: Social Constructions and Social Realities', ERCOMER, Utrecht, 18–20 April.

European Forum of Left Feminists and Others (1993), *Confronting the Fortress. Black and Migrant Women in the European Community*, a report to the European Women's Lobby, September.

Farinelli, F. (1993), 'Pari opportunità in Italia e Gran Bretagna. Teoria e pratica', in Conferenza INCA, CGIL and TUC, *Pari opportunità e diritti dei lavoratori in Italia e Gran Bretagna*, London: Trade Union Congress, pp. 13–19.

Favaro, G. and Bordogna, M. (1989), *Politiche sociali ed immigrati stranieri*, Rome: La Nuova Italia Scientifica

Favaro, G. and Bordogna, M. (1991), *Donne dal mondo. Strategie migratorie al femminile*, Milan: Guerini.

Favaro, G. (1994), 'Avere un figlio altrove', in Vicarelli, G. (ed.), *Le mani invisibili. La vita e il lavoro delle donne immigrate*, Rome: Ediesse, pp. 141–53.

Fekete, L. and Webber, F. (1994), *Inside Racist Europe*, London: Institute of Race Relations.

Ferrera, M. (1986), 'Italy', in Flora, P. (ed.), *Growth to Limits. The Western European Welfare States since World War II*, Berlin, New York: Walter de Gruyter, pp. 388–499.

Finan, T. and Henderson, H. (1988), 'The Logic of Cape Verdean Female-headed Households: Social Response to Economic Scarcity', *Urban Anthropology*, 17, 1, pp. 87–103.

Finocchiaro, A. and Rizza, A. (1993), 'La maternità in Sicilia', in *Il tempo della maternità*, Relazioni al convegno organizzato da Area Politiche Femminili Direzione Pds, Roma, 9–10 January 1992, pp. 137–42.

Fossati, R. (1976), 'La maternità come destino', in Bruzzichelli, P. and Algini, M.L. (eds), *Donna, cultura e tradizione*, Milan: Mazzotta, pp. 67–76.

Foy, C. (1988), *Cape Verde: Politics, Economy and Society*, London: Pinter.

Frankenberg, R. (1993), *White Women, Race Matters. The Social Construction of Whiteness*, Minneapolis: University of Minnesota Press.

Friese, M. (1995), 'East European Women as Domestics in Western Europe: New Social Inequality and Division of Labour Among Women', *Journal of Area Studies*, no. 6, pp. 194–202.

Gaiotti De Biase, P. (1993), 'Sostenere le scelte procreative delle donne: quali politiche', in *Il tempo della maternità*, Relazioni al convegno organizzato da Area Politiche Femminili Direzione Pds, Roma, 9–10 January 1992, pp. 79–102.

Gallagher, T. (1994), 'The Regional Dimension in Italy's Political Upheaval: Role of the Northern League 1984–1993', *Parliamentary Affairs*, vol. 47, 3, pp. 456–68.

Garassini, S. (1992), *Un uomo, un'idea. Il contributo di Padre Erminio Crippa s.c.j. alla promozione del lavoro domestico in 36 anni di attività tra le colf*, API-COLF.

Gibson, K. and Graham, J. (1986), 'Situating Migrants in Theory: The Case of Filipino Migrant Contract Construction Workers', *Capital and Class*, no. 29, pp. 130–49.

Gilroy, P. (1993), *Small Acts*, London: Serpents Tail.

Ginsborg, P. (1990), *A History of Contemporary Italy*, London: Penguin.

Ginsborg, P. (1994a), 'Familismo', in Ginsborg, P. (ed.), *Stato dell'Italia*, Milan: Il Saggiatore, pp. 78–82.

Ginsborg, P. (1994b), 'La famiglia italiana oltre il privato per superare l'isolamento', in Ginsborg, P. (ed.), *Stato dell'Italia*, Milan: Il Saggiatore, pp. 284–90.

Ginsborg, P. (1995), 'Italian Political Culture in Historical Perspective', *Modern Italy*, vol. 1, no. 1, pp. 3–17.

Giorgio, A. (1997), 'Real Mothers and Symbolic Mothers: The Maternal and the Mother-Daughter Relationship in Italian Feminist Theory and Practice', in Bedani, G., Baranski, Z., Lepschy, A.L. and Richardson, B. (eds), *Sguardi sull'Italia*, Occasional Papers of the Society for Italian Studies, pp. 222–41.

Glenn, E.N. (1990), 'The Dialectics of Wage Work: Japanese American Women and Domestic Service, 1905–1940', in DuBois, E.C and Ruiz, V.L. (eds), *Unequal Sisters: A Multicultural Reader in U.S. Women's History*, New York: Routledge, pp. 345–72.

Glenn, E.N. (1992), 'From Servitude to Service Work: Historical Continuities in the Racial Division of Paid Reproductive Labor', *Signs*, vol. 18, no. 1, pp. 1–43.

Glenn, E.N. (1994), 'Social Constructions of Mothering: A Thematic Overview', in Glenn E.N., Chang, G. and Forcey, L.R. (eds), *Mothering: Ideology, Experience and Agency*, London: Routledge, pp. 1–29.

Goddard, V. (1987), 'Honour and Shame: the Control of Women's Sexuality and Group Identity in Naples', in Caplan, P. (ed.), *The Cultural Construction of Sexuality*, London: Tavistock Publications, pp. 166–92.

Goddard, V. (1996), *Gender, Family and Work in Naples*, Oxford: Berg.

Golden, M. (1988), *Labor Divided. Austerity and Working-Class Politics in Contemporary Italy*, Ithaca/London: Cornell University Press.

Golini, A. (1986), 'La famiglia in Italia: tendenze recenti, immagine, esigenze di ricerca', in ISTAT (1986), *Atti del convegno la famiglia in Italia*, Rome, pp. 15–44.

Gordon, V. (1985), *Black Women, Feminism and Black Liberation: Which Way?*, Chicago: Third World Press.

Goss, J. and Lindquist, B. (1995), 'Conceptualizing International Labor Migration: A structuration perspective', *International Migration Review*, vol. xxix, no. 2, pp. 317–51.

Goutier, H. (1996), 'Cape Verde: Making the Best of History', *The Courier*, 158, pp. 15–31.

Governo Ombra (1990), *Donne Immigrate. Proposte di iniziativa su politiche Sociali*, Rome, April.

Graham, H. (1991), 'The Concept of Caring in Feminist Research: the Case of Domestic Service', *Sociology*, vol. 25, no. 1, pp. 61–78.

Gramaglia, M. (1993), 'Il tempo della maternità', in *Il tempo della maternità*, Relazioni al convegno organizzato da Area Politiche Femminili Direzione Pds, Rome, 9–10 January 1992, pp. 173–80.

Gregson, N. and Lowe, M. (1994), *Servicing the Middle Classes*, London: Routledge.

Gribaudi, G. (1996), 'Images of the South', in Forgacs, D. and Lumley, R. (eds), *Italian Cultural Studies*, Oxford: Oxford University Press, pp. 72–87.

Gruppo delle donne migranti (1989), 'Normali condizioni di vita', in Federazione delle chiese evangeliche servizio migranti (ed.), *Casa o fortezza? Italia, L'Europa del 1992 and l'immigrazione*, pp. 73–4.

Guadagnini, M. (1993), 'A "Partitocrazia" Without Women: the Case of the Italian Party System', in Lovenduski, J. and Norris, P. (eds), *Gender and Party Politics*, London: Sage, pp. 168–204.

Haraway, D. (1991), 'Situated Knowledges; The Science Question in Feminism and the Privilege of Partial Perspective', *Feminist Studies*, 14, no. 3, pp. 575–99.

Hellman, J. (1984), 'The Italian Communists, The Woman Question, and the Challenge of Feminism', *Studies in Political Economy*, 13, pp. 57–82.

Hellman, J. (1987), *Journeys Among Women*, Cambridge: Polity Press.

Hewitt, Nancy A. (1990), 'Beyond the Search for Sisterhood: American Women's History in the 1980s', in DuBois, E.C. and Ruiz, V.L. (eds), *Unequal Sisters: A Multicultural Reader in U.S. Women's History*, New York: Routledge, pp. 1–14.

Hine, D.C. (1990), 'Rape and the Inner Lives of Black Women in the Middle West: Preliminary Thoughts on the Culture of Dissemblance', in Du Bois, E.C and Ruiz, V.L. (eds), *Unequal Sisters: A Multicultural Reader in U.S. Women's History*, New York: Routledge, pp. 292–297.

hooks, b. (1981), *Ain't I a Woman: Black Women and Feminism*, London: Pluto Press.

hooks, b. (1989), *Talking Back*, London: Sheba.

Hornziel, I.M. (1990), *La condizione degli immigrati stranieri in Italia*, Milan: Franco Angeli.

Hoskyns, C. and Orsini-Jones, M. (1995), 'Immigrant Women in Italy. Perspectives from Brussels and Bologna', *The European Journal of Women's Studies*, vol. 2, pp. 51–76.

Il X Congresso API-COLF (1979), Documentation in *Donna e Società*, anno. 11, no. 51, pp. 60–77.

IREF (1994), *La condizione delle collaboratrici familiari in Italia.*

IREF/ACLI-COLF (1994), *La condizione delle collaboratrici familiari in Italia.*

ISCOS-CISL (1993), *Il secondo sesso e il terzo mondo. Ricerca-Inchiesta sull'immigrazione femminile nel Lazio.* Rome.

ISFOL (1988), *Percorsi femminili. Lavoro, formazione e famiglia nel Lazio*, Franco Angeli: Milan.

ISTAT (1991), *Gli immigrati presenti in Italia. Una stima per l'anno 1989.*

Italia-Razzismo (1990), *Gli Italiani e l'immagine dell'immigrato*, Rome.

Iyob, R. (1995), *The Eritrean Struggle for Independence*, Cambridge: Cambridge University Press.

Jewell, K.S. (1993), *From Mammy to Miss America and Beyond: Cultural Images and the Shaping of US Social Policy*, London: Routledge.

Kichelmacher, M. (1990), 'Immaginario e stili di vita delle donne degli anni '80', *Donna e Società*, January–March, pp. 23–7.

King, D. (1988), 'Multiple Jeopardy, Multiple Consciousness: the Context of a Black Feminist Ideology', *Signs*, vol. 14, no. 1, pp. 42–72.

King, R. and Andall, J. (1999), 'The Geography and Economic Sociology of Recent Immigration to Italy', *Modern Italy*, 4 (2), pp. 135–58.

King, R. (1987), *Italy*, London: Harper and Row.

King, R. (1993), 'Recent Immigration to Italy: Character, Causes and Consequences', *Geo-Journal*, 30.3, pp. 283–92.

Korsieporn, A. (1991), *International Labor Migration of Southeast Asian Women: Filipina and Thai Domestic Workers in Italy*, Phd dissertation, Cornell University.

Kosack, G. (1976), 'Migrant women: the Move to Western Europe – a Step towards Emancipation?', *Race and Class*, XVII, 4, pp. 369–79.

L'Agenda Ottomarzo 92/93 (1992), Area delle politiche femminili del Partito Democratico della Sinistra e da Eletta.

La politica e l'organizzazione dei comunisti italiani. Le tesi e lo statuto approvati dal XV Congresso nazionale del Pci (1979), Rome: Editori Riuniti.

Labate, G. (1985), *La crisi dello stato sociale: Il punto di vista delle donne*, Sezione formazione e scuole di partito del Pci.

Labate, G. (1993), 'Donne, salute, procreazione: linee ed. indirizzi per un programma di interventi per la salute della donna', in *Il tempo della maternità*, Relazioni al convegno organizzato da Area Politiche Femminili Direzione Pds, Roma, 9–10 January 1992, pp. 119–36.

Laitin, D. and Samatar, S. (1987), *Somalia*, Gower: Westview Press.

Le donne comuniste (1989), *Carta delle donne immigrate*, March.

Lega Nord (1992), *Programma elettorale. Immigrazione, cooperazione allo sviluppo*.

Levy, C. (1996), 'Introduction: Italian Regionalism in Context', in Levy, C. (ed.), *Italian Regionalism*, Oxford: Berg, pp.1–30.

Libere, Insieme (1991), *Documento politico dell'Associazione 'LIBERE, INSIEME'*, May 1991.

Livraghi, R. (1992), 'Le famiglie e la produzione di servizi', *Quaderni di Azione Sociale*, July–August/September–October, no. 88–89, pp. 115–27.

Lobban, R. (1998), *Cape Verde: Crioulo Colony to Independent Nation*, Boulder: Westview Press.

Luciano, A. (1994), 'Una presenza che ci interroga', in Vicarelli, G. (ed.), *Le mani invisibili. La vita e il lavoro delle donne immigrate*, Rome: Ediesse, pp. 221–6.

Macioti, M.I. (1990), 'Stato e volontariato nell'intervento a favore degli immigrati', *Inchiesta*, October–December, pp. 83–8.

Mafai, M. (1992), 'Mamma è più bello. La capriola delle donne pds', *La Repubblica*, 10 January, p. 15.

Maffioli, D. (1994), 'Il matrimonio e la nascita dei figli', in Vicarelli, G. (ed.), *Le mani invisibili. La vita e il lavoro delle donne immigrate*, Rome: Ediesse, pp. 110–27.

Mancina, C. (1986), 'Autonomia senza separatezza', *Donna e Politica*, 2–3, pp. 39–42.

Mancina, C. (1993), 'Riflessioni sull'autodeterminazione (prendere sul serio l'esperienza delle donne)', in *Il tempo della maternità*, Relazioni al convegno organizzato da Area Politiche Femminili Direzione Pds, Rome, 9–10 January 1992, pp. 25–38.

Maraini, D. (1976), 'Quale cultura per la donna', in Bruzzichelli, P. and Algini, M.L. (eds), *Donna, cultura e tradizione*, Milan: Mazzotta, pp. 60–6.

Maricos, A. (1990a), 'Essere genitori eritrei a Milano', in Demetrio et al. (eds), *Lontano da dove. La nuova immigrazione e le sue culture*, Milan: Franco Angeli, pp. 125–33.

Maricos, A. (1990b), untitled conference intervention, in Regione Emilia-Romagna, *L'Emigrazione al femminile*, Atti del Convegno, Bologna, 12–13 January, pp. 87–98.

Martelli, C. (1991), 'Da clandestino a cittadino: relazione di base', in Presidenza del consiglio dei ministri (1991), *Atti della conferenza nazionale dell'immigrazione*, Rome, 4–6 June 1990, Rome: Editalia, pp. 49–69.

Martin, P. (1993), 'The Migration Issue', in King, R. (ed.), *The New Geography of European Migrations*, London: Belhaven, pp. 1–16.

McBride, T. (1976), *The Domestic Revolution*, London: Croom Helm.

McCarthy, P. (1997), 'Italy: A New Language for a New Politics?', *Journal of Modern Italian Studies*, 2 (3), pp. 337–57.

Melandri, E. (1991), 'Nigeriana negra prostituta "picchiala"', *Avvenimenti*, 14 August.

Melotti, U (1990), 'Migrazioni, divisione del lavoro, cultura', in Demetrio et al. (eds), *Lontano da dove. La nuova immigrazione e le sue culture*, Milan: Franco Angeli, pp. 15–65.

Menniti, A., Palomba, R. and Sabbadini, L. (1997), 'Italy: Changing the Family from Within', in Kaufman, F., Kuijsten, A., Schulze, H. and Strohmeier, K. (eds), *Family Life and Family Policies in Europe*, Vol. 1, Oxford: Clarendon Press, pp. 225–52.

Michetti, M., Repetto, M. and Viviani, L. (1984), *UDI Laboratorio di politica delle donne*, Rome: Cooperativa Libera Stampa.

Miles, R. (1982), *Racism and Migrant Labour*, Routledge: London.

Montecchi, E. (1993), 'Maternità e servizi', in *Il tempo della maternità*, Relazioni al convegno organizzato da Area Politiche Femminili Direzione Pds, Rome, 9–10 January 1992, pp. 103–10.

Monticelli, G. (1983), 'L'emigrazione femminile italiana', *Affari sociali internazionali*, no. 4, pp. 95–113.

Moravia, A. (1959), *Nuovi racconti romani* (1978 edn), Milan: Bompiani.

Morokvasic, M. (1983a), 'Women in Migration: Beyond the Reductionist Outlook', in Phizacklea, A. (ed.) (1983), *One Way Ticket: Migration and Female Labour*, London: Routledge, pp. 13–32.

Morokvasic, M. (1983b), 'Why do Women Migrate? Towards Understanding of the Sex-selectivity in the Migratory Movements of Labour', *Studi Emigrazione*, 70, pp. 132–8.

Morokvasic, M. (1984), 'Birds of Passage are also Women', *International Migration Review*, vol. xviii, no. 4, pp. 886–907.

Morokvasic, M. (1991), 'Fortress Europe and Migrant Women', *Feminist Review*, no. 39, pp. 69–84.

Morokvasic, M. (1995), 'In and Out of the Labour Market: Immigrant and Minority Women in Europe', *New Community*, 19 (3), pp. 459–83.

Moussa, H. (1993), *Storm and Sanctuary. The Journey of Ethiopian and Eritrean Women Refugees*, Ontario: Artemis Enterprises.

Nanetti, R. (1988), *Growth and Territorial Policies: The Italian Model of Social Capitalism*, London: Pinter Publishers.

Natale, L. (1991), 'Atteggiamenti dei datori di lavoro nel Lazio nei confronti dell'immigrazione straniera', *Rivista italiana di economia demografia e statistica*, July–December, pp. 257–69.

Nikolinakos, M. (1975), 'Notes Towards a General Theory of Migration in Late Capitalism', *Race and Class*, XVII, pp. 5–18.

Okin, S. (1997), 'Families and Feminist Theory: Some Past and Present Issues', in Nelson H.L. (ed.), *Feminism and Families*, London: Routledge, pp. 13–26.

OMCVI (1989), *Capo Verde: Una storia lunga dieci isole*, Milan: D'Anselmi.

Orsi, R. (1987), 'Forte, nera, potente: il discorso razzista nella cultura di massa italiana', *I Giorni Cantati*, January–March, pp. 27–30.

Ortner, S. (1974), 'Is Female to Male as Nature Is to Culture', in Rosaldo, M.Z. and Lamphere, L. (eds), *Women, Culture and Society*, Stanford: Stanford University Press, pp. 67–87.

Paci, M. (1983), 'Struttura e funzioni della famiglia nello sviluppo industriale "periferico"', in Paci, M. (ed.), *Famiglia e mercato del lavoro in un'economia periferica*, Milan: Franco Angeli, pp. 9–70.

Paci, M. (1989), 'Public and Private in the Italian Welfare System', in Lange, P. and Regini, M. (eds), *State, Market, and Social Regulation*, Cambridge: Cambridge University Press, pp. 217–34.

Padoa Schioppa Kostoris, R. (1993), *Italy. The Sheltered Economy*, Oxford: Clarendon Press.

Padoa Schioppa, R. (1977), *La forza lavoro femminile*, Bologna: Il Mulino.

Pajetta, G. (1990a), 'Nere, emancipate, invisibili', *Il Manifesto*, 15 November.

Pajetta, G. (1990b), 'Le mamme della domenica', *Il Manifesto*, 21 November.

Pajetta, G. (1990c), 'Immigrare a Rebibbia', *Il Manifesto*, 28 November.

Palazzi, M. (1990), 'Donne extracomunitarie in Emilia-Romagna', in Regione Emilia-Romagna, *L'emigrazione al femminile*, Atti del Convegno,. Bologna, 12–13 January, pp. 19–37.

Parca, G. (1964), *Le italiane si confessano*, Milan: Feltrinelli.

Parmar, P. (1989), 'Other Kinds of Dreams', *Feminist Review*, 31, pp. 55–65.

Partito Democratico della Sinistra (1991), *Lo Statuto*.

Pasero, A. (1991), 'Madamismo, Meticciato and the Prestige of the Race in Italian East Africa', *The Italianist*, pp. 180–93.

Pasini, G. (1974), *Le ACLI dalle origini*, Roma: Edizioni Coines.

Pasquinelli, C. (1984), 'Beyond the Longest Revolution: The Impact of the Italian Women's Movement on Cultural and Social Change', *Praxis International*, 4:2, pp. 131–6.

Passerini, L. (1994), 'The Interpretation of Democracy in the Italian Women's Movement of the 1970s and 1980s', *Women's Studies International Forum*, vol. 17, no. 2/3, pp. 235–9.

PDS (1991), *Immigrazione*, Ufficio Immigrazione/Aree Iniziative Sociali.

Pelaja, M. (1988), 'Mestieri femminili e luoghi comuni. Le domestiche a Roma a metà ottocento', *Quaderni Storici*, 68, vol. XXIII, no. 2, pp. 497–518.

Perrotta, A. (1988), *Emigrazione e cooperazione allo sviluppo: Il caso Capo Verde*, Rome: Lega italiana per i diritti e la liberazione dei popoli.

Perrotta, A. (ed.) (1991), *Bambini immigrati. Inchiesta fra i piccoli immigrati nelle scuole di Roma*, Rome: Datanews.

Pestalozza, L. (1975), *La costituzione e lo stato*, Rome: Editori Riuniti.

Petilli, S. (1993), 'Il ruolo del diritto nella regolazione del conflitto', in Delle Donne, M., Melotti, U. and Petilli, S. (eds), *Immigrazione in Europa*, Rome: CEDISS, pp. 627–57.

Petracou, E. (1996), 'Undocumented Migrants', paper presented to conference on 'New Migration in Europe: Social Constructions and Social Realities', Utrecht University, 18–20 April.

Phizacklea, A. and Wolkowitz, C. (1995), *Homeworking Women. Gender, Racism and Class at Work*, London: Sage.

Phizacklea, A. (ed.) (1983), *One Way Ticket: Migration and Female Labour*, London: Routledge.

Phizacklea, A. (1996), 'Migration and Globalisation. A Feminist Perspective', paper presented to conference on 'New Migration in Europe: Social Constructions and Social Realities', Utrecht University, 18–20 April.

Piazza, M. (1992), 'Le implicazioni attuali del concetto di doppia presenza', *Quaderni di Azione Sociale*, November–December, no. 90, pp. 105–11.

Piazza, M. (1994), 'L'esperienza di un incontro', in Vicarelli, G. (ed.), *Le mani invisibili. La vita e il lavoro delle donne immigrate*, Rome: Ediesse, pp. 216–20.

Picchio, A. (1990), 'Il lavoro domestico. Reale meccanismo di aggiustamento fra riproduzione sociale e accumulazione capitalistica', in Nassisi, A.M. (ed.), *Il lavoro femminile in Italia tra produzione e riproduzione: 1º rapporto*, Rome: Istituto Gramsci, pp. 171–95.

Picciolini, A. (1992), 'La donna migrante', in Sergi, N. and Carchedi, F. (eds), *L'immigrazione straniera in Italia. Il tempo dell'integrazione*, Rome: Edizioni Lavoro, pp. 79–94.

Pinto, P. (1992), 'L'inserimento di lavoratori stranieri in imprese italiane: il caso di Bologna', *Il Corriere Calabrese*, vol. 2, no. 1, pp. 33–339.

Pisciotta, E. (1986), 'Challenging the Establishment: The Case of Abortion', in Dahlerup, O. (ed.), *The New Women's Movement*, London: Sage, pp. 26–47.

Pitch, T. (1990), 'Rape Reform in Italy: the Endless Story', in Nannetti, R. and Catanzaro, R. (eds), *Italian Politics: A Review. Volume 4*, London: Pinter, pp. 162–73.

Pittau, F. and Reggio, M. (1992), 'Il caso Albania: Immigrazione a due tempi', *Studi Emigrazione*, XXIX, no. 106, pp. 227–39.

Pomeranzi, B.M. (1991), 'Cercando ciò che ci unisce', *Noi Donne*, July–August, p. 4.

Portes, A. and Borocz, J. (1989), 'Contemporary Immigration: Theoretical Perspectives on its Determinants and Modes of Incorporation', *International Migration Review*, vol. xxiii, no. 3, pp. 606–30.

Presidenza del consiglio dei ministri (1990), *L'immigrazione nella stampa italiana*, March–May, Rome.

Presidenza del consiglio dei ministri (1991), *Atti della Conferenza Nazionale dell'Immigrazione*, Rome 4–6 June, Rome: Editalia.

Prima Conferenza delle donne del Pds (1993), *Essere sinistra. Diventare governo*, Atti del convegno, 9–11 December.

Pucci, R. (1992), 'Gli albanesi nel Lazio', *Lazio immigrazione*, Supplement to Lazio nel mondo, January, p. 32.

Pugliese, E. (1990a), 'Dove lavorano e che lavoro fanno gli immigrati', in Demetrio et al. (eds), *Lontano da dove. La nuova immigrazione e le sue culture*, Milan: Franco Angeli, pp. 238–41.

Pugliese, E. (1990b), 'Italy as a Particular Case of Emigration and Immigration', paper presented to conference on 'Italian Migrant Labour in the European Context: Looking Towards the 1990s', University of Bristol 27 April.

Race and Class (1991), *Europe: Variations on a Theme of Racism*, Special Issue.

Raffaele, G. (1992), 'Le immigrate extracomunitarie in Italia', *Studi Emigrazione*, XXIX, no. 106, pp. 194–223.

Ramazanoglu, C. (1989), *Feminism and the Contradictions of Oppression*, London: Routledge.

Randazzo, R. (1986), 'Strategie familiari, ruolo e identità femminili in trasformazione nell'Italia meridionale', *Inchiesta*, October–December, pp. 25–31.

Rath, J. (1993), 'The Ideological Representation of Migrant Workers in Europe: A Matter of Racialisation?', in Solomos, J. and Wrench, J. (eds), *Racism and Migration in Western Europe*, Oxford: Berg, pp. 215–32.

Ravasio, A. (1989), 'L'associazionismo femminile di ispirazione cristiana impegnato nel sociale', in CIF, *Società italiana e associazionismo ieri e oggi: 40 anni di storia delle donne del CIF*, Centro Italiano Femminile, pp. 57–72.

Regione Emilia-Romagna (1990), *L'emigrazione al femminile*, Atti del convegno, 12–13 January, Bologna.

Regione Lazio and Provincia di Roma (1986), *1° Conferenza provinciale per l'emigrazione e l'immigrazione*, 14 November.

Regione Lazio (1988), *Rapporto Lazio 1988*, Osservatorio del mondo di lavoro.

Regione Lazio (1992a), *Piano regionale degli interventi a favore degli immigrati*.

Regione Lazio (1992b), *III Rapporto Lazio sul mercato del lavoro*, Osservatorio del mondo di lavoro.

Reyneri, E. (1989), 'The Italian Labor Market: between State Control and Social Regulation', in Lange, P. and Regini, M. (eds), *State, Market, and Social Regulation: New Perspectives on Italy*, Cambridge: Cambridge University Press, pp. 129–46.

Riviello, A.M. (1993), 'Soggettività femminile e procreazione: quale società' in *Il tempo della maternità*, Relazioni al convegno organizzato da Area Politiche Femminili Direzione Pds, Roma, 9–10 January 1992, pp. 15–24.

Rollins, J. (1985), *Between Women: Domestics and their Employers*, Philadelphia: Temple University Press.

Roma Caritas (1990), 'Roma vuole solidarietà e pace con i cittadini immigrati', Mensile a cura della Caritas diocensana di Roma, no. 3–4–5, March–June.

Romero, M. (1992), *Maid in the USA*, London: Routledge.

Romero, M. (1997), 'Who Takes Care of the Maid's Children? Exploring the Costs of Domestic Service', in Nelson H.L. (ed.), *Feminism and Families*, London: Routledge, pp. 151–69.

Romito, P. (1993), 'The Practice of Protective Legislation for Pregnant Workers in Italy', *Women's Studies International Forum*, vol. 16, no. 6, pp. 581–90.

Rosci, E. (1994), 'Le lunghe adolescenze dell'Italia d'oggi', in Ginsborg, P. (ed.), *Stato dell'Italia*, Milan: Il Saggiatore, pp. 301–3.

Rossanda, R. (1987), 'Politica: significati e progetti. Le diverse strade della Carta e dell'affidamento', *Reti*, September–October, pp. 39–44.

Rossi Doria, A. (1991a), 'Primi appunti sulle donne dell'immigrazione', *Politica ed Economia*, 22 (7–8), pp. 80–81.

Rossi Doria, A. (1991b), 'Per costruire città multietniche: I diritti delle donne immigrate', Comunicazione alla conferenza nazionale delle elette, Rome, 3–4 May.

Russo Jervolino, R. (1990), 'Famiglia e Dc: una storia coerente', *Donna e Società*, 82, pp. 33–7.

Ryan, B. (1992), *Feminism and the Women's Movement: Dynamics of Change in Social Movement, Ideology and Activism*, London: Routledge.

Sacconi, R. (1984), 'Le colf, queste sconosciute', *Politica ed economia*, January, no. 1, pp. 39–46.

Salatto, P. (1992), 'La formazione professionale per gli extracomunitari', in *Lazio Immigrazione*, Supplement to Lazio nel mondo, January, p. 6.

Samatar, A. (ed.), *The Somali Challenge*, London: Lynne Rienner.

Sanna, A. (1993), 'L'applicazione delle leggi 194 e 405', in *Il tempo della maternità*, Relazioni al convegno organizzato da Area Politiche Femminili Direzione Pds, Rome, 9–10 January 1992, pp. 111–18.

Saraceno, C. (1987), 'Division of Family Labour and Gender Identity', in Showstack Sassooon, A. (ed.), *Women and the State*, London: Hutchinson, pp. 191–206.

Saraceno, C. (1988), *Sociologia della famiglia*, Bologna: Il Mulino.

Saraceno, C. (1994), 'Crescita zero: un fenomeno, molte cause', in Ginsborg, P. (ed.), *Stato dell'Italia*, Milan: Il Saggiatore, pp. 298–301.

Scalfaro, O.L. (1988), 'Solo un lavoro', *Le Colf*, May, p. 3.

Schioppa Kostoris, F. (1996), 'Excesses and Limits of the Public Sector in the Italian Economy', in Gundle, S. and Parker, S. (eds), *The New Italian Republic*, London: Routledge, pp. 273–93.

Schmidt di Friedberg, O. and Saint-Blancat, C. (1998), 'L'immigration au féminin: les femmes marocaines en Italie du nord. Une recherce en Vénétie', *Studi Emigrazione*, XXXV, no. 131, pp. 483–96.

Segal, L. (1987), *Is the Future Female?*, London: Virago

Sergi, N. (ed.) (1987), *L'immigrazione straniera in Italia*, Rome: Edizioni lavoro.

Seroni, A. (1984), *Donne comuniste: identità e confronto*, Collana dalla sezione formazione e scuole di partito del Pci.

Sezione femminile della direzione del Pci (1986), *Dalle donne la forza delle donne – Carta itinerante*, Cles (Trento),: Nuova stampa di Mondadori.

Sezione Femminile Nazionale del Pci (1990), *Le donne cambiano i tempi*.

Solomos, J. (1989), *Race and Racism in Britain*, London: Macmillan.

Song, M. and Parker, D. (1995), 'Commonality, Difference and the Dynamics of Disclosure in In-depth Interviewing, *Sociology*, vol. 29, no. 2, pp. 241–56.

Stacey, J. (1985), 'Big White Sister. Sexuality and Racism in the Women's Movement', Women's Studies Occasional Papers, No. 7, University of Kent at Canterbury.

Strozza, S. (1991), 'I lavoratori extracomunitari a Roma: ipotesi di lavoro e primi risultati di una indagine nel settore della ristorazione', *Rivista italiana di economia demografia e statistica*, July–December, pp. 305–21.

Susi, F. (1991), *I bisogni formativi e culturali degli immigrati stranieri*, Milan: Franco Angeli.

Taamallah, K. (1981), 'L'émigration tunisienne en Italie', unpublished paper presented to seminar 'La situation actuelle des migrations en Italie', Institut Colorni, Rome, 1 June.

Tan, T. and Devasahayam, T. (1987), 'Opposition and Interdependence: The Dialectics of Maid and Employer Relationships in Singapore', *Phillippine Sociological Review*, 35 (3–4), pp. 34–41.

Ter Wal, J. (1996), 'The social representation of immigrants: The *Pantanella* issue in the pages of *La Repubblica*', *New Community*, 22 (1), pp. 39–66.

Tiso, A. (1976), *I comunisti e la questione femminile*, Rome: Editori Riuniti.

Tiso, A. (1983), 'Marxismo, politica comunista, femminismo', in Dal Pont, R. et al., *La Questione Femminile*, Sezione scuole di partito, pp. 9–70.

Tobìo, C. (1997), 'Women's Strategies and the Family-Employment Relationship in Spain', paper presented to research seminar on 'Family, Identity and Society in Europe', Bath University, 28–29 November.

Togliatti, P. (1965), *L'emancipazione femminile*, Rome: Editori Riuniti.

Tognetti Bordogna, M. (1994), 'La famiglia che cambia', in Vicarelli, G. (ed.), *Le mani invisibili. La vita e il lavoro delle donne immigrate*, Rome: Ediesse, pp. 128–40.

Trifiletti, R. (1995), 'Family Obligation in Italy', in Millar, J. and Warman, A. (eds), *Defining Family Obligation in Europe*, Bath Social Policy Papers, no. 23, pp. 177–206.

Turco, L. (1990), ' I tempi e la Carta (intervista a Livia Turco),' in *Viaggio nel cuore del Pci*, Supplement to *Rinascita*, no. 17, 3 June.

Turco, L. (1993), 'Introduzione', in *Il tempo della maternità*, Relazioni al convegno organizzato da Area Politiche Femminili Direzione Pds, Rome, 9–10 January, pp. 3–14.

Turnaturi, G. (1987), 'The Role of the Italian Family after 1968', *Newsletter of Association for the Study of Modern Italy*, Spring, pp. 20–21.

Turone, S. (1981), *Storia del sindacato in Italia*, Bari: Laterza.

Turri, C. (1988), 'L'esperienza delle ACLI-COLF', *Quaderni di Azione Sociale*, no. 62, pp. 85–104.

Turrini, O. (1977), *Le casalinghe di riserva*, Rome: Coines Edizioni.

Vaiou, D. (1995), 'Women of the South After, Like Before, Maastricht?', in Hadjimichalis, C. and Sadler (eds), *Europe at the Margins*, Chicester: Wiley, pp. 35–50.

Van Dijk, T. A. (1993), 'Denying Racism: Elite Discourse and Racism', in Solomos, J. and Wrench, J. (eds), *Racism and Migration in Western Europe*, Oxford: Berg, pp. 179–94.

Venturini, A. (1988), 'An Interpretation of Mediterranean Migration', *Labour*, 2 (2), pp. 125–54.

Vicarelli, G. (1994), 'Prefazione', in Vicarelli, G. (ed.), *Le mani invisibili. La vita e il lavoro delle donne immigrate*, Rome: Ediesse, pp. 7–9.

Warren, C. (1988), *Gender Issues in Field Research*, London: Sage.

Wieviorka, M. (1993), 'Tendencies to Racism in Europe: Does France Represent a Unique Case, or is it Representative of a Trend', in Solomos, J. and Wrench, J. (eds), *Racism and Migration in Western Europe*, Oxford: Berg, pp. 55–66.

Willson, P. (1993), *The Clockwork Factory: Women and Work in Fascist Italy*, Oxford: Clarendon Press.

Woody, B. (1992), *Black Women in the Workplace: Impacts of Structural Change in the Economy*, New York: Greenwood Press.

World Bank (1994), *The World Bank Atlas 1995*, Washington: International Bank for Reconstruction and Development/The World Bank.

Wubneh, M. and Abate, Y. (1988), *Ethiopia*, Avebury: Westview Press.

XVII Congresso del partito comunista italiano. Firenze 9–13 aprile 1986 (1987), Rome: Editori Riuniti.

Yaya, B. (1994), *Transracial Fostering: A Black Perpsective*, Norwich: Social Work Monographs.

Yeoh, B. and Huang, S. (1999), 'Migrant Female Domestic Workers: Debating the Economic, Social and Political Impacts in Singapore', *International Migration Review*, pp. 114–36.

Zannatta, A.L.F and Mirabile, M.L. (1993), *Demografia, famiglia e società*, Rome: Ediesse.

Zannini, F. (1970), *Presupposti per una novazione legislativa del lavoro domestico*, Presentato al VII congresso nazionale delle collaboratrici familiari ACLI, April 1970.

Zewde, B. (1991), *A History of Modern Ethiopia 1855–1974*, London: James Currey.

Ziglio, L. (1988), 'Le donne eritree a Milano: dati e confronti', in Melotti, U. (ed.), *Dal terzo mondo in Italia*, Milan: Centro Studi Terzo Mondo, pp. 60–78.

Zincone, G. (1993), 'The Political Rights of Immigrants in Italy', *New Community*, 20 (1), pp. 131–45.

Index

331